MW00451651

Memorials Matter

Memorials Matter

Emotion, Environment, and Public Memory at American Historical Sites

JENNIFER K. LADINO

UNIVERSITY OF NEVADA PRESS *Reno & Las Vegas*

University of Nevada Press | Reno, Nevada 89557 USA

www.unpress.nevada.edu

Copyright © 2019 by University of Nevada Press

All rights reserved

Cover art by jericl cat

Cover design by TG Design

All photos are by the author unless otherwise indicated.

LIBRARY OF CONGRESS CATALOGING-IN-PUBLICATION DATA

Names: Ladino, Jennifer K., author.

Title: Memorials matter : emotion, environment, and public memory at American historical sites / Jennifer K. Ladino.

Description: Reno ; Las Vegas : University of Nevada Press, [2019] | Includes bibliographical references. |

Identifiers: LCCN 2018039125 (print) | LCCN 2018041049 (ebook) | ISBN 9781943859986 (ebook) | ISBN 9781943859962 (pbk. : alk. paper) | ISBN 9781943859979 (cloth : alk. paper)

Subjects: LCSH: Historic sites--Social aspects--West (U.S.) | Memorials--Social aspects--West (U.S.) | Monuments--Social aspects--West (U.S.) | Collective memory--Social aspects--West (U.S.)

Classification: LCC F590.7 (ebook) | LCC F590.7 . L33 2019 (print) | DDC 909--dc23

LC record available at https://lccn.loc.gov/2018039125

The paper used in this book meets the requirements of American National Standard for Information Sciences — Permanence of Paper for Printed Library Materials, ANSI/NISO Z39.48-1992 (R2002).

FIRST PRINTING

Manufactured in the United States of America

to Doug, with love and gratitude

Contents

Illustrations

Illustrations

Preface

I can still picture the tattered scrap of paper my National Park Service (NPS) supervisor had thumbtacked to her gray cubicle wall:

> Climb the mountains and get their good tidings. Nature's peace will flow into you as sunshine flows into trees. The winds will blow their own freshness into you, and the storms their energy, while cares will drop off like autumn leaves.[1]

These inspirational lines from John Muir's *Our National Parks* were a favorite among rangers I worked with, if a bit too saccharine for my tastes. My twenty-something self had chosen the wry prose of Edward Abbey to grace my own gray cubicle wall. I found it refreshing to re-read his polemic about letting tourists take risks (like getting "lost, sunburnt, stranded, drowned, eaten by bears, [and] buried alive by avalanches") and, more happily, letting park rangers *range*,[2] while I hammered out press releases, designed employee newsletters, or planned for special events—from behind my desk. During my thirteen seasons working for the NPS in Grand Teton National Park, I "ranged" whenever I could. As I hiked and climbed all over the Tetons, I felt the peace, freshness, energy, and carefree mood Muir had championed. I wanted park visitors to feel those things, too, and to appreciate firsthand the mysterious ways that the more-than-human world acts upon us—ways that researchers today are beginning to understand much better than when Muir was adventuring in the Yosemite Valley.

Romantic though they may be, Muir's words anticipate one of my goals for this book: to consider how the physical environment makes people feel things, how it shapes the "flows" of peace and many other affects at NPS sites. *Memorials Matter* is not about big-ticket destinations like the Tetons or Yosemite National Park, which rely mainly on striking natural beauty and recreational opportunities to draw crowds.

This book is about Western memorials where education, rather than recreation, is the main attraction. When it comes to memorials, everyone's a critic; that is, nearly everyone I spoke with about this project had a favorite memorial I simply *must* include. Seldom are those favorites in the American West. Civil War battlefields in the South are popular suggestions, as are the 9/11 Memorial, the Vietnam Veterans Memorial, and others in big East Coast cities. So why the West? For one thing, the region has long been tied to national identity, and in a book about public memory, national identity is very much at stake. For another, considering the West's signature environments—its open spaces, vast deserts, towering mountain ranges, lush coasts, and idyllic islands—adds a new dimension to the study of public memory.

Memorials serve a range of functions. Most are meant to be redemptive in some way: to confront loss, trauma, or violence; to provide healing for those involved; and, sometimes, to promote justice for the victims. Jay Winter describes a memory site as a "moral message" in material form.[3] More recently, Erika Doss explains how memorials in the United States have increasingly become places of contestation, "subject to the volatile intangibles of the nation's multiple publics and their fluctuating interests and feelings."[4] Many memorials today are designed to bring previously silenced voices to the fore or to promote cultural pluralism. But do they succeed? And if so, what is the role of the physical environment—both natural and built—in shaping our feelings at these "archives of public affect"?[5]

With these questions in mind, I visited selected sites managed by the NPS, the agency that paid and housed me through thirteen of my best summers and inspired my research in ways I didn't anticipate at the time. More importantly, it's an agency with a huge responsibility for narrating the intense history of the U.S., and so, for managing the relationship between public memory and national identity. I initially wanted to constrain my study to war memorials, but I worried this narrow designation would limit the range of sites I could access. I soon realized, however, that if I thought instead about *conflict* then the designation wasn't narrow at all. Nearly every landscape in the West bears witness to, and contains physical traces of, historical conflict. There was no way, in a project like mine, to catalogue all the wars and other forms of violence that mark the region's history. Confining my data set to Western memorials run by the NPS was a way of keeping the scope manageable, and it worked, although I quickly learned how complicated the category of "memorial" can be.

While the NPS uses "park" as a catch-all word for the more than 400 sites it manages, I claim "memorial" for my umbrella term. The NPS loosely defines a memorial as "commemorative of a historic person or episode."[6] "Memorial" also tends to be the colloquial choice for sites of national significance that commemorate trauma, as most of those in my study do.[7] In a broad sense, then, the label fits for all the sites in this book: three national historic sites, two national memorials, one national monument, and a national recreation area. But even sites that share an official designation—for instance, the relatively obscure Coronado National Memorial and the iconic Mount Rushmore National Memorial—don't necessarily have much else in common. And in some cases, as with Mount Rushmore, it's not clear why "memorial" is the right word at all.

Although "memorial" and "monument" are often used interchangeably in popular discourse, they mean different things. At some sites in the West, the landscape itself is deemed "monumental" because of its extraordinary size and beauty. More often, monuments refer to built structures on a grand scale (think Washington Monument), which tend to (but don't always) celebrate dominant national narratives and reinscribe official histories.[8] Memorials, by contrast, can be as simple as a plaque and tend to mark sites of grief or trauma. Memorials recognize a messier past and give expression to American publics that are "diverse and often stratified."[9] With increasing attention to identity politics, the trend in American commemorative culture has been toward memorials. Some monuments contain memorials, as is the case with WWII Valor in the Pacific National Monument, which encompasses the USS *Arizona* Memorial. And some memorials contain monuments: Coronado National Memorial includes several obelisks that function as monuments marking the U.S.–Mexico border. In short, it's complicated. I make it a priority to be clear about my own terminology in each chapter.

The NPS has a challenging job. The agency was formed and began managing natural and cultural resources in 1916, and attention

xiv   Preface

to the latter has increased substantially since then. Its responsibility for public lands is vast, not only in terms of the types of national sites it manages—now including wild and scenic rivers, scenic trails, historical parks, parkways, lakeshores, and seashores, among others—but also in terms of the amount of total land area in the system, which has doubled since 1973.[10] The fact that the NPS is not supposed to have a political agenda—uniformed rangers are prohibited from talking about politics or even so much as recommending local restaurants—also makes it an interesting case study. Not only do NPS managers have to negotiate a contradictory mission dedicated to both enjoyment and preservation, but NPS employees are also supposed to practice an ideological and political neutrality intended to ensure democratic access for all visitors.[11]

Still, the NPS wants to engage visitors emotionally as well as intellectually.[12] Even if the agency's neutrality means its staff can't tell us exactly how we should feel, emotions themselves are never neutral. The NPS manages more than just natural and cultural resources, then: It also manages *affects*. One goal of *Memorials Matter* is to flesh out those feelings. Terry Tempest Williams pursues something similar in her book, *The Hour of Land: A Personal Topography of America's National Parks*, a project that explores the value of parks at the agency's centennial anniversary. She asks: "What are [park visitors] searching for and what do we find?"[13] My own answer to this question is in some ways similar to hers: "perhaps it is not so much what we learn that matters in these moments of awe and wonder, but what we *feel* in relationship to a world beyond ourselves, even beyond our own species."[14] I am less focused on moments of "awe and wonder" than Williams is, though. Some of the landscapes in my project are quite subtle, not awesome or wondrous in the way the nation's most dramatic parks (and many of its earliest public lands) typically are.

I thought I might be able to detect a singular NPS tourist affect, a mood that remains more or less consistent across NPS-managed sites. For one thing, most tourists are on vacation, so aren't we predisposed to enjoy ourselves, or at least to bring a certain carefree mood to our travels? What other common affective ground might there be among NPS visitors? Is NPS tourism a genre? Does it have a grammar?[15] Are there affective stages—perhaps a progression from inquisitiveness to horror (or grief, or anger) and contemplation to catharsis—one is supposed to go through at sites of tragedy, like Sand Creek Massacre National Historic Site or the USS *Arizona* Memorial at Pearl Harbor?[16] What about at others, like Golden Spike National Historic Site, which are mainly celebratory? Could I come up with a grand theory of NPS tourist emotions, something like the stages of grief made famous by psychiatrist Elisabeth Kübler-Ross,[17] which applies across a range of memory sites?

As intriguing as such a model might be, the reality of commemoration is much more complex. In exploring a diverse group of landscapes and an array of NPS designations, I've discovered that awe and wonder are only two among a wide range of affects that happen at sites of public memory. In fact, awe or wonder inspired by a landscape might actually detract from the commemorative experience we're meant to have at a memorial. I suspect that even at the most sublime parks—like Grand Teton National Park, a beloved favorite of both mine and Williams's— awe and wonder can be elusive. Crowds, construction, or other frustrations can stand in the way during high tourist season. Or, we stand in our own ways, preoccupied with sending texts, taking selfies, reading roadside displays, or looking for the nearest coffee vendor. As I argued in my first book, *Reclaiming Nostalgia: Longing for Nature in American Literature*, most visitors are technological tourists: We come equipped with GPS devices, cell phones, headsets, and Fitbits.[18] We visit video rivers, go on e-hikes, and take headset tours. Most visits to national parks these days start online, with third-nature representations and virtual texts ranging from the official narratives and images on the NPS website to a friend's snapshots on Instagram and a stranger's video on YouTube. We prepare. We learn about the area. We chart our course. We make reservations. We create a checklist of things to see. All this preparation predisposes us to encounter the site in a particular way— the way laid out for us by these texts.

But that predisposition is only one facet of the experience, and it can change. A lot can happen on the way to a destination, for starters. Kids fight in cars, souring a family's collective mood. Couples bicker about directions or other logistics. (As an entrance station ranger, I was once asked to settle an argument about what the "white stuff" in the mountains was. I politely declined.) The onslaught of information at visitor centers, roadside signs and plaques, local towns peddling souvenirs and ice cream cones, and the company of other people (either the ones we brought with us or those we encounter for the first and probably only time at the site) all influence visitors' experiences. With so many factors involved, it's safe to say that what we feel at a memorial site is hardly ever what we prepared for.

Still, it is possible to say something about what happens affectively at these sites of memory. *Reclaiming Nostalgia* grew out of my NPS experiences and my corresponding desire to analyze the literary and cultural uses of nostalgia, including the more politically progressive ones. *Memorials Matter* picks up where that book left off in its attention to tourists' emotional responses to nature, but this project features a focused emphasis on NPS sites, a wider range of affects, and a larger theoretical toolbox. I draw on affect theory across the spectrum, from cultural theory to cognitive science, to ask things like: What kinds of narratives about the West, and the nation, do landscapes convey? What affects and emotions do the natural and built environments at memorial sites encourage? What happens when these affects are in tension with what a site's written texts recommend? To answer these sorts of questions, I think we have to learn to talk in clearer and more nuanced ways about affect and emotion, and about the physical environments at these sites. I hope to model that clarity and nuance in what follows.

I've placed environments at the center of my project by organizing the book around type of landscape. Together, the chapters emphasize the ways in which a desert, or a mountain range, or an island, or a coast, or a national border, shapes how public memory feels. All landscapes are, like national parks, "discursive apparatuses"[19] through which politics are negotiated at local, regional, national, and international scales. Landscapes impact how visitors react to NPS sites at least as much as the written rhetoric and other overt attempts to regulate tourists' experiences. But unlike other "display technologies"[20] — including park brochures (known as "site bulletins"), designated overlooks, and the various interpretive tools at visitor centers — landscapes have an unruly, unpredictable influence on tourists who visit these sites. Along with landscapes, I look at the built environment, including structures that appear finite and stable, to see how these features can work against the NPS's goals, complicating, or even contradicting, the written rhetoric.

As tourists, our bodies are carefully managed along with the natural resources NPS sites celebrate and enclose. My own body is no exception, which makes accounting for my corporeal experience a methodological necessity. I don't presume to write about *the* visitor experience. I focus instead on how each site constructs what I call an "implied tourist," a subject position I often, but don't always, fit. Like Wayne Booth's implied reader, the "bearer of the codes and norms presumed in [a text's] readership,"[21] the implied tourist is the visitor to whom memorials and their managers direct their rhetoric, the audience the visual and written rhetoric anticipates. Assuming that the implied tourist to Coronado National Memorial would not have read extensively on the history of the Coronado Expedition, for example, I did minimal research before visiting the sites. I think this helped me be more attuned to the mixed, even contradictory affects that are not only represented in a site's visual and written rhetoric but also, in a sense, communicated by the environment itself. What I found is that often the textual and environmental registers of affect are in tension with one another, and those tensions are instructive to map out.

Of course, an actual tourist interacts with a site in all kinds of ways that deviate from the ideal, or "authentic,"[22] NPS-constructed experience. I cannot possibly account for all of those ways. A particular challenge in this project has been how to deal with the fact that a veteran, or a Japanese descendant of an internee, or an Indigenous member of a tribe that was expelled from what's now an NPS site or whose ancestors were killed there, would no doubt react much differently than I did. Where possible, I draw on firsthand accounts. I also turn to literature. While I acknowledge the limitations of my own experiences in the West—and the limitations of the white male nature writers (like Muir and Abbey) who initially framed my own relationship to the region—my chapters reflect the region's diverse inhabitants, including American Indians as well as people of Chinese, Japanese, Mexican, and African descent.

A more explicitly environmentally justice-oriented project than mine might focus on historical and ongoing injustices with which the NPS is associated, such as Indian expulsion, racial segregation, and sexual harassment.[23] But it's the present-day sites and how they shape tourists' emotions, not the agency itself, that concern me here. My aim is neither to romanticize nor to condemn the NPS, though I do reflect on its future and its "rogue" branch, the Alt-NPS, in this book's postscript. *Memorials Matter* takes up Margret Grebowicz's call, in *The National Park to Come*, for a "new cartography of affects" at NPS sites, beyond the spectacular and historically exclusive "wilderness affect."[24] I hope that drawing attention to the politics of public affects makes a small contribution to much larger anti-racist and decolonial projects, and that the theoretical framework I lay out will be useful in future studies of affect in NPS sites (and other environments) that continue to grapple with these important issues.[25]

I've attempted to combine affect theory, a notoriously dense interdisciplinary body of work that appeals primarily, if not exclusively, to academics, with what ecocritics call narrative scholarship: a type of research-based writing that integrates personal stories and is meant to reach a wider audience. This unconventional hybrid approach was a challenge, but I took inspiration from Kathleen Stewart's evocative ethnographic approach in *Ordinary Affects* and from Rebecca Solnit's "passionate impurity."[26] Intellectually as well as stylistically, my foundations are shaky: the categories of analysis in this study—landscape, place, affect, public memory, built environment—are big, shifty ones, which I unpack in the introduction but can't finally pin down. Like Williams, I've approached my project with "humility"[27] and an openness to what Jane Bennett calls "moments of methodological naivete," in which critique is postponed in order to be more perceptive in the present.[28] I tried, as Bennett recommends, to "cultivate the ability to discern nonhuman vitality, to become perceptually open to it," a process I agree is an "ethical task."[29] For me, this perceptual openness meant letting my intellectual guard down and allowing myself to be surprised by how each memorial site affected me. Some of the arguments in the chapters struck me immediately while I was there; others emerged after much reflection. None was exactly what I expected.

If we listen and look for it, the matter at memorials tells us how to feel, and it is insistent in its calls for our ethical attention. Beyond memorials, I hope the insights in this study apply more broadly to our everyday environments.

Notes

1. John Muir, *Our National Parks* (Berkeley, University of California Press, 1991), 42. This passage is especially meaningful because it's in the chapter on Yellowstone National Park, Grand Teton's northern neighbor.

2. The lines are from the chapter "Polemic: Industrial Tourism and the National Parks." Abbey suggests rangers should be liberated from our offices and "put to work"—*outside.* "They're supposed to be rangers," he grumbles, "make the bums range." He then recommends prying tourists from their cars where they can "take risks," which he claims is "the right and privilege of any free American." Edward Abbey, *Desert Solitaire: A Season in the Wilderness* (New York: Ballantine Books, 1968), 63–4.

3. Jay Winter, "Sites of Memory and the Shadow of War," in *Cultural Memory Studies: An International and Interdisciplinary Handbook,* eds. Astrid Erll and Ansgar Nünning (Berlin: Walter de Gruyter GmbH & Co., 2008), 62. Like Winter, I use the phrase "sites of memory" (or memory sites) to mean, simply, "physical sites where commemorative acts take place" (61). I don't mean to align myself with Pierre Nora's use of the term (which I see as essentialist) to describe sites artificially produced to compensate for a lack of "real environments of memory." "Between Memory and History: *Les Lieux de Mémoire,*" *Representations* 26 (Spring 1989), 7–24. I also don't distinguish in binary terms between memory and history but rather understand "historical remembrance" as an approach in which history and memory critically inform one another as ways of making sense of the past. Jay Winter, "Historical Remembrance in the Twenty-First Century." *Annals of the American Academy of Political and Social Science* 617 (2008): 6–13.

4. Erika Doss, *Memorial Mania: Public Feeling in America* (Chicago: The University of Chicago Press, 2010), 45–6.

5. Doss, 13. Doss notes she is paraphrasing Ann Cvetkovich here, from *An Archive of Feelings: Trauma, Sexuality, and Lesbian Public Cultures* (Durham: Duke University Press, 1998), 7.

6. https://www.nps.gov/goga/planyourvisit/designations.htm. Accessed 15 January, 2017. This website echoes what several rangers told me on my site visits: a memorial "need not occupy a site historically connected with its subject."

7. I'm thankful to park historian Dr. John Sprinkle for directing me to what he says is the definitive NPS source, *The National Parks: Shaping the System* (Washington, D.C.: U.S. Department of the Interior, 2005). The different designations correspond to a distinct legislative and institutional history. For instance, a national monument can be established by a U.S. President using the Antiquities

Act of 1906, which enabled preservation of "historic landmarks, historic and prehistoric structures, and other objects of historic or scientific interest" (15). Initially, many monuments were American Indian "antiquities" (ruins and artifacts) or military forts. Nearly a quarter of NPS units "sprang in whole or part from the Antiquities Act," with more than 100 national monuments proclaimed by the beginning of this century (16). A national historic site is a broad designation for historically significant sites in the U.S. following the Historic Sites Act of 1935. Most, but not all, NHS sites are managed by the NPS. A national recreation area, a very recent designation, can be "based on roads or reservoirs—modern developments rather than natural or historic resources. Others were based on natural resources that did not necessarily meet national park or monument standards and that were set aside primarily to be developed for intensive public use. Hunting and other activities traditionally barred from national parks might be permitted in these places" (54). Recreation areas include things like reservoirs, parkways, and national seashores.

8. For instance, in his essay A. Huyssen identifies monuments with the search for origins, for a kind of "deep national past" that could suggest stability in an increasingly transient world (200). He claims an "anti-monumentalism" emerged in the twentieth century due to the aesthetically, politically, socially, ethically, and even psychoanalytically "suspect" nature of monuments (198). "Monumental Seduction," in *Acts of Memory: Cultural Recall in the Present*, eds. Mieke Bal, Jonathan Crewe, and Leo Spitzer (Hanover: Dartmouth College, 1999), 191–207.

9. Doss, 37.

10. *The National Parks*, 84.

11. This neutral philosophy is encoded in the NPS's *Interpretive Development Program*, available online at: https://www.nps.gov/idp/interp/theprogram.htm. The modules, which are used for training NPS interpreters, contain advice about helping "audiences to *make their own intellectual and emotional connections* to the meanings and significance of the resource." Accessed 3 June, 2018, my emphasis. The "visitor bill of rights" clarifies that visitors should "have their privacy and independence respected; retain and express their own values; be treated with courtesy and consideration; [and] receive accurate and balanced information." https://www.nps.gov/idp/interp/101/howitworks.htm. Accessed 9 June, 2018.

12. Emotional engagement is often yoked to intellectual engagement in NPS management literature, though specific emotional responses are rarely articulated. A close look at the *Interpretive Development Program* training modules yielded one document containing an impressive list of emotions interpreters might aim to elicit—an a-to-z list from "admiration" to "yearning." "Opportunities for Intellectual and Emotional Connections," NPS *Interpretive Development Program*, https://www.nps.gov/idp/interp/101/resources.htm. Accessed 4 June, 2018.

13. *The Hour of Land: A Personal Topography of America's National Parks* (New York: Sarah Crichton Books, 2016), 8.

14. Williams, 8 (my emphasis). I also shy away from the binary between learning and feeling that her statement implies. I discuss the relationship between cognition and emotion in the introduction.

15. Sabine Wilke, for one, suggests there is a "visual rhetoric associated with the parks and monuments of the American West [which] follows *a certain grammar* that can be articulated systematically and studied by individual examples" (101, my emphasis). "How German is the American West?: The Legacy of Caspar David Friedrich's Visual Poetics in American Landscape Painting," in *Observation Points: The Visual Poetics of National Parks*, ed. Thomas Patin (Minneapolis: University of Minnesota Press, 2012), 100–118.

16. Scholarship on "dark tourism" is worth a mention here. While some sites in my study might be understood through that framework, it's a bit tangential to (and too narrow for) my purposes.

17. Elisabeth Kübler-Ross, *On Death and Dying* (New York: Routledge, 1969).

18. *Reclaiming Nostalgia: Longing for Nature in American Literature* (Charlottesville: University of Virginia Press, 2012), xii.

19. Thomas Patin, "Introduction: Naturalizing Rhetoric," in *Observation Points: The Visual Poetics of National Parks*, ed. Thomas Patin (Minneapolis: University of Minnesota Press, 2012), xiii.

20. I invoke Robert M. Bednar's phrase. "Being Here, Looking There: Mediating Vistas in the National Parks of the Contemporary American West," in *Observation Points: The Visual Poetics of National Parks*, ed. Thomas Patin (Minneapolis: University of Minnesota Press, 2012), 2.

21. This definition comes from the Interdisciplinary Center for Narratology's online "Living Handbook of Narratology" (Hamburg: Hamburg University Press), accessed 8 January, 2015, http://wikis.sub.uni-hamburg.de/lhn/index.php/Implied_Reader. Thanks to my colleague and friend Erin James for inspiring the "implied tourist" idea.

22. Michael S. Bowman gives a useful overview of debates surrounding the concept of "authenticity" at a memory or heritage site—a concept that tends to be treated in essentialist terms, as opposed to "artificiality." "Tracing Mary Queen of Scots," in *Places of Public Memory: The Rhetoric of Museums and Memorials*, eds. Blair, Carole, Greg Dickinson, and Brian L. Ott (Tuscaloosa: The University of Alabama Press, 2010), 191–215. Like Bowman, I pursue a "more mobile, contingent, and performance-oriented conception" of tourism (208).

23. I devote some space in this book to the first two issues, but I don't attend to the agency's problems with sexual harassment. *High Country News* led an investigation of the NPS and found a systemic pattern of gender discrimination, an alarming number of sexual harassment allegations, and inadequate response by agency officials. Grand Canyon National Park has since dismantled its River District, and the House Committee on Oversight and Government Reform has begun holding high-level NPS officials (including Director Jon Jarvis) accountable. See Lyndsey Gilpin's articles in *HCN*, including an overview of the inves-

tigative process and its results as of 12 December, 2016: http://www.hcn.org/
articles/how-we-investigated-the-national-park-services-long-history-of-sexual-
harassment-and-discrimination. A follow-up feature cites a shocking report by
Secretary of the Interior Ryan Zinke that 40 percent of the National Park Service
workforce has been the victim of sexual harassment, intimidation, or discrimination. https://www.nationalparkstraveler.org/2018/01/updated-oig-finds-sexual-
harassment-continues-grand-canyon-national-park. Accessed 21 May, 2018.
Clearly this is a concerning problem, but it's not my focus here.

24. Margret Grebowicz, *The National Park to Come* (Stanford University Press, 2015),
58, 15.

25. In addition to historical work such as Mark David Spence's *Dispossessing the
Wilderness: Indian Removal and the Making of the National Parks* (New York:
Oxford University Press, 1999), scholars are assessing contemporary NPS and
other agencies' public lands management strategies for diversification. See, for instance, Randall K. Wilson, *America's Public Lands: From Yellowstone to Smokey
Bear and Beyond* (Lantham: Rowman & Littlefield, 2014). The agency's role as
an institution of settler colonialism, and the work the NPS is doing to diversify
its staff and its sites aren't my main concern. Others are taking up these issues in
more depth. Sarah Wald's monograph-in-progress examines Equity, Diversity, and
Inclusion efforts among public lands agencies and public lands advocates, and a
recent symposium Wald organized at the University of Oregon on "Environmental
Justice, Race, and Public Lands" brought together dozens of scholars invested in
these timely issues: https://blogs.uoregon.edu/ejrpl/. Accessed 29 May, 2017.

26. Stewart models the kind of scholarly experimentation she also recommends.
Ordinary Affects (Durham: Duke University Press, 2007). I appreciate Solnit's
ability to weave together "three voices" (memoirist, journalist, and critic), 2. She
encourages similarly "passionate impurists" (2) to "feel the conflicts" of a complicated world (3). Solnit, *Storming the Gates of Paradise: Landscapes for Politics*
(Berkeley: U C Press, 2007).

27. Williams, 11.

28. Jane Bennett, *Vibrant Matter: A Political Ecology of Things* (Durham: Duke
University Press, 2010), 17.

29. Bennett, 14.

Feeling Like a Mountain

Scale, Patriotism, and Affective Agency at Mount Rushmore National Memorial

When I first saw Mount Rushmore National Memorial (NM) in the fall of 1996, I was underwhelmed: It was so much smaller than I'd expected. Apparently, this is a common reaction. In films like *North by Northwest* and *Skins*, on billboards and postcards, on television shows, in cartoons, on T-shirts and souvenirs, Mount Rushmore is larger than life, the quintessential national monument,[1] the ultimate signifier of American history, patriotism, and liberty. These second-order representations isolate the mountain from its context—the visitor center, the tourists behind ropes and barricades, the roads that lead up to it, and the Black Hills themselves—and simply show four huge faces staring blankly from an enormous rock wall. Having seen so many images of the iconic foursome, there is almost no way seeing them in person can live up to expectations. Don DeLillo's Murray Jay Siskind observes something similar in *White Noise* when he arrives at "The Most Photographed Barn in America" and declares: "No one sees the barn . . . Once you've seen the signs about the barn, it becomes impossible to see the barn."[2] The same goes for Mount Rushmore.

In *Great White Fathers: The Story of the Obsessive Quest to Create Mount Rushmore*, John Taliaferro describes the "four-lane funnel" of Highway 16, the most popular approach to Mount Rushmore NM, as "one of the most orgiastic tourist corridors in the world."[3] Here you'll find a consumer-oriented "buffet of roadside attractions"[4] advertised by billboards for such places as Reptile Gardens, Old MacDonald's Farm, Cosmos Mystery Area (slogan: "See It! Feel It! Survive It!"), and Bear Country USA, where too-small enclosures house charismatic megafauna like mountain lions, wolves, grizzlies, and wolverines, and where lumbering black bears brush sides with your car door. You have to run the Highway 16 "gauntlet" before seeing Rushmore itself, and the "buildup virtually guarantees some degree of anticlimax."[5] Taliaferro likens arriving at Mount Rushmore NM to "driving up to any shopping mall in America. All the goodies are on the inside; the exterior is generic and bland." Its aesthetic is gray and "institutional" with smooth surfaces such as glass and granite. Under these circumstances, it's no wonder that, for many visitors, the experience is one of "confirmation,"[6] a kind of emotional ticking of a box. Many tourists stamp passport books, earn Junior Ranger badges, spend a polite amount of time reading each NPS display, buy a souvenir or two, and perform the compulsory but "cruel" optimism in which, Margret Grebowicz warns in *The National Park to Come*, national parks are implicated.[7]

Grebowicz challenges the reduction of public lands to "wilderness-as-spectacle," in which nonhuman nature is commodified and fetishized, and NPS sites are reified as "political states of exception," innocent of human history and conflict.[8] While not a wilderness area, Mount Rushmore NM does exemplify how the "spectacle" of public lands can falsely attest to political neutrality. The website's "History and Culture" page articulates the goal of the Memorial with a simple epigraph from Mount Rushmore's mastermind, sculptor Gutzon Borglum: "*The purpose of the memorial is to communicate the founding, expansion, preservation, and unification of the United States with colossal statues of Washington, Jefferson, Lincoln, and Theodore Roosevelt.*"[9] This simplistic description aptly matches each man to his most celebrated mythic achievement: Washington founded; Jefferson expanded; Lincoln unified; Roosevelt preserved. For rhetorician Carole Blair, the memorial generates a "Rushmore effect" in its "equation of scale and worthy commemoration."[10] Building on Blair's reading, Erika Doss notes Rushmore's "national ethos of masculinity, militarism, and gigantism," a kind of imperialistic monumentality.[11] Most distressingly, the location of the memorial is an affront to Lakota, for whom the Black Hills, and this particular mountain, known as Six Grandfathers, are sacred ground that the tribe never willingly relinquished. Despite the efforts of former superintendent Gerard Baker (Mandan/Hidatsa) and the establishment of a Lakota, Nakota, Dakota Heritage Village at the Memorial,[12] Rushmore remains, for many Indigenous peoples, a symbol of domination and disrespect.

Both Rushmore and its neighboring memorial to Crazy Horse[13] "invite us . . . to overlook their problematic ideological contents,"[14] and both "are meant to be looked at, and revered, from a distance."[15] The observations Blair and Doss make share optic and environmental assumptions: that *how we look at things*, ideologically, depends, in part, on *where we are* when we look at them. That is, our relationship to dominant ideologies is influenced by our spatial orientation. Scholarly critiques by Blair, Doss, and others are important in exposing and challenging problematic ideologies, but they miss the big picture, literally, by only seeing the mountain from one perspective, one scale.[16] Like Grebowicz's approach, these don't adequately account for the messiness of tourism, including the impacts of the landscape, the weather, and the individual tourists themselves. As Thomas Patin reminds us, tourism often "disrupts, destabilizes, unfixes, and critiques the dominant cultural schema," and tourists are never "simply and blindly mystified about the true nature of their activities."[17] Sometimes being a tourist means the images we've seen of Mount Rushmore and the ideologies we've internalized about it are "validated, *revised*, [and] *refined*."[18] What happens at Mount Rushmore NM when our perspective changes, our sense of scale shifts, and reverence isn't the affective response?

Sherman Alexie's poem, "Vilify," offers a shifty way of reading the site, leveling its own critique of the Rushmore effect and modeling an irreverent approach to the sculpture. He uses a loose villanelle form to ridicule the Memorial's ideological function by repeating versions of the line: "Who's on that damn Rushmore anyway?"[19] Like many of the poems in *Face*, "Vilify" is hybrid in form. Lengthy prose footnotes dwarf the actual verse. These footnotes range from tirades against blown glass art, to theories about President Bill Clinton's impeachment, to a mock court case featuring President Andrew Jackson discussing his penchant for duels, to a list of which presidents owned slaves—a list that includes two of the men on Rushmore. The footnotes are often quite funny. In the second one, Alexie tells about the time he was kicked out of school for wearing the T-shirt of Rushmore with "the presidents' faces on the front and their bare asses on the back." (Any tourist who's been to Rushmore will have seen this shirt.) Alexie's poetic persona tells us what he thinks of Rushmore in footnote four: The sculpture is "so literal," not like a work of art. It is one-dimensional: It "screams at us, 'These four guys are heroes.'" This kind of "epic sculpture" doesn't allow for the subjects' humanity, for their flaws, to show.[20] Rushmore "doesn't change [his] mind about the world. It exists only to be admired." Alexie's poem enhances scholarly critiques by taking the sculpture seriously as an aesthetic object: The Rushmore effect isn't just our association of scale with greatness; the effect is also bad art.

More than that, "Vilify" disrupts the in-your-face "epic" affect of the sculpture by modeling other ways to think and feel about it. Alexie claims "Native Americans are notoriously and ironically patriotic," and he models that ironic patriotism with his signature affect: "funny grief." The first footnote informs us that villanelles are the best poetic form for expressing "the painful and powerful repetitions of grief." Alexie's repetition of the question "Who's on that damn Rushmore anyway?" can thus be read as a rhetorical reenactment of the trauma of genocide and a reminder that Indigenous visitors to the site likely feel "painful grief" here. Alexie's repetitions negate the power of the "great men" by rendering them forgettable, and so, replaceable. By the end of the poem, the ambiguous "it" in the refrain "It's just too silly" could refer to the nationalistic impulse of the memorial itself as well as to its message about "heroes." Any number of the other white male presidents (who he suggests, bitterly, may have "owned a / heart chewed by rats") might be substituted for the actual four men honored on Rushmore, without altering its meaning.

With "Vilify," Alexie aligns himself with other protesters who have used Rushmore as a symbolic stage. Most visibly, American Indian Movement (AIM) protesters in the 1970s challenged the ongoing oppression of Indigenous people atop Rushmore. Greenpeace activists have held protests there as well. Alexie would be the first to admit that these acts of "reclamation" are more politically expedient than writing a subversive poem, but Alexie's approach is more attainable for most

FIGURE 1. View from the Peter Norbeck Overlook

visitors. Tourists can emulate the kind of disorientation in "Vilify." It is possible to "refine" rather than simply confirm our expectations of Rushmore through relatively simple acts of "revising its remote symbolism with supplemental meanings."[21] Driving around the Black Hills is one way to get "off the beaten path" and defamiliarize the memorial.[22]

The perspective from the Peter Norbeck Overlook, for instance, shrinks the faces to a blip in the vista, rendering them unnatural and much less significant amidst the vast Black Hills landscape. One can hardly make out the sculpture at all from this vantage point, never mind distinguish whose faces are on it. Alexie's persona in "Vilify" would no doubt love this view. Even strolling along the relatively popular Presidential Trail at the sculpture's base offers some unusual views. Features of the landscape help you re-see the faces. You can visually separate the heads and isolate one "great man" at a time. You can sneak up on George Washington and get a stunning view of his profile. You can frame a face with a quaking aspen or pair it with an unusual rock formation.

FIGURE 11. Lincoln's face framed by funky rocks

For me, traveling with a young child—my then-four-year-old son, Evan—disrupted the implied tourist's suggested perspective. Evan was fascinated by the authentic nineteenth-century steam engine that still runs out of Keystone. He was awestruck (indeed, his only assessment was: "It's awesome!") when he first saw and heard it, and I captured him on video stutter-yelling something in train language, a four-year-old elated version of "toot toot!" (and yes, of course, we rode the rails ourselves). The technologies for mountain carving showcased in the visitor center were also a hit, especially the hands-on exhibits designed for kids like him. He was not immune to the allure of the simulated dynamite detonation, for instance; he must have pushed the plunger and watched images of Rushmore rock explode onscreen at least a dozen times during our visit. But what fascinated him the most were the sculpture's lifelike visages. "What if they really came to life?" he demanded over and over again. He never tired of seeing them and he agreed with the NPS's now defunct "Moods of Rushmore" exhibit, which suggested the men's expressions are contingent and changeable.[23]

And they are. Lincoln's notably irregular eyes, for instance, communicate different moods; the left eye can look, as Borglum noted, "open, noncommittal, dreamy" while his brow appears "anxious, ever slightly elevated and concerned."[24] In the light of one particular evening, Taliaferro notices "how withdrawn Roosevelt seem[s], as if expressing his disdain for the present muster of rough riders."[25] He concludes that "the faces of Rushmore have expressions: Washington is stern, Jefferson is bemused, Roosevelt is avuncular, and Lincoln is resolute."[26] Taliaferro's labels sound definitive, but they are only his perspective on a certain day. Things like weather conditions and variations in light can make the difference between a smirk and a smile, or between a twinkling eye and a disdainful one. The facial expressions are dependent on scale, perspective, and environmental features as well as the personal predisposition of a given tourist—the "moodiness" we each bring to the site. In Sara Ahmed's words, our bodies "never arrive in neutral; we are always 'moody' in some way or another."[27] So, too, the mountain. As the "Moods of Rushmore" exhibit put it, "the Memorial has many moods, only a few of which are seen by a visitor on a given day."

The affective capacity of the memorial is one of the things the NPS wants to advertise to visitors. The website names "love" as one desirable affective response: "One of the most important gifts we can give our visitors at Mount Rushmore National Memorial is an understanding and love for our nation's history and cultures and an appreciation of the importance of caring for that legacy." Certainly patriotism, generally associated with "love of country," is one of the dominant affects circulating at Rushmore. In *Understanding Nationalism*, Patrick Hogan explains that "one function of nationalist history has been to associate our thought about the nation with emotionally powerful exempla—for instance, leaders and soldiers who protect us, thus figures that we can trust and admire."[28] Emotional reactions to exempla (Hogan tellingly names Abraham Lincoln as one) help determine our feelings about the nation as a whole, to the point where how we feel toward "real, individual Americans" matters very little. Seeing the faces on Rushmore can involve "emotion-triggering ideas and memories that will arise spontaneously when we think about the nation." Specifically, Hogan claims, nationalism can involve trust or pride, "a sort of joy derived from imagined superiority to others, first of all in emotionally consequential areas, such as greater power, which itself bears on both anger and fear."[29] Already a richer tapestry of emotions about the nation is emerging; "love of country" is one thread, but pride, trust, and joy, as well as anger or fear might also be interwoven.

Ahmed adds more emotions to the list of nation-directed feelings: "One loves the nation," she posits, "out of hope and with nostalgia for how it could have been."[30] Ahmed's nod to what we might call a *counterfactual nostalgia*, a nostalgia directed toward alternate unrealized possibilities, is prominent in American literature.[31] Perhaps the best example is Langston Hughes's "Let America Be America Again," a poignant call for America to "be the dream it used to be," a dream that "never was" but nevertheless, Hughes proclaims, "will be" realized.[32] This sort of counterfactual nostalgia is also pervasive at national memory sites. As we lament the violent aspects of our nation's history, we are asked to feel nostalgic not for the past as it actually happened but rather for a past that might have been, for an ideal version of our country that has not yet existed, but could.

Many memorials offer both a designated place to grieve a trauma and a kind of affective consolation, an affirmation of the hope that is foundational to a love of nation. The place itself matters. Just as Hughes assigns environmental features to the unrealized dream of an America we must "redeem"—"The land, the mines, the plants, the rivers," the "mountains and endless plain," and all the "great green states"—Hogan, too, ties nationalism to place as well as time. He notes how "national-ism cultivates an aestheticization of the nation as a physical place, first of all *as a landscape*" in order to "foster a sense of wonder."[33] Certainly many national memorial sites are chosen, if not explicitly to "foster wonder" then to perform the aesthetic, emplaced, ideological work of nationalism. Landscape is central to my consideration of nationalism and patriotism, these two unstable "historical, political, social, cultural, religious, and psychological construction[s]."[34] One goal of my project is to tease apart these two terms by reassessing and clarifying their en-vironmental and their affective dimensions.

I'd like to distinguish between *nationalism* as a political formation, an "idealized sociopolitical principle of 'the nation'" and *patriotism* as part of "its lived, *felt*, reality."[35] The affects in this book—patriotism, most obviously, but also shame, regret, grief, pride, fear, anger, guilt, and others—can feed into or contest nationalism, or they can do some-thing else entirely. I'd like to isolate and put pressure on patriotism as an affect that can sometimes, but doesn't always, bolster nationalism. Isn't it possible to feel patriotic, in the sense of loving one's country, but refuse to feed in to political nationalism in its more troubling man-ifestations: xenophobia, colonialism, war, and genocide? I think it is. Especially if we understand patriotism, following Ahmed, as an always deferred, unreciprocated love of country, we can more easily imagine connecting that "felt" sense of country to other objects, other collec-tives, other ideals that are neither grounded in heterosexual, white norms, nor marked by a "love for one's own kind . . . [that leads to] hatred for others."[36]

Patriotism is never a simple or a singular emotion. The sooner we acknowledge its complexities the more likely we are to find greater co-herence as a nation going forward—and increased coherence is crucial for confronting issues of social and environmental justice. One way to rethink patriotism is to foreground the physical environment's role in its production.[37] Perhaps, for example, it's possible to feel, at some me-morials, what Terry Tempest Williams calls "eco-patriotism,"[38] an affect she alludes to but doesn't fully develop in her chapter on Theodore Roosevelt National Park. This intriguing new affect is inspired, for her, by that monument's grasslands and the "openness, these unending views, the silences, the empyreal sky" that so impress her. Unlike conventional patriotism (and Williams acknowledges the tendency of "our national parks [to] make fetishes out of their founders and run the risk of turning history into kitsch"),[39] eco-patriotism is "a breathing space central to the health and wealth of our nation."[40] At Mount Rushmore NM, awe and wonder seem to preclude eco-patriotism, since the very "'awe'-inspiring artistic and technological feats" celebrated there fetishize founders, obscuring the "audacity of carving up rocky peaks held sacred by American Indians [and] embracing manifest destiny, militarism, and masculinity as appropriate tropes of national allegiance and identity."[41] For "breathing space" to be cultivated at Rushmore, it's probably necessary to be a different kind of tourist: one who views the mountains at unusual times and from unusual scales, adopts perspectives that encourage contemplation of the landscape's geologic and political history, and deliberately seeks out encounters with the Memorial's many "moods," even the bad ones.

Individual affective reactions will always vary, of course. Surveys from visitors to Mount Rushmore NM in 2013 suggest most visitors are impressed and moved by the site but can't really articulate why—a trend that holds true for all the surveys I read for this project.[42] Because of the questions the surveys pose, the majority of comments tend to be about the logistics of visiting.[43] At Mount Rushmore, visitors assess the parking facilities (too expensive, by many accounts), entry fees (should be free, many protest), ranger-led programs (by most accounts, fantastic), and other incidentals. Some urge more concessions, more conveniences, more spectacle; one visitor proposed that "live eagles and flags," and perhaps a "live band," would "give more entertainment value." Others lament the ever-growing facilities (especially the huge parking lot) and worry that the site has become "too commercialized."

There is space in the surveys for visitors to write in comments, but even in these sections emotion words are infrequent, and, for the most part, affective responses are vaguely formulated. Besides rhetoric about "enjoying" the visit, words related to "awe" are the most common. Unless you witness it firsthand, as I was fortunate to do with my son's awe at the steam engine, it's hard to distinguish a felt affective response from the colloquial use of the word "awesome"—

a word that's been robbed of its ties to the sublime and made interchangeable with other relatively empty signifiers like "cool" and "great." This casual use seemed to me to be far more prominent.[44] I will spend more time with awe and the related affect of wonder in later chapters. I also revisit the topic of patriotism—along with pride in labor-related technologies, including more mountain-moving dynamite and nineteenth-century steam engines—in chapter four, in which I describe a reenactment ceremony I attended at Golden Spike National Historic Site.

Affect theory, I'll suggest, can lend us a richer, more precise vocabulary for our emotional lives and complicate one-dimensional ways of reading memory sites. Even my quick sketch of affect at Mount Rushmore shows that "love of country" is inadequate to describing how affect circulates there. Analyzing NPS survey data offers little by way of conclusive information, since the data is sparse—most sites only do the surveys once a decade or so—and the questions aren't designed to gauge visitors' emotional responses. Still, it is possible to make some general observations about what happens at particular sites. In addition to writing about my own experiences and uncovering broad trends and insights from the surveys and other NPS data, I analyze a figure I call the "implied tourist," the theoretical cousin of Wayne Booth's "implied reader," the person who's hailed by the site's rhetoric. At each memorial, I track several affective registers: the *textual*, as represented emotion; the *corporeal*, as affect and/or emotion felt in my own body; and the *environmental*, as affect emanating from landscapes, built structures, and objects on-site. Repurposing Aldo Leopold's famous mandate to "think like a mountain," I want to consider what it would mean to *feel* like one. Even though he uses the verb "think," Leopold implies an affective dimension to this phrase. It's something we "know . . . in our bones." It might also be something "only the wolf" can manage, he admits.[45] What would it take for humans not only to think but also to feel like, or feel *with*, our environments? What particular emotions are encouraged at memorial sites? What about the affective registers that don't take emotional form, that aren't cathartic, or narrated, or easy to identify? How do landscapes and built structures shape and even facilitate affective responses to war, conflict, and national identity? To answer these kinds of questions, we need a better grasp of what affect is, its relationship to emotion, and how both circulate in the world.

———◆◆◆———

Affect is a slippery, nebulous, downright confusing term. It's been described as an "intensity," a "flow," an "atmosphere," and a "becoming." Affect can "jump," "stick," or accrete.[46] Affect can function as an umbrella term, covering things like "mood."[47] Affect can describe the way our moods make others feel, as in "the thing you display (emote) or experience (feel) toward an object or situation, any day of your life whether you are moody or not."[48] Or it can simply be used as a synonym for emotion. Kathleen Stewart's delightful ethnography *Ordinary Affects* doesn't try to define affect, but it does provide a methodological model for tracing affective "intensities" in the world—intensities that she finds are "more fractious, multiplicitous, and unpredictable than symbolic meanings."[49] Writing about such intensities requires a sense of affect as a corporeal "impression"[50] that is more immediate, more visceral, and less explicitly cognitive than emotion.

I treat affects as feelings that precede or elude consciousness and discourse, at least temporarily, and can transcend the individual body.[51] In geographer Ben Anderson's words, affects are "the transpersonal or prepersonal intensities that emerge as bodies affect one another."[52] In order to track and write about such intensities, I retain a definition of affect as an impression that is not explicitly narrated—in the late psychologist Teresa Brennan's words, a "physiological shift accompanying a judgment,"[53] where that judgment is a kind of corporeal rather than an intellectual appraisal, a physiological response to one's environment. I treat *emotions* as consciously interpreted or narrated affects— "feelings that have found the right match in words."[54] I am persuaded by Brian Massumi's distinction between emotion and affect, in which the former is but one possible form—albeit the "most intense (most contracted) expression"—affect can take.[55] Emotions are one manifestation, one coalescing, of affect in a particular body.

Melissa Gregg and Gregory J. Seigworth, co-editors of *The Affect Theory Reader*, declare no fewer than eight "affectual orientations" and insist there are "infinitely multiple iterations" affect theory might take.[56] Even for these broad-minded thinkers, it's possible to identify "two dominant vectors" in the humanities: "Silvan Tompkins's psycho-biology of differential affects" (a "quasi-Darwinian" approach) on the one hand, and "Gilles Deleuze's Spinozist ethology of bodily capacities" on the other.[57] These vectors "resonate" and, at times, "interpenetrate" with each other.[58] Despite the tendency to silo affect theory into different strands, I cite promiscuously from all varieties of the theory. As an intellectual pragmatist trained in cultural studies, I believe that the efficacy of a concept or approach depends upon what questions we're asking it to address.[59] To get at complicated social and political issues concerning emotion, a cultural theorist is probably the best resource; other times—such as when trying to understand what's happening in an individual body—it makes sense to draw on cognitive narratology or neuroscience. There are tensions between the cognitive science and cultural studies approaches to affect (the two dominant vectors), to the degree that some scholars see them as irreconcilable.[60] While my own approach tends toward the cultural theory vector, I remain committed to the insights of cognitive approaches. We need to understand how mirror neurons work, for instance, *and* how embodied encounters with environments generate impressions, intensities, and affective atmospheres. We need, I believe, an "all hands on deck" approach.

Affect theory is certainly not a utopian cure for the "hermeneutics of suspicion" that arguably constrains academic writing, but it does invite attunement to the "wonders that might emerge if we [scholar-writers] were not so attached to pragmatic negativity" in our scholarship.[61] Like Ruth Leys, who has produced one of the most incisive critiques of affect theory to date, I struggle with the idea that affect is "independent of signification and meaning," a view she condemns both neuroscientists like Antonio Damasio and cultural theorists like Massumi for championing.[62] I'm also, like Leys, skeptical of the idea of affect as entirely "free" or "autonomous." A strict interpretation of those terms implies that there is nothing helpful we can say about affect. By that logic, "you cannot read affects; you can only experience them," and, as Clare Hemmings explains in her own important critical assessment of affect theory, affect is then only "valuable to the extent that it is not susceptible to the vagaries of theoretical whim."[63] However,

I see little evidence of anyone seriously espousing such a strict interpretation.[64] I ultimately uphold several of the claims Leys critiques,
including that "affect is a matter of autonomic responses that are held
to occur below the threshold of consciousness and cognition and to be
rooted in the body," and that "there is a gap between the subject's affects and its cognition or appraisal of the affective situation or object."[65]
For me, it makes sense that affect operates "below the threshold"; much
of our affective life doesn't percolate into conscious thought. But just
because it's unpredictable and pre-cognitive doesn't mean we can't assess it; nor does it mean affect is wholly asignifying. Affect works in
mysterious ways, but those ways are neither random nor democrat-
ically distributed. With that in mind, it's crucial to attend to how racially marked and otherwise marginalized subjects, as Hemmings puts
it, "have a critical and affective life that resonates differently."[66]

Too often, affect scholars' own rhetoric works against our liberatory
impulses, even perpetuating misunderstandings and mystifications
with its opacity. Even books I love, like *Ordinary Affects*—which, at
one point, describes affect as a "kind of contact zone where the over-
determinations of circulations, events, conditions, technologies, and
flows of power literally take place"[67]—can be off-putting to students
and other scholars. A premise of my book is that ecocritical theory can
clarify how affect "takes place" on multiple scales and in diverse environments, and so help calibrate the relatively abstract definitions that
have pushed some scholars away from affect theory. I draw on insights
from ecocriticism's recent theoretical evolution: material ecocriticism,
an approach that "takes matter as a text, as a site of narrativity."[68]

Material ecocritics understand matter in an unconventional way.
More than raw material for human use, matter—the food we ingest, the
soil in which we grow food, the natural and human-made structures we
see, hear, smell, and touch—has agency in the form of profound impacts on the world and its occupants. Agency, in this humbling redefi-
nition, is not a product of individual consciousness or will but rather a
collective process, shared between human and nonhuman actors. This
conception of agency enhances scholarship on public memory by helping to theorize in more precise, nuanced terms the impacts of the extra-
textual, of physical matter, at sites of commemoration. So far, though,

ecocritics have focused on *narrative* agency and shortchanged other ways that matter affects our embodied experiences with other "things," the multitude of agential beings with which we come into contact every day. Perhaps the best-known proponents of material ecocriticism, Serenella Iovino and Serpil Oppermann, have held up "storied matter" and narrative agency as the main way of understanding matter as "agential."[69] As a trained literary studies scholar, I am tempted by this attribution of narrative agency to matter. But while I have no problem thinking of matter as a "site of narrativity,"[70] I am not convinced that matter is agential in a narrative sense. Things like rocks, for instance, are not narrators in the same way humans are, even if they might be "vibrant," in Bennett's words, or in Jeffrey Jerome Cohen's, "a spur to affect, cognition, and contemplation."[71] Moreover, we humans don't always narrate our experiences; a lot of what we feel goes unspoken and *un*storied. Finally, as any narrative theorist will tell you, narrative is a specific term, carrying particular (and contested) meanings. If we are to use it as a frame for understanding matter's agency, then narrative needs to be theorized much more carefully.

Since I want to emphasize its rhetorical dimensions, I draw on James Phelan's relatively narrow definition of narrative as "somebody telling somebody else on some occasion and for some purpose(s) that something happened."[72] Although it may seem hard to imagine an experience at a public memorial that escapes narration, I contend that we often do *not* convert bodily sensations into emotions by giving our feelings "narrative complexity." Sianne Ngai describes affect and emotion as slippery, dynamic forms of feeling: "affects [can] acquire the semantic density and narrative complexity of emotions, and emotions [can] conversely denature into affects."[73] This transmutability hinges on "narrative." If emotions require "semantic density" and affect doesn't, then affect touches tourists differently than narrative does. By bringing physical matter to the fore, I hope to extend and perhaps trouble Heather Houser's work on "narrative affect" (her shorthand for the way affects "are attached to formal dimensions of texts"[74]) by attending to the extra-textual, atmospheric dimensions of tourism that may arise from, but ultimately exceed and sometimes run counter to, the narrative dimensions. It's not sufficient to conjoin the two terms;

narrative and affect operate in tandem sometimes, but other times they are in tension and demand separate consideration. I share Houser's goal of achieving "an ecocriticism that accounts for the full affective spectrum of environmental fiction, from restorative place sense to techno-anxiety,"[75] but I extend the data set beyond fiction to include the material world. I wonder: How, and under what circumstances, do affect and narrative work together with an environment to shape experiences? What happens when they're at odds with each other? If the emotions we feel and contemplate, consciously, at sites of public memory often "denature into affects" once we head home, leaving us with only a vague set of impressions, then how do we measure the enduring emotional impacts of the site?

I propose ecocritics extend our conception of matter's agency to account for what I'm calling *affective agency*, understood as matter's capacity to generate felt impressions on other bodies even while remaining recalcitrant. This phrase might sound redundant to some theorists, especially those for whom affect is, by definition, a force or impact in the world.[76] I use it to engage the ecocritical phrase "narrative agency" directly and to encourage another angle. More than that, I attribute affective agency *to matter* in order to differentiate that kind of affect from other kinds, like background feelings and moods, which tend to be contained (and to linger) within an individual human body. The phrase affective agency, then, articulates the affective forcefulness of physical environments, which have too often been neglected in affect theory but are clearly major players in the assemblage theories and object-oriented ontologies that have captivated scholars in many disciplines.[77] Affective agency treats both affect and matter as contingent forces that are always in the process of taking shape. Just as affect can take many forms—including, but not limited to, emotion—matter, too, "is a *tendency* toward spatialization," not a stable formation.[78]

Memorials are a sort of "hard case" for ecocritics who want to talk about matter's agency, since most memorials feature sculpted, built structures, which appear static, not dynamic, and do not seem to "act" in a traditional sense. Following scholars like Bennett, who recognizes "an affect intrinsic to forms," and Erika Doss, for whom affect is "embodied in . . . material form,"[79] I ask: How does matter generate affect, exactly? I understand memorials as generating contingent "affective atmospheres," a phrase Anderson (via Nigel Thrift and others) champions and I use here to describe "singular affective qualities that emanate from but exceed the assembling of bodies."[80] Anderson likes the ambiguity of "atmosphere" because it "unsettles" the emotion-affect distinction and, significantly for my project, encompasses situations and conditions that "mix together narrative and signifying elements and non-narrative and asignifying elements."[81] Brennan challenges us to acknowledge that even the most banal places have atmospheres: "Is there anyone who has not, at least once, walked into a room and 'felt the atmosphere?'"[82] I want to push on what it means to "feel the atmosphere" not just *in* a place but *of* a place as I move to examine some of the environmental catalysts involved in the transmission of affect.

Atmospheres are shaped by the built environment as well as the natural one, but it's not enough to simply look at design plans or management strategies. Memorials (like literary texts) generate affective intensities that are not reducible to an architect's (or an author's) intentions. I approach the landscapes and the built structures at memorials in a similar way as I do literature, including assessing what Ngai calls "tone": a "literary or cultural artifact's . . . global or organizing affect, its general disposition or orientation toward its audience and the world."[83] Whereas an affective atmosphere is generated by a whole assemblage, *tone* is more particular: "the dialectic of objective and subjective feeling that our aesthetic encounters inevitably produce" when we encounter an artifact.[84] Tone doesn't so much resolve this dialectic, for me, as much as it foregrounds the processive, negotiable nature of aesthetics. I emphasize, too, that if tone is an "affective relay" between self and object,[85] there is always an environment in which this relay takes place—an environment that is affective in its own right. Even as I center the natural and built environments as affective agents at public memory sites, I read tone as a contributing feature of perpetually emergent affective atmospheres, a feature that's sometimes legible and sometimes elusive.

In addition to relying on concepts and approaches from literary studies (my primary discipline) I rely on literature itself to enhance my analysis in each chapter. As I indicated in the Preface with my recollection of poignant quotes pinned to park rangers' office walls, stories, words, even just fragments of remembered lines, shape how many of us understand our connections to natural environments. The "good tidings" Muir wants us to get from "Nature" are in part *stories*, the ones we hear, read, and tell about the landscapes we visit. With that in mind, I cite from relevant literature—poetry, memoir, short fiction, essays, and/or novels—to develop fuller descriptions of the different environments in my study. Not all of the literary texts directly address the history or perspectives represented at the NPS sites, though most do. I selected literature that best conveys the affective qualities of the particular environments at stake. In the cases where the texts shaped my personal experiences at the sites and, in some cases, the experiences of other tourists as well, those narratives become a small part of the cultural and emotional memory we bring to the sites. Perhaps most significantly, the authors I cite here—Terry Tempest Williams, Sherman Alexie, Luis Alberto Urrea, Lauret Edith Savoy, Simon Ortiz, Maxine Hong Kingston, Joan Didion, James Jones, Jeanne Wakatsuki Houston, Shelton Johnson, Carolyn Finney, and others—teach readers, in powerfully affective terms, about the rich diversity and breadth of experience that has always characterized the American West. While most of the chapters give more space to physical environments, chapter six foregrounds a novel—Shelton Johnson's *Gloryland*—as itself a kind of memorial, a powerful way of locating emotions about a history that has yet to be adequately commemorated in a particular place. In all the chapters, literary voices shed invaluable light on this region's complicated history and urge us to bring that history to bear on present-day conflicts.

Tourism is both informed by literary texts and is itself *a kind of reading*: We "read" a landscape, we follow its cues for rhythms and pacing, we detect the tone of a place. Being a tourist can feel like performing in what David Seamon calls a "place ballet": "an interaction of time-space routines and body routines rooted in space, which becomes an important place of interpersonal and communal exchanges, actions, and meanings."[86] Visiting the USS *Arizona* Memorial, for instance, involves a fluidity of movement that is ballet-like in its pacing; we do a dance carefully choreographed for us. Other times, the awkwardness of negotiating tourist sites feels more like my first ballet classes as a five-year-old girl in which I followed the leads of more experienced dancers, learned the motions by mimicry, but never quite found a graceful rhythm of my own. Every NPS site contains its "conversion points," a phrase Ahmed uses, in "Happy Objects," to refer to the moments in a narrative (in her essay, the film *Bend it Like Beckham*) at which "bad feeling (unhappy racism)" is converted into "good feeling (multicultural happiness)."[87] In her reading, it's a character that functions as a conversion point. For my project, it's the features of an environment that convert our affects: the display signs, walkways, trails, overlooks, benches, and other physical aspects of a site that direct our affective itinerary. Sometimes being a tourist feels like being one of those metal balls in a pachinko machine, ricocheting from one conversion point to another, our affective states evolving with each bump.

Literary texts may have an advantage over critical theory when it comes to describing matter and more-than-human phenomena in terms of both emotions and agency. In literature, storms can be angry, trees can harbor sad memories, or a boulder can plummet down a mountainside, nearly crushing a slumbering camper. Indigenous writers are particularly adept at expressing matter's agency in terms of narrative and affect. Every time I read Leslie Marmon Silko's "Landscape, History, and the Pueblo Imagination," I am struck by her description of rocks as mobile and, to a degree, animate. For the ancient Pueblo people, Silko explains, survival "depended upon harmony and cooperation not only among human beings, but also among all things—the animate and the less animate, since rocks and mountains were known to move, to travel occasionally."[88]

I suspect many ecocritics are persuaded by Silko's assertion that "a rock has being or spirit, although we may not understand it,"[89] and I know many of us aim for our scholarship to express how the "less animate" world has value, sovereignty, and agency. For environmental historians, the agency of nonhuman nature is a foundational premise.[90] Geographers, too, like to see agency as a property of the natural world, and that world as always in process. Theories of place typically understand it as space (imagined as "empty" by contrast) that is used, narrated, and personalized in particular ways.[91] Places, especially commemorative places, can be thought of as palimpsests,[92] where history accrues in layers over time, or as assemblages, sites where things "gather."[93] I'm most interested in places as produced by, and as themselves participants in, our embodied, felt encounters with a designated landscape, encounters that change both the observer and the observed. "Landscape" is an essential term in a project on NPS sites, since these have historically been created around impressive landscapes, and landscape architecture has steered management, sometimes to the dismay of park scientists.[94] I recognize the limitations to the term landscape; its static and optic connotations usually prioritize the "shape—the material topography—of a piece of land" and reduce it to something we look at.[95]

Yet, landscapes can be thought and experienced in more fluid terms. In Doreen Massey's view, for instance, a landscape is "the (temporary) product of a meeting up of trajectories out of which mobile uncertainty a future is—has to be—negotiated."[96] Yi-Fu Tuan's influential formulation of "topophilia" is especially attuned to the affective pull, or force, of particular landscapes.[97] Rhetoricians offer useful approaches to memorial landscapes as well. In addition to Carole Blair's influential work on memorials, Greg Dickinson, Brian L. Ott, and Eric Aoki argue for treating memorials as "experiential landscapes": "intersections of both physical and cognitive landscapes" that "invite visitors to assume (to occupy) particular subject positions."[98] I'll take up their phrase and foreground the affective dimensions of this formulation in chapter two. When I say that I'm diversifying the book by type of landscape, then, I refer both to the visual aspects of the environments—part of what makes them NPS sites in the first place—and to the unstable physicality, the materiality, and the agency of each, where the experiential, touristic shaping of public memory that occurs in it makes it a "place."

Despite the important work of scholars across the disciplines who've influenced my thinking about physical matter and affect at public memory sites, exactly *how* affect "happens"[99]—who or what initiates it, how agency is negotiated, and what role the physical environment plays—remains hard to say, especially when the bodies in question are nonhuman or inanimate. Bennett's description of the "small agencies" Darwin attributed to worms is useful to bear in mind; at a memorial, we might say a wall of the missing, an obelisk, or a flower left behind by previous visitors, has the kind of small agency that "when in the right configuration with other physical and physiological bodies, can make big things happen."[100] My project extends her thinking by foregrounding the agencies of both built structures and nonhuman nature, including things like landscape, nonhuman animals, and weather. I'm also inspired by Brennan, for whom affect transmission is a kind of emotional contagion "that is social in origin but biological and physical in effect"—a process dependent on "an interaction with other people and an environment."[101] Environments surely modulate fear, awe, joy, wonder, sadness, and every other emotion.

That said, an environment is not the sole agent of affective determination. I share Ahmed's concerns about an "outside-in" model of affect transmission: It ignores the "moodiness" of the embodied subject and risks "transforming emotion into a property, as something that one has, and can then pass on, as if what passes on is the same thing."[102] Rather, affect transmission is a kind of "world making,"[103] a mobile and fluid process in which objects become "sticky," or "saturated with affect, as sites of personal and social tension."[104] Indeed, affect might be *defined* as "what sticks, or what sustains or preserves the connection between ideas, values, and objects."[105] The objects[106] then circulate in culture, accruing more or less affective power (or a different valence) with each movement, through each conversion point. Although static in comparison to, say, a tweet that goes viral, a memorial site can itself be understood as an object in Ahmed's terms—saturated and intense—even as it contains myriad "sticky" objects that transmit affect as they exist and acquire meaning at the site and, later, in visitors' memories. Objects and other "things" have affective agency. What Bennett calls "thing-power" is increasingly a force to be reckoned with at sites of memory, as events recede into the past, survivors pass away, and tourists' memories become, more and more often, "prosthetic."[107]

At sites of public memory, affect transmission is especially complex. Grebowicz calls for a "deeper understanding of how mood, or mode of attunement, is at the center of our collective experience of an environment," by way of a more "self-reflective mapping of our nostalgia, mourning, and desire, and our experiences of futurity and internal coherence in relationship to instituted nature-spaces."[108] These are central concerns in *Memorials Matter*. However, the notion of a "wilderness affect," which Grebowicz defines by "our participation in wilderness-as-spectacle as a form of social relation,"[109] doesn't quite map on to sites of public memory. While social relations are certainly negotiated at memorials, these sites are seldom spectacular and much less likely to foster "fantasies of our own coherence" as a nation. In fact, sites like Manzanar NHS and Sand Creek NHS are set up precisely to contest the "wellness, sanity" and "social order" so often implied at national parks.[110]

I propose a new phrase, *affective dissonance*, to describe the unruly affects felt at memory sites.[111] A counterpart to what psychologists term cognitive dissonance, affective dissonance is the unsettled state in which we experience more than one *feeling* at the same time, often with a sense of conflictedness or irony but not necessarily with a consciously "storied" understanding of what we're feeling. Bennett suggests (following Latour) that the experience of modern "entanglements" precipitates a "cognitive dissonance between the everyday experience of [the] commingling [of agents] and the rubric of an environment that we direct from above and outside."[112] This is certainly one way to think of it, but I find affective dissonance is necessary for conceiving of our *feelings* about this disjunctive experiential entanglement.

I am inspired again by Ngai, whose *Ugly Feelings* uses literary terminology to gauge complex, and often mixed, emotions, including the "noncathartic" and "ambient" ones.[113] Affective dissonance is similar, in some ways, to what Houser identifies as "discord": an "irritating affect" that can produce a "suspicious stance" with "implications for oppositional politics."[114] Affective dissonance, as I define it here, can certainly be irritating, produce suspicion, and—like Houser's discord—mark our embodied situatedness in space; it also has "an intensity belied by its subtlety."[115] I appreciate Houser's point that discord "sets us outside of ourselves such that we become checks on our own habits of thought." I am convinced that all affects, to some degree, "bridge gut and mind" and have the potential to "check" our thoughts and behaviors.[116] However—and here's where I part ways with Houser's formulation of discord—affective dissonance is not a *singular* affect. It's characterized by an ironic doubleness, or even multiplicity; it's an affective state of being rather than an emotion itself.

Most of us experience affective dissonance fairly often in everyday life, especially now that "global weirding"[117] is producing strange new atmospheres. Say you're at a gasoline pump in northern Idaho, and gas costs less than $1.00. Outside it is sunny and 70 degrees Fahrenheit—in February. You are enjoying the cheap prices and the lovely weather, but, at the same time, you feel uneasy, a sense of what DeLillo's character Jack Gladney, when faced with a sudden "airborne toxic event," describes as "a vague foreboding." That's affective dissonance. Or, it is 108 degrees outside and too hot to sleep on the main floor of your house. With a sense of joy and naivete—having not yet seen news coverage of displaced people living in gyms, deserts, or temporary cities—your young children erect what they call a "tent village" in the basement. How did your seven-year-old know this phrase? Was he somehow anticipating, and adapting to, a future of climate refugees? You are proud of their intuitive resourcefulness, but you feel a simultaneous anxiety, a low-level panic—not quite dread but something close to it. That's affective dissonance.

At memorials, affective dissonance is common. Consider the irritated Rushmore visitor who did not feel the "emotional patriotism that had been felt on each previous visit" due to glitches in the affective atmosphere: a repositioning of the flags in the Avenue of Flags, crowds at the bookstore, and some disruptive children during the evening program. Or the righteous visitor who declared the site "underwhelming," then elaborated: It's "a surprisingly good indicator of why the Native Americans were, have been, and remain against this type of colonialism. White supremacy. We were far more intrigued by the nature than by this giant, clearly out of place, white rock with heads of dead white guys in the middle of the Black Hills."[118] An Indigenous visitor to Mount Rushmore NM, especially a Lakota, likely brings with her a feeling for the Black Hills as sacred, but perhaps also a measure of anger at the U.S. appropriation and desecration of this space.[119] Forced into the role of a tourist at this site of settler colonialism, she might feel affective dissonance, an unsettled mood, or a set of conflicting emotions.

Indigenous visitors might be among those who feel like *affect aliens* at NPS sites. I borrow this phrase from Ahmed to describe a person whose emotions are out of synch with what's expected— usually, happiness, or another affect that reflects and reinforces dominant social norms.[120] Being an affect alien is complicated and exhausting. As Ahmed explains, "You can be affectively alien be- cause you are affected in the wrong way by the right things. Or you can be affectively alien because you affect others in the wrong way: Your proximity gets in the way of other people's enjoyment of the right things, functioning as an unwanted reminder of histories that are disturbing, that disturb an atmosphere."[121] The Lakota visitor who brings anger to Mount Rushmore would likely feel like an af- fect alien during the memorial's evening program, at which veterans are routinely invited up on stage for a standing ovation and patri- otism is the dominant mood. Being an affect alien can be a useful way of diagnosing and critiquing dominant ideologies. In the case of this hypothetical visitor, we're reminded that members of tribes need not be merely "ironically patriotic," in the way Alexie's poem models, but can feel genuinely patriotic about their own tribal na- tion and potentially about the U.S. as well. This affect alien could foreground the fact that this country is, after all, a nation of nations, or that patriotism is a form of unrequited love, which works so well because it's perpetually deferred.[122]

While select tourists may function as "unwanted reminders" of re- pressed histories, many more of us have had the sensation that we are being affected "in the wrong way" by a site. Broadly speaking, feeling like an affect alien as a tourist often means something more like *affect imposter syndrome*: a sense of inadequacy, of being unqualified to assess a situation, or of "not getting it" on some fundamental level. The affect imposter feels in over her head, not in a professional capacity, which is the context the phrase usually refers to,[123] but in relation to a place. The imposter's anxiety is of merely passing as an insider, of not really belong- ing at all. While I don't want to diminish the important work being done on imposter syndrome in other contexts, especially related to gender in the workplace, I think tourism of memory sites is especially conducive to affect imposter syndrome. For most of us, sites of trauma are places of "second-order memory" where we "remember the memories of others, those who survived the events marked there."[124] Affect imposter syndrome is important to track as part of this process.

———————

These conversations matter not just for the relatively narrow scholarly category of material ecocriticism, but for the environmental humanities, Indigenous studies, American studies, and public memory studies. As should be clear by now, I believe public memory studies can be enriched by more attention to environmental and affect theory. I treat "public memory" like Edward Casey does, as memory that occurs "out in the open . . . where discussion with others is possible—whether on the basis of chance encounters or planned meetings—but also where one is exposed and vulnerable."[125] For me, as for Casey, "platial parameters" are "central, if not primary" to the production of public memory.[126] Affect has garnered some attention from public memory scholars, but it often remains undertheorized,[127] showing up in scholarship as an unexplored assumption or a catchy buzzword.[128] Environments, likewise, certainly do feature in some public memory studies, but not typically with an explicitly ecocritical focus. Because it is organized around a comparative study of landscapes and built structures and draws directly on affect studies and ecocritical theory, *Memorials Matter* makes a unique contribution to public memory studies.

Public memory is increasingly understood as contingent and processive, and today's memorials are often ambivalent. This marks a shift in the history of commemoration in the U.S. Doss sketches the history of memorial production over the last century and a half in the first chapter of her book *Memorial Mania*, "Statue Mania to Memorial Mania." Statue mania, dominant during the decades after the Civil War, presumed a unified sense of history and a more cohesive nation, frequently celebrating "great men" (and so, too, masculinity and war) in order to bolster nationalism. Memorial forms have diversified along with the demographics they represent, and official national narratives have mostly given way to "the subjective symbolic expressions of multiple American publics."[129] Statues to famous men have not been entirely displaced, but statues have been supplemented by commemorative trees, plaques, parks, benches, quilts, candlelit shrines, roadside markers, and websites. Commemoration has shifted in scale, too, from the predominantly local in the nineteenth century, to the national, and now, at least in some cases, to the global. Doss identifies our contemporary moment's "memorial mania," the "obsession with issues of memory and history and an urgent desire to express and claim those issues in visibly public contexts." She notes that this mania is shaped by the "affective conditions of public life in America today: by the fevered pitch of public feelings such as grief, gratitude, fear, shame, and anger."[130] Not all the sites in my study could be described as "fevered," but they all deal with public feelings that warrant clarification.

In addition to highlighting a distinct landscape, each chapter features a constellation of related affects, which I theorize via a range of disciplinary approaches. As tempted as I was by the idea of a one-affect-per-chapter framework, I've found it impossible to isolate one at a time. To echo (clumsily) John Muir, when I tried to pick out any affect by itself, I found it hitched to everything else, if not in the whole universe, at least in the immediate environment, and to other affects as well. Affects are never static; they precipitate, emerge from, merge with, and fade or intensify into, other affects. And affect only rarely takes the form of a singular emotional response; more often we are "moody" in a complex sense. My methodology assumes that our affective lives are perpetually in flux and that even an apparently singular emotion, like fear, can be felt differently in an individual body, depending on present circumstances.[131] With the exception of entrenched moods or background feeling such as depression, we flit, or morph, from one affective state to another, sometimes rather quickly and sometimes slowly. As I map the shifts and flows within particular environments and around the many conversion points that direct a tourist's encounter with a memory site, I find myself moving between affiliated affects—such as fear, awe, and anxiety, or guilt, regret, and compassion—in any given chapter.

I've organized the chapters chronologically by historical event, for several reasons. For one, it's difficult to decide how to mark the official beginning of a site. Would I use the date when legislation was first introduced, when legislation was approved, when the visitor center opened, when people first began to create makeshift memorials, or when the most recent NPS designation was made? Although the book isn't structured around NPS history, I try to think about why particular memorials were designated when they were, and to say something about the emergence of the NPS in the twentieth century and its shifting priorities as an agency. My (admittedly limited) data set suggests it takes longer to deal with sites that more directly address racism or confront American Indian genocide.[132] Sand Creek Massacre National Historic Site was the last in my study to receive official designation, and there are, as of yet, no sites in the U.S. West devoted exclusively to African American experiences in the region.

Since memorialization in the U.S. typically involves "rights claims and demands for respect,"[133] this lag time tells us something about what (and who) the American public deems worthy of respect, who belongs in that public, and whose rights matter. Minority groups in the U.S. have nevertheless found ways for their voices and experiences to come through, even in a region—the West—to which their contributions have too seldom been recognized. To its credit, the NPS often works closely with the groups whose history is being remembered; in my study, Manzanar and Sand Creek National Historic Sites are examples of long-term NPS partnerships with victims and their descendants. Too often, though, despite well-intentioned managers and site designers, Indigenous and other nonwhite groups' experiences in the U.S. West remain elided, downplayed, or romanticized. Contemporary politics—whether along the coasts, on islands, or at our national borders—can be elusive, even at sites where the *historical* significance of these politics is clear.

It's not enough, then, to simply presume that "healing" happens. We need to grasp how the physical environment and the emotions generated at sites of public memory have serious implications not only for how we remember the past but also for how we understand the present. In her brief overview of affect, Cvetkovich ties it to public memory: "In seeking to address traumatic histories, public cultures of memory raise questions about what emotional responses constitute a reparative relation to the past and whether it is ever possible to complete the work of mourning, particularly while social suffering is ongoing."[134] No one project can answer those questions definitively, but I hope, in comparing diverse sites across the American West, mine makes strides toward contextualizing the social suffering of the region's diverse inhabitants and moving toward "a reparative relation to the past."

The first chapter of *Memorials Matter*, "'Fears Made Manifest': Desert Creatures and Border Anxiety at Coronado National Memorial," opens in an especially fraught environment: at the U.S.–Mexico border, site of President Donald Trump's highly controversial proposed wall. Initially envisioned as a collaborative memorial between the two nations, today's Coronado National Memorial is managed solely by the NPS. Textual displays highlight the cultural exchange that resulted from Francisco Vázquez de Coronado and other explorers in what is now the American Southwest, but that rhetoric masks deep anxieties. I invoke a range of research on fear to argue that a more precise understanding of fear, as well as its more moderate register, anxiety, helps reveal how these affects work culturally, and how they "stick" to some landscapes and bodies, but not others. Citing Luis Alberto Urrea's *The Devil's Highway*, Lauret Edith Savoy's *Trace: Memory, History, Race, and the American Landscape*, and other texts, I argue that cultural associations with deserts and their inhabitants (specifically, rattlesnakes) as well as fear of immigrants coming from Mexico—reinforced by NPS literature and the presence of Border Patrol vehicles—may stoke an anxious affective atmosphere. At the same time, the vast desert landscape exposes the arbitrariness and contingency of national borders as well as the complexity of fear itself. This opening chapter outlines an array of approaches in affect theory—from cognitive science to cultural theory—that I draw on, to varying degrees, in the other chapters.

In chapter two, "Placing Historical Trauma: Guilt, Regret, and Compassion at Sand Creek Massacre National Historic Site," I turn to an especially violent episode in the history of Westward expansion, the Sand Creek Massacre. Putting Simon Ortiz's poignant poetry collection, *from Sand Creek*, in dialogue with the representations of the massacre at today's National Historic Site, I suggest that this remote, quiet landscape may be ideal for contemplation, but that the NPS's reliance on primary historical documents and overarching minimalist approach risk quieting the violence of the actual massacre. The calm landscape and the history of trauma it contains are in tension here for the implied tourist, encouraging an affective dissonance for non-Native visitors that makes it difficult to imagine what happened there. For most non-Native tourists, I suspect, white guilt slips into a self-congratulatory form of patriotism without necessarily feeling compassion for, or taking responsibility for, either past or present Indigenous struggles. For the affected tribes, even for some members for whom the creation of the site marked a positive step, healing remains prospective, contingent on apologies and reparations yet to be made. I suggest that compassion and regret, rather than guilt, may be the affects most likely to support real healing and justice for the tribes.

Chapter three, "Performing Patriotism: Reenactment, Historicity, and Thing-Power at Golden Spike National Historic Site," shows how the reenactment ceremony at Promontory Point creates a public united, affectively, around the historicity of the occasion and the patriotic enthusiasm for labor and technological progress the site celebrates. Even while the NPS tries to be sensitive to the exploitation and loss of life that were by-products of the railroad building—for instance, by constructing a small monument to the Chinese laborers and featuring the "Chinese Arch" as a stop on the driving tour—the site ultimately champions Westward expansion in spite of its human sacrifices. That violence is historicized out of existence through the celebratory affects of pride and patriotism. I situate Maxine Hong Kingston's memoir, *China Men*, especially the chapter about her Chinese ancestors building railroads in the West, as a provocative challenge to NPS managers to step up their efforts to honor the victims of "progress" and generate more nuanced understandings of patriotism.

In chapter four, "Remembering War in Paradise: Grief, Aloha, and Techno-patriotism at WWII Valor in the Pacific National Monument," I examine the difficult, even ironic task of commemorating war in an environment often thought of as a kind of paradise. I incorporate vibrant descriptions of the Oʻahu landscape, weather, and flora from Native Hawaiian authors and scholars, from James Jones's *From Here to Eternity*, and from Joan Didion's "The Islands," to argue that there is a strong sense of affective dissonance involved in being asked to grieve lost lives in a "paradise" setting. The natural beauty and tropical atmosphere work at cross-purposes with the kind of solemnity most of us associate with war memorials—and which the NPS and military managers prepare visitors to feel at the USS *Arizona* Memorial. I read the Memorial's "black tears"—the oil that still leaks from the sunken USS *Arizona*—as an instigator of affective dissonance that challenges the patriotism encouraged at the site. The celebration of war technology on the mainland is also at odds with the contemplation of loss visitors are meant to undertake at the Memorial itself and with the historic move "from [military] engagement to peace" with Japan that NPS managers have lately emphasized. The site's tendency to sideline Indigenous Hawaiian knowledge and ignore how Kanaka Maoli feel about the militarization of their sacred landscape means that peaceful resolution is promoted without a fuller picture of historical and present-day concerns.

Chapter five, "Mountains, Monuments, and Other Matter: Reckoning with Racism and Simulating Shame at Manzanar National Historic Site," grapples with the aftermath of Pearl Harbor: internment (incarceration) of Japanese Americans in the West. It also probes attitudes about national identity and raises concerns about how violent attacks spark extreme, sometimes racist, responses. This chapter uses former incarceree Jeanne Wakatsuki Houston's memoir *Farewell to Manzanar* as a touchstone as I explore the environmental features of Manzanar: the extreme desert weather, the mountain vistas, the incarceree-created rock gardens, the reconstructed barracks, guard tower, and barbed wire fence, and the cemetery/monument. My analysis shows how powerful affects of shame, anger, and grief circulate at the site and how spatial ironies are embedded in the environment. I question under what circumstances shame actually happens at sites like this or whether, as Ahmed suggests, shame too often morphs into patriotic affirmation, both of oneself as a "good citizen" and of the nation as a progressive, liberal democracy.

Chapter six ends at the watery Western edge of the nation, in the Presidio of San Francisco, a place almost as fraught as the border featured in chapter one. The Presidio has been a staging ground for imperialism abroad and incarceration at home, and it bears the traces of this history. In this chapter, "'We have died. Remember us.': Fear, Wonder, and

Overlooking the Buffalo Soldiers at Golden Gate National Recreation Area," I compare the Presidio's official WWII Memorial, a wall of the missing inscribed with names of soldiers whose bodies were lost at sea, to a more subtle one: a stone wall at the nearby cemetery overlook engraved with excerpts from Archibald MacLeish's poignant poem "The Young Dead Soldiers Do Not Speak." Among the 30,000 buried in the cemetery are 450 buffalo soldiers, whose graves conjure a "black West" that is often invisible. I invoke Shelton Johnson's NPS career and his historical novel *Gloryland* to flesh out the too-seldom acknowledged service of these soldiers at the Presidio and elsewhere in the West, including their involvement in frontier expansion and their roles as some of the first NPS rangers. *Gloryland*, I argue, confronts the affective dimensions of racism, exposing fear as both a justifiable response to racism and one of the negative affects that fuels it. At the same time, the novel tracks more positive emotions—including joy and wonder— African Americans feel in natural environments. Even at a site of recreation, overlooked histories and other matters of life and death are brought to the fore in surprisingly affective ways. I end by encouraging readers to pay attention to our everyday environments, to become attuned to the features and feelings we tend to ignore, and to increase our receptivity to the emotional memories embedded in all landscapes.

Finally, a short postscript entitled "'Going Rogue' with the Alt-NPS: Managing Love and Hate for an Alternative Anthropocene" considers the NPS's role in the polarized political climate following the election of President Donald Trump in 2016. In this "alt-conclusion" of sorts, I track the emergence of the Alt-NPS as a participant in movements to resist the Trump administration's stances not only on environmental issues but also on social issues. I discuss the events in Charlottesville, Virginia, surrounding the removal of a statue of Robert E. Lee from a public park, as a tragic reminder of what powerful affective agents memorials continue to be and a contemporary example of how love and hate are enlisted as emotional allies for various activist groups. I conclude with a call for a clearer understanding of what love and hate are, how they inform the politics of social and environmental justice in particular, and how expanding love's boundaries might be the most crucial call to action in our new epoch, the Anthropocene.

Notes

1. Despite its designation as a "memorial," Mount Rushmore illustrates the power of "monument" as a colloquial term for a site of memory. I still find it hard not to call it a "monument," since, after all, it is nationalistic, conventionally celebratory, and of course, enormous in scale. Ideologically, it fits. But it does correspond to the NPS's definition of a memorial in the broadest sense.

2. Don DeLillo, *White Noise* (New York: Penguin, 1984), 12.

3. John Taliaferro, *Great White Fathers: The Story of the Obsessive Quest to Create Mount Rushmore* (New York: Perseus, 2002), 15.

4. Taliaferro, 15–16.

5. Taliaferro, 18.

6. Taliaferro, 397–8.

7. Margret Grebowicz, *The National Park to Come* (Palo Alto: Stanford University Press, 2015). Grebowicz draws on Lauren Berlant's well-known formulation of "cruel optimism" to argue that national parks participate in a consumer-oriented affective economy, 66.

8. Grebowicz, 29.

9. https://www.nps.gov/moru/learn/historyculture/index.htm. Accessed 15 October, 2016.

10. Carole Blair and Neil Michel, "The Rushmore Effect: Ethos and National Collective Identity," *The Ethos of Rhetoric,* ed. Michael J. Hyde (Columbia: University of South Carolina Press, 2004), 175.

11. Doss, 346.

12. Baker consulted tribal elders before taking the job; he admits there are still "hard feelings" today but says that the elders approved, because, as they put it, "what a better place to heal." The Ken Burns's film, *The National Parks*, features interviews with Baker along with footage of his interpretive talks and dancers performing the Lakota Hoop Dance, all of which makes the Indigenous presence at the memorial seem more substantial than perhaps it is. Baker speaks movingly about the sacredness of the site, the persistence of racism in the U.S., and the prospects for "healing our nation," in scenes like "Untold Stories: Mount Rushmore: Telling America's Stories": http://www.pbs.org/nationalparks/watch-video/#857. Certainly hearing him speak at the Heritage Village would have been a special experience. The NPS website hardly mentions the Indigenous presence, though, and I was hard pressed to find information on the village online. The village itself was closed when I visited.

13. I visited Crazy Horse, but it doesn't fit my project's parameters since it's not managed by the NPS. The fact that it isn't complete—while raising interesting questions about temporality and affect—also makes it problematic for me.

14. Blair, 175.

15. Doss, 348. Rushmore has garnered plenty of attention from other scholars and critics. Essays on Rushmore feature prominently in *Observation Points*, tracing the powerful rhetorical work done by visitor center orientation films, tourist bro-

chures, documentary and feature films shown at, or containing, park sites, even the visual arts (like paintings) that influence the design of NPS structures into the present. I don't have space here to attend to the many interesting readings of Rushmore. If I draw heavily on Taliaferro, it's because his blend of personal encounter and history is especially pertinent to my approach, and because he seems most attuned to the "moodiness" of the site.

16. To be fair, Blair conducts a thoughtful, nuanced analysis of other rhetorical features of the site, including the visitor center and its displays. One of the benefits of affect theory, though, is that it complicates standard ideology critique by highlighting embodied experiences in the world. That's the piece of the "big picture" I foreground.

17. Thomas Patin, "America in Ruins: Parks, Poetics, and Politics," in *Observation Points: The Visual Poetics of National Parks*, ed. Thomas Patin (Minneapolis: University of Minnesota Press, 2012), 286.

18. Taliaferro, 18, my emphasis.

19. Sherman Alexie, "Vilify," *Face* (New York: Hanging Loose Press, 2009).

20. As this book went into production, Alexie's own "flaws" are being exposed: Multiple women have accused him of sexual harassment, including predatory behavior such as unwanted sexual advances. He denies some accusations but admits to having "harmed" women. One overview, including a link to Alexie's official response to the accusations, can be found here: https://www.npr.org/sections/thetwo-way/2018/03/09/592480180/ beset-by-sexual-harassment-claims-sherman-alexie-declines-literary-prize. Accessed 3 June, 2018. The topics of toxic masculinity, sexual assault, and the #metoo movement are beyond the scope of this project. For a thoughtful analysis of the challenges scholars face when citing authors accused of sexual assault, see Nicole Seymour's piece in Edge Effects: "Citation in the #MeToo Era" http://edgeeffects.net/metoo-era-citation/. September 11, 2018. Accessed 20 September, 2018.

21. Doss, 348.

22. Walker Percy's essay "The Loss of the Creature" outlines solutions to the problem of tourism DeLillo gestures toward. Percy arguably reinforces what I'd argue is a false idealization of authenticity in this essay; he implies that there is a "sovereign" place there that we can ultimately "recover" with the right tactic. Still, his points are intriguing as tips for becoming attuned to how the landscape and its features have a kind of affective agency. He is also smart to note an "anxious" feeling among tourists that stems from the sense of not "getting it" at some crucial level. I'm less concerned with wresting a sovereign memory site from its NPS "packaging" than I am with gauging the complex affective atmospheres that emerge there. Percy, "The Loss of the Creature," *The Message in the Bottle: How Queer Man Is, How Queer Language Is, and What One Has to Do with the Other* (New York: Farrar, Straus, and Giroux, 1975).

23. The exhibit we saw—which featured moody instrumental music but few words— has been taken down and is meant to be replaced with what park officials say will be a "more interactive" one. Email correspondence, 17 January, 2017, Maureen McGee-Ballinger, chief of interpretation and education.

24. Cited in Taliaferro, 105.

25. Taliaferro, 20.

26. Taliaferro, 20. Taliaferro gestures toward the mountains' affective agency when he says it can "grow on you in a way that cannot be measured in feet or tons" (17). Whether one reads his look as "more judgmental than gentle," it's hard to avoid "feel[ing] the force of his magisterial gaze" (Taliaferro, 125). William Chaloupka's "Thinking Like a Mountain: Mt. Rushmore's Gaze," discusses Rushmore as having a perspective and a gaze. The positioning of their faces "implies that there is something to be seen from there, that the four presidents are watching" (198–9). *Observation Points: The Visual Poetics of National Parks*, ed. Thomas Patin (Minneapolis: University of Minnesota Press, 2012), 187–206. His analysis is echoed in one NPS film clip I heard as I wandered through the visitor center, which informed visitors that the faces on the mountain "look back at you."

27. Sara Ahmed, *The Cultural Politics of Emotion* (New York: Routledge, 2004), 36.

28. Patrick Hogan, *Understanding Nationalism: On Narrative, Cognitive Science, and Identity* (Columbus: Ohio State University Press, 2009), 96.

29. Hogan, 96.

30. Ahmed, *Cultural Politics*, 131.

31. While I focused on what I call "counter-nostalgia" in my earlier book, *Reclaiming Nostalgia*, I gestured toward nostalgia's ability to facilitate the imagination of better futures in this "counterfactual" sense. My thinking about nostalgia has been inspired by Svetlana Boym's *The Future of Nostalgia* (New York: Basic Books, 2001).

32. Langston Hughes, "Let America Be American Again," https://www.poets.org/poetsorg/poem/let-america-be-america-again. Accessed 17 January, 2017.

33. Hogan 104, emphasis added.

34. Doss, 54.

35. Doss 53, emphasis added.

36. See Ahmed, "In the Name of Love," *Cultural Politics*, 122–143. Ahmed rethinks Freudian concepts of parent-child affective bonds, which are transferred to other authority figures, such as the nation; she urges us to think instead about "how love moves us 'towards' something in the very delineation of the object of love, and how the direction of 'towardness' is sustained through the 'failure' of love to be returned" (124).

37. Martha Nussbaum prefers the term patriotism, which she defines as "love of nation," to nationalism. Nussbaum implies nationalism is "divisive" because it "involves deifying one's own nation and pitting it against other nations" (85). *Political Emotions: Why Love Matters For Justice* (Boston: Harvard University Press, 2015). I generally agree with her distinctions, though I hope tying patriotism to landscape can push us toward new prospects for that affect.

38. Williams, 62.

39. Williams, 49.

40. Williams, 65.

41. Doss, 56.

42. Margaret Littlejohn and Yen Le, "Mount Rushmore National Memorial Visitor Study," University of Idaho Park Studies Unit. U.S. Department of Interior, 2013.

43. One interesting reaction, which occurs a handful of times on the 2013 survey, is resentment about being asked to self-identify by racial demographic. In the words of one frustrated respondent, who was merely trying to enjoy a nice day with his grandchildren: ". . . And you make it political." Another respondent flat-out calls the race question "insulting." Survey designers might want to do a better job of explaining what this information is used for.

44. A few visitors did seem to find the memorial genuinely "awe-inspiring." One writes that their "Dominican wife was awestruck." It's difficult to gauge the feelings behind these words, but many comments have a cursory, perfunctory, if positive, tone to them.

45. Leopold, *A Sand County Almanac, with Other Essays on Conservation from Round River*. New York: Ballantine Books, 1970.

46. I define each of these (and give citations) below, with the exception of "jump," which I attribute to Alphonso Lingis, cited in Kathleen Stewart, *Ordinary Affects* (Durham: Duke University Press, 2007), 40. "Accrete" is a term I will take up, especially in relation to physical matter, but to which I have seen only scattered references. Gregory J. Seigworth and Melissa Gregg mention how "affect accumulates" and how an "ever-gathering accretion of force-relations" constitutes "the real power of affect." "An Inventory of Shimmers," in *The Affect Theory Reader* (Durham: Duke University Press, 2010), 2. The editors of *Places of Public Memory: The Rhetoric of Museums and Memorials* mention that memory sites not only have histories but also "*accrete* their own pasts." Greg Dickinson, Carole Blair, and Brian L. Ott, *Places of Public Memory: The Rhetoric of Museums and Memorials* (Tuscaloosa: The University of Alabama Press, 2010), 30, original emphasis. Jessie Oak Taylor describes ice cores as "an archive of accretion, in which the passage of time is rendered visible as accumulating matter." Taylor, "Auras and Ice Cores: Atmospheric Archives and the Anthropocene," *Minnesota Review* 83 (2014): 73–82.

47. I follow Antonio Damasio in distinguishing moods by their endurance: They are "modulated and sustained background feelings as well as modulated and sustained feelings of primary emotions—sadness, in the case of depression." In other words, moods are "dragged-out emotions along with the consequent feelings." Damasio, *The Feeling of What Happens: Body and Emotion in the Making of Consciousness* (Orlando: Harcourt, 1999), 286, 342. Moods are often associated with treatable disorders and are usually thought of as objectless, or as emotions that are, as Sianne Ngai puts it, "searching for appropriate objects." Ngai, *Ugly Feelings* (Cambridge: Harvard University Press, 2005), 179.

48. Damasio, 342.

49. Stewart, 3.

50. I like the word "impression" for reasons similar to Ahmed's—among them, its connotations of both thought and emotion help avoid reinforcing a mind-body split when thinking about affect. Ahmed, *Cultural Politics*, 6.

51. Ngai's *Ugly Feelings* offers a useful overview of the distinction between the two terms. See 25–28.

52. Ben Anderson, "Affective Atmospheres," *Emotion, Space and Society* 2 (2009): 78.

53. Teresa Brennan, *The Transmission of Affect* (Ithaca: Cornell University Press, 2004), 5.

54. Brennan, *Transmission*, 5.

55. Brian Massumi. *Parables for the Virtual: Movement, Affect, Sensation* (Durham: Duke University Press, 2002), 35.

56. Gregg and Seigworth, 4–9.

57. Ibid., 5.

58. Ibid., 6.

59. I've always thought of cultural studies as "pragmatic, strategic, and self-reflective," and my "choice of research practices depends upon the questions that are asked." Lawrence Grossberg, Cary Nelson, and Paula Treichler, eds., *Cultural Studies* (New York: Routledge, 1991), 2.

60. I rely for evidence of this on my own experience with peer reviews (I was asked, for instance, to cut certain cognitively oriented scholars from an article because I was using primarily cultural theorists) and informal conversations, though the split is implicitly reified in much scholarship as well.

61. Clare Hemmings, "Invoking Affect: Cultural Theory and the Ontological Turn," *Cultural Studies* 19.5 (2005): 563. For a recent engagement with the "hermeneutics of suspicion" (Paul Ricoeur's phrase), see Rita Felski, *The Limits of Critique* (Chicago: The University of Chicago Press, 2015). For a thoughtful intervention in these debates that attends to affect in relation to suspicion, see Heather Houser, *Ecosickness in Contemporary U.S. Fiction: Environment and Affect* (New York: Columbia University Press, 2014), 69–71.

62. Ruth Leys, "The Turn to Affect: A Critique," *Critical Inquiry* 37.3 (2001), 443.

63. Hemmings, 563. The first quotation, which Hemmings uses for her epigraph, comes from Simon O'Sullivan, "The aesthetics of affect: thinking art beyond representation," *Angelaki* 6.3 (2001): 125–125.

64. Clearly Massumi and Sedgwick don't; after all, they both "read affects" in various ways. My discussion of fear in chapter one cites Massumi doing exactly that in regard to fear's management post-9/11.

65. Leys, 443. I'm not sure how much I disagree with Leys at all, really. She admits that her main problem with Massumi and his ilk isn't "the idea that many bodily (and mental) processes take place subliminally, below the threshold of awareness"; rather, she takes issue with the implications they attribute to that idea, namely that they "idealize the mind by defining it as a purely disembodied consciousness" and end up reifying a mind-body split (456). I hope to avoid this mistake by thinking not about "mind" in some kind of "highly abstract and disembodied" sense (458, note 43) but rather in terms of its capacity to narrate our feelings.

66. Hemmings, 564.

67. Stewart, 3.

68. Serenella Iovino and Serpil Oppermann, "Theorizing Material Ecocriticism: A Diptych," *ISLE: Interdisciplinary Studies in Literature and Environment* 19.3 (2012): 451.

69. Iovino and Oppermann define material ecocriticism as "[d]ealing with the narrative dimension of . . . agential emergences"—the way matter is "at once material, semiotic, and discursive," 451.

70. Iovino and Oppermann, 451.

71. Jeffrey Jerome Cohen, *Stone: An Ecology of the Inhuman* (Minneapolis: University of Minnesota Press, 2015), 11.

72. James Phelan, "Rhetoric/Ethics," *The Cambridge Companion to Narrative* 14 (2007), 203. Erin James recognizes the complexity of the word "narrative" in her glossary entry: "Traditionally, the representation of a story consisting of an event or a sequence of events, fictional or otherwise. Narrative is a notoriously difficult word to define . . ." She references scholars for whom narratives are "defined by the presence of one or more narrators speaking to one or more narratees"; others, for whom "narrative can be distinguished from description by the representation of a sequence of events, as opposed to one event"; and still others, for whom "experientiality is the defining component of narrative." Erin James, *The Storyworld Accord: Econarratology and Postcolonial Narratives* (Lincoln: University of Nebraska Press, 2015).

73. Ngai, *Ugly Feelings*, 27. She doesn't herself prefer to distinguish between affect and emotion, but her overview of the terms is useful.

74. Houser, 3.

75. Houser, 170.

76. If we follow Silvan Tomkins and consider affect as a kind of drive enhancer, or if we follow Spinoza's definition of *affectus* as the power to affect or be affected, agency is presumed by definition. Eve Kosofsky Sedgwick and Adam Frank, eds., *Shame and Its Sisters: A Silvan Tomkins Reader* (Durham: Duke University Press, 1995). Baruch Spinoza, "The Ethics." In *A Spinoza Reader: The Ethics and Other Works*, ed. and trans. Edwin Curley (Princeton: Princeton University Press), 85–265.

77. I approach the agency of assemblages and objects mostly by way of Stewart and Jane Bennett, *Vibrant Matter: A Political Ecology of Things* (Durham: Duke University Press, 2010). I mainly use the term assemblage in the Deleuzian sense, described by Bennett as "living, throbbing confederations" of "diverse elements, vibrant materials of all sorts," that are "not governed by any central head," yet still have agency (Bennett, 23–24). Other influential sources on these topics include (for assemblage theory) Bruno Latour, Karen Barad, and Gilles Deleuze and Felix Guattari, and for object-oriented ontology, Ian Bogost, Graham Harman, and Timothy Morton, among others.

78. Bennett is paraphrasing Henri Bergson here. *Vibrant Matter*, 77.

79. Bennett, xii. Doss, 13.

80. Anderson, 77. Nigel Thrift, *Non-Representational Theory: Space, Politics, Affect* (New York: Routledge, 2008).

81. Anderson, 80–81.

82. Brennan, 1.

83. Ngai, 28.

84. Ngai, 30.

85. Ibid., 87.

86. Cited in "*A Geography of the Lifeworld* in Retrospect: A Response to Shaun Moores," *Particip@tions* 3.2 (2006). http://www.participations.org/volume%203/issue%202%20-%20special/3_02_seamon.htm. Accessed 18 March, 2017. Seamon, who considers himself a phenomenological geographer and a phenomenological ecologist, coined the phrase "place ballet" in *A Geography of the Lifeworld* (London: Croom Helm, 1979).

87. Sara Ahmed, "Happy Objects," in *The Affect Theory Reader*, eds. Melissa Gregg and Gregory J. Seigworth, (Durham: Duke University Press, 2010), 50.

88. Silko, "Landscape, History, and the Pueblo Imagination," in *At Home on the Earth: Becoming Native to Our Place: A Multicultural Anthology*, ed. David Landis Barnhill (Berkeley: University of California Press, 1999), 33.

89. Silko, 31.

90. For treatments of agency in environmental history, see, for instance, Linda Nash, "The Agency of Nature or the Nature of Agency?," *Environmental History* 10 (2005), 67–69; and, for a recent (and more critical) take, Paul Sutter, "The World with Us: The State of American Environmental History," *Journal of American History* (2013), 94–119.

91. Tim Cresswell provides a useful overview of work on place in geography over the past several decades. *Place: A Short Introduction* (2004), (second edition, Wiley Blackwell, 2015).

92. Lucy Lippard takes a palimpsestic view of places, as local geographies at which histories and memories layer upon each other: "histories which sediment in place and become the bedrock for future action" (cited in Cresswell, 72).

93. Cresswell mentions specifically "things, emotions, people, memories, etc." that can be said to "gather" in place. He credits Edward Casey, *Getting Back into Place* (1993) and Arturo Escobar, who writes: "places gather things, thoughts, and memories in particular configurations" (2001, 143). Kim Dovey approaches architectural theory by way of assemblage theory. For her, "All places are assemblages" (2010, 16). In this project I draw on whichever framework for place seems most salient in any given chapter.

94. For a history of the agency that attends to the role of landscape architects in NPS history, see Richard West Sellars, *Preserving Nature in the National Parks: A History* (New Haven: Yale University Press, 1997).

95. Cresswell, 17–18.

96. Doreen Massey, "Landscape as a Provocation: Reflections on Moving Mountains," *Journal of Material Culture* 11, no. 1-2 (2006): 35, 46.

97. Among the many geographers I could mention here, W. J. T. Mitchell is perhaps the most commonly cited by scholars on national parks.

98. Greg Dickinson, Brian Ott, and Eric Aoki, "Spaces of Remembering and Forgetting: The Reverent Eye/I at the Plains Indian Museum," *Communication and Critical/Cultural Studies* 3 (2006), 30.

99. Ahmed's discussion of the "hap" of "happiness" comes to mind. She recalls the Middle English root of the word, "hap," which suggests "chanciness" and contin-

gency ("Happy Objects," 32–34), both of which are important to bear in mind when thinking about affect more broadly.

100. Bennett, 94.

101. Brennan, 3. Brennan admits that there are "environmental factors at work" in affect transmission, but these are outside the scope of her analysis (8). Her cursory examples are telling: the "ancient peace" of Delphi and the "pavement" of NYC. She describes physical matter as only passive by our standards, because we see objects in the environment as not able to "carry out intentions of their own" (93)—as lacking "free will or agency." She does not take the step of disassociating free will from agency and redefining the latter, but her argument aligns, more or less, with material ecocritical views.

102. Ahmed also makes the case that the "inside-out" model of emotional transference, in which emotions are inherent to individuals, is flawed for different reasons: it ignores the sociality of emotions (and so risks essentialism). *Cultural Politics*, 10.

103. Ahmed, *Cultural Politics*, 11. Anthropologist Kay Milton argues, similarly, that emotions are ecological, "induced when an organism interacts with objects in [its] environment." *Loving Nature: Towards an Ecology of Emotion* (New York: Routledge, 2002), 4.

104. Ahmed, *Cultural Politics*, 11.

105. Ahmed, "Happy Objects," 29.

106. Following Damasio and others, I use "object" loosely. For Damasio, "objects" can include "entities as diverse as a person, a place, a melody, a toothache, a state of bliss." Objects are fodder for the multi-sensory mental patterns he calls "images" (9).

107. Alison Landsberg, *Prosthetic Memory: The Transformation of American Remembrance in the Age of Mass Culture* (Columbia University Press, 2004).

108. Grebowicz, 58.

109. Grebowicz, 15, my emphasis.

110. Grebowicz, 55.

111. This is not to be confused with "ecoambiguity," a term Karen Thornber develops in regard to East Asian literature. Karen Laura Thornber, *Ecoambiguity: Environmental Crises and East Asian Literatures* (Ann Arbor: University of Michigan Press, 2012).

112. Bennett, 115.

113. Ngai, 6, 21.

114. Houser, 34, 39.

115. Houser, 66.

116. Houser, 67–69.

117. Thomas Friedman, to whom "global weirding" is often attributed, credits Hunter Lovins, of the Rocky Mountain Institute, for coining it. Friedman believes "weirding" better encapsulates the "crazy things" manifesting in disparate forms in different locations. http://www.nytimes.com/2007/12/02/opinion/02friedman.html. Accessed 18 January, 2017.

118. Obviously a non-Native (as indicated by the reference to "the Native Americans"), this respondent brings an interesting, but rare, perspective to the surveys.

119. I tried repeatedly to reach park managers at Mount Rushmore to see what records they have on Lakota and other Indigenous responses to Rushmore, and to the Heritage site, but I did not manage to get a response.

120. Ahmed uses the phrase to indicate people who are "alienated from the affective promise of happy objects" and so help expose political inequities.

121. Ahmed, *The Promise of Happiness* (Durham: Duke University Press, 2010), 67.

122. Ahmed, "In the Name of Love," *Cultural Politics*, 122–143.

123. The phrase "imposter syndrome" was coined in 1978 by two women psychologists, but it has received tremendous attention in recent years. Pauline Rose Clance and Suzanne Imes. (1978). "The Impostor Phenomenon in High Achieving Women: Dynamics and Therapeutic Interventions." *Psychotherapy: Theory Research and Practice*, 15: 241247. http://www.paulineroseclance.com/pdf/ip_high_achieving_women.pdf. Accessed 25 March, 2017.

124. Winter, *Sites of Memory*, 62.

125. Casey, "Public Memory in Place and Time," in *Framing Public Memory*, ed. Kendall R. Phillips (Tuscaloosa: University of Alabama Press, 2007), 25.

126. Ibid., 41.

127. The editors of *Places of Public Memory* claim affect is "perhaps the most under-developed of public memory's assumptions, [but] it may also be one of the most central" (7). That collection is indebted primarily to Ahmed's work on affect as "sticky."

128. Cvetkovich notes that "affect" as a term carries more "neutrality" (even sophistication) than "emotion" or "feeling" and so perhaps lends it more credibility.

129. Doss 43.

130. Doss, 2.

131. Lisa Feldman Barrett's recent book, *How Emotions are Made: The Secret Life of the Brain*, argues that emotion research is on the verge of a paradigm shift, which will overturn the model of emotions as generated in discrete parts of the brain and cross-culturally recognizable (e.g. using facial recognition software). Her work proposes a much more complex theory involving multiple brain regions and an individual's prior experiences. She explains her view of emotions in a compelling interview: "I have an entire vocabulary of sadness. I don't have one happiness, one feeling of awe, or one feeling of gratitude; I have many. And they're highly specific to the situation." Individuals' brains draw on whichever previous version of a single emotion is most useful in the contemporary situation. "How emotions are 'made': Why your definition of sadness is unlike anyone else's," Emma Bryce, *Wired*, March 23, 2017, *http://www.wired.co.uk/article/lisa-feldman-barrett-emotions*. Accessed 3 June, 2018.

132. A glance at the more recent NPS site designations upholds this speculative conclusion, as it shows a clear spike in sites devoted to more diverse cultural histories.

133. Doss, 353.

134. Cvetkovich, 15.

CHAPTER ONE

"Fears Made Manifest"

Desert Creatures and Border Anxiety at
Coronado National Memorial

Perched on a bench at the Coronado Peak overlook (elev. 6,864 feet), near Montezuma Pass, I am doing my best to follow the NPS instructions: Take in the view, imagine the history, contemplate its legacy. The panorama, as a sign at the trailhead had promised it would be, is "stunning": The San Pedro River Valley spreads out to the south and east, the Huachuca Mountains rise to the north, and the San Rafael Valley extends to the west. This is a "timeless landscape," another NPS display in the parking lot claims, which "has barely changed since the Coronado Expedition passed near here in 1540–1542." The international border is "off toward the horizon," that sign continues, though the actual border is "difficult to see."

A few feet from where I sit, another sign, titled "A Lasting Exchange," celebrates the cultural exchange initiated by Spanish "conquest." It hails me in the second person: "Can you imagine Italy without tomato sauce, Belgium without chocolate, and Ireland without potatoes?" Photos of these European specialties—and, representing the American Southwest, a few ears of corn—supplement the text. The sign hits home for this hungry hiker. My stomach rumbles, and I realize I haven't eaten since I left my hotel in Sierra Vista, a nearby town of about 45,000, near Fort Huachuca. This quiet overlook seems worlds away from Sierra Vista's traffic lights and strip malls, with their eclectic mix of gun and knife stores, tattoo parlors, pawnshops, bail bondsmen, and Asian food buffets. The Coronado Peak overlook is an idyllic place to have lunch and listen to the wind brush the dry grasses.

FIGURE 1.1. View from Coronado Peak Overlook

It's mid-April in Coronado National Memorial, and the weather is lovely: not quite 90 degrees Fahrenheit, with a soothing breeze up high. The unbearably hot temperatures will be here soon, and park visitation is winding down in anticipation. Ranger-led tours have already stopped for the season, so I won't be able to go on a guided tour of the Coronado Cave or hear a ranger interpret the overlook displays. Sitting here alone, I am nevertheless confident that I'm getting one of the most important experiences at this park. According to the NPS's website, the Memorial's location "was chosen for the panoramic views of the U.S.–Mexico border and the San Pedro River Valley, the route believed to have been taken by Coronado in 1540."[1] This location is why I'm here. What better place to begin a project like mine than along a national border, at an ecological confluence?

A large "Welcome" display just outside the visitor center (VC) below had oriented me that morning by situating the Memorial at the "crossroads" of four natural ecosystems: the Rocky Mountains ("high and cool"), the Sierra Madre Mountains ("high and tropical"), the Sonoran Desert ("low and hot"), and the Chihuahuan Desert ("high and dry"). Another helpful panel outside the VC calls the mountains here "sky islands": isolated high-elevation habitats "in a sea of low-elevation desert and grass-lands." I hadn't heard that phrase before, but I am taken with the idea of mountains as islands in a "desert sea." I count myself among the plants and animals that prefer the "wetter, cooler climes in the sky islands." Even the so-called dry heat of the desert makes me wilt; I consider myself more mountain woman than desert rat. Of the four ecosystems outlined on the display, the Rockies are the place I've spent most of my outdoor time. At the overlook, I am sunshaded and comfortable enough to convince myself that deserts are not so inhospitable—at least if I can stick to the sky islands.

As the international food references on the "Lasting Exchange" sign suggest, Coronado NM's implied tourist is, among other things, educated, perhaps well traveled; she is intellectually curious as well, if not necessarily well informed about Francisco Vázquez de Coronado or his historical expedition. These are criteria I fit. But I am also part of a small subset of park visitor—what managers call a "subject matter enthusiast,"[2] here for a professional research project—which means I am not the primary target audience, not exactly the implied tourist. Although I would never claim special access to an "untrammeled ontological" realm of experience, I want to experience the site with fresh eyes and minimal expectations.[3] I'd come to Coronado NM with little preparation aside from a glance at the website. I trust the displays and the rangers will tell me what I need to know. From the time I had stepped out of my car earlier that day, it was clear to me that imagination and contemplation were meant to be central to my experience.

The very first word on the prominent "Welcome" display is the imperative "Imagine," urging us to consider what being part of the expedition would have been like. Tourists inside the visitor center can try on chain mail armor to see how that feels (hint: it's heavy). Rangers I spoke with mention this is a favorite activity for children, especially, and comment books confirm that. Similarly, on the way up the trail to the overlook a sign had prompted me to count my steps and do some basic multiplication to see how much distance the Coronado expedition covered. For today's Fitbit fans, this analog version of counting steps engages our desire to quantify and measure. It hooks us with numbers then sneaks in the history. The embodied experience of re-treading someone's footsteps or trying on their armor is meant to help us imagine the past by feeling our way into it. We learn that it was someone's job to count all the steps they took, every day, while we walk the same terrain. We feel the weight of the armor and imagine how hot it must have been, how exhausting to wear.

Inviting visitors to physically immerse themselves in the history of a site is a common NPS strategy for inspiring connection. Facilitating contemplation is another. At Coronado NM, the "Welcome" display panels are set up in a comforting circular arrangement and are partially shaded, creating an atmosphere conducive to pausing, reading, and reflecting. Here at the Coronado Peak overlook, too, the physical environment encourages quiet thought. There are benches, a shelter to shade us from the sun, and written displays to spur reflection. Our typical state of continuous partial attention[4] is temporarily shut down—especially if, as is the case for me, we're alone and out of cell phone range. But the "imagine" mandate is not so easy to achieve. As hard as it is to spot the border, it's also difficult to envision Coronado and his entourage of more than 1,000 men—nearly two-thirds of whom, one NPS sign reminds us, were "Indian allies and slaves"—passing through this valley. No one's sure exactly where the expedition crossed the river, for one thing; I don't even know where to look. But where, or even whether the crossing took place within (or merely "near") the current park boundary, is in some ways beside the point.

The Memorial's managers have a plan for us visitors, an official "Long-Range Interpretive Plan," and in that plan what matters is less the expedition itself (which was considered a "failure" in 1542, the plan informs us[5]) than this contemporary landscape, the sweeping vistas that highlight the boundaries, as well as the present-day connections, between the U.S. and Mexico. In addition to "inspir[ing] visitors to imagine distant places, or people seeking their fortunes or a new life,"[6] the NPS plan aspires to international amity, something also mentioned on the website and in the Memorial's site bulletin: "It was hoped that this proximity to the border would strengthen bi-national cooperation and the bonds, both geographical and cultural, which continue to link the two countries."[7] A main goal of NPS managers is to broaden out from the event itself to its legacy of transnational connection.

Understanding this legacy is meant to be an affective experience, not just an intellectual one. The interpretive plan strategizes explicitly about the "visitor experience," defined as "what people do, sense, feel, think, and learn. It is affected by experiences prior to the visit and affects behavior after the visit. The ultimate goal of interpretation is for visitors to experience strong *emotional and intellectual connections* with the meanings represented in park resources and as a result become better stewards of these places which characterize our national heritage."[8]

There's an assumption here and throughout the NPS plan that the landscape, this site's most important "resource," will facilitate not only contemplation but also some unspecified "emotional connection" that will encourage stewardship. By definition, it seems, an emotional response is at least as important to the visitor experience as an intellectual one (it is even listed first in the text), even if the prior experiences of visitors will remain, to some extent, idiosyncratic and hard to predict. The NPS wants us to "sense" and "feel" something. But what?

Any answer must take into account the physical environment. As Camilla Fojas claims in *Border Bandits: Hollywood on the Southern Frontier*, the southern border is "one of the most emotionally charged zones of the United States."[9] How, then, do the desert landscape and its nonhuman inhabitants shape the "emotional connections" here? What cultural and sociopolitical narratives influence tourists' encounters with the border? How does what we "sense" and "feel" here work alongside, or in tension with, the memorial's written rhetoric to shape an affective atmosphere? To answer these questions in regard to Coronado NM, I suggest we need to understand fear as well as its more diffuse, more moderate register, anxiety.

A more precise understanding of fear helps reveal how it works culturally, how it "sticks" to some objects and some bodies (but not to others), and how it might be transmitted across local, regional, national, and global scales. It's my contention, here and throughout this book, that affect theory can clarify how emotions are felt individually and at these various scales. Coronado NM is a place at which, to borrow Grebowicz's description of a different NPS border site (Big Bend National Park), "assumptions about belonging, security, and safety, expectations of surveillance and reporting, and even ecological concepts like native and invasive species are all inflected with the tensions particular to keeping undocumented Mexican migrants out."[10] I'll explore how these "tensions" infuse desert landscapes, reinforcing a sense of the environment itself as threatening and dangerous. These affective attributes are influenced by culture and politics, then, but I'll submit that they're compounded by direct experience of the intense heat, the relentless aridity, and even the presence of certain nonhuman inhabitants. I'll suggest that the vast desert landscape combines with the built environment to expose the contingency of national borders and of fear itself—a misunderstood affect with complex material, environmental, and political dimensions. Finally, I'll speculate on why it might matter which affective terms—fear, anxiety, or something else—we use to describe the nation as a collective.

⬤

The southern frontier might not be as famous as its western cousin, but it's equally mythic. In his powerful book *The Devil's Highway: A True Story*, Luis Alberto Urrea explains:

> In North America, the myth tends west: the cowboys, the Indians, the frontier, the wild lands, the bears and wolves and gold mines and vast ranches were in the west. But in Mexico, a country narrow at bottom and wide at the top, the myth ran north. The Mayas pushed north, and the Aztecs pushed north once they'd formed an empire. Later, the Spaniards pushed north. The wide open spaces lay northward. The cowboys and Indians, the great Pancho Villa outlaws, the frontier, lay north, not west. That's why norteño people are the cowboys of Mexico—not westerners. The Spanish word for 'border' is, after all, *frontera*. The frontier.[11]

If frontiering has historical roots in European conquest (Coronado, of course, was one of the Spaniards who "pushed north"), then "immigration, the drive northward, is a white phenomenon." How ironic that contemporary ancestors of these early frontiersmen now seek to prohibit would-be migrants from following in their footsteps by perpetuating tales of "sinful frontier towns with bad reputations. Untamed mountain ranges, bears, lions, and wolves. Indians. A dangerous border."[12] Mexico and its people, in today's southern frontier narratives, are cast as fearsome and dangerous, like the megafauna and Indigenous people in the U.S. western frontier myth. Indeed, these inhabitants are primarily what mark the border as "dangerous."

The U.S.–Mexico border is often portrayed in literary, filmic, and other cultural texts with "phobic" images.[13] Some of these texts add fuel to the fearful fire, and others challenge it. Fear of Mexican migrants is too often kindled by political figures, including when high-profile men such as President Trump make fear-mongering comments about "bad hombres" coming across the border.[14] I don't want to minimize the impacts of that kind of fear, but I would like to suggest that another kind of fear arises from associations with the plants, the heat, the nonhuman animals—in particular, rattlesnakes—and the unforgiving nature of the desert environment. In her book, *The Hour of Land: A Personal Topography of America's National Parks*, Terry Tempest Williams contests the first kind of fear (the "bad hombres" variety) but sometimes reinforces the second kind, the fear of the desert environment. For instance, she warns:

> Yucca with leaves like quivering swords stand next to cholla, the devil's club. In the desert, success is the understanding of limits. One false move and you die. You can't talk your way out of thirst. Bare skin burns. Face-to-face with a spitting rattlesnake, the only thing you have to negotiate is your escape. There are rules in the desert. Pay attention. Adapt or perish.[15]

Her book makes a broader case for refusing fear in favor of humility: "the nature of our national parks is bound to the nature of our own humility, our capacity to stay open and curious in a world that instead beckons closure through fear."[16] Still, Williams affirms that if you aren't at least a little scared in the desert you aren't paying attention.

David Taylor's *Monuments* project, for which he traveled to and photographed all 276 official border monuments along the 690 miles of land boundary from El Paso to San Diego, also challenges fear at the southern border by humanizing those who cross into the U.S.[17] The essays at the back of Taylor's impressive collection of photographs acknowledge that fear is still very often tied to both people and landscape. For example, in "Straddling the Fence," Claire C. Carter describes the desert border as a landscape of contradictions: "fences demarcate territory, but the sheer length makes trespassing unenforceable; the desert is sparsely inhabited but also a transit path for illegal migrants; it's a fragile habitat but a deadly climate." She notes the increase in anxious, nationalistic affects at the border post-9/11. Today, as President Trump continues to champion his border wall and bully leaders around the world—including Mexican president Enrique Peña Nieto, who Trump repeatedly insists will pay for the wall's construction (but who repeatedly refuses to do so)[18]—we once again "feel the rumblings of fear, suspicion, and xenophobia," both regionally "and on a national scale."[19]

As a longtime seasonal ranger, I am not inclined to feel these "rumblings" in any NPS site. My visitor experience is (to cite the park's interpretive plan again) "affected by experiences prior to the visit" in significant and unique ways: My thirteen idyllic summers in the Tetons lend the familiar colors and fonts of the signage a nostalgic valence. My heart flutters with excitement and joy when I see the rustic NPS "parkitecture,"[20] the friendly fonts, or a buttoned-up ranger wearing the traditional green and gray. Visiting an NPS site is, for me, like returning home—even better, to a home not haunted by fraught family relationships. Let me hasten to add that I recognize the privilege in my positive affiliation with the NPS, and I am well aware of the uncomfortable fact that the parks' formation relied upon the colonial project of Manifest Destiny, including the displacement of, and sometimes violence against, Indigenous peoples who lived in or used these particular places.[21] That awareness is unsettling, an uneasy guilt I feel most strongly when I'm immersed in my research. But when I'm at an actual NPS site, with its comforting signage, mild-mannered authority figures, and romantic uniforms, my positive emotional memories tend to overshadow negative affects like guilt and fear in the present.

My research also makes me less afraid of this border landscape. My familiarity with Urrea, Taylor, Williams, Francisco Cantú, and others who depict the complexities of the border makes me sympathetic to migrants. I'm more worried that I wouldn't have enough water to offer a migrating person (or more likely, people) than that they'd cause me any harm. The harsh aridity, the brutal heat, the prickly plants, and the possibility of running into a rattlesnake or *el tigre* are more pressing concerns. I worry that in an "adapt or perish" situation, I might find myself unprepared. Perhaps most significantly, my relative lack of fear is due to not being an *object* of fear. While hiking alone as a woman is always a little disconcerting, I am not one of the bodies who, as Franz Fanon, Audre Lorde, Ta-Nehisi Coates, and many others have patiently explained, moves through the world as a target of racialized fear, anger, or hate.[22] The uniformed officials I might encounter in Coronado NM are likely to be friendly toward me. My whiteness also gives me a measure of freedom as a researcher. As Clare Hemmings puts it, "the autonomy of the critic" is in part "dependent upon their being the subject rather than object of affective displacement."[23] Because negative affects like fear and hate are not "displaced" onto me, I have more agency, including the luxury of tracing affects with a degree of critical autonomy many people of color would not have, especially in this border landscape. Both the positive affective predisposition my personal history affords me and my relative methodological freedom are bolstered by my white privilege.

All that said, a sense of danger is heightened at Coronado National Memorial, even for me, by at least two things, one environmental and the other textual. The environmental manifestation of fear happens when I turn into the parking area at Montezuma Pass and discover two large Border Patrol vehicles parked at the trailhead.

FIGURE 1.2. Border Patrol vehicles at Montezuma Pass

With their darkly tinted windows, it's impossible to tell whether anyone is in the trucks—itself an unsettling fact—and their motion-detecting cameras are pointed out at the expanse of the desert. I find myself following the cameras' gaze, scrutinizing the landscape for signs of movement. Seeing the Border Patrol trucks parked at the pass might make some visitors feel safe; however, that response requires some measure of fear to begin with. You have to be aware of a threat—in this case, the threat of migrating Mexicans—before you can feel reassured that you're protected. Perhaps a supporter of Trump's border wall would feel a sense of security at the sight of the trucks. Regardless of one's political affiliation, the vehicles and their cameras urge a kind of vigilance that could align the implied tourist with the "legal" Border Patrol by implicitly asking visitors to be on the lookout for "illegal" activity.[24] There's an "other" being constructed—the fearful "them" who might be out there, poised to cross the border at any moment.[25] If you are that "other," the vehicles will register quite differently, a point to which I'll return.

The textual manifestation of fear comes in the frequent warnings on NPS literature not to hike alone in remote areas due to illegal activity. It's common for NPS maps, brochures, and displays to contain safety reminders to hikers about carrying sufficient water and other supplies, and, where appropriate, warnings about bears or other potentially dangerous nonhuman animals. I always feel a tinge of anxiety when starting out on a hike or climb, an anxiety with a positive valence—which we might just call "excitement"—associated with the anticipation of healthy adventure and reasonable risk-taking. But that anxiety can turn negative when I link it to specific risks. What if the weather takes a sudden bad turn? What if I sprain an ankle? What if I encounter one of the dangerous animals I've been warned about—or worse, a human predator, a solo male hiker intent on doing me harm?

The literature here at Coronado NM lists distinct risks tied to the border location. This excerpt from a prominent display at the Coronado Peak overlook trailhead features a warning I saw in several pieces of NPS literature:

> Hike Safely. Smuggling and/or illegal entry is common[26] in this
> area due to the proximity of the international border. Be aware
> of your surroundings at all times and do not travel alone in
> remote areas. Report suspicious behavior to a park ranger or
> border patrol agent at 1-877-872-7435.

The active diction is striking, with three imperatives and an implicit suggestion that the border actually causes the illegal activity, which is true in a sense—at least, insofar as it's an arbitrary line, historically contingent and far from "inevitable."[27] These frank imperatives, especially the instruction to "be aware," rhetorically align visitors with the NPS and the Border Patrol. The imperatives could easily spark or compound anxiety. The mention of "poisonous snakes" (introduced with the more polite, less urgent, mandate to "Please be alert") a bit farther down on the same trailhead sign reiterates the sense of danger. But after seeing the Border Patrol trucks and reading the textual warnings in multiple places, it's clear whom "we," the implied tourists, are supposed to fear: "illegal" migrants and/or smugglers coming from Mexico.

At this point in my trip, I haven't consciously sifted through the forms of fear in play—fear of snakes and other desert creatures, fear of brown people, fear of hiking alone as a woman, fear of being unprepared, and the fear a migrant would feel during a border crossing—but I can feel myself becoming anxious, as my typically positive NPS visitor mood is tinged with unease. What follows is my attempt to sort out these forms of fear, to attend to how they compound, displace, or exacerbate one another, and to distinguish between fear and anxiety as they register corporeally and are represented textually. Fear is most often theorized as one of the primary, or basic, emotions, an evolutionarily useful response to a threat, shared by all sorts of animals. Many scholars use encounters with nonhuman animals—often bears or snakes— to explain how fear works in human bodies. Like all longtime hikers, I have my share of animal stories, including some far more exciting than the one I'll recount here. While it may seem like a detour to turn to the nonhuman in a space that's so culturally and politically fraught for humans, this "tale of two snakes" from my hike to the U.S.–Mexico border allows me to survey a range of approaches to fear and anxiety within affect theory and to demonstrate how my corporeal experience of these affects in the desert is alternately compounded and assuaged by the Memorial's environmental and textual registers. After laying that foundation, I'll return to the cultural politics of the border and the different forms of fear and anxiety attached to this site.

———◆———

Walking to the border hadn't been my plan. I had thought I'd hike to the overlook along the Coronado Peak Trail, and maybe walk for a bit along the Yaqui Ridge Trail, saving the border for the next day. But five minutes into my hike I see the trail sign pointing to the "U.S-Mexico Border" (just a mile away!) and I change course, unable to resist its allure. Partly, it's the monument that attracts me. Border monuments are erected, in part, to delineate, materially and legally, an otherwise chaotic border region. In this desert they are material and symbolic lines in the sand that mark "the outer limit of the nation beyond which there is land that cannot be readily conquered."[28] Establishing the border markers was a bi-national project. After the 1848 Treaty of Guadalupe Hidalgo, the U.S. and Mexico worked together, through the temporary International Boundary Commission, to install the original 52 masonry monuments. They renewed their efforts in 1882, constructing another 206 cast-iron obelisks. Today there are 276.[29] Three are in Coronado NM, and it is to number 102, the one most accessible by trail, that I've decided to hike. In Taylor's words, the border monuments are "curious objects that are somehow totally inscrutable but ultimately point to all the other issues that surround them. That's part of what draws [us] to them."[30] I'm drawn to it by a kind of affective as well as an intellectual curiosity; I want to understand the "issues" it points to and to know what it *feels* like to stand in front of it.

Committed to my revised itinerary, I begin anticipating the obelisk that marks the spot. I waver between expecting to see it around the next bend and worrying that it's all the way down in the valley—a good ways down, from the looks of it. I'm not sure I brought enough water to make it comfortably back up. I register a fleeting twinge of familiar hiker anxiety, comparable to coming upon a steep snow field and realizing I've forgotten my ice axe. But the ranger at the visitor center had said the hike involved only 600 feet of elevation change. Trusting in the green and gray, I continue down.

I move along the trail at a good clip, kicking up loose rocks and dust, the breeze instantly drying my sweat. I absorb the views, but the atmosphere is more than just visual; the nonhuman world exerts its agency on me in ways I can hear and feel as well. The rustling of shifting rocks underfoot, the wind in the grasses, and the occasional call of a canyon wren make a soothing soundtrack, and the sun warms my bare skin with its unfathomable energy. Even though it's not hot by desert standards, this fair-skinned north-Idahoan is feeling the sun's intensity. I count three shade trees and plan to stop under them on the way back up. My thoughts wander from one quotidian topic to the next—to my sons, who have a soccer game that night, to my husband, who will coach for me and bring the snacks, to the pictures I might post later, to how fortunate I am to be here on a grant-funded research trip. I am physically healthy, able-bodied.[31] I am alone outside, walking, content in what neuroscientists call my default mode network.[32] As I'll discuss in chapter six, research in environmental psychology has isolated a pleasurable feeling called "soft fascination," which the more-than-human world inspires in hikers. The break from technology (I'm out of cell range here) is probably a factor in my good mood as well.

Just when I'm confident I have the trail to myself, I round a corner and see a white man, about my height but stockier and strong looking, on the trail just ahead. My heart jumps and accelerates until, a few seconds later, I am relieved at the sound of a small voice, and I catch a glimpse of a young boy. I catch up with the pair at the border, where I offer to photograph the man and the boy I suppose is his son. They accept, and I snap their picture by the obelisk, making sure to get as much of the landscape into the shot as I can. Then I put my foot tentatively through the barbed-wire fence and take a photo, muttering something about whether I've just illegally crossed into Mexico. The father follows suit, reaching through the barbed wire with his arm and taking a picture with his phone. The boy, an awkward tween, stays silent, shuffling from one foot to another in his too-big backpack. I put my own pack down to get a swig of water and enjoy the satisfaction of being at my destination. I eat a power bar for quick energy. I learn that the father is stationed at Fort Huachuca and that the boy is visiting from Wisconsin. I hope the duo will start back up the trail, and they soon do, the father taking off at a jog and the boy following at a slow trudge. I enjoy some time to myself at the border monument, something I'll say more about shortly.

As I hike back up the trail toward the parking area, I feel the backs of my calves burning and regret not putting sunscreen on them. A dull headache is starting, and I loosen my ball cap to let in the breeze. Lucky for me, the shade along the trail has increased as the sun shifted position, and I stop below each tree to rest and scribble any insights that have occurred to me since the last water break on a scrap of paper. I keep my eyes on the trail, careful not to twist an ankle or slide on the loose dirt and gravel. I soon catch up to the father-son team. They are peering off the trail's edge at something in the brush. I wonder if it's that lizard I photographed on the way down. But no—it's a snake, about three feet long, I'd estimate, with black stripes and a spectrum of yellow-orange coloring from head to tail. I stop and stare with them as it sidewinds along the edge of a dried-out bush and finds a gap beneath a rock outcropping.

I'm not the kind of naturalist who's equally in awe of, or equally unfazed by, all critters. Despite my best efforts, I startle easily around yellow jackets, wasps, spiders, and any creature that makes a sudden move, including snakes. In his essay, "Snaketime," Charles Bowden recounts his attempts to educate himself out of his own fear of snakes— reminding us, for instance, that what snakes spend "at most one minute of time in decades of life" doing, striking at prey, has somehow come to stand in for their entire identity, from a human perspective.[33] But even he concedes that "no matter how much we learn of them the fear never completely leaves."[34] Since this particular snake hadn't startled me and is a safe distance away, I feel only a mild curiosity and, when it starts to move, a creepy sensation as the hairs on my arms and neck bristle. I recall, briefly, Edward Abbey's lengthy list, in *Desert Solitaire*, of the scorpions, black widows, and other critters lurking in pit toilets and other dark desert crevices, shiver a bit, and am grateful for my dehydration and the lack of a toilet. I am eager to use this opportunity to leapfrog the other hikers (the young boy is really dragging by now) so, after what seems like a polite amount of time to stand and look, I pass them and continue up the trail, head down, at a slow, even pace. I lapse back into the meditative, contemplative state I'd been in before the snake encounter.

A switchback or two later, though, I feel full-on fear when, rounding a switchback, something long, dark, thin, and spotted, suddenly appears in my peripheral vision. I catch my breath, feel my heart start to pound and race, and a severe startle reflex stops me in my tracks. It's the classic fight-or-flight response, and I am momentarily paralyzed as fear is activated in my body. Only retrospectively, after what Brian Massumi describes as a "half-second delay,"[35] do I begin to assess the situation and perceive my surroundings clearly. As he puts it: "Objects in spatial configuration begin to appear, distinguishing themselves from the fear in which they were enveloped" only a moment earlier.[36] I now register the object as a stick—in my defense, a long, thin burned-out piece of wood with a striking pattern of spot-like holes. Perhaps because I've been conditioned by the actual snake I'd just seen—and prior to that, by the NPS warnings to "be aware," which (I suddenly remember) *did* mention "poisonous snakes"—to feel more anxious, this stick has the capacity to prompt what the snake didn't. In any case, the initial fear response is short-lived. By the time I get to the next switchback, I am breathing regularly again, and my heart rate has slowed to as normal as can be expected for someone hiking uphill at nearly 7,000 feet above sea level. But I don't fully relax until I'm back at the trailhead. I'm jumpy, tense, anticipating another surprise around every bend.

—————•••—————

What caused my bodily response to the snake-like stick? It depends who you ask. Neuroscientist Antonio Damasio would say fear is one of our emotions: "complicated collections of chemical and neural responses, forming a pattern" and helping regulate our behavior.[37] Fear and other emotions serve evolutionary functions, helping us stay safe in the world. Fear is an automatic response to external stimuli that we can observe in the brain, in the amygdala; it's typically short-lived and common to a wide range of species. In his essay "Fear (The Spectrum Said)," an analysis of the color-coded terrorist alerts that followed the

September 11th attacks, Massumi describes fear "at this level of pure activation" as merely the "*intensity* of the experience and not yet a content of it." He elaborates: "Threat strikes the nervous system with a directness forbidding any separation between the responsiveness of the body and its environment."[38] At the activation stage, affect and environment are, for a moment, conjoined. Moreover, there is not immediately an emotional content to our affective experience. Only after we begin to act, and enjoy the "luxury of a pause," do we recognize our fear for what it is.

Things get even more complicated when we consider the cognitive and cultural dimensions of fear. If you ask an appraisal theorist, for whom emotions are produced through cognitive evaluation of objects or situations, she might say I didn't fear the real snake because I appraised the situation, including my proximity to the snake, the company of other hikers, and my (perhaps ill-informed) assessment of it as not poisonous.[39] This may explain my encounter with the real snake, but it's not what happened with the snake-like stick. No single theoretical approach to fear is adequate to describe both situations. We need to think through fear as both a "basic" emotion *and* what some term a "social-evaluative" one,[40] an affective judgment of how we feel about others. We also need to understand both the initial affective response—what Massumi refers to as an "activation," the moment at which affect is, in his words, "autonomous" and unpredictable—*and* the emotional aftermath of that corporeal impression, the evaluative, cognitive, often (but not always) narrative, process that follows.

Patrick Hogan is helpful with the latter task. Hogan agrees with scientists who suggest our fear mechanisms are "adaptive," though he warns that fear and other emotions' functionality for evolutionary purposes is "very circumscribed."[41] In particular, we often fear objects or situations that are not dangerous; he mentions the fear of snakes that we know are not poisonous as one example of this phenomenon. The reverse is also true: We trust objects and situations we probably shouldn't. Hogan presents these insights to show the limitations of appraisal theory. His model, by contrast, insists emotional response is more immediate and direct, and that it often doesn't involve extended appraisal or goal evaluation. He argues for a "'neurobiological sensitivity'

account of emotions" that suggests they result from "the concrete imagery they recruit and the emotional memories they trigger."[42] For him,
fear results from triggers that may be innate, genetically organized, or a
result of an individual's emotional memories—all of which are shaped
to some degree by culture. This model is much more helpful in assessing why I reacted in fear to the snake-like stick.

Hogan differentiates himself from Martha Nussbaum, whom
he counts as an appraisal theorist. Still, her recent book, *Political
Emotions: Why Love Matters for Justice*, is a useful reference point in
beginning to think about fear and politics. In it, she calls fear "a narrow-
ing emotion" and an "unusually primitive" one.[43] She argues that fear
and shame block compassionate politics, and she suggests that for gov-
erning bodies to use fear "well," they need to combine it with sympathy, which means moving from individual scales to more general ones.
If this isn't done deliberately and carefully, fear "can often distract us
from general sympathy." Certainly it's true that governments too often
create "the perception of danger" where it doesn't exist.[44] Fear tends
to produce self-interest—and the problematic othering, the drawing
of social lines that all-too-often are racially based. When we're afraid,
this argument goes, we go into self-preservation mode. Nussbaum, following this logic, claims that fear is "centrifugal; it dissipates a people's
potentially united energy."[45] I think it's more accurate to say, along with
Massumi, that fear does, in fact, unite people (sometimes in narrowly
defined groups; other times as a nation) based on perceived risk and
susceptibility to a threat.

But exactly who is this "we"? Which "people" are "potentially
united"? Here is where cultural theorists of emotion can help fine-tune
the more general observations neuroscientists, philosophers, and cognitive narratologists make. Working from a theoretical grounding in
feminism and cultural studies, Sara Ahmed also sees fear as, initially,
a "shrinking" of the body away from a perceived threat.[46] Our own
mobility may be restricted at the moment of a fearful encounter, as
mine was when I saw the stick-snake. Contrary to common beliefs that
fear is a universal human emotion rooted in individual bodies, though,
Ahmed challenges us to understand fear in more complex terms as
a cultural and political process. Ahmed "troubles" emotion the way

Judith Butler did gender: She destabilizes it, denaturalizes it, and un-
moors it from individual bodies.[47] Fear isn't "in" bodies; it's relational
and processive. Fear emerges, in Ahmed's model, when distinctions
between those who are threatening and those who are threatened are
created. Importantly, fear is "an effect of this process [of distinction],
rather than its origin."[48] Put another way, fear is a product of social
relations rather than their cause.

What tends to happen, Ahmed explains, is that whoever is not included as the sufferer of the fear becomes marked as its origin. When
the object of fear is racialized, those bodies take on the status of a threat,
an anticipation of hurt or injury that's by definition "unknowable."[49]
Fear also involves "an *anticipation* of hurt or injury"[50] and, as such, is
future-directed as well as object-oriented. It becomes attached—or in
Ahmed's terms, it "sticks"—to specific objects, to specific bodies, and
I'd stress, to specific landscapes. Then these objects make their way into
individuals' thoughts and memories, and circulate in culture, where
they can trigger emotions like fear in the way Hogan describes.

Moments of individual fear can accumulate at collective scales. For
Massumi, the color-coded terrorist alerts that followed the 9/11 attacks
offer an instructive example of fear management or, as he terms it,
"affect modulation."[51] His theory of how fear goes from individual to
other scales is intriguing if a bit hard to parse: it moves "from activation to feeling-in-action, from feeling-in-action to pure expression of
affect, from pure expression of affect to branchings into perception,
reflection, and recollection, then on to affective containment." After
that, the accretive process gets even more complex, as fear "attache[s]
itself to signs, then to thought-signs."[52] The end result of this process
can culminate in fear becoming self-generating and entirely virtual
("ontogenetic")—in a sense, entirely without an object.[53] In my snake
encounters, it's easy to see how I contained the fear through a process
of reflection on, and recollection of, the initial activation experience.
At the same time, it seems that my misrecognition of the snake-like
stick was more than simple misrecognition. Massumi might say it was
an instance of fear's "emergent self-reflective capacity to be its own beginning and end," and a contributor to a "background mood of fear"
that carries an "ontogenetic charge."[54] This, Massumi explains, is how

the "affective attunement" of a public occurs. In the case of post-9/11 America, and perhaps also now, in the age of Trump, that attunement is toward nervousness—although *not*, Massumi emphasizes, a uniformity of action or behavior.

In my faux snake encounter, I wouldn't say the fear occurred ontogenetically (after all, there was a real stick there to trigger it) but I would say my "background mood" was one of fear, or at least, anxiety. But which was it? Massumi uses fear and anxiety interchangeably; however, I suggest it's important to differentiate between the two. Fear and anxiety share symptoms, including "nervousness, uncertainty, excitability, blind resentment, and unreasoning hysteria."[55] While they may both be "expectant emotions," they aren't the same thing.[56] As Ahmed points out, fear and anxiety are often distinguished by their relationship to objects. Fear is commonly understood to have a clear object,[57] whereas anxiety can be a more ambiguous sense of unease without a single identifiable object. Ahmed revises this model to suggest anxiety is *"an approach to objects"* while fear is *"produced by an object's approach."*[58] In either case, there is a spatial dimension that must be accounted for; the physical environment influences the approach, the objects, and the bodies in question. It's telling that the colloquialisms we use to describe anxiety are often material and linked to movement; we say we're "jumpy," "unsettled," "on edge," or "on pins and needles." Both fear and anxiety are environmentally modulated, even if anxiety seems to be a longer-lasting feature of a particular human body, a predisposition to environments and the objects within.

Another way to distinguish them is temporally, in terms of duration. A healthy person cannot exist in an actual state of fear, in the basic sense of organism activation, for very long; we must downgrade it to anxiety. Anxiety, unlike fear, can be an enduring background feeling or a mood that one may or may not be conscious of. Anxiety might be a more appropriate response to a threat, if we define "threat," along with Massumi, as a virtual "quasicause" of fear.[59] In my case, the trajectory (my own "line of fright," to borrow Massumi's clever Deleuzian pun[60]) was a bit different. Fear did not "slide" into anxiety after a fearsome object passed me by.[61] In my experience at the Coronado, the anxiety I felt after reading the signs, finding the Border Patrol vehicles, and seeing the real snake made me more susceptible to a fear response when I saw the snake-like stick. Fear flickers but anxiety lingers, creating a sort of feedback loop that fuels a collective affective atmosphere: Once attuned to anxiety, we then become predisposed to feel fear more readily, and those startling flickers of fear in turn compound the anxiety.

Nussbaum's, Massumi's, Hogan's, and Ahmed's approaches to fear and anxiety are different, but I read them as complementary rather than mutually exclusive. To recap: Damasio's scientific framework provides an essential starting point for explaining what happens in the body when we're afraid. Massumi takes the discussion outside of the individual body to broader scales and reminds us that environment and affective response are, at least at the moment of activation, united. Emotion happens after, if at all. Hogan's trigger theory lends a cognitive vocabulary to Massumi's understanding of affective activation. Hogan also foregrounds the emotional memories and cultural associations that contribute to individual affective responses. Nussbaum's formulation is interesting for its critique of fear as socially prohibitive and for her strategic movement toward compassion, but her democratic utopianism can't work without directly confronting the more difficult racial politics that Ahmed grapples with. Ahmed explains how fear is often read as originating in particular bodies, despite it being, in actuality, relational; she also helpfully differentiates between it and anxiety. All are most useful, I find, when we pay attention to the emergence and circulation of fear and anxiety within particular environments and in relation to particular objects.

------◆------

Back we go, then, to Coronado National Memorial. Here, tourists will be more or less inclined to fear or anxiety depending on the emotional memories of deserts they bring, on the cultural associations they have with the landscape, and on how mobile they are in this particular environment: a militarized NPS site in a desert, near a tense national border. Mobility here is a privilege of U.S. citizens—the Border Patrol vehicles aren't looking for citizens with those rotating cameras—and of white bodies in particular. In American culture, border stories often "elicit fears about the hydra of villainy: drug traffickers, 'illegal' immigrants, and terrorists."[62] These "illegals," to use the charged (and highly problematic) term in political discourse, are "read as the origin of fear."[63] In reality, though, the fear does not come from their bodies, just as (to return to my snake example) fear does not originate in me, or in the snake, or in the desert landscape. Ahmed explains that "fear is felt differently by different bodies, in the sense that there is a relationship to space and mobility at stake in the differential organization of fear itself."[64] Who should be afraid here? To return to the NPS warnings, whose bodies are "illegal" here? Whose behavior qualifies as "suspicious"?

On the one hand, as a white U.S. citizen hiking in a national park, I can traverse this space more or less uninhibited; because I am not likely to be profiled as a drug trafficker, would-be migrant, or terrorist, my body occupies a relatively privileged position in this border environment. On the other hand, as a woman, my relative freedom to recreate is constrained, if only slightly. The NPS sign counseling vigilance resonates with solo women, in particular, since we are often warned to be aware of our surroundings when in public—especially when walking alone and/or at night. It's our responsibility, we're taught, to take precautions to stay safe. This is a cultural norm, not a natural one, and it spatializes and reinforces patriarchy. Ahmed clarifies: "Vulnerability is not an inherent characteristic of women's bodies; rather, it is an effect that works to secure femininity as a delimitation of movement in the public, and over-inhabitance in the private. In this way, fear works to align bodily and social space: it works to enable some bodies to inhabit and move in public space through restricting the mobility of other bodies to spaces that are enclosed or contained."[65] The same could be said of racialized bodies at the border. Race, like gender, is "not an inherent characteristic" of bodies, but whiteness is nevertheless both privileged—white bodies can move through this space without suspicion—and "vulnerable," insofar as we are told we face dangerous threats by doing so.

But prospective migrants are far more vulnerable. They are the ones risking their lives to cross the border in this brutal environment. They are the ones who rightly feel afraid here, not only of the desert but also of the government officials who police it. I have no way of accessing that fear or comprehending the anxiety of being led by a "coyote" who cares next to nothing for your safety, or the terror of seeing a Border Patrol agent or vehicle. I can only imagine it, with the help of other people's stories. Francisco Cantú's controversial memoir tells some of these stories from the perspective of a former Border Patrol agent.[66] While the book itself is fascinating—it features, among other things, discussions with his mother, a former park ranger and the daughter of a Mexican immigrant[67]—the criticisms of it are even more so. One critic, 31-year-old Jesús Valles, who was smuggled into Texas as a child and later gained legal permission to stay, chastises Cantú for not fully grasping "the fear that the Border Patrol instills in people like me," a fear Valles describes as "a dread of being hunted down like an animal, of seeing your siblings deported."[68] Having never experienced anything close to that feeling myself, I can't claim empathy with that kind of vulnerability.

My own associations with the border are frivolous by comparison. As I walk steadily toward monument 102, two visual images pop into my head and float there as unbidden thought-signs. The first, an image of a delirious Chevy Chase (playing Clark Griswold in the 1983 film *National Lampoon's Vacation*) stumbling over a sand dune wearing his blue jeans on his head, alternates with the second, a disturbing image of an amputated human head hinged to the back of a tortoise, who's slowly crossing into the U.S. from Juarez (from the "Tortuga" episode of HBO's hit show *Breaking Bad*). Clearly I've been out in the heat too long. But actually, this is the kind of strange, idiosyncratic imagery each of us brings to a landscape. Predicting which cultural associations and emotional memories will shape an individual's affective encounter with an environment is tricky, if not impossible. We can't deny that these factors matter, though, even if this facet of the affective atmosphere can't be reliably used to promote a general theory.[69] Some speculations feel safe to make, anyway—for instance, that increased exposure to violence at the border, in shows like *Breaking Bad* and other readily available visual texts, feeds in to associations of racialized fear with this landscape and reinforces, for some Americans, the ideological (us versus them) boundary between nations.[70]

In a funny way, the two images do illustrate my fluctuating mood. As I hike alone in the desert, I waver between a vague sense of anxiety—the "Tortuga" episode represents that—and the delirious elation seen in Chase's character. Like poor Clark, I've been horribly lost in the desert (though I've never gotten so hyperthermic that I've worn pants on my head). One of my emotional memories is of spending the better part of a night wandering from slot canyon to slot canyon without water or shelter, utterly unable to find my way back to the parking area. The desert can be not just physically but also emotionally disorienting, offering up a mirage of pleasure to obscure the fact that you're courting death. But aren't the stakes high in any relatively wild place? Deserts are risky for recreational hikers and other walkers, sure, but so are mountains, if you're a mountaineer, and so are oceans, if you're a scuba diver. Like the bodies that move through these spaces, the environments themselves do not contain fear, even if they do house some dangerous creatures; neither the places nor their inhabitants are inherently fearsome. Still, for me, its relative harshness, its intense heat and relentless aridity, combined with the cultural texts I associate with it, links the desert more closely with fear than these other environments.

When I reach monument 102 and spend some time alone there, something odd happens: The cultural associations and the affective predisposition they give me start to fade. The built environment—the obelisk and barbed-wire fence—has the most affective agency here; the natural landscape becomes, for the moment, just a backdrop. There is minimal text, aside from a legal warning engraved on the monument itself (a reminder that it's a misdemeanor to destroy or displace it) and a friendly sign to the north welcoming "all users" to explore the Arizona National Scenic Trail, which goes for 800 miles, all the way to Utah. To be sure, a barbed-wire fence connotes fear, linked as it is to prisons of all kinds. But this one is ragged, broken-down, clearly futile. Any fear it might inspire is canceled out by its neglect and ineffectualness.

The monument—an obelisk—has a different, more historical tone. Carter traces the use of obelisks by ancient Egyptians and Greeks, and the more contemporary (and common) use of the form to "signal historical events and mark a time and place,"[71] a goal in keeping with the NPS's designation of historic sites. Obelisks have been popular

FIGURE 1.3. Border monument 102 with barbed-wire fence

boundary markers in the U.S. since at least the 1790s, when they were used to differentiate between the District of Columbia, Virginia, and Maryland. The Washington Monument (another NPS-managed site) is perhaps the U.S.'s most high profile obelisk. Carter suggests an obelisk can "communicate conciliation and unity" (as the NPS mission promotes) and still be "a reminder of bloodshed and sovereignty."[72]

Despite the scattered graffiti on monument 102 (much of which I unfortunately can't read since it's in Spanish), this one feels benignly symbolic, a material incarnation of a treaty, its historical tone editing out the bloodshed and death. Perhaps if there had been *things* there, the water bottles, scraps of serape fabric used for smuggling marijuana, or other "trappings of contemporary activity"[73] Taylor captures so evocatively with his camera lens, I'd feel differently. Objects like these mark the border with traces of the stories—and the affects—of migrants' journeys. For me, on this day, the "tone" of the obelisk counteracts the fear-inducing warnings and the Border Patrol cars. There is something about this obelisk—perhaps an "affect intrinsic to [its] form"[74]—that inspires quiet contemplation. I feel calm standing to look at the monument in this breezy, warm weather. The affective atmosphere is a serene one.

I decide to step through the fence and see what the monument looks like from that side—and to see how it feels. I'm not the first to do it. The barbed-wire fence has been split apart, and a nice big gap beckons to the curious. Will I feel different on the other side? And suddenly, as I start to extend my leg between the wires, the anxiety returns: Is anyone watching? Will I hear an authoritative voice calling sternly to me through a loudspeaker? Will somebody pull a gun on me? These are not conscious thoughts (yet), nor are they logical, but they register corporeally as a sense of unease. My heart rate increases as I gingerly ply the rusty wire upwards and ease my body through without getting scratched.

Other than the fact that the official language on this side is Spanish, it looks and feels the same. The view is just as lovely—better actually, since I no longer have to peer through barbed wire to see the Sonoran Desert and an unpeopled landscape extending to the horizon. For me, as for Taylor, standing at the border monument exposes "the contrast between the *idea* of a border and the experience of how a boundary functions on the ground . . . One step south and you are in Mexico; one step north and you are in the United States. The place doesn't change, but you are in a different country."[75] The landscape doesn't suddenly change; it doesn't look "Mexican," whatever that might mean. (Actually, a ranger would tell me later, I'm not even in Mexico; there is a 150-foot easement before the actual boundary.) There are no brown bodies below, except the ones I imagine might be resting in the shade, waiting to walk across at night. Perhaps Americans who support President Trump's wall imagine these bodies as "slobbering rapists and murderers"[76] walking zombie-like across the border to steal jobs, dodge taxes, and inflict violence on God-fearing Americans.

What strikes me most at border monument 102 is the way the natural landscape defies the national border, exposing it as the arbitrary political construction it is. Williams ponders similar things at the border in Big Bend National Park: "No map can orient us here. Where does America end and Mexico begin? This is its own country, borderless by nature, unowned, unbowed, complete. Boundaries are fears made manifest, designed to protect us. I don't want protection, I want freedom."[77] The fence is surely a false indicator of protection; any motivated human could get through at this point, provided they could survive the desert environment. It's also just plain strange, out of place in this contoured valley. To me, the fence looks utterly unnatural against the otherwise uninterrupted desert landscape, which doesn't suddenly change at the fence line. Landscape, and the nonhuman animals that live here, render the notion of national boundaries and fences—or walls—not just unnatural but absurd. I think back to the NPS display about the four ecosystems that come together here, a complex intersectionality that also gives the lie to any kind of artificial, quasi-linear, national boundary here.

Visitors who have been reading the NPS displays may recall, at this point, the one called "Life on the Border," located just outside the visitor center. In its visual and written rhetoric, the border is an obstacle the NPS must "help" overcome. Photos from elsewhere along the border depict much more substantial walls, illustrating text that foregrounds the obstacles to mobility. The negative consequences for the wildlife the agency is supposed to keep safe are especially important to mitigate: The fence "restricts large wildlife that once roamed freely," the sign reads. Invoking a bit of nostalgia for the free, unfenced past, the display reminds us of borders' power to "define the land and the life that resides here. Borders can be natural, like rivers and mountain ranges. Or they can be legally drawn, like the border between Mexico and the United States." The rest of the display spells out which wildlife migrations are most constricted by fences, and the negative impacts for diversity and population. The rhetorical implication that "natural" and "legally drawn" borders are an either/or binary is important for my reading of the site. Even without knowing the shifting history of this border—and even without the conscious recognition that one is standing in what used to be Indigenous and later, Mexican lands—there's no way to see a "legally drawn" border (or the fence that marks it) as anything other than unnatural.[78]

No matter how many treaties we sign, there is no *tabula rasa* at this border, as Lauret Edith Savoy reminds us:

> Not with tribal peoples Indigenous to these basins and ranges. Not as so many other peoples came. Mexican citizens, then "immigrants." Chinese immigrants who labored in mines and laid tracks but couldn't live in sundown towns like Bisbee. And those of African heritage, from as early as the 1530s when a man named Esteban or Estevan de Dorantes, survivor of the disastrous Narváez expedition in Florida, may have passed this way. Africans certainly trudged north on Coronado's *entrada*, for it was reported that "negros y indios" died of thirst and hunger. People of mixed African Indigenous, African Mexican, and African European ancestry arrived and stayed. William 'Curly' Neal built the famous Mountain View Hotel, a resort in Oracle frequented by Buffalo Bill Cody and other celebrity guests. Jazz legend Charles Mingus, son of an African American soldier and a Mexican woman, was born in Nogales. Black homesteaders settled along the San Pedro River.[79]

Savoy's brilliant memoir, *Trace: Memory, History, Race, and the American Landscape* tracks her family's history in the region and fleshes out the history of a multiracial West, including the "negros y indios" on the Coronado expedition. It was from *Trace* that I first learned that all four of the African American military regiments known as "buffalo soldiers" were stationed at Fort Huachuca at one time or another. I take up this history in chapter six, where I explore the role of the buffalo soldiers in other parts of the West. There's little trace of this multiracial history in Coronado NM today, though.

Although arbitrary by ecological measures and not "inevitable"[80] by historical standards, today's legal border is quite real, and the stakes are high for those who attempt to cross it illegally. In Savoy's words, "borders erected here long ago—borders of history, of possession, or meaning—still seem sharp and unyielding. They cut."[81] As border checkpoints in major towns become increasingly militarized, would-be migrants are forced more and more into the desert to make their crossings. Deaths have increased as a result.[82] Urrea's *The Devil's Highway* offers a nuanced and profoundly moving look at the desperate economic circumstances that compel people to attempt such a risky crossing by telling an especially powerful story of death in the desert: the story of fourteen Mexican migrants, known as the "Yuma 14" (part of the "Wellton 26," for those who want to reflect the initial number of walkers—though that may actually have been 29) who died trying to cross the border in southern Arizona in May 2001.

Urrea's intertextual and thickly contextualized approach emphasizes the physicality of walking, as Amy Hamilton shows in her book, *Peregrinations*, by turning "repeatedly to the metaphoric, emphasizing the men's trans-corporeality, their intermeshment with Christian stories, Indigenous histories, and economic contexts."[83] Urrea's deft mixing of genres—including interviews, news stories, and speculative fiction—illustrates the complexity of the tragic journey. Confusion surrounds the Yuma 14 tragedy and reveals one reason "why it's so difficult to enforce immigration law on the border. Of the men confirmed to have survived from the group, none can agree on where, exactly, they entered the United States."[84] It's partly the walkers' disorientation that's to blame for this, but it's also the desert itself, in which, even in the best circumstances, it can be easy to lose your bearings. (I hear Williams again: "No map can orient us here.")

Urrea's is an unusually affective portrayal of the desert's agency. *The Devil's Highway* captures what the NPS interpretive plan describes as "the ethereal beauty of a harsh land."[85] His gripping account emphasizes the harshness. The desert is a ruthless, unforgiving place, a "terrible landscape" housing "a vast trickery of sand."[86] It is a place where "heat sizzle[s] at the edges of things".[117] In one particularly horrifying passage,[87] Urrea uses second-person point of view (like many NPS signs do) to address readers. His description of the stages of hyperthermia is terrifyingly vivid. In the early stages, victims are clumsy;

they fall down awkwardly, a kind of "funny stumbling."[88] But as the stages progress, the suffering does too: "Your legs suddenly ache . . . You tumble."[89] After describing hallucinating victims who bury themselves underground to escape the heat (and are "bake[d] like a pig at a luau") or try to swim in the sand, "thinking it's water," he ends with the victim's "system clos[ing] down in a series. Your kidneys, your bladder, your heart. They jam shut. Stop. Your brain sparks. Out. You're gone."[90] With this second-person address he confronts readers with our mortality and positions the desert as merciless killer, a move that feeds in to environmental narratives of fear even as it helps humanize the walkers.

Urrea's narrative also highlights the arbitrariness of political boundaries. The actual border crossing is anticlimactic: "No matter where they entered, they had only to step over a drooping bit of wire fence, or across an invisible line in the dust."[91] The material presence of the landscape exposes the symbolic nature of the border crossing as akin to a "myth" or a "fairy tale"; "One step, and presto! You're in the EEUU. Los Estados Unidos. The Yunaites Estaites. There's nothing there. No helicopters, no trucks, no soldiers. There's a tarantula, a creosote bush, a couple of beat saguaros dying of dry rot, some scattered bits of trash, old human and coyote turds in the bushes now mummified into little coal nuggets. Nothing."[92] Of course, even Urrea's "nothing" is composed of many "things," from dried turds to tarantulas. And each of these things has a kind of agency in the desert environment.

Indeed, many of his descriptions are music to the ears of material ecocritics, who understand physical matter as having narrative agency. Urrea tells of Border Patrol agents who "read the land like a text. They search the manuscript of the ground for irregularities in its narration. They know the plots and the images by heart. They can see where the punctuation goes. They are landscape grammarians, got the Ph.D. in reading dirt."[93] Taylor, too, refers to the landscape as a text to be read and the obelisks as "punctuation" on the landscape.[94] Like Urrea and Taylor, material ecocritics are dedicated to reading the stories embedded in landscapes. For tourists who are not expert "landscape grammarians"—indeed, many of us may be inclined to read only the display signs and other written texts, not to seek out stories in landscapes—our response might be less like reading a book and more like watching a film, or reacting to a work of landscape art. It is a primarily affective reaction, which we narrate to ourselves only after an affective response is activated. Some of our affective impressions are never narrated.

For those, like me, who can't fathom what it would feel like to hire a "coyote" to guide me across the border, to walk through miles of dry land in incapacitating heat, to begin the agonizing descent into hyperthermia, or to watch others succumb to painful, delirious deaths, Urrea's book makes crossing the border visceral in a way that NPS visitation cannot. My "tale of two snakes," with its bourgeois soccer-mom daydreams and indulgent selfies at the border, is certainly banal and privileged, by contrast. I am one of the border writers Urrea condemns as "tourists."[95] Of course, mine is a book about tourism. I include my thoughts and experiences in a spirit of honesty and humility, and with the understanding that my hiking excursion resembles the experiences of at least some of the many recreational visitors to the memorial—most of whom will not have migrated illegally themselves nor have read Urrea's troubling account of the border. I hope the discussion of my personal fear and anxiety makes visible a darker reality: that speciesism and racism can infiltrate the psyches of even the most politically progressive and well-intentioned among us. Encounters with others can bring those harmful ideologies out into the light. Snakes may trigger fear, but—as with most people—when we are face-to-face with them they rarely strike. Borders negotiate the question of which animals—human and non—are considered to belong on which side of the fence. Fear and anxiety referee our answers.

In *Between Two Countries: A History of Coronado National Memorial: 1939–1990*, Joseph P. Sánchez, Jerry L. Gurule, and Bruce A. Erickson claim that ongoing concerns about migrants trampling grasses and harming the natural environment, about visitor safety, and about political and economic inequality contribute to a "tense and dangerous atmosphere."[96] I don't detect any tension in NPS ranger Christopher Bentley during my visit in April 2016. A trained historian with long dark hair, clear blue eyes, and a guitar leaning casually in the corner of his office, Bentley has been leading tours in Coronado

NM for two years when we meet. He tells me, among other things, that the Coronado Peak overlook would be the ideal place to pilot the new "facilitated dialogue" approach to interpretation that he learned in a recent NPS training. This approach brings visitors into a conversational format, where they're invited to share their individual perspectives on controversial issues. Sadly, he hasn't had the opportunity to try it out when we talk, and I don't imagine he'll want to risk such open dialogue at the border in the current political climate.

Rangers in uniform are not supposed to talk about politics, and Bentley is appropriately vague about his. He explains that the park was initially proposed as an international memorial, jointly managed by the U.S. and Mexican governments. It's easy to imagine why this plan fell through, he says, but does not elaborate other than to suggest the nations have "different versions of the conquistador history."[97] The Memorial's signs are all bilingual and the languages take up equal space on the displays, but, since Mexico opted out of the international plan, this isn't their story. As Bentley points out, the relief map at the entrance to the VC stops abruptly at the Mexican border. I hadn't noticed it at first, but when I go back to confirm I see he's right. To the north, on the U.S. side, intricate mountains, streams, and trail systems wrinkle and texture; at the southern border, a smooth black cliff breaks off cleanly, at a 90-degree angle.

While this map brings border politics into, well, stark relief, NPS written displays use more subtle language to describe those politics. I wonder if they get around their "no politics" mandate by embracing a strategy of coded, but potentially subversive, suggestions. The Coronado Peak overlook, where I began this chapter, features three display panels titled, from left to right: "A Lasting Exchange," "The Legacy of Coronado," and "Movement Provides Opportunities." Taken together, the trio conveys a story of cultural exchange with a lasting (and positive) impact: "in the United States, we feel the impact daily—millions speak Spanish, horses and cattle are essential to our economy, and the guitar is an important component of American music." The "Movement Provides Opportunities" display punctuates the story with a strong hint that various kinds of migrants, including human ones, still cross the border for many reasons. It reads:

> Coronado set out on his dangerous mission to earn wealth and honor. His soldiers, servants, and allies saw the expedition as an opportunity for financial gain and higher social standings. Many species continue to move for opportunities: people, to find work, go to school, raise a family; animals, to find more favorable habitats; and plants, to take root and thrive.

Although "people" are listed as the first migratory "species" (a clever reminder of our own animality), the images are all of flora and fauna. The javelina, coues deer, and a rather unhappy looking mountain lion stare at us from the display, confronting us with their gazes. Nonhuman animals do the ideological work here, which again could be savvy strategy, since many comments in the visitor surveys note the significance of the site for preserving wildlife and their habitat. The language here is ambiguous, but that leaves room for us to jump from Coronado and his crew to present-day immigrants from Mexico, taking advantage of this "migratory corridor" like the wildlife does.[98] The signs may fail to address the essential economic contributions made by the large numbers of migrant workers in the U.S. in its eagerness to celebrate their cultural contributions, but perhaps the NPS hopes visitors will make that connection themselves.

Not surprisingly, some visitors do think of human migration here. Survey comments are generally positive, with many mentions of the "significance" and "beauty" of the site, a few references to "contemplation" (though scant specific emotion language), and ample praise for NPS managers. There are quite a few allusions to immigration, too, ranging from concerns about access (one observed that the Memorial contains "a good road for illeagles (sic) to enter our country"); aesthetics and cleanliness (another attributes the "TRASHED" backcountry to "illegal immigrant traffic"); and safety: one man (self-identified male, age 21–30) "would like to see more armed park rangers patrolling park, so as to feel safer from Mexican drug cartels." A related comment (from a woman) believes the "biggest problem" with the site is "the illegals and associated danger to park users." Another claims the park "Establishes a foundation for our God-given patriotic beliefs." These don't necessarily reflect the majority view,[99] but they show that I'm far from the only visitor reading the signs, thinking about the politics, and grappling with feelings of fear, anxiety, and other affects. On the other side of the spectrum are calls to tell history from nonwhite perspectives, including one to "END THE BORDER WAR/END THE MILITARIZATION OF OUR PUBLIC PARKS."

The majority of the Memorial's 70,000–100,000 annual visitors are local residents coming for a recreational experience, and most, from what I can gather, do not have all-caps-worthy affective reactions. But because sites like Coronado NM commemorate a national heritage, they're especially useful in assessing how fear works in a country that claims freedom and democracy as foundational values. Touring public memorials like this one, it's easy to locate fear or the actions it motivates (like the incarceration or destruction of fearsome bodies) in the *past* but fail to see it in the present. But when I read the survey comments about "illegals" and the NPS warning about "suspicious activity," I am reminded that fear is here, now, in the present.

Fear and anxiety have accrued at this border since September 11, 2001. When Taylor took the photographs for his *Monuments* project, the Secure Fence Act of 2006 had authorized hundreds of miles of new fencing along the southern border. Taylor witnessed as nearly 237 miles of new fencing was erected. George W. Bush's goofy appropriation of Robert Frost's "Mending Wall" (he cited the "good fences make good neighbors" line) in support of that act seems relatively benign, even quaint, next to the context for my own project: the dictatorial insistence by President Trump that he will build a wall and have Mexico pay. From my viewpoints in Coronado NM—Montezuma Pass, the Coronado Peak overlook, and border monument 102—a wall is the ultimate in human hubris.

The environment creates, for me, a visceral understanding of the arbitrariness and temporariness of borders. The broken barbed wire speaks to its futility. Even the wind is a subtle but persistent reminder that natural forces are far more powerful than any human being, even the POTUS. Everything about the desert, from the landscape's vastness to the weather-worn stone of the border obelisk, reminds us of our temporariness here on earth. I'm grateful to Indigenous writers, such as Tohono O'Odham poet Ofelia Zepeda, who convey native inhabitants' respect for the desert's agential powers.[100] I appreciate, too, how writers like Urrea and Cantú tell stories that help realign our affects about the border and humanize the people and communities on both sides. I am glad that this desert is unwilling to differentiate itself along nationalistic lines.

But not everyone in the U.S. agrees. The freedom I find in the diffuseness of the natural landscape may be anxiety producing for others. Fear at the national level can increase when the symbolic, nationalistic "homeland" appears to be violated, by something dramatic like a terrorist attack or by something less so, like a broken fenceline at the border.[101] Certainly part of President Trump's success was due to his ability to manipulate fear—in Massumi's terms, to perform an "affective modulation of the populace."[102] President Trump knows how to stoke fear; there will be no fear fatigue under his watch. Fear can certainly cause some people to want to retreat into safe havens, to shut themselves off from others, or to pledge allegiance to tyrants.

The actual, material homeland is a physical place, though, and it functions unpredictably in relation to ideology. Even at the Arizona border, many people may not be as scared as they're said to be.[103] Fear, at its most ethically evolved, may be a kind of affective disorientation that never stabilizes, never congeals into nationalism. What if fear, instead, as Doss suggests it might in her chapter on fear and terrorism memorials, could "generate a counternarrative of empathy and hope"?[104] I have to confess this prospect sounds naively optimistic in our present sociopolitical moment. Still, fear can alert us not only to rattlesnakes but also to racism, something that is clearly a problem in the contemporary U.S. And I hope—Bowden's essay notwithstanding—that knowledge of how fear works *can* help us overcome irrational fears, whether of desert creatures or of human "others."

The profound ways that fear registers differently for gendered, sexualized, classed, and raced bodies, and in various environments, demands more attention than I can give it here. For white people like me, I suspect fears about border violence are mainly trumped up, ascribed to an imagined (white) community that may be, collectively, pretty *anxious* but not, at least day to day, in the grips of actual *fear*. What difference might it make, politically, to say many white Americans are anxious, rather than afraid? Isn't anxiety more accurate to describe a complicated geopolitical reality? Perhaps, too, anxiety is less likely to "suspend action" than fear is; rather, anxiety could be a form of "discord," in Houser's terms.[105] Unlike fear, anxiety is not necessarily paralyzing or "anaesthetizing"[106] but—in small doses—can even be motivating. As a "discordant" affect, anxiety can be both diagnostic and generative, in the sense that it doesn't "just help us choose between available ethical and social possibilities" but also "sparks the creative work that generates new ones."[107]

If Ahmed is right that anxiety is less attached to particular objects and bodies, then anxiety might be less inclined to point fingers at particular (always "othered") bodies as fearsome, and more open to pointing out the broader sociopolitical forces that are to blame. Perhaps, then, shifting the discourse about white Americans (who too often claim to be spokespeople for "the nation" itself) to be about anxiety would turn attention to forces, rather than "races," to systems rather than individuals. Perhaps white Americans would discover that "our" anxieties are more about our budgets than our borders, or more about global weirding than the shade of our neighbors' skin. Perhaps, then, the very real anxieties of people of color might be heard and understood. One thing is certain: Both the diagnostic capacity of fear and anxiety and a skeptical evaluation of their circulation are urgently needed in the post–November 8, 2016, United States.

Notes

1. https://www.nps.gov/coro/index.htm. Accessed 3 April, 2016.
2. *Coronado National Memorial Long-Range Interpretive Plan* (Washington, D.C.: Department of Interior, 2007), 13.
3. Clare Hemmings, "Invoking Affect: Cultural Theory and the Ontological Turn," *Cultural Studies* 19.5 (2005): 559.
4. This is Linda Stone's phrase for the way we pay partial attention to many things, continuously. She ties it to the desire to be connected, to be "a LIVE node on the network," and distinguishes it from multitasking: https://lindastone.net/qa/continuous-partial-attention/. Accessed 19 May, 2018.
5. *Coronado National Memorial Long-Range Interpretive Plan*, 9.
6. Ibid., 9.
7. Ibid., 2.
8. Ibid., 10 (my emphasis).
9. Camilla Fojas, *Border Bandits: Hollywood on the Southern Frontier* (Austin: University of Texas Press, 2010), 2.
10. Grebowicz, 9.

11. Luis Alberto Urrea, *The Devil's Highway: A True Story* (New York: Little, Brown, and Company, 2004), 48.

12. Ibid, 8.

13. Fojas, 5.

14. Trump's suggestion that Mexico is "not sending their best" to the U.S., including the assertion that "they're rapists," is infamous by now. For one record of these statements, with a video and some crime statistics, see: https://www.washington-post.com/news/fact-checker/wp/2015/07/08/donald-trumps-false-comments-connecting-mexican-immigrants-and-crime/?utm_term=.f231b3f60aeb. Accessed 21 January, 2017. The irony in the "no taxes" stereotype is rich, too, given Trump's boasting in the presidential debates about not paying taxes himself. Urrea provides economic numbers that challenge these stereotypes.

15. Terry Tempest Williams, *The Hour of Land: A Personal Topography of America's National Parks* (New York: Sarah Crichton Books, 2016), 197.

16. Williams, 13.

17. David Taylor, *Monuments* (Reno, Radius Books, Nevada Museum of Art, 2015).

18. For one of many news sources on this subject, see Kate Linthicum, "Mexican president rejects Trump's border wall—and says he won't pay for it," *Los Angeles Times*, January 25, 2017. http://www.latimes.com/politics/washington/la-na-trailguide-updates-mexican-president-rejects-trump-s-1485404143-htmlstory.html. Accessed 18 May, 2018.

19. Claire C. Carter, "Straddling the Fence," in David Taylor, *Monuments* (Radius Books, Nevada Museum of Art, 2015), 287.

20. For an overview of NPS architectural trends, see Robert Frankenberger and James Garrison, "From Rustic Romanticism to Modernism, and Beyond: Architectural Resources in the National Parks," *Forum Journal: The Journal of the National Trust for Historic Preservation*, 2002. http://forum.savingplaces.org/viewdocument/from-rustic-romanticism-tomodernism. Accessed 26 March, 2017. Gregory Clark offers a fascinating account of the rustic aesthetic of NPS architecture and the nostalgic ideologies it promotes. "Remembering Zion: Architectural Encounters in a National Park," in *Observation Points: The Visual Poetics of National Parks*, ed. Thomas Patin (Minneapolis: University of Minnesota Press, 2012), 29–54.

21. For a good historical overview of the parks' formation, see Mark David Spence, *Dispossessing the Wilderness: Indian Removal and the Making of the National Parks* (New York: Oxford University Press, 1999).

22. Sara Ahmed cites Franz Fanon's well-known description of an encounter with a white child who becomes "frightened" in his presence. In this case, the signs "Negro, animal, bad, mean, ugly" are associated historically in ways that produce the black man as an object of fear for the child. Ahmed, *The Cultural Politics of Emotion* (New York: Routledge, 2004), 66. Clare Hemmings cites this same example as proof that affect is not wholly unpredictable or virtual, certainly "not random," 561–2. Both Ahmed (53) and Hemmings (561) cite Audre Lorde as well, who registers "hate" coming from a white woman on a bus. Coates write movingly

about the fear felt by black men he knew growing up in Baltimore, the "vulnerability of the black teenage bodies," and his fear for his son's safety. *Between the World and Me* (New York: Spiegel & Grau, 2015), 15.

23. Hemmings, 562.

24. I don't have space to analyze tourists' attitudes toward law enforcement in general or Border Patrol in particular. For instance, Carter describes many Border Patrol agents as first- or second-generation immigrants who "intimately understand both immigration enforcement and the economic drive to migrate to the U.S. Some see themselves as humanitarians, hopeful that they can rescue lost migrants before they die from exposure and dehydration" (291). Urrea's descriptions concur, although he devotes more space to imagining what migrants see and feel when they encounter Border Patrol agents. Francisco Cantú's book, *The Line Becomes a River: Dispatches from the Border* (New York: Riverhead Books, 2018) is another important contribution to borderlands literature.

25. Lauret Edith Savoy recounts meeting an African American Border Patrol agent at this very same overlook, and she notices he speaks of migrants as "other"—a "third-person plural as object of his daily business," a "them" to our "us." Savoy, *Trace: Memory, History, Race, and the American Landscape* (Berkeley: Counterpoint Press, 2015), 122.

26. The interpretive plan (which I'd not yet read when I set out for my first hike in the park) actually warns that illegal activity happens "daily."

27. Savoy, 124.

28. Fojas, 25.

29. http://www.ibwc.state.gov/About_Us/history.html. Accessed 20 October, 2016.

30. Interestingly, echoing Ahmed's definition of affect, Taylor calls his photographs "sticky": They're meant to be "adherent," he says, "They'll stick. They'll stick tenaciously" and maintain a "resonance that changes over time" (314–15).

31. I don't mean to fetishize walking or to be ableist. I am indebted to disability studies scholars for, among other insights, the reminder that all of us are only temporarily able-bodied. The late Lucia Perillo's work, *I've Heard the Vultures Singing: Field Notes on Poetry, Illness, and Nature* (San Antonio: Trinity University Press, 2007), is especially impactful for me, since she was a park ranger who struggled with multiple sclerosis later in life.

32. Default mode network, a connected network of brain regions, is a kind of wakeful resting state, the one in which our thoughts wander freely, when we are not engaged in a goal-oriented task. Default network is thought to be involved in awareness of both our own and others' emotions; it often entails thinking about oneself and others, remembering the past, and anticipating the future. For one of many resources on the subject, see Jessica R. Andrews-Hanna, "The brain's default network and its adaptive role in internal mentation," *The Neuroscientist* 18.3 (2012): 251–270.

33. Charles Bowden, "Snaketime," in *The Charles Bowden Reader*, ed. Erin Almeranti and Mary Martha Miles (Austin: University of Texas Press, 2010), 34.

34. Ibid., 37.

35. Brian Massumi, *Parables for the Virtual: Movement, Affect, Sensation* (Durham: Duke University Press, 2002), 195. He draws on scientific experiments to support this statement.

36. Brian Massumi, "Fear (The Spectrum Said)," *positions* 13.1 (2005), 38.

37. Antonio Damasio, *The Feeling of What Happens: Body and Emotion in the Making of Consciousness* (Orlando: Harcourt, Inc., 1999), 51.

38. Massumi, "Fear," 37.

39. Narratologists, such as Keith Oatley, are also helpful in describing how readers approach fiction, suggesting that "we respond emotionally to literature because we mentally simulate the experiences of a character from his or her point of view" (Hogan, 245).

40. Mark R. Leary, "Affect, Cognition, and the Social Emotions," in *Feeling and Thinking: The Role of Affect in Social Cognition*, ed. Joseph P. Forgas (Cambridge: Cambridge University Press, 2000), 334.

41. Patrick Hogan, "On Being Moved: Emotion and Cognition in Literature and Film," in *Introduction to Cognitive Cultural Studies*, ed. Lisa Zunshine (Baltimore: The Johns Hopkins University Press, 2010), 242.

42. Ibid., 245.

43. Martha Nussbaum, *Political Emotions: Why Love Matters for Justice* (Boston: Harvard University Press, 2015), 320.

44. Ibid., 322. Like Hogan, Nussbaum warns that errors in perceiving fear can occur at a number of points. She paraphrases Aristotle: "We may have misidentified the threat, or misestimated its size. Or we might be right about the threat but wrong about who has caused it. Or we might have a conception of our well-being that is off-kilter, which makes us fear something that is not bad at all (for example, the inclusion of new ethnic groups in our nation)" (322).

45. Ibid., 323.

46. Ahmed, *Cultural Politics*, 69.

47. Judith Butler, *Gender Trouble: Feminism and the Subversion of Identity* (New York: Routledge, 1990).

48. Ibid., 72.

49. Massumi, "Fear," 35.

50. Ahmed, *Cultural Politics*, 65, original emphasis.

51. Massumi, "Fear," 34.

52. Ibid., 44–45.

53. Ibid., 42.

54. Ibid., 45.

55. Erika Doss, *Memorial Mania: Public Feeling in America* (Chicago: The University of Chicago Press, 2010), 147.

56. Sianne Ngai classifies both fear and anxiety as "expectant emotions" but differentiates them by their relationships to psychological projection. Her chapter "Anxiety" in *Ugly Feelings* makes a fascinating argument about anxiety as a form of "distanciation" for "male knowledge-seekers," a kind of psychological projection from the

feminine and other "sites of asignificance or negativity" (246–7). Ngai spatializes anxiety by linking it to projection—a move that is quite different from my interest in anxiety's relationship to actual physical spaces and objects. She also draws on Freud, of course, for whom anxiety meant a range of things, a descriptor for "psychic suffering of all kinds" (Tomkins, 236). Ngai identifies the need to attend to the spatial dimensions that "haunt anxiety's temporal definition" (215) and complicate its anticipatory character—priorities I share—but her main argument is tangential to mine. Ngai, *Ugly Feelings* (Cambridge: Harvard University Press, 2005).

57. Ruth Leys characterizes Damasio's views otherwise when she writes that, for him, "the basic emotions are inherently objectless in the sense that they are bodily responses, like an itch." Leys, "The Turn to Affect: A Critique," *Critical Inquiry* 37.3 (2001), 463. I'm not sure I buy her analysis, though, since a bodily response does imply an object that initiates it.

58. Ahmed, *Cultural Politics*, 66, original emphasis.

59. Massumi, "Fear," 35–36.

60. Ibid., 37.

61. Ahmed, *Cultural Politics*, 73.

62. Fojas, 2.

63. Ahmed, 71.

64. Ibid., 68.

65. Ibid., 70.

66. Francisco Cantú, *The Line Becomes a River: Dispatches from the Border* (New York: Riverhead Books, 2018).

67. She tells her son why she joined the NPS: "I wanted to be outdoors . . . because the wildlands were a place where I could understand myself. I hoped that as a park ranger I could awaken people's love for nature, that I could help foster their concern for the environment." She adds, "I wanted to guard the landscape against ruin . . . to protect the places I loved." Cantú, 5.

68. Simon Romero, "Border Patrol Memoir Ignites Dispute: Whose Voices Should Be Heard from the Frontier?" *The New York Times*, May 19, 2018. https://www.nytimes.com/2018/05/19/us/francisco-cantu-border-patrol.html. Accessed 20 May, 2018.

69. This is one place at which skeptics, including Hemmings, push back against affect theory. I try to manage this problem with my theoretical formulation of the "implied tourist" and attention to "tone" as a feature of environments.

70. Urrea does not shy away from tragic retellings of real-life violence. He notes, too, how our exposure to violence ("it's all on YouTube") makes shootings "a bore" and "even beheadings . . . passé" (224). Urrea's text is expert at pointing the finger not at some "hidden wickedness" (225) in people of color but rather at economic desperation and a basic human impulse to survive.

71. Carter, 287.

72. Ibid., 291.

73. Taylor, *Monuments*, 314.

74. Bennett, xii.

75. Taylor, 314.

76. Urrea, 233.

77. Williams, 181.

78. If one explores the visitor center, she will likely see the display there inviting visitors to learn about the shifting historical borders of this region. We can scroll through images on a screen that offer a kind of hands-on cartographic tour of the shifting border, as the land goes from Spanish to Mexican to U.S. control.

79. Savoy, 158.

80. Savoy, 124.

81. Savoy, 116.

82. For one account of this, see Wayne A. Cornelius, "Death at the Border: Efficacy and Unintended Consequences of US Immigration Control Policy," *Population and Development Review* 27.4 (2001): 661- 685.

83. Amy Hamilton expertly contextualizes Urrea's work within frameworks of pilgrimage, Aztlan, and migration, in particular. *Peregrinations: Walking in American Literature* (Reno: University of Nevada Press, 2018), 134.

84. Urrea, 57.

85. *Interpretive Plan*, 10. Exposing visitors to this is one of the NPS's stated goals.

86. Urrea, 4.

87. Urrea mentions, in his 2013 "Afterword," that this is the section of the text that has garnered the most attention, "the most traction" (222).

88. Urrea, 121.

89. Ibid., 123.

90. Ibid., 128–9.

91. Ibid., 56.

92. Ibid., 57.

93. Ibid., 29.

94. Taylor, 333.

95. These tourists, he goes on, "think they're going to hell to take snapshots of the devil. Or worse, it's like a visit to the zoo. All them l'il brown critters doing crazy brown things" (234). Cantú tells a very different story, beginning with a Prologue that finds him and his mother (a former park ranger) in "dangerous" Juarez, where they're greeted not by devils but rather by a community of compassionate people (4).

96. Joseph P. Sánchez, Jerry L. Gurule, and Bruce A. Erickson, *Between Two Countries: A History of Coronado National Memorial: 1939–1990* (Rio Grande Books, 2007), 177.

97. Sánchez et al. chronicle this history in detail. See also Sánchez's newer book, *Coronado National Memorial: A History of Montezuma Canyon and the Southern Huachucas* (Reno: University of Nevada Press, 2017).

98. The Coronado interpretive plan links both humans and wildlife as using this corridor, 6.

99. While I am not trained, or interested, in coding data, the NPS does sort comments into "positive," "neutral," and "suggested improvements." It's clear they use the data to try and improve services.

100. See, for instance, Zepeda's *Ocean Power: Poems from the Desert* (Tucson: University of Arizona Press, 1995).

101. Doss explains how the "homeland" is a symbolic geography that helps assuage fears at the national level, 147.

102. Massumi, 32. I wonder, too, if there's something to the findings in certain recent psychology studies that political conservatives have larger amygdalas. See, for instance: https://www.psychologytoday.com/blog/mind-in-the-machine/201609/the-psychology-behind-donald-trumps-unwavering-support. Accessed 18 October, 2016.

103. For instance, a vimeo clip shows border residents protesting at a visit by Arizona governor Jan Brewer, there to campaign for Trump and his wall. They hold signs that read "We are not afraid," among other things. https://vimeo.com/190337086. Accessed 21 November, 2016.

104. Doss, 181.

105. Houser, 16. Houser's discussion of anxiety in the novel *Almanac of the Dead* suggests that "the very emotion that triggers revolutionary fervor about the dancers of emergent technologies in fact suspends the capacity to resist them," 170. I think she conflates anxiety and fear, and so limits the possibilities of anxiety.

106. Houser, 216.

107. Houser, 25.

CHAPTER TWO

Placing Historical Trauma

Guilt, Regret, and Compassion at Sand Creek Massacre National Historic Site

Sand Creek Massacre National Historic Site (NHS) isn't on the way to anywhere. Located 175 miles southeast of Denver—hours away from the world-class ski areas and mountain parks that draw outdoor enthusiasts to the Rockies—and on a remote stretch of Colorado's high plains in the southeast corner of the state, this place is its own destination. Terry Tempest Williams suggests that today's tourists don't spend enough time approaching our NPS sites. We greet them, she thinks, as "'pop-up parks,' a spot of entertainment and commerce instead of an unfolding geography."[1] This may be true of, say, Grand Teton National Park, the only national park with an airport inside its boundary. Williams needn't worry about Sand Creek Massacre NHS, though. Visitors won't stumble across it as part of a larger NPS tour, and you can't simply turn off at a major interstate exit and snap a few photos. This place promises neither entertainment nor commerce. There is nothing "pop-up" about it.

When my Miami, Florida-based sister, Liz, visited me in Wyoming for the first time, she said it made her feel "claustrophobic." She would probably feel the same way in this Colorado prairie as she did in the high-elevation, mountain-ringed valley of Jackson Hole: isolated, remote, helpless, vulnerable without her usual resources. I doubt the nearby town of Eads, where I'm staying, would offer her any consolation. Eads is "typical" of many small Western towns, Ari Kelman reports in his history of the Sand Creek Massacre NHS, with its "fiercely proud residents [who] love their community while worrying over its future; and a fragile agricultural economy [that] threatens to blow away in the next drought."[2] Eads is also 98 percent white. I'm reminded of Kent Haruf's fictional Holt County, about which he's written: "This country isn't pretty, but it's beautiful."[3] Surely my love of Haruf's spare but wonderful prose is part of why I appreciate the "austere beauty"[4] of this environment. Whatever words we use to describe this subregion of the Great Plains (and we'd later diagnose Liz with a mild case of *agoraphobia*[5]), the Colorado high plains are unique. A landscape of shortgrass prairie and scrub, with low moisture and at a relatively high elevation, this place is known for extreme temperatures, tornadoes, and near-constant wind. Perhaps these harsh conditions account for the low population density in what some no doubt consider flyover country. As I'd seen for myself when my first teaching job landed me in Omaha, Nebraska, the prairie is an acquired taste.

Since opening to the public in 2007, Sand Creek Massacre NHS receives just six or seven thousand visitors in a typical year. Of the two demographics known among NPS rangers (affectionately, of course) as "the newlywed and the nearly dead," this site attracts the latter: roughly 75 percent of its visitors are over the age of 50, and 42 percent of those fall into the 61–70 age group.[6] These are people who've lived long enough to be curious about the past, and they have time enough to make this out-of-the-way place a destination. The massacre site itself encompasses 3,025 acres and is situated twenty long miles northeast of Eads. In Kelman's evocative words, the site "sits on a rolling prairie, a place transformed by seasons. From late summer till winter's end, it remains a palette of browns, grays, and dusty greens: windswept soil, dry shrubs, and naked cottonwoods. In early spring through the coming of autumn, though, colors explode. Verdant buffalo and grama grasses, interspersed with orange, red, and purple wildflowers, blanket the sandy earth, and an azure sky stretches to the distant horizon."[7]

Most visitors come in July and discover this "vivid quilt," although they have to contend with rattlesnakes and intense heat. My own visit, just a few days before Christmas in 2015, brings me face-to-face with the more desolate landscape Kelman cleverly describes as looking "like the NPS had made a bulk buy of olive-drab scenery at a local army-navy surplus store."[8] Given my longtime associations with the NPS "olive-drab" (or what rangers lovingly call the "green and gray"), this aesthetic endears it to me. I'll take drab over hot, any day. I'm glad I'm here in the same wintry season in which the November 29, 1864 massacre took place, so the landscape looks about like it did on that dreadful day, aside from a more recent gallery of cottonwood trees.[9]

Today's Sand Creek Massacre NHS is firmly embedded in the Great Plains, and that natural environment shapes tourists' impressions. As Greg Dickinson, Brian Ott, and Eric Aoki argue in their provocative reading of the Plains Indian Museum, most visitors are prepped to encounter "the West" (in particular, for their analysis, Wyoming) with awe, to feel "dwarfed" by its immensity and vastness, and to perhaps experience a "feeling of isolation," like my sister did.[10] This sense of the West is part of what these rhetoricians theorize as our "experiential landscape": a term that includes cognitive landscapes, physical landscapes, and "dreamscapes," which I understand as akin to what I discuss in chapter one (following Patrick Hogan) as the emotional memories and cultural associations that shape a tourist's encounter with a place.[11] I, of course, want to add the affective landscape to their intersectional approach. In this chapter, I'll try to pinpoint what makes the Colorado plains, and the particular landscape at the Sand Creek Massacre NHS, distinctly affective. Since this landscape is so closely tied to the trauma of the massacre, it is inseparable from negative affects, especially grief. But in what follows I'll draw on Simon Ortiz's powerful collection, *from Sand Creek*, and my own experience at the site to show how the place inspires resilience and perhaps invites compassion as well.

Dickinson, Ott, and Aoki critique the Plains Indian Museum for fostering "a rhetoric of reverence" that encourages visitors to "adopt a respectful, but distanced observational gaze."[12] This "rhetorical mode," they argue, lets non-Native viewers off the hook, "absolv[ing] Anglo-visitors of the social guilt regarding Western conquest."[13] To some degree, and at certain of its "conversion points" (to return to Ahmed's useful phrase), Sand Creek Massacre NHS invites a similar gaze. Because the landscape is both sacred and archaeologically significant—like the USS *Arizona* Memorial, the subject of chapter four, this site contains human remains—we are kept at a distance from portions of the massacre site. And we are certainly meant to be respectful.

However, while Dickinson, Ott, and Aoki are right that a respectful but distanced experience at a site of memory is insufficient—and that a polite sense of "reverence" can compound that distance—I disagree with the implication that "guilt" is the optimal affective response. The NPS faces a challenge here. The interpretive talks and displays at Sand Creek Massacre NHS assume an implied tourist who is non-Native, who's come to understand, and perhaps even to atone for, what happened here. How can managers tell the story of the massacre appropriately to this audience? What affects are desirable for a visitor who is not innocent in this history but who might nevertheless resist guilt, or perform it politely, respectfully, but ultimately without consequence? How might the NPS sidestep the touristic impulse to "compulsory compassion"[14] and a perfunctory white guilt and instead foster a connection to this place that might facilitate more sincere concern?

The NPS is well aware of its high-pressure role as "national narrator."[15] Despite managers' understandable reluctance to prescribe any particular emotions for tourists, the NPS is also an affect manager, and Sand Creek Massacre NHS has a very traumatic story to tell.[16] As if to illustrate the way trauma tends to be relived, visitors find versions of the massacre story in several places, beginning in the town of Eads at a roadside pullout. Those who stop here, as I did, can orient themselves with maps and read about ways to "Explore Colorado's Canyons and Plains." They can also read about Colonel John Chivington, an ordained Methodist minister from Ohio, and his 675 men—a posse of temporary volunteers, the Colorado 3rd Regiment—and how they rode all night from Fort Lyon to the place where approximately 750 Cheyenne and Arapaho were camped, peacefully, along Sand Creek, and how they surprised the tribes at dawn, and—despite Cheyenne Chief Black Kettle having raised an American flag and a white one, signaling peace—slaughtered 230 of these human beings, indiscriminately and without mercy, and how they mutilated their bodies, and how they burned the camp to the ground, scattered the horses, and looted what they could, and how they took scalps and other body parts as trophies. Among the 230 killed were nineteen chiefs, thirteen of whom were Cheyenne Council Chiefs.[17] About two-thirds of the victims were women and children, shot down as they fled the scene or desperately dug pits in the sand in a futile attempt to take cover from the bullets. This was a brutal massacre. How could it happen?

The mood in Colorado Territory was one in which "gold fever" set the stage for conflict, and in which "widespread fear and panic in Denver and the territory" had taken root, due in part to the high-profile murder of a rancher, Nathan Hungate, and his family, as well as to Governor John Evans's wish to make non-Native inhabitants feel safe enough to support his push for statehood. While the soldiers' orders came from the federal government, Governor Evans's proclamation that "all citizens of Colorado" should "go in pursuit, kill and destroy all hostile Indians that infest the plains" must have bolstered some soldiers' sense of righteousness. Some didn't know where they were headed or what they were in for when they left Fort Lyon. It was a surprise attack for them too. Still, they brought howitzers. Some of the soldiers must have been eager for battle, their egos bruised by the nickname "the Bloodless Third."[18]

Later, at the site, I'd learn that not everyone participated in the massacre. Chivington's orders were to take no prisoners, but Captain Silas S. Soule and Lieutenant Joseph Cramer refused to follow his orders. Their testimony was crucial to the Congressional Joint Committee on the Conduct of the War, which collected firsthand accounts, nearly all of which decried the appalling behavior of the troops. But justice was never done. No one was put on trial in either military or civilian court. Chivington, whom the committee accused of perpetrating a "foul and dastardly massacre which would have disgraced the veriest savage among those who were the victims of his cruelty," resigned from military service, unpunished.[19] Soule was shot and killed five months after the massacre, shortly after testifying against Chivington.

It is a hard story to hear, traumatic for survivors and descendants, and emotionally unsettling in different ways for non-Native visitors who bring with them cultural associations of the West with Manifest Destiny and pioneer heritage. The massacre site belies an enduring belief in American exceptionalism by casting as villains some of those who are usually lionized, including "citizen soldiers, rugged pioneers, [and] Union officials."[20] At the Sand Creek NHS opening ceremony, Kelman found most of the speeches were "utopian" about the site's prospects:

"By remembering the dead and pondering the nation's history of racial violence, site visitors would fuel cultural pluralism's ultimate triumph over prejudice, brokering a rapprochement between long-standing enemies." He also detected a similar risk to the one that concerns me here, namely that "visiting the memorial landscape would exculpate the perpetrators' heirs, because of their willingness to mourn while admitting their forebears' guilt in a tragedy."[21] In other words, white guilt might be acknowledged and simultaneously forgiven by the "willingness to mourn" here. Grief and mourning might be merely "palliative," an opportunity to move quickly from guilt to a self-congratulatory form of patriotism without feeling compassion for, or taking responsibility for, either past or present Indigenous struggles.

I am even more suspicious than Kelman. Do even this fleeting mourning and this temporary admission of guilt actually occur? If so, do they facilitate compassion, prosocial behavior, or a "rapprochement"? Or do they represent merely a "hollow offer of painless healing and quick reconciliation"?[22] And what role do the natural and built environments play in refereeing visitors' emotions? These are difficult questions, and they resonate at other memory sites; I take up a similar set of concerns in regard to shame at Manzanar National Historic Site in my fifth chapter. Here at Sand Creek Massacre NHS, the NPS is careful not to over-interpret the site, and managers have worked closely with the Cheyenne and Arapaho tribes to honor their visions for the place. Visitors are asked only to read, to listen, to get a feel for the place, and to contemplate the history. The minimalism of the management approach mirrors the stark, seemingly timeless landscape, which couldn't be a more ideal place to reflect if it were custom-made. The affective atmosphere is rarely tense here; for the most part, the environmental register of affect aligns with and bolsters the solemnity of the textual register.

Indeed, it would seem that all the NPS has to do is stand aside and let the affective agency of the landscape do its emotional work on tourists. Yet the minimalism of both the built and natural environments may quiet the violence of the massacre too much, so that some visitors won't hear it, or feel it, at all. In the remainder of this chapter I speculate that the optimal affective responses for non-Native visitors include neither a simulated and necessarily false empathy, nor a performance of guilty but patriotic atonement, but rather a contemplative compassion. For the implied tourist, I suggest, regret rather than guilt might be more effective at fostering positive feelings about Indigenous peoples, a "rapprochement," and, potentially, justice.

—◆—

The road to Sand Creek NHS is graded dirt and gravel, surrounded on all sides by dead sage, dry grasses, and scrub. Even the topography is minimalist. The horizon is flat as far as I can see, the wide sky a faded blue. I'm traveling with my good friend Amy, a whip-smart professor of rhetoric and disability studies, whom I've known since graduate school. We are enjoying being together and reminiscing, our memories of those days tinged with nostalgia. Our lives were simpler then, if not actually better. We're parents and associate professors now, with present-day concerns and their attendant feelings: nerve-wracking career decisions, child-related guilt and anxiety, and most immediately, a slightly stunned sense of disbelief that the last town we passed through on our way to the site is called "Chivington." It's hardly a town—it looks, more or less, like a junkyard, with apparently deserted buildings, a dilapidated set of mobile homes, and a smattering of broken-down cars—and it's more than a little strange that the last place you pass through on the way to the massacre site is named for its perpetrator.

We stop at the entrance sign, which is tucked behind a buck-and-rail fence, about twenty yards back from the road. I've watched visitors pose for photos in front of the Grand Teton National Park entrance sign many times. But this sign's placement discourages selfies, even if someone were to think them appropriate. We gaze out at the prairie instead, and I sneak a shot of Amy looking reflectively into the distance. Leaning on the entrance sign are what look like a bundle of teepee poles, lashed together at their midpoints. I'd soon learn that these lodgepoles did, in fact, function as frames for teepees, and that, when dragged along the ground while tied to the backs of horses as tribes changed location, they formed what are now known as lodgepole trails: rough, two-lined trails in the dirt that eventually formed the origins of many roads used in the

FIGURE 2.1. Welcome sign at Sand Creek Massacre NHS

state today, including portions of I-25. The lodgepole trails are among the many traces of the past embedded in this landscape.

On this December morning, we are the second people to park in the unpaved lot at Sand Creek Massacre NHS. There's a moment of silence after we close the car doors. Our ears adjust to the bit of white noise provided by the steady wind, and our eyes take a minute to stop squinting in the hazy brightness. Amy's always been able to make me laugh, but the familiar chitchat we enjoyed in the car isn't appropriate here. Already the atmosphere is solemn. The visitor experience begins at the edge of the lot, where a few interpretive signs are stationed to orient us. We're drawn first to the large sign titled "Welcome to the Sand Creek Massacre" (and, in smaller print) "National Historic Site." Its top third introduces the massacre as a "national tragedy," and the words of survivor George Bent form a prominent epigraph, telling of a "terrible sight: men, women, and children lying thickly scattered on the sand, some dead and the rest too badly wounded to move." The tone is set. Something "terrible" happened here, and it involved children. Bent's phrase "terrible sight" reinforces his authenticity as firsthand witness, and his details, like the "thickly scattered" bodies, suggest a historical accuracy and certify the magnitude and depth of the violence. In case our imaginations aren't vivid enough, the bottom third of the display includes part of an elk hide painting of the massacre.[23] Right in the center of the painting, a soldier holds up either a scalp or, more likely, a slain Indian's genitals; the body lies at the soldier's feet, naked from the waist down, legs spread, a bloody hole at its middle. There's no way to unsee this image.

The middle section of the "Welcome" display provides a brief overview of the site's history, along with the claim that "the sound of birds and wind replace [sic] those of pain and anguish." The last sentence tells us that "Cheyenne and Arapaho tribal members still gather here to pay homage to ancestors, to heal, and to educate future generations." Just above the painting are the words "Enjoy a Safe Visit," though it seems incongruous to speak of enjoyment here. I notice the tornado shelter on the map (good to know) and I make a mental note to visit the area near the overlook. Several of our senses are aroused by this unconventional "Welcome." We are meant to listen for the sounds, which "replace" the pain and anguish but also carry them forward, and to look at the landscape for affective clues. I can't help but think the education of future generations of tribal members alluded to in that last sentence constitutes something very different from the education I'm meant to receive here. I feel like an outsider—not an affect alien, exactly, as I have no wish to disrupt the affective atmosphere here or challenge its norms, but rather an affect imposter. As neither a tribal member who pays homage and pursues healing here (nor, I might add, do I feel a kinship with the rattlesnakes or biting insects who, another sign tells us, also call this place "home") I'll never really understand the experiences this place commemorates. I may not feel what I'm supposed to feel here, and that makes me nervous. My only possible course of action is to be humble, to be a respectful outsider at this unique place.

Nestled amidst a small grove of cottonwood trees just behind the "Welcome" sign we find two more displays. The first is the transcript of a long letter, reproduced at a scale nearly as large as the "Welcome" sign itself, against a dusty yellow parchment paper background, penned by Captain Soule—the one who, along with Lieutenant Cramer, disobeyed Chivington's orders. Soule's account includes even more appalling details, such as the stand-out last line of the middle paragraph, which reads: "One woman was cut open and a child taken out of her, and scalped." Capital letters attract our eye to other words. We read, for instance, about how chiefs had "Ears and Privates cut off." Soule's handwriting reinforces the letter's authentic feel and assures us of his honesty. The second sign positions Soule and Cramer as heroes. Framed by the official NPS banner and titled "Conscience and Courage," it features a portrait of Soule, with furrowed brow and slightly downturned lower lip, as if he's recalling something distasteful. Soule is an attractive martyr in this tale of honesty and moral choice; he was "shot in the streets of Denver" after testifying to the outrages he witnessed. Already I imagine non-Native visitors are aligning themselves with Soule against the evil Chivington. Who wouldn't identify with moral courage instead of the painted soldier brandishing an unidentifiable body part?

While we're taking in the orientation materials, we're joined both by Ranger Craig Moore, who begins an informal orientation of his own, and by the two other tourists whose car we'd seen when we pulled in. Moore tells the four of us about the site and what we might do here, but while he's still talking the other visitors wander off abruptly, without so much as a nod to Moore. Amy observes that they treated him more like a sign than a person. While I'm no stranger to being seen as more informational resource than human being—it's one of the awkward things about being an NPS ranger—I can't help but think that here, even more than at most NPS sites, the ranger uniform blends aesthetically with the natural landscape. Both are "olive-drab," with a nuance that's easy to miss. It's as though Moore himself was designed and built in the "Park Service Rustic" architectural style, which encouraged harmony between the natural and human-made environment.

Between the roadside signs in Eads, Moore's overview, and the first set of texts at the site, I am starting to grasp the broad strokes of the history. I'm also getting a sense of what the implied tourist's affective itinerary might, ideally, include: feelings of horror, disgust, and sadness at the appalling events rendered in detail here; perhaps anger about not only the violence but also the multiple failures of justice; and maybe also a smidgeon of pride at the story of heroic resistance. Not all of our ancestors were bad people. Some resisted the "hell on wheels" violence of Westward expansion. So far, the tone of the signage matches the solemn, historical mood of the site; indeed, it helps create that mood. The landscape here is as "historical" as the archival documents on the signs. The historical tone mutes the violence, making it hard to picture the graphic details of the massacre and even harder to conjure the emotions I suspect we're meant to feel. NPS historicity might itself be an affect—an "olive-drab," serious, even boring feeling that's transferred from signage to tourist, and to landscape as well. Like Moore himself, the landscape and its violence are easy to overlook, dulled by their very historicity.

Moore gives Amy and me the start time for his official interpretive tour, which we plan to attend, and I head inside for a meeting with Chief of Interpretation Shawn Gillette. I have a long list of questions for Ranger Gillette, so I turn Amy loose to wander the grounds. Moore steers me to Gillette's office, which is inside a pale trailer serving as a bare-bones visitor center. Inside are a couple of shelves housing books, rolled-up posters, and a few other tokens for sale. A complete framed version of the elk hide painting on the "Welcome" sign, also for sale, hangs next to the posters. There's a comment book and an NPS passport stamp, an ancient-looking cash register, a couple of small offices, an even smaller library, and a staff room/kitchen, where I can smell cheap coffee burning. Gillette greets me with a warm smile and a firm handshake, and we sit down at a wood laminate table in the staff room.

Every ranger can tell you the most frequently asked—and most oddball—questions at the site where he or she works, and Gillette opens our conversation with two he's heard at Sand Creek: How did the Indians get way out here? And where are the majestic mountains and teepees? These impressions, Gillette says, are shaped by Dee Brown's *Bury My Heart at Wounded Knee*[24] and by film and television. Gillette mentions the TV series *Into the West* (2005), one episode of which depicts the Sand Creek massacre against a backdrop of craggy peaks. Some visitors are disappointed. This is not the dramatic landscape they associate with "the West" or with Colorado, he explains. I'm fascinated, and I tell him about my family back East, who—when I first moved "out West"—could never keep track of what state I was in and seemed to think of the region as still a territory.

An English major and former junior high school English teacher, Gillette knows how to tell a good story, and he knows that words matter. It matters that this is the first NPS site to be named for a "massacre." And it matters that there are some who still prefer to legitimize it as a "battle"—though Gillette reports, anecdotally, that those numbers are decreasing. Gillette is a typical ranger, as genial as they come, and I can easily imagine him talking and listening to a visitor from any point on the American political spectrum. As he tells me about the NPS partnership with the Cheyenne and Arapaho tribes over the years, I am convinced of the agency's sincere efforts to honor the tribes' sovereignty, their claims to the place and its history, and their visions for its future. He is wary of presentism as he explains that he wants visitors to understand what happened here, including the context, the way people understood it then. While there are plans for a few more signs, he tells me that the NPS and the tribes agree they should keep impacts at the site minimal (not "jammed with exhibits"), so they're opening a new research and interpretive center in Eads. That will become the official visitor center, which will let the massacre site remain a place for quiet contemplation. Contemplation, Gillette affirms, is one of the interpretive goals for visitors, but—like at Coronado NM—there is no singular affective goal attached to that contemplative process.

Suddenly, an alert in the front office begins chiming Für Elise (one of only three songs I can still play by heart after ten years of piano lessons) and I hear the sound of tires on gravel. Gillette pushes himself up to a stretchy stand, rolls his shoulders back, and excuses himself to greet the visitors who have just arrived. Inside the trailer's foyer, Gillette offers this family of four his "10-minute interpretive talk." He is engaging; even the two teenagers seem to be listening. I resume my scanning of the visitor use surveys and comment books. I'm thinking about the distractions, interruptions, and banalities of NPS tourism when I stumble across a scribble in the "remarks" section from back in May: "another stamp in our book!" Later I'd see an actual visitor stamping his national parks passport book; he would give me a big grin and allow me to take his picture. For some tourists, this place is just another box to check on their NPS circuit. For them, tourism is a kind of verification; to count as genuine a visit has to meet expectations and be certified with stamps, photos, and souvenirs. As Walker Percy puts it, many tourists want to leave a site "having the experience in the bag, so to speak—that is, safely embalmed in memory and movie film," or, in this case, in a passport book.[25] Perhaps this desire partly explains why one survey respondent seems so upset by the inability to visualize what happened here: "We actually could not view the encampment site nor the sand creek. So we could not visualize in our minds the actual slaughter. The limited view was a great disappointment. Cutting down some foliage or erecting a tower would have greatly helped." For visitors like these, a landscape should be sculpted to promote "enjoyment" above all else.[26]

I only have access to the last year or so of comment books in the visitor center and two years' worth of the more extensive surveys collected on site. My method of skimming through and noting all the emotion words I can find might be enhanced by a more scientific approach, including coding the data. But even this wouldn't be conclusive. The data is too sparse, for one thing. Moreover, my approach brings advantages that only a human reader can: a greater sensitivity to visitors' less-articulate affective impressions, an ability to closely read the tone of their words, and a willingness to speculate. The visitor center comment books leave little room for lengthy thoughts, but among the words that stand out are "sad," "sobering," "poetic and poignant," "truly awesome," and an "emotional sacred place." Many write no comments at all. The survey comments, which are longer than the "remarks" in the comment book, occasionally reference the "shamefulness" of the massacre and the "unmitigated hatred" out of which it arose. From what I can gather, though, it isn't so much guilt that circulates, or even grief. It's a sense of poignancy without clear emotional valence. There is a tone of righteousness in some comments, and seldom a mention of a desire, or responsibility, to learn more. Overall, the comments feel to me like visitors are trying to say the "right" things, to prove they've gotten the message. For some, certainly, the act of coming here is an act of atonement. Once it's done, they can check it off the list.

Out in the lobby, today's visitors seem sincere in their desire to understand. I overhear the woman, whom I take to be the mother of the two older boys, asking Gillette "why" this happened. He's diplomatic. He mentions gold in Colorado, a young Republican administration, momentum toward Colorado statehood, and railroad development through the territory, fueling more competition over the land. He doesn't place blame; he lays out context, including connections to the Civil War.[27] The visitors are nodding. I imagine here, more than at other sites, visitors self-select. In reading through the comments, I find just one who was unsympathetic. Asked about the site's national significance, he responded: "To lie about the Indian Wars and make up history to make the Indians feel good." A staunchly conservative American who believes the massacre story is revisionist history is unlikely to visit. These are also the visitors who most need to come here, to listen to the stories and feelings of "the Indians" with an open mind and heart.

Perhaps *from Sand Creek*, should be required reading at the site. Simon Ortiz is Acoma Pueblo, not Cheyenne or Arapaho, but his collection of poetry framed by prose gets to the heart of the massacre, the landscape, and the violence and suffering that continue to plague our world. He wrote these poems while in a drug and alcohol rehabilitation unit of the Veterans Administration Hospital in Fort Lyon, Colorado, in 1974–5—twenty-five miles from the original Fort Lyon, the town from which Chivington and his men set out for Sand Creek just over a century prior.[28] The writing comes, literally, "from" a place of trauma, but it moves toward resilience and healing. First published in 1981 and reissued the same year Sand Creek Massacre NHS was authorized by Congress, in 2000, *from Sand Creek* casts a unique light on this site. Grief is a presence in Ortiz's poems, whether personified (as when it "memorizes this grass"[29]), or vocalized as the anguished cry of a veteran for his mother. Memory, too, is a main character, rendered as an agential force in Ortiz's descriptions. The collection combines poetry and prose—a move that enables "distilling moments of emotion based on the prose lines"—and adopts a tone that is "often sad but tender,"[30] even hopeful.

It's Ortiz's natural environment that most fascinates me, his lyrical descriptions that render both the trauma and indigenous resilience visceral. The wind is "abrupt" in one poem, "blunt and sad" in another.[31] Elsewhere Ortiz simply notes Colorado's singular beauty, as in autumn, when "like a golden dusk, rich with smell, the earth settling into a harvest, and one could feel like a deep story."[32] It's interesting to compare Ortiz's landscape language to the NPS's description of Sand Creek on its site bulletin as "a windswept place haunted by violence and broken promises." That opening paragraph concludes: "This remains sacred ground—a place to honor the dead and dispossessed, a place where they are not forgotten." The NPS text's tone is solemn and respectful, but it can't convey the affective agency of the landscape, the way affects accrete here, the way Ortiz's poetry can. With meter that often evokes "a handful of heartbeats," Ortiz's poems are more evocative of the moments that constitute felt memory than the "unwieldy narrative accounts"[33] the NPS uses to tell the story—or the dozens of pages of firsthand testimony that never led to justice.

When I teach poetry, I ask students to look and listen for (among other things) the poems' pacing, rhythm, tone, and intensity. These same terms apply to tourism. It's during our corporeal movement over, across, and through landscapes that an affective atmosphere—that assemblage of interacting bodies, objects, and other actants—emerges. The built environment delineates the pace and rhythm of our movements and helps set the tone; as we pass by display signs, walk the trails, pause at overlooks, or sit on benches, these conversion points prompt affective shifts in us. The natural landscape, too, contributes, especially in shaping the intensity and the overall tone, mood, and atmosphere at a site. As with poems, there is no singular meaning waiting to be uncovered at a memory site, and the tone of a landscape emerges via an "affective relay" between self and object, or self and text.[34] My own subject position and my "moodiness" matter; a Cheyenne visitor would interact with the landscape in an entirely different way.

Affect is not exactly "in" the landscape, then, even if there's a sense in which I'm saying affects accrete in a place. The sage doesn't, on its own, elicit sadness, and a dry creek bed doesn't automatically conjure anger. This landscape does seem resilient, though; it persists, perseveres, and survives. And it doesn't get in the way of the emotional stories I am about to hear from Ranger Moore. If "cultural materials in national parks and monuments can . . . be presented in such a way as to naturalize history,"[35] then a landscape, too, especially a minimalist one like the one at Sand Creek Massacre NHS, can naturalize history, can lend it authenticity, and can allow us to transpose a range of emotions onto it. As I'll suggest below, this landscape mitigates any guilt the non-Native visitor might feel, but it doesn't foreclose regret. It enables visitors to feel compassion and sense cultural resilience as well. I can imagine that in the spring, when it's filled with new life, the impression of resilience is even more intense.

<hr>

Today, after sitting in the NPS trailer and talking with Ranger Gillette, smelling the familiar aroma of employee-purchased Folgers coffee sitting on a hotplate too long, recognizing the NPS graphics and fonts I'd worked with in the Grand Teton NP Public Affairs Office and its visitor centers, and hearing the opening notes of Für Elise I'd memorized during my formative years, my own mood is melancholic. As I make my way to the overlook to hear Ranger Moore's interpretive talk, "Walking Through the Fire," the persistent wind across an otherwise quiet setting intensifies this mood. As I slowly walk the trail, I approach a display sign titled simply "Why?"

Like Gillette's, this narrative rehearses some context: the "gold fever" of 1858, the murder of Hungate and his family, which created "widespread fear and panic" in Denver and the Territory, and

FIGURE 2.2. "Why?" display

Governor Evans's instructions to "kill and destroy all hostile Indians that infest[ed] the Plains." Only this, Evans apparently believed, would ensure "a permanent and lasting peace." A large black-and-white portrait of Evans looms large next to his words. Weirdly, he meets the visitor's gaze with eyes that are intense but almost kind looking, with a grandfatherly twinkle. A tiny squint, a hint of the double-crease of concern between his eyes, and a barely perceptible drop of the eyebrows betray an emotional depth behind his confident gaze, and maybe even something like sorrow.[36]

There are only a handful of visitors at the site today, and Amy and I are among the few who've come to hear Moore's talk. This is the most photographed spot at the site. It features a memorial plaque mounted on conglomerate stone, a ring of rocks that signifies its sacredness, and a seating area shielded from the sun or other elements with a slatted wooden ceiling, much like the one at the Coronado Peak overlook. The plaque lists two dates for the massacre, reminding us that the suffering went on for many hours. In case anyone wants to look more closely into the creek bed, there are spotting scopes set up at the edge of the overlook rise. No one does, while we're here.

Robert M. Bednar describes how overlooks "discipline" our bodies in space, allowing a "distanced but still embodied relation" to what we are seeing. He's right, I think, that overlooks facilitate "a dissonance between ways of seeing, photographing, and knowing, on the one hand, and ways of inhabiting, being, and knowing, on the other."[37] I suggest they fuel not only that sort of dissonance between the epistemological and the ontological, but also what I've been calling affective dissonance.

In fact, adding an emotional register to Bednar's formulation helps clarify what I mean by affective dissonance. Ontologically, the way I'm situated to inhabit, be in, and know this natural landscape inspires me to feel calm and peaceful, reassured by the historical constancy of this place. Epistemologically, though, I am aware of twinges of sadness, anger, and disgust at what I am hearing, seeing, and reading about on the signs. Put simply, the natural environment and its affective register is in tension with the emotional details in the stories of what happened

FIGURE 2.3. Sand Creek Massacre NHS memorial plaque and overlook

here. That said, the overall *tone* of the textual register is still historical and solemn, much like the landscape itself; both reflect that historical aesthetic that, as I said earlier, quiets the details of the violence. Any felt dissonance resolves, then, into a mood of solemn receptivity, a proclivity toward contemplation, and for me, accentuates my background feeling of melancholy.

Because the landscape below is so subtle (thankfully, devoid of teepees or other signs of reenactments) it is unlikely to spark the "reverence" that Dickenson, et al. are concerned about, at least for a non-Native visitor. There are no obvious instructions coming from the creek bed. Once Ranger Moore begins to tell the massacre story (this is the fourth time I've read or heard about it by now), it becomes clearer how we are being cued to feel. He wants us to understand, and to imagine, the savagery, the brutality, the utter horror of this event. "Spread out before you," he says, "as far as you can see, is where the massacre took place, nearly 30 square miles." Moore asks us to visualize the "carnage" of people huddled in sand pits along the creek, shot dead at point blank range. He pauses for dramatic effect, then adds: "There is no sound worse than the sound of babies crying."[38] Just as the display signs down below had done, Moore asks us to use all our senses to create this historical simulation, and to feel horror, disgust, and grief at the suffering that took place right here, where we stand.

Perhaps to counterbalance the inclusion of troubling details, Moore titled his talk in honor of Chief Black Kettle, whom he describes as a symbol of peace and reconciliation. His comments end on a hopeful note. Visitors, Moore tells us, have "scribbled out" the phrase "Colorado soldiers" on the display that explains who's commemorated here five or six times since the site opened. Even so, when Cheyenne chiefs come here to pray they insist on commemorating everyone; "soldiers are at the top of the list." This is, Moore concludes definitively, "an American place." His story moves us from horror to patriotism, via this reassurance of the country's essentially peaceful, forgiving, and capacious nature. If a tourist were here to atone, Moore's words might afford her the opportunity to walk away feeling pretty good about herself and the U.S.

At several moments during the talk, I respond to the story's affective triggers. I'd like to say I recalled some of the Indigenous literature

I read and teach, that I thought of the trauma of Zitkala-Ša's child narrator being taken from her mother, off to boarding school. Or that I connected this story to other narratives, like Urrea's description of migrants deliriously digging holes in sand in the blistering desert heat, to fend off imminent death. But it was only later that I'd make these connections. At the talk, I just listen and feel the story. My shoulders tense at the word "carnage," and something stirs unpleasantly in my stomach at the mention of babies crying, although to associate the sound of my own children's crying with violence of this magnitude is too much for me to imagine. I can't claim empathy for the victims. What I can and do feel is compassion, especially for those who watched family members suffer or who lost children or other loved ones that day, and for those still alive today who feel the reverberations of this trauma in all sorts of ways.

Psychologists and philosophers alike have become more interested in compassion in recent decades. Martha Nussbaum ties compassion to justice and names guilt, along with shame and fear, as one of "compassion's enemies." (I return to her work in chapter five.) According to psychologist Paul Bloom, author of the provocatively titled *Against Empathy*, we should cultivate "positive feelings toward others, a desire that others do well and do not suffer, as when you wish an anxious friend would feel more calm without necessarily feeling any anxiety yourself. This is also known as 'kindness,' 'compassion,' or 'concern,'" and Bloom claims it "should replace emotional empathy as a moral motivation."[39] Compassion, provided it isn't compulsory, is more likely to produce concern for the present-day tribes as well as, perhaps, prosocial behavior.[40] It is also, I suggest, a feeling more likely to arise in non-Native visitors to Sand Creek Massacre NHS than other more poignant, cathartic, affects, like anger, sadness, or guilt.

Guilt in particular is not very likely here. As I noted earlier, most visitors aren't going to align themselves with the perpetrator's perspective, especially when Soule's story offers a more palatable alternative. Like many professors of American studies, I've heard my share of white students disavow their complicity with U.S. history; "my grandparents didn't own slaves," they say, or, in reference to Indigenous peoples, "they lost the war." The refusal to acknowledge the complexities of history or how they benefit from that history is, of course, part of their white privilege. Ortiz puts it this way: "The victors (discoverers, settlers, real estate developers, government leaders, etc.) can afford" the kind of "amnesia" that edits out the "atrocious" parts of the past, "as long as they maintain control and feel that they don't have to face the truth."[41] But maybe guilt is not the best way to own up to an "atrocious" past.

Recent research on guilt and regret suggests that regret, like compassion, might be better suited to promoting "positive intergroup relations."[42] A series of studies summarized in the *European Journal of Social Psychology* examined collective feelings of regret versus collective guilt in relation to historical atrocities—in these studies, the Holocaust. The findings suggest not only that regret and guilt are distinct affects but also that they have different antecedents, and different capacities for generating positive social results. They argue that guilt is "an aversive self-focused emotion following from appraisals of responsibility and motivating individuals to commit to reparation intentions. In contrast, regret is assumed to be a less aversive, primarily empathic emotion that follows from taking a victim's perspective, ultimately resulting in greater openness to intergroup contact."[43] There is interesting common ground between Bloom's argument for compassion (as opposed to empathy) and this group of researchers' suggestions that regret has advantages over guilt: namely, both empathy and guilt are "unpleasant" for the one experiencing them. That unpleasantness usually motivates self-interest. In the case of empathy, it can cause compassion fatigue; or, if we are distressed, we'll do what it takes to alleviate that distress. In short, we don't care about others so much as we just want to feel better ourselves.

Like the NPS surveys that form my data set in this project, these researchers relied largely on self-reported data. They're inconclusive. But they make convincing points about guilt's questionable potential. At best, it might lead to reparations. At worst, it shirks justice in the interest of alleviating the suffering of the one who feels guilty. Americans are notorious amnesiacs, which partly explains why we tend to dismiss regret as a self-indulgent emotional response. It looks backward. We feel regret because we imagine how much better it would have been if it had been otherwise. But if regret, this "counterfactual emotion," is less tainted by "aversive arousal" and the "feelings of distress" that go with guilt—physical reactions like a pounding heart and other markers of bodily tension[44]—then perhaps regret best describes the cognitive-emotional experience many tourists must feel at a site like this one. Regret, which is less tied to responsibility, seems much more likely to appeal to those who refuse guilt over something they didn't directly have a hand in. Perhaps it can be a way of "facing the truth" that's more effective because it feels less painful.[45]

With this in mind, the abundant images of human faces at the Sand Creek Massacre NHS—faces are all over the literature and the displays—might encourage us to "face the truth" about what happened here, including acknowledging the emotional impacts of the trauma, even on its perpetrators. For instance, the NPS site bulletin includes a rather distraught looking Chivington, staring over the reader's left shoulder, refusing our gaze, but with a creased brow and downturned mouth that make him appear worried. He resembles Governor Evans and Captain Soule, in fact; all three look concerned. Among the Indigenous faces, there are some that perpetuate the common past-tensing and romanticizing of tribal cultures. For instance, the faded image of an Indigenous man's face, a man who doesn't quite meet our gaze, is superimposed on the landscape on the display titled "Healing." I suspect the idea is to merge the face with the environment to remind us of Indigenous worldviews, in which humans and nature are not separated. However, its effect is to imply that healing means forgetting, even, I'd argue, in spite of the text's reminder that "atrocities . . . continue to be inflicted on cultures across the world." Yet, some of the Indigenous faces are more confrontational. On "The Sand Creek Massacre" display, a close-up of Cheyenne Chief War Bonnet, who was "slain at Sand Creek" shortly after visiting Abraham Lincoln in D.C., looks at us with eyes that somehow seem both sad and a tiny bit accusatory—as if to ask, "do you see?" Or maybe, since this was taken during a visit to meet with President Lincoln, the eyes are distrustful: "You've betrayed us many times; please don't do it again." His eyes evoke the title of a different display sign: "Pleas for Peace."

Despite psychologists, including Paul Ekman, who suggest recognizing other people's emotions can make us more compassionate, and perhaps even more likely to help others, many facial expressions aren't so easy to read.[46] I'm editorializing mine, and others would no doubt interpret them differently. Even if there is a way in which mirror neurons work automatically in a kind of emotional mimicry when we are face-to-face with another live organism, there is no simple affective transfer between me and these faces. The ones that look directly at us seem the most confrontational and the most resistant to emotional capture. They refuse resolution and catharsis in favor of reflection and contemplation. Taken together, these human faces transmit a range of negative affects, which we then associate with the surrounding landscape.

Despite all the disturbing imagery, nothing I've seen so far has implicated me. On the contrary, I feel, as I suspect the implied tourist is meant to, affectively aligned with the NPS, and the agency is clearly horrified by what happened here. Visitors to Sand Creek Massacre NHS seem appropriately contrite in their comments. As one notes: "It is important to know the unsavory portions of our history, not just the things we can be proud of." It's hard to say whether comments like this one reflect the righteous patriotism meant to "exculpate the perpetrators' heirs," and a kind of "compulsory compassion," or whether they indicate a genuine lesson in social justice. Compassion and regret afford us the opportunity to understand someone else's pain or to process a historical tragedy in which we are, however remotely, involved, without feeling so terrible that we disengage. In the next section, I'll assess the landscape's potential to prompt regret by facilitating contemplation without requiring guilt.

———•◦•———

On my second day, I return to Sand Creek alone. I want to see, and feel, the landscape by myself. My plan is to walk every trail, which should be doable; there's only one. The repatriation area, where I stop first, is the most clearly designated sacred ground here, even though its boundaries are hardly visible. Only the four corners are marked; the rest of the burial ground is indistinguishable from the surrounding prairie. A small sign tells us about the massacre (again) and explains that human remains and objects taken from the site are being recovered and interred here. The emotional register here is muted, unclear. I am pleased to see the inclusion of Arapaho and Cheyenne words here, in their native languages, but I can't understand what they say. English speakers can only access the sentiment that "The land here is our home—we have come back home."

The subtlety is partly pragmatic: Vandals can't disturb the gravesite if they can't see its boundaries. It's hard to fathom that there are people who would. But it's easy to see how non-Native tourists feel like outsiders here. Those without a history here require substantial prompting to feel anything at all. I recall Ranger Moore's invitation to hear and see the ghosts here. As I set out along the bluff overlooking the dry creek bed, I do sense ghosts. I understand the faces of Indigenous people I'd seen on the signs in another way. Maybe they are not romanticized or rendered past tense. Could they actually be made more present by their superimposition against images of the landscape, so that when we encounter the actual landscape, we sense these resilient people still in it?

Ortiz's poems champion resilience as they call for compassion. Perhaps that's why he doesn't dwell on the horrific details of the scalping, castrating, and eviscerating in his poems. His bloodiest poem reclaims blood as a life force, a replenishing liquid streaming from the landscape. In Linda Helstern's reading of it, the poem shows us "not the blood of death but the blood of life, brilliant red, literally uncontainable."[47] The prose on the preceding page sets us up for the poem: "The blood poured unto the plains, steaming like breath on winter mornings; the breath rose into the clouds and became the rain and replenishment."[48] Already we have not death but *breath*, and *replenishment*. The poem continues to revivify the landscape, as "awed" witnesses see blood

> Spurting,
> sparkling,
> splashing, bubbling, steady
> hot arcing streams.
> Red
> and bright and vivid
> unto the grassed plains.

The water imagery flows throughout the poem, and Ortiz carries it through with similes: "it kept pouring / like rivers, / like endless floods from the sky." Compared to the most prominent image of the slaughter on site—the hand-painted scene I'd first observed on the "Welcome" sign—Ortiz's tone is "bright and vivid," almost festive. The scene is more "magical" than awful.

While that poem refuses to allow the soldiers access to this life force "to replenish / their own vivid loss"—their "helpless hands" are "like sieves," unable to hold the liquid[49]—his other poems alternately criticize and sympathize with the settlers of this country that "has been a burden / of steel and mad / death" but that he nonetheless chooses to love.[50] The townspeople of La Junta "volunteer nothing, no compassion, no love."[51] A Texan stares at the poetic speaker with "murderous eyes" in one poem.[52] Yet, another poem invites compassion even for these "murderous" invaders. Ortiz reveals their "dread" as the frontiers "ended for them."[53] They are "self-righteous," "complex liars. / And thieves."[54] They are full of "greed and callousness" but desperate, too, "like lost children."[55] Even Chivington seems to warrant a little compassion. Ortiz describes him as "this Colonel" who was "giddy with patriotism," imagining himself a hero, rewarded with "medals and admiration."[56] Reading these poems, you get the sense that the poetic persona feels for these people, who are too "frightened by emotion" to learn to listen to the land and live with it.[57]

Refusing to be frightened, Ortiz embraces and works through emotion on every page. He even sounds a bit like an affect theorist in one poem. Condemning "scholars" and "intellectualism" for being "barriers to emotion," he articulates what many affect scholars now acknowledge as a serious downside of an intellectual history in which rationality and emotionality have been cast as binaries, with women (and nature), linked to the latter, and so feared, domesticated, and denigrated. Scholars, Ortiz writes, were "thieves" who stole "compassion" and "anger" and made people afraid of losing power, susceptible to myths like Theodore Roosevelt's "race suicide," which Ortiz shorthands as the fear that whites "would be trivial / as their blood diminished."[58]

Despite its important critiques, its depictions of anguish, and its "honest and healthy anger,"[59] *from Sand Creek* claims hope as its dominant tone. The book is capacious enough to make room, some-times even within the same poem, for both "a train that carries dreams / and freedom away" and "a world / peopled with love."[60] These are poems that sing a new America into being; the Whitman references are no accident, and echoes of Langston Hughes's "I, Too" are there as well. Ortiz reinvents America, reclaims it, beginning with "flowers, grass, spring wind rising" and ending with a "dream" of "love / and com-passion / and knowledge" that "will rise / in this heart / which is our America."[61] Ortiz names compassion as both one of the "stolen" affects and a key feature of the "dream" he carries for the country. Part of his brilliance is that he asks us to have compassion for people and events that are more recent: both the victims of Sand Creek and a different, but not unrelated set of sufferers: U.S. military veterans. Veterans are not just a bridge to get us feeling for the Cheyenne and Arapaho vic-tims, though they might serve that function for some readers. They are worthy of compassion as suffering humans and as witnesses of pain and anguish unimaginable to many tourists. Ultimately, Ortiz's poems "call forth compassion deep enough to begin a national healing."[62]

There is mounting evidence that compassion, "a prosocial response that involves both recognizing that another person is suffering and being motivated to reduce the suffering," can be cultivated by contem-plative practices.[63] Reading poetry is one such practice. Compassion needs words, stories, reflection, and some kind of empathic connection to someone or something else. Compassion is not a cathartic emotion, not a punch-to-the-gut response of fear, disgust, or surprise. It is a non-cathartic affect, with a strong cognitive component. It requires contem-plation. At Sand Creek Massacre NHS and at many other NPS memory sites, contemplation is an important interpretive goal.

Contemplation is shaped by narrative, of course. Narratives pro-vide us with details to mull over, but there's an affective dimension to contemplation as well, a level at which there is "a gap between the subject's affects and its [my] cognition or appraisal of the affective sit-uation or object."[64] Part of contemplation is *feeling* something. Even though the tone of the NPS display signs and text I'd read elsewhere on site have conditioned my mood, actual narratives fail to capture what I'm feeling on the ridge. My contemplation exceeds story, even while it is shaped by what I have read and heard about the Sand Creek massacre. My affective life has very little "narrative complexity" at the moment.[65] It's only after the fact, in this case a year and a half after, that I process the felt affects at the site and begin to make connections to texts, to affect theory, and to other scholarship. Much of this "reaction" comes in hindsight, as a kind of speculation, closer to memoir or to travel writing than conventional scholarship. This is how I'm arguing affect theory works: as an always belated diagnostic of a felt experience of a world (or as Stewart would have it, a "worlding"[66]) that was, at the time, imprecise, devoid of the "semantic density" we later assign to it.[67]

If the natural landscape is a prompt for contemplation and compassion, then—like the faces on the signs—it isn't easy to read. We have many opportunities to try, though. As I walk the bluff trail, I find a series of benches, each overlooking the creek bed. They seem casually placed at intervals along the ridgeline. They are not "the" overlook, where the memorial rock stands and NPS displays guide our affective response. After an initial double take at seeing the rather large "Look before you sit" warning sign—which includes a silhouette of a forked-tongue rattler—I'm able to approach each bench as a welcome respite. The benches beckon us like friends; here, sit down, take a load off, have a seat, and contemplate. The spacing of the benches dictates "a certain pace as well as a sequence to the experience of [this] landscape."[68] Our pace is meant to be slow, meandering, like the creek bed itself. The spaced-out seating is less sequential than it is expansive; the series of benches renders the entire ridgeline an overlook. Everywhere along the bluff is an appropriate place to observe, to look, to contemplate.

Because it's changed very little since the massacre, this landscape has that sacred quality unique to "blood-soaked ground," a quality of connecting past to present because "the landscape appears permanent, unchanging through the years, and thus capable of trapping history in amber."[69] What seems trapped here, too, are affects. Toni Morrison's well-known formulation of "re-memory," the felt presence of the past in a place of trauma, is especially helpful in understanding what I mean. A traumatic memory is, Morrison's protagonist Sethe explains, "still out there. Right in the place where it happened."[70] The independent, material existence of memory seems as pronounced here as on the Southern plantation in her masterpiece, *Beloved*, "Sweet Home." As the "Healing" sign at the overlook says, "memories live on" long after the event is over. Memories make the landscape affective. Scientists are beginning to affirm what humanists have long suspected: that trauma exists in our bodies and can be passed down through generations.[71] Perhaps they will confirm that trauma lives in landscapes, too. Nowhere has this seemed more probable to me than here.

I feel far less affective dissonance at Sand Creek Massacre NHS than I'd expected. The moments of unease at the overlook during Ranger Moore's talk have faded as I wander the bluff and stop at each bench. I am not picturing "carnage" now. To the contrary, my background as a hiker—and I'd say, my education in the genre of NPS tourism, with its rules about how to walk a trail—has trained me to look for signs of life: nonhuman animals, colorful foliage, striking colors, and contrasts in the sage. Although I find very few of these signs during my visit, I'm still predisposed to seek out life, not death. The wind in my face is the most obvious agent in this touristic assemblage, and it lends a feeling of intensity to the affective atmosphere. Wind has always increased my anxiety if I'm high on a mountain climb, especially if it's bringing storm clouds with it. Here, though, the wind contributes to the sense of authenticity; it seems appropriate, rather than threatening, for it to be windy. It contributes to my impression of the historical continuity and the passage of time—from the bench I'm sitting on, the wind direction even follows the progressive, left-to-right motion of reading text. The affective agency of the physical environment quiets the trauma of the massacre story and facilitates, instead, an atmosphere of resilience, peace, and healing.

It's partly solitude that allows me to pick up on this affective agency. I wouldn't notice these things, at least not in the same way, if Amy, or anyone else, were with me. I check my watch. I've left Amy at the hotel, but we need to get back to Denver to pick up her son from daycare by 5:00 p.m. I am, as usual, running late. I'm at the last bench on the ridge, and I realize that if I'm going to get back to her in time I'll need to run back to the car. I'm a recreational runner, and I've been wanting to get out for a jog anyway, so I pick up my pace and begin a slow trot across the rough ridge trail to the parking area. The landscape and my own scattered thoughts recede to the background, and I start to enter a state of concentration, a "flow" state, somewhere between boredom and anxiety, intently focused on where to place each foot and on regulating my pace.[72] Before long, things start to feel strange. Jogging disrupts the expected pacing of the site; this is not how visitors are meant to use this trail. Now I *do* feel like an affect alien. In the same way that jogging through a cemetery—especially if a mourner is there—can feel wrong, this gives me pause. I have little choice but to continue (understandably, many daycares charge exorbitant fees if you're late for pickup) despite feeling out of synch with my environment for the first time here. I'm relieved to get back to the parking lot and drive off.

The car ride seems longer going than it did coming, and it highlights how remote this place is. I worry the geography isolates the massacre in history, that the remote location reifies it as an anomaly, an event far afield from an otherwise progressive historical timeline. While the site isn't conducive to an easy patriotism in the way that, say, Mount Rushmore NM can be, Sand Creek Massacre NHS might still feed into the assurance that, while the massacre was truly a tragedy, the course of history ran in a more or less straight line, and that the sins of the past have been atoned for in the creation of this site and our pilgrimage to it. How easy it must be for some tourists to leave it behind, to check it off their list and never look back. That said, I'm sure I'm not alone in having "mixed emotions," like those with which Kelman opens his book.[73] I'm left with what Ngai describes as a "meta-feeling," in this case "disconcertedness," a "feeling of not being 'focused' or 'gathered.' "[74] With the plains extending around me in all directions, that feeling intensifies.

At Sand Creek Massacre NHS, non-Native visitors should avoid the mistakes of their ancestors, who "Never thought / that guilt was a partner."[75] Visitors need to engage and feel responsible in ways that are productive and enduring. Guilt is too easy to assuage with a kind of box-ticking patriotism, which would replicate the "self-righteousness" Ortiz alludes to repeatedly in his book. Ortiz also rebukes the westward migrants who "deny regret / for the slaughter / of their future."[76] What would it mean for non-Natives to embrace that regret? Could that be a necessary step toward real healing? What else could Sand Creek

Massacre NHS do to facilitate that? Could patriotism become an affect rooted in regret and compassion, rather than in fear and nationalism?

————•◦•————

This is an appropriate moment for such questions. Sand Creek Massacre NHS is still a relatively new NPS site, and contemporary management is a work in progress. Research into the history is ongoing, and generative inquiry continues. Only very recently, for instance, have the NPS and tribes reconciled conflicting research about where, exactly, the village site was located.[77] Thus, the site challenges us to consider memorials not as places that freeze time in space and render history static, but rather as evolving, accretive landscapes that prompt continual reassessment of the past. In the case of Sand Creek Massacre NHS, this reassessment must mean continuing to let the tribes help tell the story, something Superintendent Alexa Roberts's oral history project is aiming to do, and the site managers seem committed to. It must also include healing and justice for the tribes.

Noncathartic affects, which offer "no satisfactions of virtue, however oblique, nor any therapeutic or purifying release,"[78] seem most appropriate for non-Native visitors. Managing for complex emotional responses seems to be in keeping with the agency's open-ended thinking about how it manages affect. The site and its managers successfully elude the cathartic discourses of shame and guilt, but there is still the chance that visitors leave feeling virtuous just for showing up. Perhaps the NPS could do more to deliberately encourage messy, dissonant, noncathartic feelings: more second-person rhetoric, more confrontational faces directly gazing at us, and less reliance on the hero-villain tropes that tend to structure stories about the nineteenth-century West. Since the NPS is a public agency, it may not have explicit political goals such as intercultural understanding (or "intergroup harmony"[79]) or long-term justice. But their partner organizations—including the International Coalition of Sites of Conscience, the U.S. Holocaust Memorial Museum, and the tribes—certainly do. I've been suggesting that regret and compassion would be more effective at facilitating those goals.

As William Walksalong, a Northern Cheyenne spiritual leader and member of the tribe's Sand Creek Massacre Descendants Committee,

claimed at the NPS opening ceremony, "justice"—in the form of recognizing and upholding existing treaties—is "necessary for genuine forgiveness and reconciliation."[80] Apologies are only a first step.
Colorado Governor John Hickenlooper offered the first public apology for the massacre at Sand Creek in the twenty-first century,[81] in
a welcome departure from Governor Evans's defense of Chivington
over a century earlier. The NPS is aware that "Healing" takes more
than apologies or even reparations. Its sign by that title encourages
justice and vigilance as ongoing processes in the future: "Sand Creek
Massacre National Historic Site reminds us not only of the atrocities
that occurred here, but those that continue to be inflicted on cultures
throughout the world. It is a place to rest torments of the past, but
moreover, to inspire us to keep them from happening again." Still,
justice is unlikely without a clearer understanding of Indigenous relationships with the more-than-human world.[82]

I was glad, then, to see an essay by Daniel Wildcat capping off
the NPS publication *American Indians and the Civil War*, which I
bought in Sand Creek Massacre NHS's visitor center. Wildcat's epi-
logue, provocatively titled "You Cannot Remember What You Never
Knew," champions Indigenous "resilience and resistance" and explains
that each tribe possesses a "resilient spirit that resides in the land, or
to speak more precisely, in the landscapes and seascapes from which
their unique tribal identities emerged."[83] Importantly for my analysis,
Wildcat suggests "there is no reason to feel guilty about the past so long
as one does not carry the prejudices of the past into the present," and
he encourages readers instead to "join the growing number of people
on the planet who are beginning to recognize that there is something
useful to be learned from tribal peoples."[84] If there's one lesson the NPS
should pass along to visitors, I think it's this one.

Sand Creek Massacre NHS reminds scholars of the various "lessons
about societal resilience"[85] to be learned from Indigenous cultures,
among them, Wildcat points out, lessons about patriotism, humility,[86]
history, and sustainability. Resilience, in particular, is frequently celebrated in the NPS literature and on signage.[87] I have my suspicions
about the way non-Natives use the word "resilient," especially in professional contexts. Whether invoked to motivate employees to work

more efficiently or to reassure anxious citizens of the Anthropocene, it too often comes across as a neoliberal mandate for individuals to rebound without rethinking the status quo, to "make do" without making waves. But indigenous forms of resilience and Indigenous scholarship challenge non-Natives to rethink what "resilience" might mean. In a scholarly essay, Ortiz describes something like resilience in his definition of "cultural authenticity" as the "creative responses to forced colonization" that "maintain tribal identity and resist loss."[88] "Survivance," Gerald Vizenor's influential portmanteau, similarly alludes to survival and endurance as an "active repudiation of dominance, tragedy, and victimry."[89] More recently, Kyle Whyte's formulation of "collective continuance" also describes a distinctively Indigenous practice of resilience.[90] The nuances of these phrases warrant more attention from non-Native scholars and, perhaps, from the NPS as well.

While it carries many different meanings in theory, resilience also takes many different forms in practice. One is the Annual Spiritual Healing Run/Walk to Denver, which begins at Sand Creek Massacre NHS and is meant to honor the tribal victims and survivors as well as to promote healing.[91] Shaping the process of public memory can also be a form of resilience for the tribes. The Remember Sand Creek organization is working to raise money for a permanent memorial on Denver's state capitol grounds. The Denver memorial would touch about a quarter million visitors each year—far more than make the trek to the massacre site. Along with the Healing Run/Walk, it would also extend the affective reach of the site, avoiding the potential for the isolated location to depoliticize trauma and cover over more quotidian acts of violence. We twenty-first-century Americans are no strangers to the "fear and panic" felt in Denver after the Hungate family's murder, the collective atmosphere that set the stage for the Sand Creek massacre. As I argued in chapter one, an atmosphere of anxiety makes people more prone to full-on fear. The borders, especially the southern frontier, tend to be the most affectively charged parts of the country, and patriotism tends to coalesce at borders—perhaps more so now that the nation's boundary lines have been drawn and seem to require constant securing.

Patriotism is never simple in a nation of nations like ours, especially when regional affiliations remain strong. The aftershocks of the

Civil War are still being felt, not only in the South and along the East
Coast but also in the West and in the Great Plains. I drafted this chapter
amidst ongoing protests on the Standing Rock reservation in North
Dakota, where tribes and allies stand strong against the Dakota Access
pipeline, which would carry hundreds of thousand of barrels of oil
from the Bakken oil fields in North Dakota to southern Illinois, crossing the Mississippi and Missouri Rivers, as well as Lake Oahe, threatening water supplies at Standing Rock. A group of veterans formed
to support the water protectors, vowing the pipeline will not be built
and, at one point, creating a human shield between them and the U.S.
military.[92] These veteran allies remind me of the men in Ortiz's poems,
working through suffering to forge healthy, resilient alliances. Given
the disproportionate service of Indians in the armed forces (a point
stressed in the *American Indians and the Civil War* book), this alliance
is not as unlikely as it may seem. It's a hopeful one, as it affirms that
justice is possible if non-Natives can learn to understand and honor
Indigenous relationships to their homelands.

Sand Creek Massacre NHS shows how affects coalesce and accumulate in lesser-known landscapes in remote pockets of regions like
the Great Plains, which don't always feature the dramatic landscapes
commonly associated with the U.S. West. Chapter three takes up another relatively out-of-the-way late-nineteenth-century site that commemorates Western settlement: Golden Spike National Historic Site.
The completion of the transcontinental railroad in 1869 signaled the
union of the country's diverse regions around a single point and even,
as the site's name implies, a single object: the last spike driven in to
join the two railroad lines. The righteous belief in Manifest Destiny,
the Homestead and Railroad Acts, and a "hell on wheels" embrace of
violence as a byproduct of Westward expansion, all fueled the "attempt
to end the Plains Indians' way of life."[93] Fortunately, that attempt failed.
In its aftermath, these historic sites tell stories about the nineteenth
century that resonate in the twenty-first. They are, like Ortiz says of his
poetry, "an indirect celebration of what is real American: America with
all of its sad and terrible history, but a real America that is more than
just a dream."[94] What America might emerge from a better understanding of tribal patriotism as an affiliation with landscapes? What would it

take to promote an eco-patriotism that might appeal to the wide range of inhabitants of today's U.S.?

Notes

1. Williams, *The Hour of Land*, 62.
2. Ari Kelman, *A Misplaced Massacre: Struggling Over the Memory of Sand Creek* (Cambridge: Harvard University Press, 2013), 1. Superintendent Alexa Roberts calls Kelman's description outdated and affirms that Eads is "rapidly becoming revitalized and vibrant." Email correspondence, November 22, 2017.
3. Max Liu, "Kent Haruf's Holt County, Colorado, in pictures," *Picador*, April 4, 2013. http://www.picador.com/blog/february-2014/kent-haruf-s-benediction-in-pictures. Accessed 5 April, 2017.
4. Kelman, 3.
5. Typically thought of as a "fear of open spaces," agoraphobia can also mean "a fear of being in situations where escape might be difficult or that help wouldn't be available if things go wrong." http://www.nhs.uk/conditions/Agoraphobia/Pages/Introduction.aspx. Accessed 7 April, 2017.
6. *Sand Creek Massacre NHS Visitor Survey Card Data Report* (Pacific Consulting Group, 2015).
7. Kelman, 1.
8. Kelman, 1.
9. Interestingly, the trees could be partly to blame for the difficulty in identifying the precise location of the massacre site. Email correspondence, Superintendent Alexa Roberts, November 22, 2017.
10. Greg Dickinson, Brian Ott, and Eric Aoki, "Spaces of Remembering and Forgetting: The Reverent Eye/I at the Plains Indian Museum," *Communication and Critical/Cultural Studies* 3 (2006), 31.
11. Ibid., 30.
12. Dickinson et al., 27.
13. Dickinson et al., 29, 27.
14. Annelise E. Acorn, *Compulsory Compassion: A Critique of Restorative Justice* (Vancouver: University of British Columbia Press, 2004). See especially chapter six, "Compulsory Compassion: Justice, Fellow-Feeling, and the Restorative Encounter." Robert Bednar also uses the term in a context close to my own, to describe the performed compassion by news media in regard to the real or potential removal of roadside memorials. See Bednar, "Killing Memory: Roadside Memorial Removals and the Necropolitics of Affect," *Cultural Politics* 9.3 (2013): 337–356.
15. Kelman, 20. These are former NPS Director Mary Bomar's words from her speech at the Sand Creek Massacre NHS's opening ceremony in 2007. Bomar also celebrated the agency's "commitment to diversity" (20).
16. The NPS does not articulate explicit affective goals; nor does it try to "steer visitors' feelings in any particular direction," as Superintendent Roberts puts it. Roberts sent me

their most recent Long Range Interpretive Plan, which affirms that teaching the history and the context are the main goals. The Plan does list the emotions that are part of that context but not those it hopes visitors might feel. For instance, the Plan states: "The Sand Creek Massacre reveals good and evil qualities such as courage, anger, depravity, grief, indifference, perseverance, fear, hate, greed, forgiveness and the quest for healing through its heroes, victims, perpetrators, survivors and descendants." Roberts emphasizes that the site is still relatively new and is constantly evolving.

17. There is still a range of numbers used in regard to the casualties, but Ranger Shawn Gillette confirms 230: they "can put names to most of these numbers." Email, April 10, 2017.

18. The quotes in this paragraph are taken from the website and from a display sign called "Why?" at the site. The NPS site bulletin explains that, "having seen no combat," they were "mockingly labeled" with the nickname. NPS, *Sand Creek Massacre*, 2014.

19. "John Chivington Biography," NPS website, https://www.nps.gov/sand/learn/historyculture/john-chivington-biography.htm. Accessed 10 May, 2017.

20. Kelman, 279.

21. Kelman, 4.

22. Kelman, 4–5.

23. The painting was done by Eagle Robe Eugene J. Ridgely Sr., descendent of Little Raven, great-grandson of Lame Man, survivor of Sand Creek.

24. Gillette explains that while the book can be credited with raising awareness of the site and Indigenous history, it also contains some erroneous information, which is why they don't carry it in their visitor center. Email correspondence, November 22, 2017.

25. Percy Walker, "The Loss of the Creature," *The Message in the Bottle: How Queer Man Is, How Queer Language Is, and What One Has to Do with the Other* (New York: Farrar, Straus, and Giroux, 1975).

26. My language here intentionally echoes that of the NPS's founding legislation, the Organic Act of 1916, which bequeathed the agency its notoriously problematic "dual mandate" balancing preservation and enjoyment.

27. The site bulletin explains how the tumultuous political context engendered by the Civil War made the Colorado plains more important to non-Natives, who wanted to stabilize the region (turning it from territory to state), to have access to gold, and to secure safe passage for railroad passengers. Kelman's book foregrounds that, "for Native people gazing east from the banks of Sand Creek, the Civil War looked like a war of empire, a contest to control expansion into the West, rather than a war of liberation." Kelman, xi.

28. Roberts clarifies that the town of Fort Lyon moved locations after a flood in 1867. Email correspondence from November 22, 2017.

29. Simon J. Ortiz, *from Sand Creek* (Tucson: University of Arizona Press, 2000), 11.

30. "An Interview with Simon Ortiz," Simon Ortiz, Kathleen Manley and Paul W. Rea, *Journal of the Southwest* 31, no. 3 (1989): 363.

31. Ortiz, 19, 25.

32. Ortiz, 18.

33. Jules Gibbs, "In the Beautiful, Violent Swirl of America: Simon Ortiz's *From Sand Creek*, Thirty Years Later," *American Poetry Review* (July/August 2012): 37.

34. Ngai, 46.

35. Thomas Patin, "America in Ruins: Parks, Poetics, and Politics," in *Observation Points: The Visual Poetics of National Parks*, ed. Thomas Patin, (Minneapolis: University of Minnesota Press, 2012), 282.

36. The conventions of nineteenth-century portraiture were, of course, very different from today's selfie culture. For helpful context, see Alan Trachtenberg, *Lincoln's Smile and Other Enigmas* (New York: Hill and Wang, 2008).

37. Robert M. Bednar, "Being Here, Looking There: Mediating Vistas in the National Parks of the Contemporary American West," in *Observation Points: The Visual Poetics of National Parks*, ed. Thomas Patin (Minneapolis: University of Minnesota Press, 2012), 9, 22.

38. These quotations come from my own notes and from Thomas Curwen, "Confronting our history and 'unspeakable acts' at the site of the Sand Creek Massacre," *Los Angeles Times*, 31 July, 2016. http://www.latimes.com/travel/la-tr-nps-sand-creek-massacre-20160731-snap-htmlstory.html. Accessed 5 April, 2017.

39. Paul Bloom, "Empathy and Its Discontents," in *Trends in Cognitive Sciences* (January 2017): 21.1, 25.

40. For a provocative critique of compassion, a "fickle emotion" and a "capricious creature" (136), in regard to restorative justice, see Acorn.

41. Ortiz, 6.

42. Roland Imhoff, Michal Bilewicz, and Hans-Peter Erb, "Collective regret versus collective guilt: Different emotional reactions to historical atrocities," *European Journal of Social Psychology* 42 (2012), 730. Regret and guilt aren't entirely inseparable. Regret is actually "likely to be 'tinged with guilt,'" and conversely, if we feel guilt we are most often going to feel regret about it. Ibid., 729.

43. Imhoff et al., 729. By "empathic" they seem to mean what Bloom describes as cognitively taking another's perspective, not necessarily feeling another person's pain in a distressing way. For them, this sort of empathic distress is a positive thing, tied to regret's potential to form more positive views of an out-group.

44. Ibid., 730.

45. For a book-length study that also acknowledges regret's potential, see Janet Landman, *Regret: The Persistence of the Possible* (Oxford: Oxford University Press, 1993).

46. Ekman, who has researched with the Dalai Lama, is one of a team of researchers that tested contemplative practices, including mindfulness meditation, on compassionate behavior; there appeared to be a link between mindfulness practice and facial recognition skills and compassionate, prosocial action. See Margaret E. Kemeny, Carol Foltz, Margaret Cullen, Patricia Jennings, Omri Gillath, B. Alan Wallace, James F. Cavangh, Janine Giese-Davis, Erika L. Rosenberg, Phillip R. Shaver, and Paul Ekman, "Contemplative/Emotion Training Reduces Negative

Emotional Behavior and Promotes Prosocial Responses," *Emotion* 12.2 (2012): 338–350.

47. Linda Lizut Helstern, "Shifting the Ground: Theories of Survivance in *From Sand Creek and Hiroshima Bugi: Atomu 57*," in *Survivance: Narratives of Native Presence* (Lincoln: University of Nebraska Press, 2008): 172. She reads Ortiz's book as laying a claim to "Deep Memory," defined as "the development of a profound emotional/psychological connection with the transpersonal traumas of native history in order to render them a source of personal strength," 164.

48. Ortiz, 66.

49. Ortiz, 67.

50. Ortiz, 9.

51. Ortiz, 36.

52. Ortiz, 63.

53. Ortiz, 43.

54. Ortiz, 50–1.

55. Ortiz, 75, 78.

56. Ortiz, 71.

57. Ortiz, 59.

58. Ortiz, 58–9.

59. Ortiz, 84.

60. Ortiz, 83.

61. Ortiz, 95.

62. Helstern, 178.

63. Kemeny, et al., 345.

64. Leys, 443.

65. Ngai, 27.

66. Kathleen Stewart, "Worlding Refrains," in *The Affect Theory Reader*, eds. Melissa Gregg and Gregory J. Seigworth (Durham: Duke University Press, 2010), 339–353.

67. Ngai, 27.

68. Bednar, 4.

69. Kelman, 4.

70. Toni Morrison, *Beloved* (New York: Random House, 2004), 43.

71. Though still quite exploratory, research in epi-genetics suggests trauma may be passed down through generations in our bodies via genes. For one recent article, see http://www.sciencealert.com/scientists-have-observed-epigenetic-memories-passed-down-for-14-generations. Accessed 25 April, 2017. For a preliminary resource on Indigenous intergenerational trauma, see Eduardo and Bonnie Duran, *Native American Post-colonial Psychology* (Albany: SUNY Press, 1995).

72. The concept of "flow" was introduced by psychologist Mihaly Csikszentmihalyi to describe the dynamic absorption in a physical task in which we float between boredom and anxiety in a kind of harmony with our environment and temporarily silence our internal monologue. Trail running is a kind of flow activity, at least for me. An overview of Csikszentmihalyi's ideas can be found here: http://

www.pursuit-of-happiness.org/history-of-happiness/mihaly-csikszentmihalyi/. Accessed 20 May, 2018.

73. Kelman, 1.

74. Ngai, 14.

75. Ortiz, 85.

76. Ortiz, 77.

77. When Kelman's book was published there was a theory that the creek itself had actually shifted, an attractive theory because it reconciled the tribes' memories of where the village site was located with NPS archaeologists' findings. The shifting creek theory has been disproven, but the tribes and the NPS now concur about the location. Roberts, email correspondence, November 22, 2017.

78. Ngai, 6.

79. Imhoff et al., 740.

80. Cited in Kelman, 33.

81. For one account of Governor Hickenlooper's apology, see http://www.denverpost.com/2014/12/03/gov-hickenlooper-apologizes-to-descendants-of-sand-creek-massacre/. Accessed 5 September, 2017.

82. NPS literature struggles to articulate that difference. In the site bulletin's "Two Cultures, One Land" section, for instance, the "two vastly different cultures" are described primarily in terms of their economic and technological differences, not their spiritual ones. Contra the "rapidly growing, expansionist nation employing industrial technology," plains Indians are described as "a nomadic people dependent on the buffalo hide trade." Again, this literature is under revision as I complete my project.

83. Wildcat, 199.

84. Wildcat, 199.

85. Wildcat, 204.

86. Wildcat describes "humility" as a "mature" appreciation of "nature as full of relatives—not resources—and responsibilities rather than only rights," toward the end of his essay (208).

87. The "Healing" sign reads: "Ever resilient, the Cheyenne and Arapaho nations of today number in the thousands." In its "Aftermath of the Massacre" section, the final sentence credits the "resilience of the Cheyenne and Arapaho people" for maintaining their way of life and thwarting efforts to "end" their "way of life."

88. Simon Ortiz, "Towards a National Indian Literature: Cultural Authenticity in Nationalism," *MELUS* 8.2 (1981), 9, 12.

89. Vizenor defined the term in *Fugitive Poses: Native American Scenes of Absence and Presence* (Lincoln: University of Nebraska Press, 2000), 15, and it has been omnipresent in scholarship and public discourse since.

90. Whyte defines this as "a way of understanding Indigenous governance as a community's aptitude for making adjustments to current or predicted change in ways that contest settler-imposed hardships and other oppressions, establish quality diplomatic relationships, bolster robust living in the face of change, and observe

balanced decision-making processes capable of dealing with difficult tradeoffs." "What Do Indigenous Knowledges Do for Indigenous Peoples?" in *Traditional Ecological Knowledge: Learning from Indigenous Methods for Environmental Sustainability*, ed. Melissa K. Nelson and Dan Shilling (Cambridge University Press, forthcoming). I heard Whyte speak in Detroit, and he defined collective continuance more broadly as: "how it is that we've been adaptive through our relationships and responsibilities to change," especially climate change. His keynote lecture was called "Resurgence within the Rust: Indigenous Science (Fiction) for the Anthropocene." https://echo360.org/media/76adf527-126c-459d-b86e-9672970ea7aa/public. Accessed 2 September, 2017.

91. For a description, see: https://www.nps.gov/sand/planyourvisit/annual-spiritual-healing-run-walk.htm. Accessed 5 September, 2017.

92. Tom DiChristopher, "U.S. Veterans Group Says Dakota Access pipeline 'will not get completed. Not on our watch,'" CNBC, 1 February, 2017, http://www.cnbc.com/2017/02/01/standing-rock-dakota-access-battle-brews-as-us-veterans-sioux-dig-in.html. Accessed 4 May, 2017.

93. NPS, *Sand Creek Massacre*, https://www.nps.gov/media/photo/gallery.htm?id=36FCF7B1-155D-451F-67C9BA8EF6734448

94. Manley and Rea, "Interview," 373. The word "American" seems like a typo but is accurately transcribed here.

CHAPTER THREE

Performing Patriotism

Reenactment, Historicity, and Thing-Power at
Golden Spike National Historic Site

"The train is a replica, right?"

I've directed my question to the first official-looking person I can find: a tall man in spectacles, a black top hat, and tails, who's standing by the rails and stroking his long, wiry beard. He taps his cane on the dusty ground, leans on it, and replies, with exaggerated patience and a deep sigh: "There are no trains here. Only locomotives." I've been at Golden Spike National Historic Site (NHS) for less than ten minutes and I've already learned one of its most important lessons: Accuracy matters. Whether we're talking about history or technology—and the replica locomotives "Jupiter" and "119" embody both—we'd better get our story straight.

The locomotives were a big draw for my family, as they are for many who make the trek out to Promontory Summit. When I told my two sons that my latest research trip would involve steam trains and tent camping, they wouldn't miss it for the world. (And when I agreed to camp with two kids, I decided my husband, Doug, wouldn't miss it for the world either.) Evan has been a lover of all things train since he was big enough to hoist his first Thomas the Tank Engine. A favorite family video shows his pure awe at witnessing a steam engine in Keystone, South Dakota, during our visit to Mount Rushmore National Memorial—words fail the then-four-year-old Evan, and he seems to become part train himself, capable only of howling a wild "toot toot!" Elliott, who's four when we visit Golden Spike NHS, follows Evan's lead in most things, and he's watched his older brother operate the model train in our basement for many an hour—though he's not allowed to touch the controls.

The boys' latest obsession is with ghost stories, provided they are titillating but not terrifying. The previous night Doug (a lapsed fiction writer and the designated family storyteller) had invented the legend of the "Ghost Train" to tell around our campfire. The ghost train's whistle can be heard from time to time in the high deserts of Utah, Doug had warned, but be sure to avoid looking directly at it. If you meet his gaze, a ghost engineer will pick you up and keep you prisoner until another victim makes the same mistake and takes your place. Around 4 a.m., as if on cue, we were awakened by an eerie and distant sound, which soon cohered into a long, slow moaning that crept into our dreams before coaxing us to full consciousness. The blasts became more urgent and more frequent (could there be that many road crossings here, or was the driver messing with the campers, we'd wonder in the morning?), and soon the two boys were sitting bolt upright in their sleeping bags, staring at us with enormous eyes. "Is it the Ghost Train?" Elliott whispered, his older brother looking equally alarmed. We reassured them that no, this one was real. They weren't sure what to believe, and sleep took its time returning to the tent.

It's hard not to have some kind of visceral reaction to the sound of a train, even if fear isn't the typical one.[1] My children are far from alone in their fascination with trains. Historian Richard White describes nineteenth-century Americans as "in love with railroads."[2] Ranger David Kilton, whom I would soon meet, tells me he often sees grown men "act like children" in the presence of the engines at Golden Spike NHS.[3] I'd timed our visit to coincide with one of the reenactment ceremonies, which happen on Saturdays and holidays from May to September, so I could witness these emotional reactions for myself. As my naive inquiry to the volunteer reenactor reveals, I'd done little to prepare for the visit other than to ensure this timing. I wanted to be ready to take it all in, to get a feel for the place, without being preoccupied with the railroad history or the politics of the nineteenth-century U.S. West.

Bringing my family with me—and meeting up with my longtime friends Kerry and Albert and their three young children—would make it even easier to approach this site as most tourists do: as a fun holiday destination, a leisurely way to combine a touch of education with our recreational tourism.[4] On our drive down from northern Idaho, we'd passed a billboard on I-15 that read: "Find Your Park." At that moment, in the backseat, my boys had been dutifully filling out the "Every Child In a Park" activity book, one of the NPS's Centennial projects. While most of our long drive had not been so picture-perfect, I am fairly confident that we are the implied tourists: a white, middle-class family, visiting an NPS site to learn about our heritage as part of a summer road trip. With our blonde-haired boys and light skin, we could even pass for Mormons, perhaps with ancestors who'd helped lay tracks. We had camped at the kid-friendly Crystal Hot Springs campground (which the children loved and Doug and I vowed never to do again), and now, we have arrived in a "family group," which nearly 75 percent of visitors do.[5] Even the entrance sign, with its childlike font and cartoonish engine, looks made for kids.

It is Saturday, May 28, 2016, and the "rough crowd" of Monday, May 10, 1869, has been replaced by a slightly more put-together bunch.[6] In colorful T-shirts of hot pink, turquoise, and patriot-red, wearing ballcaps of orange, green, and white, carrying backpacks full of snacks, windbreakers, and water, and holding cell phones aloft, poised, and primed to take video, these tourists sit patiently atop wooden benches awaiting the ceremony. Parents corral squirmy kids on their laps, and an anxious dog tugs on its human's leash, but otherwise all is politely anticipatory. Those of us awakened by ghost trains the night before clutch coffee, not the champagne that the 1869 celebrants purportedly drank. The weather on this day is uncannily similar to that of May 10, 1869, with a gentle breeze, sunshine, a few scattered clouds, and a pleasant temperature of around 70 degrees Fahrenheit.

We'd only had time to read one display on our way to the reenactment: a cracked, sepia-toned NPS sign called "Jubilation," stationed about 100 yards from the present-day tracks. It tells us how the 1869 witnesses "exploded with hurrahs" as the final spike was driven and how, after the official announcement—a telegraph signal set up to be triggered by the hammer's last blow—the "nation went wild": "In city after city, church bells rang, trains hooted, fire engines howled, gongs clanged, and cannons thundered. Citizens thronged the streets to watch parades. People sang "The Star-Spangled Banner," prayed, and shouted themselves hoarse. Countless orators hailed this as a 'great day' of national destiny." David Nye's account of the day the railroads came together echoes the "Jubilation" sign. At this historic moment, Nye writes, "people literally felt united by the railway." A *New York Times* article pinpoints the emotional register: "Joy was expressed on every face."[7] Evidence from regional telegraphs decorates the sign, with all-caps statements so faded they are barely readable. (Some of the site's displays are from 1969, Kilton admits, though the 2014 "Long-Range Interpretive Plan" has developed outlines for replacements.) "Jubilation"'s worn-out aesthetic could be seen as strategic, since it certifies the historicity and authenticity of the narratives.

Today's ceremony is not exactly "wild." It feels more like the NPS signs look: historical, detail-oriented, and somewhat outdated. While the reenactors inhabit their roles with gusto, no one in the crowd is going to be hoarse after this. Still, there is an atmosphere, if not of jubilation, at least of happy enthusiasm, much like the one at the Mount Rushmore evening program. The mood intensifies when we hear the noise of the approaching locomotive, 119. The engine does a drive-by, its steam whistle piercing our ears and our viscera. Children line the tracks and wave eagerly to the engineer, who returns the gesture. "Just listen," a ranger gently urges, gazing intently at the oncoming 119, "she speaks for herself." The ranger describes the chuffing as a "signature" sound, made as the locomotive exhausts the steam up the smoke stack. The bell clangs. Visitors take videos. Locomotive 119 parks next to the rails with a loud sigh-like hiss, and an enthusiastic MC in impeccable period dress (Edgar Mills, a Sacramento banker) welcomes us to the ceremony with the declaration that on this day, "America changed." Here in Utah Territory, we mark the "end of the old west and beginning of the new." It's a story of "vision, determination and hard work." We are not meant to be bystanders, though. The dozen or so of us are to participate: We are to be the 600 to 800 people that were in the crowd that day in 1869.

We do our best. We yell "hip-hip-hooray" with increasing confidence and volume, growing more unified with each repetition. ("Yell from your diaphragm!" the MC urges.) We clap together. The "here here!"s from the reenactors compel our allegiance. Like sports fans, we root for our team. We boo the "bad guy," Dr. Thomas Durant, vice president of the Union Pacific Railroad, when we're told he hasn't paid his crew. The locomotive hisses rhythmically in the background, setting a pace for our enthusiasm. The reenactors have created a temporary public, and we are part of it. Citing Émile Durkheim, Nye suspects that moments like this are produced by emotional contagion, that these public feelings "do not originate in any one particular individual consciousness," but rather "come to each one of us from without and can carry us away in spite of ourselves."[8] If there's an affect alien in our midst, I can't detect her. Even the dog's bark seems to signal approval.

This place ballet is a familiar one to anyone who's been part of a crowd: All it requires is that we act as part of the whole, move our hands at the same time, and synchronize our voices when called upon. When the MC claims it's a "sacred occasion" that brings us together today, I'm reminded of Murray in *White Noise*, who explains that tourists "agree to be part of a collective perception." We create and "maintain" the image of the place; our behavior "reinforce[s] the aura." He also claims all tourism is "religious." Any "religious" quality here is surely tied to authenticity. The reenactment ceremony is historically accurate, its script pieced together from telegraph messages, news reports, and other meticulously researched historical records.[9] The "aura" here is historicity, and as Murray observes, "We can't get outside the aura. We're part of the aura. We're here, we're now."

Even so, there are moments that threaten to push us out. Some reenactors ad lib, Ranger Kilton explains, to connect with the audience. For instance, with a bit of levity, today's reenactors joke about "self-inflicted headaches" and make drinking gestures with their hands. When Leland Stanford misses the spike, as he did, famously, some laugh and mutter things like "get a real railroad man up here." Stanford suggests there may be a time when we'll need three tracks across the nation. Reenactors respond with mock disbelief, sparking a self-aware chuckle in the crowd as we recognize the huge chasm between past and present. We watch as the telegrapher taps in the final message and narrates it for us: "D-O-N-E – Done!" Another round

FIGURE 3.1. Our "Kodak moment" at Golden Spike NHS

of three cheers for each railroad company marks the finale. The MC invites us to take advantage of a "Kodak moment," another reminder of our temporal distance, which pushes us out of the history and back to the present.[10]

Sadly for us, the other engine, Jupiter, is out of commission, confined for repairs in a shed nearby. With only one engine present, the "Kodak moment" so carefully staged on May 10, 1869 (and captured by photographer Andrew J. Russell) won't happen for us. For me, this discrepancy proves a rule: Tourism inevitably "gets it wrong" somehow, and authenticity is an impossible goal. Walker Percy blames planners, "expert" knowledge, and various media for spoiling tourists' "sovereign experience" of a place. One way to "recover" this experience, for him, is by "avoiding the approved confrontation of the tour and the Park Service." Another is an unplanned "breakdown of the symbolic machinery by which the experts present the experience to the consumer."[11] Unexpected events, like national disasters, disease outbreaks, or—in my case, when I visited the Presidio for this book in 2013—government shutdowns, might prompt a re-seeing of a place. Perhaps the absence of

Jupiter would serve this function for other tourists, giving us an "Inside Track," so to speak, to Golden Spike NHS.

Although I'm not convinced such a track is ever laid, Percy might applaud my approach. As a former ranger, I'm familiar with "the beaten track" but have been away from it for a while. Returning now, I'm able to approach the experience of tourism with fresh eyes, as a kind of participant ethnographer revisiting a culture she once knew well. Because of this perspective, I am not as susceptible to the emotional contagion as the people I'm with. However, I have to admit that there's *something* about the sound of that locomotive that escapes narration, that is undeniably affective. Locomotive 119 bears the burden of a whole history, with its shiny, heavy iron and curling steam, dissipating into an enormous cerulean sky. As Nye rightly notes, machines that once inspired sublime emotions "soon cease to seem remarkable, and the next generation demands something larger, faster, or more complex."[12] Tourists at this site are unlikely to feel our ancestors' awe, and certainly we don't "fear" such antiquated technology. What, then, do we feel?

Kerry (who, despite being a nurse, is not prone to sentimentality) was surprised at her own emotional reaction. She'd tell me a year later that she got teary-eyed when she first heard the sound of the whistle. Distractions (kids, dogs, thirst) fell away instantly as the urgent presence of the locomotive gripped her. Her husband, Albert, reacted similarly; they felt that sense, as Murray wisely puts it, of "We're here, we're now." The whistle, for them, also connoted adventure and exploration. Albert attributes this, in part, to watching Western films, but Kerry hasn't seen any. It reminds her, she'd explain, of the way she feels when she's traveling or on an outdoor adventure—hiking, mountaineering, backpacking—and the sound made her yearn for days when she had those adventures more regularly. As someone who's been on many such adventures with her—we spent our twenties (plus a few more years) blissfully exploring the Teton Range in summers—I know what she means. There's something very personal about this reaction. Yet I suspect that even these seemingly idiosyncratic feelings are tied to national narratives of frontier adventure and nostalgia, insofar as outdoor recreation, especially in its adventurous or risky forms, is a kind of modern-day frontiering.

Not all affects "gather themselves into what we think of as stories and selves"[13] as coherently as Kerry's retrospective account. Many of the visitors surveyed in the 2006 Visitor Services Project appreciated the authentic feel (or, conversely, were "disappointed" that the site doesn't house the real golden spike); however, only one of the dozens I read mentioned a specific feeling (beyond more generic words such as "cool" and "wonderful") in relation to the place. That visitor "loved the simple design and letting the area speak for itself" and noted a "remote and serene feeling."[14] Utah Public Radio's Resa Ledbetter, who interviewed me at Golden Spike NHS the day of my visit, caught up with other visitors immediately after the reenactment, and they were able to articulate their feelings more precisely. For these visitors, the affective atmosphere coalesced into a clearly identifiable emotion: pride. One woman described it as "amazing to be here and hear the words that were spoken . . . certainly I feel very proud."[15] Another echoed that, saying he felt "extremely proud of our country." Another said: "I feel overwhelmed by the magnitude of the achievement." Still another, seemingly a young child, put it in terms of basic emotions, saying simply: "It makes me happy."

Despite their differences, these affective responses share a positive valence. However, as the MC points out in the reenactment ceremony, there would have been "mixed emotions" in this commemoration: "joy that in a combined effort and common cause, the brains, the sweat, and the muscle of thousands of men have joined together this great adventure under the guidance of Almighty God," but also "profound sorrow," as we "remember and pay homage to the hundreds of men who, in construction of the Pacific Railroad, gave their lives that you and I might stand here at this moment and share, one with another, this sacred occasion." Amidst the celebration of labor and masculinity, there's meant to be sadness, too, a sense of the "sacred" more appropriate to a memorial service for the dead. Certainly some of the laborers, especially those who had lost family or friends in the process, would have heard the sorrowful note struck in 1869.

For a glimpse into the less joyous aspects of the railroad history, I rely on Maxine Hong Kingston's memoir, *China Men*, particularly its chapter "The Grandfather of the Sierra Nevada Mountains." For today's

FIGURE 3.2. Locomotive 119

visitors, the human losses involved in this historic technological feat are easy to overlook in the face of the atmosphere of "joy." The locomotive is so large, so impressive, so progressive, that it feeds into this atmosphere.

As it whines, exhales, and creeps its way toward us (at a safe speed of course; a common NPS slogan is "safety first!" and rangers make a point of watching out for small children whose parents may be distractedly taking photos or videos), it feels very animate. The locomotive possesses, in Jane Bennett's words, a material vitality or "thing-power": "a shimmering, potentially violent vitality intrinsic to matter."[16] The allure of the engine's vitality, to my mind, poses a challenge for NPS managers to the degree that it simplifies the "mixed emotions" the site intends to promote into a single one: patriotism.

This landscape, the things in it, and the "sense of wonder" it generates—especially at ceremonies like the one I participated in—can certainly contribute to patriotic nationalism.[17] As I've been suggesting, NPS tourism has a special relationship to patriotism. Not only do visitors tend to align themselves with the NPS, and with the nation, but also, as Cindy Spurlock suspects, we feel like we're doing our patriotic duty simply by visiting. Even just watching a film (in Spurlock's essay, Ken Burns's *The National Parks* documentary) certifies us as "park supporters and as good citizens simply by tuning in."[18] In what follows, I'll evaluate this claim as it works at Golden Spike NHS. I'll try to pinpoint the emotions and affects that come together here, in the texts, landscapes, objects, and bodies that converge to create an affective atmosphere. I'll ask: How are the reenactments and NPS signage directing our affective reactions? How might we describe the visceral response to the locomotives, and to the landscape, in more precise affective terms? Does the allure of the train pique visitors' interest in the bigger story of this place, including the multicultural—and not entirely joyful—historical narrative? Or is it a diversion from that history, a sexy sideshow for railroad buffs and small children, which covers over the violence of the past? I'll suggest that a prideful, nostalgic relationship to the technology does divert attention from the "sorrowful" elements of the history, and that the thing-power of the locomotives and other material objects on-site encourages this as well. I'll speculate, more hopefully, that a patriotic affective atmosphere does not necessarily have to congeal into nationalism. The feeling of unity during the reenactment ceremony could evolve in unpredictable, and potentially more politically progressive, ways, especially if visitors get away from the main visitor center complex and encounter a less manufactured landscape.

———◆———

At the entrance to the visitor center stands an obelisk: bright white, wide at the base, and more than head-high, protected from the hands of the masses by a gleaming metal chain tied to four wooden posts around its perimeter. Obelisks are common at memory sites, monolithic monuments to the past with a vertical reach that signals "striving."[19] The "Significance of the Monument" is spelled out for us in a display along the walkway. Placed near the site of the last spike in 1916, the same year the NPS was formed, the obelisk "stood there, a lonely reminder" of the 1869 ceremony until it was "handsomely restored" and reclaimed as "an icon of westward expansion," a marker of "an historic event that transformed America." It's the perfect icon for the progress narrative told here. Like the locomotives, this material object embodies the site's historical significance, testifies to authenticity and progress, and invites national pride, all at once.

Inside the visitor center, more material objects abound. The center is set up like a museum, full of display cases featuring authentic objects from the period or, in some cases, convincing replicas. These include various sizes of spikes, in silver, gold, and other metals; surveying equipment; hand tools; a Link and Pin Coupler; pocket watches, their mainsprings separated and bared; copper wire from the 1869 telegraph; and photography equipment—tripods, lenses, plate holders, and prints. One case displays tiny gold splinters from the original golden spike, which were made into seven "memento spikes" and used as watch charms and rings. One of these miniature spikes is encased in a glass cube. And, of course, there's a model train, set amidst a scale model of the town of Promontory and showing the two engines coming together at the May 10 ceremony.

In her scholarly classic *On Longing: Narratives of the Miniature, the Gigantic, the Souvenir, the Collection,* Susan Stewart describes how miniatures signify "the labor of the hand, of the body," and how their uniqueness becomes "a stay against repetition and inauthenticity."[20] Her analysis resonates with the feeling of authenticity this NHS fosters, in which the objects (not all of which are miniatures, but many of which are small and encased in glass) participate. Miniatures, including the model trains, manage to both showcase and cover over manual labor. Model railways operate in the realm of "play" and "amusement," she writes. Reducing the scale means a "corresponding increase in detail and significance, and we are able to transcend the mechanical as well as the natural that forms its context."[21] Miniatures serve ideological functions, like anything else that's tied to human narratives. Stewart describes their "double effect." "First, the object in its perfect stasis nevertheless suggests use, implementation, and contextualization. And second, the representative quality of the miniature becomes a stage on which we project, by means of association or intertextuality, a deliberately framed series of *actions*."[22] The handmade quality of a miniature, including a model train, makes it nostalgic, "a representation of a product of alienated labor" that has, ironically, been made by hand, "constructed by artisanal labor."[23] These objects elicit a "nostalgia for pre-industrial labor, a nostalgia for craft."[24]

The miniature "erases not only labor but causality and effect" as well. The model train offers us "spatial transcendence," much like the actual transcontinental railroad did to the nineteenth-century Americans who fell in love with it. But we lose a sense of the real history, the real context, and the real conditions of labor that produced the thing itself. If we compare this to the dynamic locomotives, an interesting similarity emerges. Both the engines and the model trains move us "from work to play, from utility to aesthetics, from ends to means." They both perform an "erasure of labor" and a "celebration of the mechanism for its own sake." Part of how this happens is that they function "to bring historical events 'to life,' to immediacy, and thereby to erase their history, to lose us within their presentness."[25] Stewart's words echo Kerry and Albert's recollection of "losing themselves" within the locomotive's "presentness."

The language of affect perhaps best approximates that feeling of being utterly present. In moments like this, nostalgia—or any other narrated emotion—has not yet set in. These are moments of pure potentiality, virtuality, what Massumi calls autonomy, during which we are poised between past and future, and in this case, between nostalgia and optimism. Affect theory can give a different perspective on the life and power of things, as well. Many of the objects on display are made of metal, reminding us, however obliquely, that the tools of progress come from the earth. Metal is also what Bennett rightly calls a "hard case" for affect theory.[26] In her short chapter "A Life of Metal," she tackles this especially recalcitrant form of vibrant matter, insisting that even metal possesses a kind of affect that is "not fully susceptible to rational analysis or linguistic representation" and that is "not specific to humans, organisms, or even to bodies: the affect of technologies, winds, vegetables, minerals."[27] She shorthands this as "geoaffect or material vitality."[28]

These objects are not strictly ideological. They retain a thing-power, an affective force in the world that escapes narration, that can't be fully captured with language. Our bodies register the affects, but they don't always crystallize into stories or identifiable emotions.

When memory sites fetishize objects and specific events they risk isolating the events in space and time and minimizing the violent parts of the past. At Sand Creek Massacre NHS, this risk is somewhat mitigated by the connections the managers make to the Civil War, to Colorado statehood, and to Manifest Destiny. Here at Golden Spike NHS, the NPS tries to complicate a simple patriotic reaction by con-textualizing the historical objects. Even so, the "spike" becomes a pa-triotic fetish, its thing-power reduced to that affective note of pride and national unity. Labor is celebrated as a sacrificial good, its tools fetishized. But railroad labor was industrial, not artisan: it prized "rep-etition over skill and part over whole."[29] It was a team effort, unlike the single-handed creation of a model train. Details of the deaths, injuries, and exploitation are all over the site. Somehow, the specifics of these stories pale in comparison to the things themselves, the locomotives, the spike, the model train.

The pieces of the past I'm most interested in are those related to Chinese labor history. I am aware, before I arrive, of the amazing work the Chinese crews did for the Central Pacific, and of their no-torious omission from the famous photo of the 1869 ceremony—even as they were relied upon to do the real work of driving in the ac-tual spike shortly afterwards. I know that the historic absence of the crews that were so crucial to the Central Pacific Railroad's successes glossed over the history of the overworked and underpaid laborers who barely survived their toil—or who didn't survive, and whose deaths were never tallied. In the back of my mind, too, is the fact that this work, and its celebration, were done on Indigenous lands, at the cost of the expulsion of Native peoples. I know from the website that the Chinese laborers are honored not only in an on-site monument and an arch, but also by a front-page spot on the NPS website. The feature story, "A Legacy from the Far East," outlines the amazing con-tributions of the Chinese work crews and explains what the NPS does to commemorate that legacy today. I'm heartened that the NPS is trying to remedy these omissions and I'm eager to see how the agency teaches visitors about the history today.

One of the first things I see inside the visitor center is a plaque donated by the Chinese Historical Society of America in the anniversary ceremony of 1998—a token of "appreciation" but, notably, not a narrative. There is also a replica of an original sign testifying to the Chinese crews' record-setting laying of ten miles of track in a single day, a record that still stands. Letters engraved in chipped wood are in a "wild West" font, now associated with clichés like "wanted" posters on swinging saloon doors. A display case showcases coins, a medicine bottle, game pieces, a soy sauce jar, a liquor bottle, and other items, along with a brief overview of their contribution. A grateful quote from one of the few authorities who acknowledged the crews' contributions in 1865, Central Pacific treasurer Mark Hopkins, serves as a title for the document: "Without Them, it Would be Impossible."[30] More than 12,000 Chinese workers were hired, constituting 90 percent of the labor force for the Central Pacific. Unlike the model trains, which play up thing-power while eliding labor, this display contains its objects within an aesthetic of "Westness" that situates Chinese culture as distinct from Euro-American culture but still "natural" in this region. The labor they signify is also naturalized, insofar as the Chinese are depicted as good Western patriots.

I stop to watch the visitor center film, which elaborates on what was known as the "Chinese experiment": to hire fifty laborers and see if they could cut it. Despite stereotypes of Chinese men as effeminate and weak, they outperformed everybody and proved to be "faithful and industrious" employees. The narration gives specifics of the work. The Chinese crews could move eight inches a day through the mountains on a good day. There were snow tunnels, and avalanches that buried the men. One especially severe one buried 100 men; their bodies weren't found until spring. Only thirty-nine miles were laid in the long winter of 1866. In 1868, Chinese graders (the film calls them "gangs") and Irish track layers did more than a mile a day, and they managed the famous ten miles in one day toward the end of the "race," as the competition between the two railroads is frequently dubbed. The film tells a story of "greed" and exploitation. It was the end of the frontier and the end of the Indian wars. "Then," the film says, a "great human tide of immigrants" was carried by the railroads. As dramatic music rises to crescendo, the final words call this "the beginning of something new," a "new force ramming forward." There is little question that this "ramming forward" is the *only* way forward. Loss is but an unfortunate byproduct of inevitable progress.

I notice a volunteer presentation called "Why Here?" is about to begin, so I take a seat. Another older male living historian sits in an auditorium surrounded by old wood paneling, flags, and historic photos. He's dressed in the requisite period attire: bowler hat, bow tie, pocket watch chain, suit jacket. He carries a cane and sports a grizzled beard. For forty-five minutes, he tells an evocative story—with no notes. At one point he passes around a few photos of where the Central Pacific crews broke through the mountains. One visitor says he recognizes the power lines in one of the photos. Despite the distractions—screaming kids, slamming doors, visitors milling about in the exhibit area outside, the noise of the machine that flattens pennies into souvenirs, and the big-haired woman in front of me, who is recording the whole thing on her phone, her manicured nails adorned with tiny Texas flags—I am mesmerized. And I am prepared to trust every word this volunteer says.

He has a one-word answer to the question "Why here?": greed. The railroads were paid by the mile, he explains, and "like all government contractors, they were gonna milk it for all it's worth." Promontory Summit was never the goal. The goal was "money and land, and that's what drove them." It's rare to hear such a blunt account of Western settlement. He spends some time laying out context: the Civil War, which competed for many of the same resources (manpower, and materials, especially); the 1862 Pacific Railroad Act, which was updated two years later to provide government bonds for every mile of track laid (and, he adds, these were scaled to match the difficulty of the terrain); the railroad barons, who skimmed off all the profits. But the bulk of his talk is about the labor itself. This feat was accomplished without steam shovels or backhoes, he reminds us; it was "manual labor, 100 percent." He dwells on the details, including how engineers navigated through mountains using both complex and simple tools: geometry, trigonometry, and "sharp pencils." In addition to the landscape, the weather was an opponent, with wind, hail, snow, or rain across the Nebraska prairie. Indians were "harassing" the Union Pacific crews, he says. More people died in the towns along the way, in the "hell on wheels" dens of vice and frontier justice, than as a result of the work itself.

For the Central Pacific crews, the Sierra Nevada stood as the biggest "obstacle." The Chinese crews, the "backbone" and "strength" of the Central Pacific Railroad, were indispensable in powering through the mountains. He spends a few minutes on the role of these crews. They "didn't fare quite as well as Caucasians." Their pay was close (though I'd later find out it was classified as "unskilled labor," which earned less), but they had to feed and house themselves. The lucky upside to this was that they didn't die of dysentery or cholera, mostly because they boiled their water for tea. They also maintained a culinary variety by hiring farmers and fishermen, and sending for dried fruits from China. Despite these specifics, I notice that by the end of the talk the volunteer is getting some of the years wrong, saying 1877 when he means 1867. I wonder what else in his account is not quite right.

Finally, I meet with Ranger David Kilton, who clarifies some of my questions. He says visitors often ask him "Did you do something wrong?" to be stationed way out here. People don't expect this place to be beautiful. Again and again, he tells me, visitors are surprised at how much is here. He urges me to walk the Big Fill Trail and look across the Wasatch Front. The beauty isn't dramatic, he says; you have to look for it. The locomotives, on the other hand, are spectacular: "nice, big eye candy," as he put it. Some employees think they're not much more than that. But Kilton finds the reenactments and locomotive demos to be a "very effective interpretive tool." People connect with them, he tells me. "Things dawn on them," he says, eyes sparkling. With all their senses involved, visitors are "smelling, hearing, seeing that history." It is, he adds, "so authentic." He clarifies that seeing the same landscape that's in the historic photos as a present-day backdrop is another "aha" moment for folks, another connection to the history.

But what "things" are dawning on park visitors? The NPS interpretive themes are not helpful in identifying any standout emotional register. Although the latest "Long-Range Interpretive Plan" alludes to the significance of the Golden Spike NHS for "the national psyche," the themes prioritize information transmission over affective knowledge.[31] Phrases like "life-long connections" and "connect with the park" appear in the text, but the emotional quality of these connections remains elusive.[32] In addition to taking "meaningful photographs," one of the stated goals is that the implied tourist gains "a positive impression of the visitor center and surroundings";[33] however, nary an emotion word is used to pinpoint what makes a photo "meaningful" or what that "positive impression" might feel like. After watching the film, hearing the volunteer's presentation, and speaking with Ranger Kilton, I'm ready to go back outside and feel it for myself.

I exit the visitor center and step out into the bright afternoon sunshine. Inside, with the tools and other objects to inspire us, we get a sense of how hard the work must have been. Outside, our bodies feel small against this open space, and the sense of scale that renders things "miniature" or "gigantic" in relation to us shifts. I breathe the crisp, dry air, and begin a slow panoramic survey of the terrain. The landscape surrounding the visitor center recalls few of the "hell on wheels" aspects of the past. There's no trace of the boomtown of Promontory, which popped up after the May 10 ceremony as a place from which "gamblers and con artists" could "victimize" passengers who changed trains here.[34] Although it was a "vital hub" for commerce and passenger exchange for a few months, Promontory was, like so many Western boomtowns, destined to become a ghost. The landscape itself isn't especially distinctive: the big sage, rocky ground, and gently contoured mountains are similar to those of many other remote, arid Western places. But, as it does at Sand Creek Massacre NHS, the landscape reinforces the sense of timelessness, the feeling that not much has changed in the last century and a half.

Because the landscape is so subtle, the tracks and the locomotives stand out. I watch as visitors ascend wooden platforms, a series of steps that brings even the littlest humans (like my boys) closer to eye level with locomotive 119. According to Nye, nineteenth-century Americans would not have felt "ironic contradictions" in the juxtaposition of this new technology with the grand nature of the American West. Rather, he claims, they would have seen "the rugged western landscape and the transcontinental railroad [as] complementary forms of the sublime that dramatized an unfolding national destiny."[35] Today, there is still no sense of irony or contradiction, but for more complicated reasons. It's true that, since 1869, more Americans have begun to conceive of nonhuman nature as something to save from the ravages of our unbridled progress. But that doesn't mean we see the railroad and landscape here as anything other than complementary. The landscape is historicized right alongside the tracks and locomotives; it's primarily the history that this NPS site protects. The landscape, it seems, achieves more or less what the signs do: It testifies to the authenticity of the place, to the accuracy of the history, and to the *feeling* of historicity. That historicity entails a kind of trust, and that trust, coupled with pride, fuels patriotism.

As it is inside the visitor center, the focus here is on the objects: display signs, the tracks, the locomotive (now parked for all to see up close), and two monument stones. The exterior objects testify to the labor required to build the railroads. On the way to the tracks, a smooth plaque attached to a rough hunk of granite rests next to the footpath. This is the Irish memorial, a small token to honor the "Irish who toiled," dedicated in the late-1990s. The rock sits atop some short grasses and is about knee-high, large enough to attract at least a glance. Its tone is subdued, though, the darker plaque blending with the gray of the rock in a quiet testimonial aesthetic. On the other side of the same path lies another monument, a much larger block of speckled granite, neatly cut with square corners, on which several more plaques share space: one from the centennial anniversary celebration, another designating this a national historic civil engineering landmark, and a third, also from the centennial, honoring the "indomitable courage" of the Chinese crews. Kilton had told me to look out for a unique rock, cuprous quartzite, which is only found in large quantities in two quarries: one in China, the other in Utah's Park Valley. I see it, but I'm not sure how it's supposed to make me feel. I worry its presence aestheticizes and naturalizes the connection between the two places—and so, the labor, violence, and death as well. That is, the Chinese were somehow fated to journey here, to work, and to sacrifice themselves for "nature's nation."

Compared to the obelisk that greets us out front, these smaller monuments have a lonelier, more melancholic tone. They are markers of loss as much as symbols of striving or progress. Like Erika Doss explains, today's memorials recognize the many smaller publics that constitute a diverse America. What Doss calls "memorial mania" is the affective context within which the specific societies that sponsored these markers—in these cases, the Hibernian Society of Utah and the Chinese Historical Society of America—gathered political energy to lobby for their inclusion and found a receptive ally in the NPS. These memorials may effectively "pay tribute," but I suspect most visitors find them less affectively stirring than the locomotives. Worse, the memorials might be dismissed as "politically correct" by a certain segment of the American public. Of course, for descendants of the workers being honored, the reaction would be quite different. Since I am not among those descendants, I turn now to someone who is: Maxine Hong Kingston.

Kingston's memoir, *China Men*, tells the story of the Chinese labor crews in poignant detail in its chapter "The Grandfather of the Sierra Nevada Mountains." In Kingston's hands, the memoir genre transcends its typically "progressive" assumptions, refusing to be "simply a matter of telling the author's version of the 'truth'" or a reflection of "one individual's lifelong process of identity formation."[36] As such, her book is an important counter-history to the NPS site's celebratory progressivism. Julia Lee explains how the railroad is an attractive topic for Kingston, Frank Chin, and other Chinese American writers, "a highly visible signifier of Chinese lives, communities, and experiences that have been otherwise made invisible." Like the small markers on-site, the railroad itself is both "a monument to the labor and ingenuity of thousands of Chinese workers" and "a manifestation of the economic exploitation that they endured." This history can be a "rebuttal to popular stereotypes about Asian American masculinity" because it proves their toughness, their work ethic, and in those, their patriotism.[37] This discourse is troubling in at least two ways, though. First, it implies immigrant groups must "'prove' their right to belong through their contributions to nation and/or empire-building projects; it turns immigration and immigrant labor into a version of model minority politics." The other major problem with it, Lee points out, is that it glorifies a particular kind of masculinity and some forms of labor as "more heroic" than others.[38] Golden Spike NHS is guilty of both of these faults. Even the well-intentioned display case filled with remnants of Chinese labor and culture and the proud claims of "Ten Miles In A Day" wrap the Chinese crews into a broader narrative of patriotism, which is grounded on perseverance, labor, risk, domination of nonhuman nature, and hyper-masculinity.

For Kingston, patriotic inclusion in the nation isn't the goal of retelling her grandfather's story, even if she sometimes appropriates frontier language to describe her ancestors' work. She depicts them in "cowboy jackets, long underwear, Levi pants, boots, earmuffs, leather gloves, flannel shirts, coats" and cowboy hats, with bandanas over their mouths in a failed attempt to keep the dirt out. But in the same breath, Kingston renders the cowboy hat a poignant symbol of the costs of frontier expansion, as she describes a hat that "skim[s] and tack[s]" against a cliff as a falling laborer screams his way to death after being blasted out of a basket.[39] As this passage makes clear, labor—its physicality, its risks, and its material reality—is the highlight of her chapter, as it is at Golden Spike NHS. But whereas the NPS displays celebrate the tools and technologies, Kingston dwells on the work itself, foregrounding its costs and risks.

Her grandfather, Ah Goong, worked as a basketman (and "some basketmen were fifteen-year-old boys," Kingston mentions), which entailed swinging from overhangs in a basket, digging holes in cliffs, inserting black powder and fuses into the holes, then lighting the fuse and hoping to avoid the blast—either by your coworkers pulling you back up or by swinging out from the cliff while the explosion happens.[40] Kingston renders this unimaginable work visible to contemporary readers. Her depictions of the history are multi-sensory and evocative of both the stubborn landscape and the laborers who worked through it. She measures years of labor by seasons and by stars. She notifies us casually about the passage of time, a move that helps readers imagine the repetition and routinization of such hard labor, the way the days, and years, must have seemed interminable. "After tunneling into granite for about three years, Ah Goong understood the immovability of the earth. Men change, men die, weather changes, but a mountain is the same as permanence and time."[41] Swinging a sledgehammer against granite teaches him the intractability of rock: "The mountain that was millions of years old was locked against them and was not to be broken into." He hits the same spot over and over, with little change in the granite. "It had no softer or weaker spots anywhere, the same hard gray." Kingston also foregrounds the sounds of work, especially the "banging" her grandfather lived with as he and many others chopped, drilled, hammered, and blasted their way through the Sierra Nevada. For Ah Goong, a sensitive and perceptive protagonist, the banging sounds of railroad work connect to New Year's celebrations and to the Civil War, "the war to decide whether or not black people would continue to work for nothing." He associates this new banging sound, ironically, with "holidays and harvests."[42]

Kingston's representations of labor function, alongside the railroad itself, as "a symbol of Chinese resistance to racist discourses."[43] Part of the text's anti-racist agenda is achieved through a transfer of affect to the reader. We are asked to imagine and to *feel* her grandfather's suffering. In an especially impactful section, her grandfather watches as "two men were blown up," and one of the men, still conscious and screaming, falls slowly to his death. He sees a different man fall into a ravine, a man whose hands "were grabbing at air. His stomach and groin must have felt the fall all the way down."[44] Readers might feel the fall in our own viscera as well. The blasting is, for Ah Goong, a way of stopping time and, if only momentarily, the anxiety that must have characterized every minute of labor in the tunnels. "He couldn't worry during an explosion, which jerked every head to attention."[45] New explosive technologies made the labor more efficient, Kingston writes: "The terrain changed immediately. Streams were diverted, rockscapes exposed." The costs, however, were huge. Kingston continues:

> The dynamite added more accidents and ways of dying, but if it were not used, the railroad would take fifty more years to finish. Nitroglycerine exploded when it was jounced on a horse or dropped.[46] A man who fell with it in his pocket blew himself up into red pieces. Sometimes it combusted merely standing. Human bodies skipped through the air like puppets and made Ah Goong laugh crazily as if the arms and legs would come together again. The smell of burned flesh remained in rocks.[47]

Kingston is relentless in her use of sensory details, asking readers to hear, feel, and even smell the violent injuries and deaths. Ah Goong emerges from the tunnel one day to find a macabre winter landscape: "The snow covered the gouged land, the broken trees, the tracks, the mud, the campfire ashes, the unburied dead." With winter came new challenges and more death: "The dynamiting loosed blizzards on the men. Ears and toes fell off. Fingers stuck to the cold silver rails. Snowblind men stumbled about with bandannas over their eyes." Men were trapped underground for weeks, or buried in avalanches, their bodies gone until spring melted the snow. This is a fact the NPS film mentions. But Kingston's description is far more vivid: "Spring did come, and when the snow melted, it revealed the past year, what had happened, what they had done, where they had worked, the lost tools, the thawing bodies, some standing with tools in hand, the bright rails. . . . They lost count of the number dead; there is no record of how many died building the railroad. Or maybe it was demons doing the counting and chinamen were not worth counting."[48] With language that aestheticizes the horror, she shows how "crazily" the labor was done, how the fragile human body can explode into "red pieces," and how expendable the puppet-like bodies really were.

Golden Spike narratives like Kingston's fill in the gaps in the historical and visual record.[49] Twice Ah Goong had occasion to "cheer and throw his hat in the air, jumping up and down and screaming Yippee like a cowboy." The first was the day they broke through the tunnel, and the second was the day the tracks met at Promontory Summit. Part of the cheering was patriotic, not unlike the cheering at the site today. For Ah Goong, "he was an American for having built the railroad," one of the "binding and building ancestors of this place." In Kingston's version of the story, the Chinese crews "Yippee'd like madmen" on the day of the railroad's completion, while the "white demon officials gave speeches." Another "white demon in top hat tap-tapped on the gold spike, and pulled it back out. Then one China Man held the real spike, the steel one, and another hammered it in."[50] Kingston seems, on one hand, to be arguing that railroad labor enabled her ancestors'—and her own—inclusion in the nation; her grandfather undoubtedly "accomplished something monumental."[51] But as Lee explains, the railroad becomes not a clearcut symbol but rather "a kind of palimpsest for the Chinese experience," one that is written and rewritten, alternately performed and done "for real" (as in the spike ceremony), "a message [that] is always just a promise and never fulfilled," like the nation itself.[52]

In tourism, as in memoir, there is likewise no access to an authentic past. The reality is always multilayered. Kingston embraces an ambivalent history, rich in possibility, refusing a singular narrative—including that of patriotic nationalism. Interestingly, Lee's overall reading of *China Men* as "an attempt to decipher what the messages left by the past might mean"[53] could describe the NPS's mission at sites like this one. While the NPS can't be expected to describe the loss of life in terms as evocative as Kingston's, the details she accentuates are precisely the ones that are invisible at the contemporary site. It's the things themselves that enable this invisibility, that simplify the past and render it static, a kind of historical still life. The railroad, along with the locomotives and other things on the site, are material reminders of the nation's history, but they can never be the real past. They are replicas only, and they signify absence and inaccessibility as much as presence. In terms of affects, this leaves a gap that is often filled by nostalgia for labor or by patriotic cheers, as in the reenactment ceremonies. Perhaps it would be better to leave it unfilled, to embrace a sense of emptiness, a failure or "not-yetness" of the American promise. I'd find more potential for these noncathartic affects when I ventured off-site the following day.

——◆——

It is day two, and my family has set out for Robert Smithson's Spiral Jetty, leaving me to explore Golden Spike NHS on my own. After revisiting the main site, I set out to take the auto tours and walk the Big Fill Trail. A wayside display along the main park entrance road (bearing the declarative title "The Track that United the States") explains that a "sharp eye" can pick out traces of the original railroad grade in today's landscape. The sign continues: "These fading remnants tell the story of a daunting engineering challenge—linking the Western states to the rest of the nation. Inscribed here, amid the sagebrush and bedrock of northern Utah is a tale of grand dreams and brute work, greed and glory." My goal for today is to compare these "fading remnants" to the ones in and around the visitor center and to, as Terry Tempest Williams recommends, walk the landscape without "crowds, without interpreters or reenactors or plaques telling us what to think and how we should feel," to "let the land tell its own story."[54]

For material ecocritics like me, inclined to read landscape as text, the rhetoric of inscription resonates. Fascinated as I am by the prospect of discovering a story here, though, the vagueness of the word "amid" betrays the fact that this landscape does not actually house any written text.[55] There are no golden plates for me to unearth, no narrative account of the "tale" hiding beneath a clump of big sage. It is affective agency I am searching for in the landscape, to complement the narratives in the NPS literature and displays. If the story the textual rhetoric tells is one of competition, the "greatest race of the 19th century," between "two hot rivals," in which nonhuman nature is an "obstacle" to be "hurtled over" in the hustle for "more capital,"[56] then does the landscape reinforce or contest this story? If the affects attached to the "hell on wheels" story of competition are primarily pride and patriotism, then what affects might the landscape itself promote? What affective register does this particular environment take?

I'm not sure a driving tour can answer these questions, and the west auto tour route is closed to accommodate a rancher's grazing cattle. As with the reenactment ceremony, I'll only witness half the story. So I begin the east auto tour somewhat warily. Minding the speed limit, I inch along in second gear, at a pace which permits the kind of multitasking that characterizes much NPS tourism: I glance down at the NPS brochure that maps the tour stops, take sips of coffee, and scan my surroundings for signs of life. The first stop on the tour is not far from the main road. A short way from the pullout I find two gently rounded piles of rock, side-by-side. A sign called "The Last Cut" explains their significance: these rocks were carefully excavated, stacked, and later used as fill to create the maximum 2 percent grade mandated by the Pacific Railroad Act of 1862. I enjoy the chance to stretch my legs and feel the dry, warm-but-not-yet-hot air on my arms and legs, but I don't feel a visceral connection to these rocks.

A bit farther along the road, though, I stop at a vista and gaze to the south and am stunned by what I see. Beyond the tufts of sage amidst which I stand lie the northern edges of Great Salt Lake—light brown pools interspersed with green patches of land—and, in the distance, Utah's Wasatch Front. I realize I'm standing on one of the benches formed by Lake Bonneville, the ancient lake I'd read about in Williams's masterpiece, *Refuge*, the lake whose waters covered this very spot—and, at its largest, another 20,000 square miles—from thrity-two to fourteen thousand years ago.[57] Lake Bonneville was, at one point, 325 miles long and 135 miles wide, and the distant mountains I see now were once islands in its waters. Mammoths "roamed its shores" along-side bison, camels, and musk oxen.[58] Cutthroat trout swam while "dire wolves called up the moon." Williams reads her beloved landscape in the bench levels, which "tell a story of old shorelines, a record of where Lake Bonneville passed in its wild fluctuations over the course of fifteen thousand years."[59] Standing here overlooking today's lake, the geologic past lies before me, a "story" in a sense, but a wordless one that I'm not sure I can call "narrative."

I can believe that the Promontory Mountains, while not "as for-midable . . . to modern eyes" as the Sierra or the Wasatch, were the toughest hurdle for the crews. From this vantage point, maintaining a 2 percent grade seems like an impossible task. In the moment, I don't think about this so much as I feel it in my body. I absorb the vastness, the wonder the landscape prompts; I take it all in. The result can be conscious thought, or it can be a felt moodiness that's hard to describe in words. "[M]ore than scenery," this place has become the "breath-ing space" Williams says all parks can be: "portals and thresholds of wonder, an open door that swings back and forth from our past to our future."[60] Situated against this landscape of "deep time," my smallness is comforting. I am invigorated, curious, and simultaneously peaceful, an affective combination that often accompanies a stunning vista.

As beautiful as the view is (I snap a picture, of course), I don't tarry long. I am antsy to get to the Chinese Arch, the next stop on the auto tour. My car's tires crunch over the gravel, which pops periodically under the weight. Then I see it—barely. Its limestone shape blends with the rock just behind it. Like Asian American history, a history of exclu-sion "in which visibility and invisibility are in constant tension with each other,"[61] the Chinese Arch is there, but it could easily be missed. I wonder how many people get out of their cars to walk over to its base.

It's a humble little arch, reminiscent of its more iconic cousins in the red-rock desert at the southern end of this state but paler in color and much smaller than most of those. At the end of the very short trail is a sign telling us that this "monument in limestone" was initially a gift from none other than Lake Bonneville. The huge lake's waves formed the arch by crashing against the "fault-fractured rocks" along what was once its shoreline. The display explains: "While the arch was created by forces of nature, today it stands as a memorial to the Chinese who worked for the Central Pacific Railroad. It is an embodiment of the strength and stamina" these men demonstrated.

Dovetailing with the display at "The Last Cut," in which nonhuman nature is depicted as passive matter, a resource for, and obstacle, to human labor, the arch is likewise instrumentalized, enlisted in the commemorative project of honoring the work of men. Like the unique quartzite used in the visitor center's walls, nature sanctions not just the men's labor but, more broadly, American technological progress. The arch seems to testify to the "strength and stamina" of nonhuman nature as well. This is no place to perform joyous patriotism, though, or even to celebrate masculinity; it's a quiet place to contemplate. The form of the arch conveys permanence, solidity, and endurance. In telling us how this arch was formed, the narrative on the sign positions the lake as a historical agent—a gift-giver, even—and situates it, and us, in a geologic timescale. Even if all we read of Lake Bonneville history is the description of the arch, we've been given another perspective and another way to feel about the history here. The construction of the railroad, and this brief, temporary workers' camp, were blips in time.

That knowledge and the act of standing beneath the arch make me melancholy, as I sense the transience of human life so heartbreakingly rendered in Kingston's book. Like at Sand Creek Massacre NHS, there are ghosts here: the railroad is "an unmarked grave"[62] for all who died building it. Here, though, there are no signs featuring black-and-white faces staring at us, challenging us to match their emotional complexities with our own. Apparently, some of the first passengers on the railroad saw the remnants of the camp and nicknamed it "Chinaman's Arch." An itinerant visitor myself, like those passengers, I feel as though the ghosts of the Chinese crews still inhabit this spot. Without being prompted to, I imagine the Chinese workers setting up camp here. This is where they ate, brewed tea, and rested their weary bodies. The arch is a sideshow, not central to the narrative being told at the visitor center, but that makes it feel more authentic in its historicity. This is their spot. The rainbow shape of the arch feels peaceful to me, like the promise it carries in its Biblical sense.

I bring this mood of solemnity with me to the Big Fill Trail, the final stage in my itinerary at Golden Spike NHS. The trailhead sign boasts "you can still see some of the violent fury of the final days of the race to Promontory, carved into unyielding limestone." As if to hammer home its insinuation about nature's "unyielding" qualities, we're also informed that "Rattlesnakes have the right-of-way." I try to take the cell phone tour, but the reception is spotty, and anyway, the narration is nearly verbatim what I can read on the signs. In places, the landscape does bear traces of the "brute work." Most visible, as I walk the trail to the Big Fill, are clean vertical lines in the rock where black powder was inserted into drilled holes to blast the rock apart, making way for the grading process. In lieu of human bodies, or even photos of human laborers, the land itself bears the burden of history in its marks of labor, and of trauma.

In narratives that associate Western landscapes with glory and "grand dreams," nonhuman nature sacrifices itself willingly for the cause. In fact, nothing about this swath of northern Utah sage flats looks like an obstacle. The scattered sage tufts, muted red grasses, dirt, and rock are unimposing. Only the aridity and heat seem remotely threatening. It's easier to perceive this landscape as a "natural memorial" than it is to see it as an "obstacle." The Big Fill Trail is, in some ways, as powerful a memorial as the Chinese Arch; both are relatively unchanged, and both commemorate the labor history this NHS preserves. Most of Golden Spike NHS's landscape is memorialized, captured and past-tensed, erased and ghosted, and in the process, reified as resource rather than agent.

The rocks, the arch, and the chiseled blast marks along the Big Fill Trail foster a kind of contemplative mood, an atmosphere that counters the playful, celebratory patriotic one on-site, in which even work is subsumed as part of the "jubilant" project of nation building. The signs in and around the visitor center channel our feelings into recognizable stories, stories in which nonhuman nature is a victim, a casualty of the "violent fury" with which Manifest Destiny was pursued. Its wounds are lamentable but necessary. The affective atmosphere on-site is largely in synch with those stories: the textual, environmental, and corporeal registers of affect cohere into a singular atmosphere of patriotic celebration, especially during the reenactment ceremony. Removed from all that, there is more room for affective dissonance. Especially if one is alone, like I am, it's possible to avoid compulsory patriotism and feel otherwise. This quieter, more remote landscape has more affective agency, whether in the pile of rocks at the "Last Cut," the subdued Chinese Arch, the palimpsestic tiers of the ancient Lake Bonneville, or here, as I walk the old grades near Big Fill. Here, the landscape's agency is amorphous and ambiguous. It registers as a non-cathartic affect, not an identifiable emotion.

Stories, identities, and even physical matter are always unstable and unsettled, and these natural memorials are the kind of "provocations" Doreen Massey says all landscapes should be.[63] They embody the processes and forces—from geology to capitalism to public memory—that temporarily stabilize in a particular landscape formation and, at the same time, foreground that landscape formation's transience and contingency. At their best, the NPS texts convey the sense that *history*, too, is an ongoing process, and that the natural world is not just an exploited "resource" but also an agent in that history. Moments of transparency can be found in the signage. One sign explains, for instance, that even as Americans celebrated their railroad the technology used to build it was outdated; iron rails were quickly replaced by steel, which was made widely available by the Civil War. The last spike would be "ceremonially undriven" in 1942 and the steel salvaged to support WWII.[64] As natural materials take new forms, they are used in the service of new wars, undergirded by techno-patriotism: an affective state marked by pride in a country understood as exceptionally tech-savvy, inventive, and forward-looking.

From "cell audio stop" number five, I can see the sprawling Orbital ATK complex, manufacturer of rocket and satellite technology. Kilton tells me the only day he's had traffic on the way to work was the day

FIGURE 3.3. Orbital ATK complex from cell phone audio tour stop #5

they launched a rocket from this site and invited the public to watch. Kids today think of the moon landing as ancient history, he points out. One way to encourage contemporary visitors to connect to the history, then, is that diverse groups came together to produce new technologies. A primary interpretive message is about diversity, he explains: "If we can all work together, we can make a difference and accomplish great things." Kilton's comments clarify something for me about this place: namely, that the landscape, museum objects, and reenactment ceremony together encourage us to feel that work itself—and more specifically, *teamwork*—is the real history here, and that ours is still a great democracy, founded on collaboration. The interpretive theme fashions democratic patriotism *as* teamwork, regardless of whether all teammates are treated as equal players. NPS rangers become, in effect, cheerleaders for team U.S.A.

The NPS's "rails to rockets" theme—a favorite for Box Elder County fairs and other public events, Kilton says—foregrounds how the railroads put this place on the map and paved the way for other technological advancements. There's an implied historical continuity between past and present, and techno-progress is the thread that runs through it. An interior display showcasing a replica of the original Golden Spike, which was taken into space during the Orbiter Atlantis's 1990 space shuttle mission, reinforces this sense of continuity. Its display sign reads: "By this gesture, the ribbons of iron that spanned America's first Frontier are united with the ribbons of fire that are spanning America's final Frontier." Beneath this grand declaration, the replica spike shines golden, encased in glass that reflects our faces back to us. A prayer for "the unity of our country" lies at the base.

After the reenactment ceremony I'd brushed shoulders with a visitor wearing a "Hillary for Prison" T-shirt. The shirt shook my mood of optimism that day, and I remember it now as a harbinger of something we know all too well after 11/8/2016: that ours is nowhere close to the "united state of humility"[65] Williams wishes we could become. Ours is, rather, a united state of techno-progress, which is too hubristic to be humble. Even so, I believe sites like Golden Spike NHS do carry the potential to create the affective foundations for humility. How might they accomplish that? What stories about humans, and about non-human nature, could generate a different kind of patriotism, perhaps something closer to what Williams calls eco-patriotism? How can the physical environment be enlisted more effectively in that project?

The NPS recognizes that the railroad was "a troubled project," and Golden Spike NHS managers are even aware of the "risk that the park's focus on the locomotives and the last spike ceremony distracts from, rather than enhances, a nuanced interpretation of the building of the transcontinental railroad and the complex issues surrounding it."[66] Managers have made strides in honoring the legacy of the Chinese and other work crews; these crews are a central part of the history told here, and the Chinese Arch in particular has the potential to pick up on the "appeal" of the locomotives and the last spike ceremony but draw visitors' feelings into new affective territories.[67] But the crews' "deeper story" is subsumed within the larger historical narrative of sacrifice, labor, and progress; that narrative lauds their heroic acts and minimizes their exploitation. The same ideologies that are celebrated here—progress, meritocracy, patriotism—enabled that violence. The ongoing challenge for the NPS is to tell that story without oversimplifying, without covering over the violence, and in a way that makes room for skepticism about those ideologies.

The NPS should take opportunities to accentuate the connections between environmental justice and social justice, too. At Golden Spike NHS, there need to be alternatives to the story of the land as an obstacle to the labor, a barrier to progress, and a resource to be exploited. Perhaps the agency could do more to foreground ancient Lake Bonneville and the sense of geologic time here. Even the dimmest sense of the geologic history enhances understandings of this place. Taking that long view slows down the progress narrative and might help disrupt the ideologies and affects attached to it. Why not include some of Williams's evocative words about the lake, and this region, at some of the pullouts? What if rangers connected the geology to contemporary debates about the Anthropocene, an epoch some date from the invention of the steam engine and other technologies new to the industrial revolution. (Indeed, the date in question is often referred to as the "golden spike" for the epoch's origin.) It wouldn't hurt to tap in to current debates in geology and reinforce the sense that there are agencies at work beyond the human, forces greater than our capacity to produce new technologies.

Along with new stories should come more opportunities for visitors to have embodied encounters with the landscape, beyond the visitor center and its object-oriented patriotism. More immersive forms of tourism are one way to get to know this landscape's depths and its history. Perhaps the NPS will reinstate its bike tours[68] or more radically, take tourists on a tour that highlights the scarred landscape: its blasted-out mountainsides, dug-out pits, and piled-up rubble. There's no substitute for having an expert, rather than a sign or a cell-phone tour, point out the historical features of an environment, and there might be something especially affective about seeing these environmental "ruins." Rangers must find more ways to cast human "mistakes and shortcomings . . . within the perspective of time," and to remind us that we "are not the only species who lives and dreams on the planet. There is something enduring that circulates in the heart of nature that deserves our respect and attention."[69] That "something" is largely affective, and bodily immersion in a landscape is one way to access it.

My kids return from the Spiral Jetty covered in salt. Evan's face looks like a Jackson Pollock canvas done all in beige paint. His shorts are crusted over and stiff; they, and his crisp sandals, are unwearable. The boys tell me about watching pelicans disappear in flight, going from white to gray to invisible, momentarily blending with the sky as they spiraled through the air. As we drive away, Elliott finds a duck in the clouds, pointing out the eye and bill in profile. We bought not a single souvenir, that quintessential proof of the "capacity of objects to serve as traces of authentic experience."[70] I suspect what Evan and Elliott will remember most from this trip are the ghostly sounds of the locomotive and the feel of the lake water drying on their skin.

Utah's welcome sign had promised us "Life Elevated." The slogan connotes the sublime and the spiritual, the striving and the adventure that make up a good life. My friend Kerry's feeling when she heard 119's whistle, that feeling of risk-taking, freedom, and exploration, is shared by many, especially in this "land of the free, home of the brave." Still, patriotism need not be "elevated" to nationalism, or inspire an excep- tionalist "America first" agenda. Eco-patriotism's potential lies, I think, in suturing patriotic feeling to love, rather than to pride. Pride, after all, tends to be self-centered and exclusive—a hierarchical affect—whereas love can be inclusive, a way of connecting to someone, or something, beyond the self.[71] Eco-patriotism means envisioning—indeed, feel- ing—one's country as the product of a different kind of teamwork, the kind where all players, including the nonhuman ones, are equally valu- able and treated as such.

I'd like to ask, along with Williams: "Can we engage in the restoration of a different kind of storytelling, not the stuff of myths, self-serving and corrupted, but stories that foster integrity within a fragmented nation? Can we change America's narrative of independence to one of inter- dependence—an interdependence beautifully rendered in the natural histories found in our public lands?"[72] What if greed and competition aren't the basis for our national identity? What if cooperative, rather than competitive, patriotism were the norm? This is a tall order, and I suspect many tourists would claim to feel more eco-patriotic at places like Grand Teton National Park, where it's easy to take pride in our nation's awe- some nature. But that isn't what I have in mind. We need new feelings about the United States that don't rely on spectacular landscapes, or on awe. Sites of trauma and national memory must harness a different set of affects: love, respect, compassion, and if there is pride, a pride in our human capacity to feel across lines of difference.

The historicity of the objects collected at the site generates a compelling affect. But those objects, and their attendant affects, don't have to certify authenticity or feed into collective patriotism. Echoing Bennett on thing-power, Williams writes: "Artifacts are alive. Each has a voice. They remind us what it means to be human—that it is our nature to survive, to create works of beauty, to be resourceful, to be attentive to the world we live in."[73] The NPS narratives at today's Golden Spike NHS reinforce humans' resilience, industriousness, and resourcefulness, but they fail to fully compel our attention to the more-than-human world. That world is becoming ever more complex. If we are to replace techno-patriotism with eco-patriotism—a tension I continue to address in the next chapter—we'll need to dwell in those complexities.

Notes

1. David Nye tracks nineteenth-century reactions to incipient railroad technologies, including fear, "unease," and a "Dickensian nervousness," in *American Technological Sublime* (Boston: The MIT Press, 1994).
2. Richard White, *Railroaded: The Transcontinentals and the Making of Modern America* (New York: W.W. Norton & Company, 2012), xxii.
3. Interview, June 28, 2016. Interestingly, Kilton says it's mostly older men who show the childlike fascination with model trains and replica locomotives; my limited experience with model train shows bears this out. When May 10 fell on Mother's Day, Kilton laughs, the site had its lowest visitation ever. Certainly there is a gendered aspect to train fascination. I wonder if it's about power and control. Why else would trains be gendered "she"? While I don't have space here to explore these questions in detail, more work on the genderedness of trains and other "things" is in order.
4. The 2006 visitor survey report shows that just under 20 percent of visitors "did not obtain any information about the park before their visit." Most others were evenly split between learning about the site from "friends/relatives/word of mouth" or from "travel guides/tour books." For 75 percent of visitors, "learning about the history" was the primary reason for coming. Jessica Evans, Michael A. Schuett, and Steven J. Hollenhorst, "Golden Spike National Historic Site Visitor Study," University of Idaho Park Studies Unit. U.S. Department of Interior, 2006, iii.
5. Evans, Schuett, and Hollenhorst, iii.
6. According to the 2006 survey, most visitors come from states in the region: Utah,

California, Washington, Colorado, and Idaho. The survey notes there are "too few international visitors to provide reliable data." Evans, Schuett, and Hollenhorst, iii.

7. Nye, 75.

8. Nye, 75.

9. The reenactment script is sold in the visitor center, a thin brochure published by the Western National Parks Association.

10. Kodak was actually formed not long after the ceremony at Promontory, in 1888, but most Americans probably associate it with the twentieth-century, when photography became more accessible and commonplace.

11. Walker Percy, "The Loss of the Creature," *The Message in the Bottle: How Queer Man Is, How Queer Language Is, and What One Has to Do with the Other* (New York: Farrar, Straus, and Giroux, 1975).

12. Nye, 60.

13. Kathleen Stewart, *Ordinary Affects*, 6.

14. Jessica Evans, Michael Schuett, and Steven J. Hollenhorst, "Appendix." The Appendix contains approximately 120 comment forms (unnumbered). Only two mentioned disappointment by name, but many others conveyed that the lack of the original spike was among the things they "liked least about the visit to Golden Spike NHS." The locomotives and reenactment were at the top of the "liked most" list on nearly every survey.

15. "Memorials Matter: The Impressions History Leaves Behind," Resa Ledbetter. Utah Public Radio interview, June 27, 2016. http://upr.org/post/memorials-matter-impressions-history-leaves-behind. Accessed May 17, 2017.

16. Bennett, 61.

17. Hogan, 104. As I noted in the introduction, Hogan ties nationalism to geography, to "powerful exempla," and to feelings of wonder.

18. Cindy Spurlock, 263.

19. Yi–Fu Tuan, *Topophilia: A Study of Environmental Perception, Attitudes, and Values* (Englewood Cliffs: Prentice-Hall, Inc., 1974), 28.

20. Susan Stewart, *On Longing: Narratives of the Miniature, the Gigantic, the Souvenir, the Collection* (Durham: Duke University Press, 1993), 39.

21. Susan Stewart, 58–9.

22. Susan Stewart, 54.

23. Susan Stewart, 58.

24. Susan Stewart, 68.

25. Susan Stewart, 59–60.

26. Bennett, xvii.

27. Bennett, 61.

28. Bennett, 61.

29. Susan Stewart, 68.

30. James Strobridge, superintendent of the Central Pacific, who hired the Chinese crews, also celebrated their achievement, but not in any publicly visible way.

31. *Golden Spike National Historic Site Long-Range Interpretive Plan: 2014–2023.* (Harper's Ferry: Department of the Interior, June 2013), 8.

32. Ibid., 13.

33. Ibid., 14.

34. We can read about it on the bare-bones NPS sign "September 1869," which contains a photo from the town and a quote from "Newspaperman J.H. Beadle," who described it as "morally nearest to the infernal regions of any town on the road" that year.

35. Nye, 76. For Nye, the railroads heralded what he calls a "dynamic technological sublime," a "triumph of machines . . . over space and time" (57).

36. Julia H. Lee, "The Railroad as Message in Maxine Hong Kingston's *China Men* and Frank Chin's 'Riding the Rails with Chickencoop Slim,'" *Journal of Asian American Studies* 13, no. 3 (2015), 267.

37. Lee, 266.

38. Lee, 272.

39. Maxine Hong Kingston, *China Men* (New York: Alfred A. Knopf, Inc., 1977): 132–33.

40. In my follow-up emails with Ranger Kilton, he emphasized that there is no "recorded documentation" of workers hanging from baskets, though it is a commonly told story. Kilton thinks it more likely that they hung from ropes, rappel style. Email correspondence, September 8, 2017. Sources at Stanford say no one knows for sure: http://web.stanford.edu/group/chineserailroad/cgi-bin/wordpress/faqs/. Accessed 12 May, 2018.

41. Kingston, 135.

42. Kingston, 128.

43. Lee, 266.

44. Kingston, 131–2.

45. Kingston, 136.

46. Kilton also told me that dynamite was not used on the construction of the Transcontinental Railroad; dynamite was still being patented at that time. Email correspondence, September 8, 2017. Kingston may be using dynamite interchangeably with nitroglycerine, which was in use and was quite dangerous. Kilton recommended this website for context: http://railroad.lindahall.org/essays/black-powder.html.

47. Kingston, 136.

48. Kingston, 137–8.

49. David Eng has shown that Kingston and Frank Chin have provided "'new methods of looking,' specifically by challenging the supposed transparency and veracity of the photography itself." Cited in Lee, 268.

50. Kingston, 144–6.

51. Lee, 279.

52. Lee, 280.

53. Lee, 278.

54. Williams, *The Hour*, 141.

55. I realize some biosemiotics scholars might beg to differ. However, my understanding of "narrative" (outlined in my introduction) is narrower than the kind of information such scholars say is conveyed by the sign systems that exist in the dynamic natural world. For one recent resource on the subject, see Wendy Wheeler, *Expecting the Earth: Life/Culture/Biosemiotics* (Dagenham: Lawrence & Wishart, 2016).

56. NPS, "The Last Hurdle" sign.

57. Gwynn, J. Wallace, *Commonly Asked Questions About Utah's Great Salt Lake and Ancient Lake Bonneville*. (Utah Geological Survey, 1996), 1. This brochure is for sale in the Golden Spike NHS visitor center.

58. Ibid., 2.

59. Williams, *Refuge*, 30.

60. Williams, *The Hour*, 14.

61. Lee, 267.

62. Lee, 266.

63. Doreen Massey, "Landscape as a Provocation: Reflections on Moving Mountains," *Journal of Material Culture* 11, no. 1-2 (2006).

64. The NPS wayside display "September 8, 1942" tells this story.

65. Williams, *The Hour*, 11.

66. *Golden Spike NHS Long-Range Interpretive Plan*, 33.

67. Ibid., The plan says rangers hope to use that "appeal" to "engage visitors in the deeper stories of the building of the railroad and its impact on the nation."

68. Kilton reminisced about the bike tours they used to offer, and how riding on the historic grade made visitors aware of the work it took to make that grade. He said the NPS tours competed with Utah's Tour de Cure, which is one reason they were canceled.

69. Williams, *The Hour*, 14.

70. Susan Stewart, 135.

71. An obvious exception here is the "pride" attached to LGBTQ identities and the politics that informed the marriage equality movement by drawing on a collective affect of love. Love, of course, is complicated and especially problematic from a psychoanalytic perspective. See Ahmed's brilliant chapter, "In the Name of Love," for a thoughtful discussion (informed by Julia Kristeva, among others) of how "love of nation" can reinforce exclusive ideals, even while it fancies itself inclusive. Ahmed, *Cultural Politics*, 122–143. I'll revisit love in my postscript.

72. Williams, *The Hour*, 12.

73. Williams, *Refuge*, 189.

CHAPTER FOUR

Remembering War in Paradise

Grief, Aloha, and Techno-patriotism at WWII Valor in the Pacific National Monument[1]

On December 27, 2016, just three weeks after the 75th anniversary of the Japanese attack on Pearl Harbor, Japanese prime minister Shinzo Abe and outgoing U.S. president Barack Obama tossed purple orchid flowers into the waters above the sunken USS *Arizona*. Reciprocating Obama's unprecedented visit to Hiroshima earlier that year,[2] Abe became the first Japanese leader to set foot on the USS *Arizona* Memorial.[3] In an emotional speech, Abe offered "condolences to the souls" of victims and their loved ones and vowed to "never repeat the horrors of war." He pledged, instead, to work for "reconciliation and peace" between the two countries—to forge, in his twice-repeated phrase, an "alliance of hope."[4]

Despite their apparently heartfelt wishes for peace going forward, neither leader apologized for their country's military actions. This is in keeping with the spirit of anniversary events in general, which, even when they profess peace, tend to applaud heroism, reaffirm patriotism, and gloss over the complicated emotions that circulate around an event and its aftermath. Among the more high-profile public memory practices, anniversaries draw prominent political leaders and often, big crowds: At the 75th anniversary memorial observation on December 7, 2016, more than 200 survivors and families showed up, compared to "a handful" in a typical year.[5] Anniversaries offer a range of conventional ways to commemorate—such as parades, floats, wreaths, music, and moments of silence—and, increasingly, less conventional ways; among the eleven affiliated events listed on Pearl Harbor's 75th Anniversary

website were two basketball games and a marathon.[6] Historian Ray
Sun warns that anniversary festivities and rhetoric can simplify past
conflicts. In the case of Pearl Harbor, they edit out the "atmosphere of
fear" that shaped policy following the attack. As Sun puts it, "the dominant, heroic memory of Pearl Harbor has no place for the ambiguous
or dark attitudes and actions that resulted from the wartime fervor."[7]
These "dark" actions included the incarceration of more than 100,000
Japanese, most of whom were American citizens, in prison camps (the
subject of my next chapter).

Nationality and other kinds of personal affiliation shape the way
individuals remember the events of December 7, 1941. Some in Japan
still laud the "heroes" who dropped the bombs, even while Japanese
veterans, including the lead pilot of the attack, were instrumental in
pushing for reconciliation at the USS *Arizona* Memorial.[8] Hawai'i was
immediately enlisted in a national project of retaliation after the attack,
despite its not yet being one of the "united" states at the time. Even
post-statehood, Hawai'i, with its rich multicultural demographics and
active sovereignty movement, does not permit neat allegiances along
national boundaries. From the perspective of many Native Hawaiians,
or Kanaka Maoli, heroes "tend not only to be great conquerors like
Kamehameha but also people like Lili'uokalani, who peacefully opposed the American military occupation of Hawai'i in 1893."[9] From that
perspective, it's strange, even offensive, to commemorate the actions of
a military that colonized and continues to occupy this place. Tensions
persist between remembering Pearl Harbor, on the one hand, as a site
of military tragedy linked to national identity and American patriotism, and, on the other hand, as a way of moving toward peace and
reconciliation between people of all nations, including the Indigenous
inhabitants of the Hawaiian islands. Public events such as the Abe-
Obama flower-throwing ceremony walk a sometimes shaky line between the two.

Chief historian Daniel Martinez confirms that reconciliation is
a key interpretive theme at today's World War II Valor in the Pacific
National Monument.[10] The NPS website's homepage and its main site
bulletin feature the prominent headline: "From Engagement to Peace."[11]
Anthropologist Geoffrey M. White's recent book, *Memorializing Pearl*

Harbor: Unfinished Histories and The Work of Remembrance, chronicles the process through which reconciliation and peace have gained traction among the historical narratives explicitly told at the site. Because public memory is a work in progress, a national monument like this one can sustain multiple ways of honoring the past, from "national military remembrance" to "transnational peace prayer."[12] Books like White's are essential in sorting through the stories that compete for dominance. But even White's intimately researched and gracefully conveyed study of what he calls Pearl Harbor's "memorial landscape" focuses almost exclusively on the site's "*semiotic* landscape," including "museum exhibits, audio and video narratives, and personal presentations."[13] Aside from an astute observation about the tendency to segregate the "sacred" memorial space from the "secular" mainland complex—an insight that aligns with my own observations—White pays little attention to the emotionality of the *natural* landscape or the way it intersects with the semiotic one.

Such attention requires an ecocritical lens. As I've been suggesting, a natural environment is never just a backdrop; it's a set of forces, an agential assemblage, that shapes individual emotions about war and the production of public memory. Hawai'i is well known among tourists as a tropical paradise, and for good reasons. O'ahu's temperatures are warm but not hot (80 degrees Fahrenheit, on average), and the island gets more than 3,000 hours of sun each year but enough rain to keep things lush. Of course, much of O'ahu is developed, there is considerable traffic in and around Honolulu, and there are military bases peppered across the island. For visitors who come to WWII Valor in the Pacific NM as part of a longer vacation,[14] it's easy to overlook the features that don't fit the "paradise" narrative.

From the moment a tourist steps off the plane—perhaps already a bit buzzed from a complimentary mai tai—she is invited into full immersion in the island's famed spirit of aloha. Traditionally, visitors are presented upon landing with a lei, a garland given "as a sign of love, respect, and honor," which can "symbolize a circle of relations or a beloved person, place, or thing."[15] A lei is also what Sara Ahmed might call an affectively "sticky" object; leis transmit aloha, the dominant affect on the island. Encoded in state law, aloha is "the working philosophy of Native

Hawaiians" and a "life force" tied to feelings of kindness, tenderness, harmony, humility, patience, modesty, and other "traits of character that express the charm, warmth, and sincerity of Hawai'i's people."[16] I suggest aloha might also be understood as a kind of affect transmission: It assumes that emotions flow between places and people, that "good feelings" should be intentionally cultivated, and that even government officials should be responsible for propagating positive, collective affects. The leis may seem like a tourist gimmick, but they are meant to spread aloha, to connect humans affectively to each other and to the more-than-human world. When visitors to the USS *Arizona* Memorial drop flowers from leis into the water, as Obama and Abe did, they extend love, respect, and honor to those who are no longer with us.

Aloha is only part of the story, though. As geographer Kyle Kahijiro explains, Pearl Harbor contains a "paradox," being at once "hypervisible as a war memorial and tourist attraction, yet forbidden and mysterious," a landscape in which "something important [is] being concealed, something more than classified secrets or critical military facilities."[17] His genealogy of Pearl Harbor demystifies that "something" by historicizing the harbor as a "lost geography," in which an ideologically neutral view of the place as "simply a beautiful portal" through which bodies, products, and military forces can move at will masks the ways in which it has been "conscripted to do the work of imperial formation."[18] Of course, this history is more visible for some than for others. For Kanaka Maoli, Pearl Harbor, or "Pu'uloa," as they've traditionally called it, is an ancestral home with a long history, very little of which is represented at the current NPS site. The harbor is part of an *ahupua'a*—a traditional landscape division structured by natural boundaries—called Hālawa,[19] one of twelve in the 'Ewa district. Today Kanaka Maoli are likely to see the harbor as a thoroughly militarized space; its story is a declensionist one of a ruined paradise that has gone "from fishponds to warships."[20] As historian and musician Jon Kay Kamakawiwoʻole Osorio explains, it is "a landscape so altered as to seem alien," "forbidding" to many Kanaka Maoli—"unless they join the armed services or the large corps of civilian workers at Pearl Harbor."[21] Osorio explains the intergenerational (and sometimes intrafamilial) rifts created by conflicting attitudes toward the armed services and U.S.

military presence in the islands. He also finds the potential for "certain values to resonate between Hawaiians and soldiers—discipline, self-sacrifice, and a willingness to commit to a deserving leader"—and describes "a kind of grace between soldiers"[22] that can be heard in some traditional *meles*, which he performs today.[23]

From a different vantage point, veteran James Jones reveals moments of "grace between soldiers" in his popular 1951 novel, *From Here to Eternity*, which won the National Book Award for its portrayal of military life on Oʻahu leading up to, and immediately following, the Pearl Harbor attack. Jones does not represent a Native Hawaiian perspective and is not particularly sensitive in his treatment of the island's multicultural demographics.[24] To 1950s readers, this novel must have felt raw, honest, and authentic.[25] It registers to me, today, as an instance of what I call counter-nostalgia: a literary or cultural artifact's tactical deployment of nostalgia to disrupt dominant nostalgic narratives.[26] Informed by his experiences serving on Oʻahu, at Schofield Barracks, and elsewhere in WWII, Jones is particularly good at challenging romantic views of soldiers as model patriots, "Our Simple Boys,"[27] by asking us to witness their deepest insecurities, most poignant emotions, and most profound existential insights. Like the veterans who survived and volunteered to tell their stories at the memorial site, Jones provides a valuable perspective on the local environment and the emotional impacts of the Pearl Harbor attack, a perspective that complicates any easy association with heroism or romance.

The elisions and gaps Osorio and Jones write about are reinforced by popular discourse, in which Pearl Harbor often stands in metonymically for the attack itself. This unfair reduction substitutes military history for a more complex one. My chapter will explore nuances within, and intersections between, three competing perspectives of Pearl Harbor: the Native, the veteran, and the touristic, each of which has a different relationship to the physical environment and the history of the place. Since my focus is on the tourist perspective, I will talk mostly about the ways in which the other two views are (or are not) incorporated into the monument complex today. I hope my inclusion of Osorio's and Jones's voices helps me avoid silencing Native and veteran perspectives, even if it falls short of doing them full justice.

Because Hawai'i is so pleasant, visiting a war memorial there is an especially disconcerting experience, one in which the natural environment plays a key affective role. In this chapter, I track how the natural beauty and tropical atmosphere contrast with the militarized landscape and often work at cross-purposes with the kind of solemnity, even grief, most of us associate with war memorials, and which the NPS and military managers at Pearl Harbor encourage. Thomas Patin suggests "national parks are essentially museological institutions, not because they preserve and conserve, but because they employ many of the techniques of display, exhibition, and presentation that have been used by museums to regulate the bodies and organize the vision of visitors."[28] The implied tourist's *emotions* are also "regulated" and "organized" at Pearl Harbor. As an ex-military friend of mine who visited recently put it, our feelings are "compartmentalized."[29] There is an affective trajectory that the built environment encourages us to follow, and it parallels the NPS theme "from engagement to peace." The implied tourist should move through the museum galleries and watch the orientation film, where we find knowledge (and perhaps, feel horror) about the attack and the war itself; then shuttle to the USS *Arizona* Memorial, where we solemnly honor (and perhaps, grieve for) the soldiers who died; and finally, return to the "Contemplation Circle" back on shore, where we achieve the cathartic "peace" of knowing the nations are now reconciled. The actual affective trajectory is complicated, of course, in part because the sun, breeze, tropical birds, swaying palm trees, and other features of the more-than-human world threaten to disrupt the visitors' emotional engagement at every turn.

NPS managers are aware of the risks posed by a built environment that's out of synch with the sacred atmosphere the memorial is meant to safeguard. For instance, when the U.S. Navy leased the shoreline to a private company, who was temporarily permitted to set up a "tent mini-mall" full of souvenirs, retail shops, and "tropical kitsch" figuring Hawai'i as "exotic paradise," the NPS and partner organizations fought alongside Pearl Harbor survivors to condemn what they saw as "desecration."[30] But the impacts of the natural environment remain harder to pinpoint and, perhaps because of that, have received less strategic attention from park managers. If the story the NPS wants to tell is in fact one of a move "from engagement to peace," then perhaps the natural environment plays exactly the right role: soothing grief-stricken tourists, assuaging our distress over the violence of the attacks, and inspiring a peaceful feeling. But is the move to peace too fast? Are we asked to dwell for long enough in the "engagement" stage of the violence? Does aloha render violence past-tense? And are aloha and patriotism compatible affects?

In what follows, I seek answers to these questions as I track how affect circulates at Pearl Harbor within the "semiotic ecology of objects, texts, and activities"[31] that together form public memory. I discover tensions between how affect registers in texts and in the physical environment. Texts on-site steer us toward conventional feelings of grief, solemnity, kinship, honor, respect, and patriotism. The military technology celebrated in the built environment tends to encourage a particular form of patriotism, which I call techno-patriotism, while erasing Indigenous perspectives on the harbor. The experience of being a tourist here seems to work against the sacredness of the memorial: Between the headphones, the crowds, the U.S. Navy-run shuttle, and the affectively didactic arrangement of the physical space, the insistent aloha of the natural environment feels out of step. In spite of the constant inducements by the trade winds, gently moving seawater, vibrantly colored flora, and mood-improving sunshine to move toward a cathartic contentment, the corporeal register is, for me, one of affective dissonance, a kind of irritation that lingers.

———◆———

When I reach the entrance to the WWII Valor in the Pacific NM, I am relaxed and refreshed from spending the previous week on Kauai. Hoping to replicate the way most tourists approach this place, the most visited site in Hawai'i, I've scheduled it as "just another tourist attraction on [my] holiday itinerary."[32] I prepurchased my tickets online, listened to an upbeat pop radio station on the drive over from Honolulu in my GPS-guided rental car, paid to park in the closest lot, and made my way to the entrance. It is mid-May, and the weather couldn't be more perfect. I'm sure I have a goofy smile on my face as I stroll past other tourists posing for photos by the flagpoles and welcome signs, rent a locker for my belongings (as the site bulletin informs me, any "bags or articles that allow concealment are prohibited"), and wait in a short line at the counter in "Aloha Court" to claim my tickets and secure a headset for the narrative tour. It's hard not to detect a bit of "the Disneyland problem" at the site: the way even a sacred memory site like this one can be reduced to an entertaining, commercialized "playground," a "recreational and pleasure-oriented" space.[33] The USS *Arizona* Memorial is embedded deep within a complex that features military technology, war history, and interactive museum displays, where visitors can simulate the perspectives of torpedo launchers or the feeling of being a soldier bunking deep within a submarine. Perhaps the USS *Arizona* is still the heart of the complex, but it takes some effort to find its pulse.

It doesn't help that the sunken ship is buried at the bottom of the main site bulletin, on its backside, below the fold. As I browse the glossy brochure's front-page images of 1930s Waikiki, photos of the smoky aftermath of the attack, and a detailed map of the military sites on Oʻahu and Ford Island, I at first see no sign of the USS *Arizona* Memorial. Finally I find it, a lovely aerial image of the gracefully lined white structure built over top of the "sunken hull" of the battleship. "Memorialization" is positioned as an afterthought here, despite the text's claim that it is "Central to the park's mission." For visitors just arriving, the textual focus on military history and imagery parallels the physical environment: Flags and giant U.S. Navy missiles dominate the visual landscape and shape my first impressions. The USS *Arizona* Memorial was once the primary destination for visitors to Pearl Harbor, and it is the "main attraction" for me. But today—since it was incorporated into the WWII Valor in the Pacific National Monument in 2008—it is but one feature in a larger memorial complex.

As White explains, the shift to monument status accomplished "in a single move what decades of contested remembrance could not—situating the Pearl Harbor bombing attack in a broader context of war that includes, in equal measure, civilian and military casualties, as well as the impacts of war for all sides involved."[34] Monument legislation expanded educational and historical opportunities and made space for new kinds of ceremonies at the site, including Japanese tea ceremonies and the evocative paper crane exhibit, first presented via ceremony and now a permanent exhibit at the museum. With that expansion, the official conception of how visitors might respond emotionally has also shifted. White recalls hearing Martinez introduce the park orientation film (for which Martinez wrote the narrative) in 1997 with the following words: "For most of you today, this journey back to the days of 1941 will probably evoke some kind of feeling or emotion: sadness, despair, maybe even anger."[35] White reflects on the order of the emotions listed, noticing that anger is now almost an afterthought, where in the Memorial's early days—and certainly prior to its monument status—it was the dominant affect underscoring a righteous call to "Remember Pearl Harbor." The re-prioritizing of affect corresponds to the shift toward a "global memorial"[36] meant to appeal to visitors from all over, not just to American patriots.

The implied tourist must accordingly be treated as a broadening demographic, a global visitor. As of 2000, approximately 20 percent of visitors were international,[37] and exhibits are increasingly multilingual. Martinez's impression is that people from all over the world, including Japanese visitors, feel more welcome at the current site than they ever have.[38] Even so, American patriots will find plenty to admire here today. The USS *Arizona* is one of many official names on the lists of historic sites. On one prominent entrance sign it is one of three ships, sharing equal space with the USS *Utah* and the USS *Oklahoma*. On another large sign, these ships vie for visitors' attention with the other sites in the monument complex: the USS *Bowfin* Submarine Museum and Park, the Battleship *Missouri* Memorial, and the Pacific Aviation Museum Pearl Harbor. The ubiquitous military technology—phallic missiles and torpedoes lining the walkways, and the giant *Bowfin* submarine dominating the skyline—combines with the signage to encourage visitors to see the NM as primarily a commemoration of the age of the battleship, just before it gave way to the age of the aircraft carrier. Though Japan gets some credit for this technological shift (their use of aircraft carriers was a major reason their covert attack of Pearl Harbor was successful), American military expertise steals the show. The physical environment inspires techno-patriotism, a love of country based on its military might and, as the monument's official name reminds us, pride in the "valor" of those who serve.

FIGURE 4.1. Military technology on shore at Pearl Harbor

My tickets to see the USS *Arizona* Memorial aren't until 1:30 p.m., so I tour the mainland complex first. I don a pair of rented headphones, orient myself with the map, and begin the narrative tour. From the moment I press "play" and hear an odd juxtaposition of traditional Hawaiian luau music and patriotic band music, I know I can expect ironies throughout the Pearl Harbor complex. Remembering war in paradise constantly threatens to render visitors affectively as well as temporally distant from the historical events that transpired here. The aloha can register as ironic in the midst of structures, images, and text that are far from peaceful. I feel affective dissonance right away, as the phenomenon of being in this lovely natural environment clashes with the celebration of war technologies I've seen so far and those I've brought with me, including familiar historical photos of the burning USS *Arizona*. I'll soon discover that images of black smoke and fire and corresponding sound effects are common throughout the museum galleries. While I do not have space to assess all of the text, displays, or film footage inside the galleries, nor the official orientation film itself, I will speculate on how these make an impression upon visitors that we carry with us to the USS *Arizona* Memorial, which is my focus here.

The implied affective trajectory begins with knowledge, so I'm on the right path by starting with the galleries. But there are certain things that, from the start, make me feel like an "affect alien." The first such catalyst for this feeling is a wayside display called "A Home To Many Peoples," which I find just outside the galleries. Native Hawaiian perspectives are rare on-site—I counted two displays devoted to Indigenous perspectives—so I'm pleased to see some information presented front and center. The "A Home To Many Peoples" sign splits its space between multicultural and Indigenous histories and features a multi-ethnic population pie chart along with black-and-white photos of immigrants and Native peoples. Native Hawaiians, the sign notes "had steeply declined" in number in the 100 years prior to 1940. At that time, "only 15 percent of the islands' population was Kanaka Maoli . . . and sacred areas were being lost to large-scale sugar and pineapple plantations, new construction and military use. Access to land and water was important to traditional Hawaiian customs, practices and beliefs. A leader in the Hawaiian community put it this way: *'It is not that the ships and armed soldiers themselves are menacing, so much as it is the sense that they belong to this place and we do not.'*" That unnamed "leader" is Jon Osorio, though I had not yet learned of him or his work.

This quote is the most direct mention of the way Native Hawaiians respond to the contemporary site. The NPS is clearly making an effort here to emphasize the damage to the landscape and loss of culture that Osorio himself sings, writes, and teaches about. Others might wonder, as I did, what kind of "paradise" this place really is if its Indigenous peoples don't feel they belong. However, the past-tense rhetoric feeds into dominant nostalgic narratives about Indigenous peoples and their cultures as always disappearing, and so undermines the power of Osorio's words. It also verges on a problematic form of multiculturalism—one that prioritizes "the cultures of Hawai'i *since* the colonization of Hawai'i" and so continues to marginalize Indigenous history.[39] One might be inclined to applaud the NPS designers for attributing equal space to multicultural and Indigenous experiences on the "Home to Many Peoples" display. But this balanced design risks setting up an opposition between "Indigenous" and "immigrant" cultures of Hawai'i that is all too common. Multiculturalism can implicitly reinforce that opposition when, in reality, there was already tremendous variety ("multiculturalism") in the Indigenous Americas, including in the Pacific Islands, before the influx of immigrants. As my former American ethnic studies professor Stephen H. Sumida puts it, when we assume Hawai'i's multiculturalism began at the "point of erasure of Indigenous history," with the introduction of immigrant labor on plantations, then it makes multiculturalism "an aspect of colonization."[40] Though this is surely not the NPS designers' intention, I suspect most non-Native tourists read this sign, perhaps chalk it up to a "superficial liberal gesture of multicultural inclusion to add local color to the unified master historical narrative,"[41] and move on.

The physical environment compounds the affective dissonance I'm already beginning to feel. The story of the attack usually begins the same way: It was a peaceful, quiet Sunday morning in paradise. Even a lieutenant on the Japanese attack ship, the *Akagi,* remarked on the lovely natural environment as they approached Pearl Harbor: the sunrise, he remembered, "looked beautiful against our national flag." At times, the NPS deliberately invokes the trope of paradise—and the corresponding aloha—in its visual and written rhetoric. NPS displays describe a formerly pristine environment—the harbor overflowing with pearl oysters, the high-rise-free horizon line, the sparsely populated beaches—in order to make the attacks themselves seem more striking and violent. The "Eve of War" is typically represented as an island paradise, with hula dancers, luau music, swaying palms, and near-empty beaches.

There's no shortage of nostalgic images in the rhetorical landscape, but there is one notable exception: a display called "Not Quite Paradise," which is meant to give a more realistic depiction of how soldiers on O'ahu spent their time. It explains soldiers "felt like foreigners, had little money to spend, and found few entertainment options. Many men struggled to fight off homesickness." Sometimes their days off were just plain "dull." Jones's novel confirms the material poverty of soldiers' lives and fleshes out these feelings. His protagonists live rich emotional lives, even if their day-to-day tends to fluctuate between monotony and hard labor. Far from lounging on the beach, Jones's soldiers are underpaid enlisted men and guilt-ridden officers doing what they can to avoid loneliness: drinking heavily, visiting brothels, and carousing with "queers" in Honolulu. I don't recognize these characters in the NPS display, which reinforces a sense of nostalgia for the era by including black-and-white images of young, smiling men in uniform alongside handwritten letters.

Restricted by its "museological" strategies, the NPS display can't achieve the counter-nostalgic lens Jones offers. In one of many thoughtful reflections, the protagonist of *From Here to Eternity*, Private Robert E. Lee Prewitt ("Prew," for short) critiques the way tourists' photographs misrepresent Hawai'i and the Army. Pictures of "quaint Wahiawa without the smells" and of his own Schofield Barracks looking "lovely enough to make you want to enlist for this happy land" prove his point that tourists can only see these places "from the outside."[42] The rift between tourists and those in the armed forces is two-sided, since Prew and the other soldiers have never "seen the insides of" many of the places the tourists visit, including big hotels like Honolulu's iconic Royal Hawaiian hotel.[43]

I may be a *haole* here on the island and an outsider to both Native and veteran perspectives, but I'm a welcome guest at the NPS site. The narrative tour offers me a handheld escort through the site. After telling me to "rest a minute" just before entering the gallery, Jamie Lee Curtis gives those of us taking the tour a kind of trigger warning. She wants to "tell [us] what to expect." When she says "stand to the left so you don't block the entrance," the direct imperative is eerie, as if she were watching over my shoulder. (I had, indeed, been blocking the entrance.) A moment later, I enter the gallery and she issues another command: "Now, look up." Above me is a replica torpedo bomber. After being told that the day of the attack was a typical one in O'ahu—sunny and warm—and a Sunday at that, the bomber, and the explosive sounds I'd hear inside the galleries, are even more striking. As one reviewer says of Jones's novel, because we know the attack is coming it "lend[s] an air of foreboding to even the most mundane events."[44] The same might be said of the tourist experience; we read everything leading up to the attack through that anticipatory framework, such that the quotidian is tinged with dread. Elsewhere on-site, the NPS display "Before the Storm" characterizes December 6 as "a balmy night" that "felt routine—the same weekend chores or duties, the same evening diversions." Black-and-white images of young soldiers in all white "swabbing the Nevada's deck" and a quiet Honolulu lined with palm trees reinforce that sense of an unsuspecting, innocent nation.

Jones's version of the attack complicates that sense of innocence. When the Japanese arrive at Pearl Harbor, Prew, a talented bugler and former boxer, is recovering from a knife wound at the home of his lover, Alma (a prostitute) and spending his days binging on books and booze. Prew awakens to the news and a hangover so bad only more alcohol (he thinks) can help. Jones provides fictionalized radio footage from the day—attributed to Webley Edwards (who did actually announce the attacks)—to compensate for Prew's foggy mind; italicized sections give us the play-by-play and reflect "the first great rush of emotion" in Honolulu.[45] Edwards, who is known for his 40-year-long radio show "Hawaii Calls,"[46] lauds the *"quiet heroism under fire"*[47] of the American servicemen and compounding Prew's guilt for not being there. Jones hits all the right affective notes in this rich scene, letting Edwards speak to the youthful innocence presumed of soldiers and used to shore up nationalism: *"They are creating a legend, these men, these boys—and most of them are just that: boys—a legend of Democracy that will for long and long remain unequalled and unsurpassed, and that will strike fear into the hearts of the enemies of freedom."*[48] He captures the patriotism and romance surrounding military service while simultaneously debunking both by revealing the real feelings of individual guilt and fear. Before long, Prew is sobbing (still clutching, and sipping from, a whiskey bottle, which he would do for the next eight days) and Alma and her roommate are cursing the "dirty yellow-bellied little Japs" for "sneak[ing] in without warning and [making] a cowardly attack."[49]

First Sergeant Milton "Milt" Warden, a noncommissioned officer who has a soft spot for Prew (and for his superior's wife, Karen Holmes), is also recovering from a boozy night when the bombs hit. Jones's description echoes the "typical Sunday morning" rhetoric mentioned elsewhere on-site, but with a dose of military realism: "It was a typical Sunday morning breakfast, for the first weekend after payday.

At least a third of the Company was not home. Another third was still in bed asleep. But the last third more than made up for the absences in the loudness of their drunken laughter and horseplay and the clashing of cutlery and halfpint milk bottles."[50] It becomes a flashbulb memory for Warden, as for those who lived through it.[51] When he hears the first blast, he stops to look at his compatriots in the mess hall. "He remembered the picture the rest of his life."[52] Their initial reaction is boyish exuberance. Warden and some of his men begin shooting back at the plane, an activity they all participate in with "pure glee."[53] They drink coffee, then more liquor, as they hoot and holler, arguing over whose turn it is to shoot the weapons like schoolchildren on a playground. After the attack is over, though, they are left with a "dead silence which no sound seemed able to penetrate."[54]

The affective atmosphere shifts again as they approach the beach. "Gradually, foot by foot, the trucks moved on down toward Honolulu and whatever waited on the beaches. Up till now it had been a day off, it had been fun. Pearl Harbor, when they passed it, was a shambles. Wheeler Field had been bad, but Pearl Harbor numbed the brain." The next paragraph puts it in terms of a different body part: "Pearl Harbor made a queasiness in the testicles. Wheeler Field was set back quite a ways from the road, but parts of Pearl Harbor were right on the highway. Up till then it had been a big lark, a picnic . . ." Despite the dawning awareness that things are far worse here, "Among the troops in the trucks there was a certain high fervor of defense and patriotism that exploded into a weak feeble cheer in the heavy perpetual wind." Nonhuman nature defeats patriotic body language here; their proudly displayed V-for-Victory signs are "feeble" in the face of the wind. In a poignant one-paragraph sentence Jones expresses how short-lived this atmosphere was: "This general patriotic enthusiasm lasted about three days." The creation of barbed-wire fences, the unlit streets and closed-down bars, the sundown curfew, the declaration of martial law, the newfound sobriety, the loss of basic comforts like beds, and the hard labor—like the maneuvers they'd done for training, but with no end in sight—depress the troops' spirits considerably. The barbed wire, in particular, Jones explains, "ate into the patriotism of the troops." Meanwhile, "All the tourists had either gone home, or else were sitting tight in their hotel rooms waiting for the Army to evacuate them."[55] Later in the novel he describes the curfews and blackouts in terms of death: "At sundown Honolulu crawled quickly into its various holes and died until morning."[56] In a poignant moment of nostalgia, these soldiers, who are now entering into a war, suddenly sense that "the golden days on this rock are over."[57]

We see a similar shift captured on the NPS display called "Hawai'i at War," which describes the affective atmosphere of O'ahu following the attack. With punchy subtitles like "Blackouts and Barbed Wire" and "From Paradise to Paranoia," the sign uses vivid imagery to represent the affective shift to "paranoia." One O'ahu resident, Violet Lai, explains that "the war years were frightening times. I think our child really felt the tension. There was a fear of invasion, and you couldn't do this and you couldn't do that under martial law." Another resident, Elizabeth Atkinson, simply remembers "We had gas masks in our arms and hibiscus in our hair." The last sentence punctuates the rest with the poignant invocation of schoolchildren, who "carried gas masks along with their books when they went to school." The transformation of O'ahu from "paradise to paranoia" was a mood shift encapsulated in an altered physical environment, including the contrast of seeing—or building, if you were a soldier—"barbed wire along beautiful beaches." It's hard to imagine that here, now, as a tourist, but the NPS does encourage us to try. Still, Jones's book throws opens a window that a tourist—even aided by these firsthand accounts—can only peak through.

Even if we can conceptualize the past, the island's aloha renders much of the history hard to feel. Although the NPS invokes the *trope of paradise* (located in the past), there is little awareness of how the natural environment shapes the embodied visitor's experience in the present. Visitors shuffle through tight gallery spaces, but these are not far from the outside air and can even feel breezy in spots. The winds blow into the attack gallery, disrupting the compartmentalization of affect by bringing the outside in, infusing patriotism with aloha spirit. The "Green Guide" wayside display (subtitled "A Design Inspired By Nature") engages us with a second-person imperative to "Notice the curved roofs that resemble the monkeypod canopy, the careful arrangement of small-scale buildings to channel the breeze, the reliance

on natural ventilation, and the generous use of shade." There is an ac-
knowledgment here that the more-than-human world continues to be
an active agent in shaping the built environment.

Those who stop and read this display are cued to pay attention to
the elements as they work on us (the winds "dry and cool" our skin, the
sign says), and to the wind, in particular, which helps establish a kind
of affective continuity across and throughout the complex. We feel the
atmosphere: the actual air, the smells it carries, even the molecular
humidity of the water on our skin. This atmospheric fluidity troubles
what White formulates as a dichotomy between the fixed/static features of the site—the exhibits, "architecture, museum, documentary
film or landscape"—and the lived/dynamic practices that turn it into
a place, an "array of commemorative and educational activities" that
happen on or near the memorial space and reveal a "striking variety
and fluidity."[58] As material ecocritical perspectives show, landscapes
are never as "fixed" as they seem to be; they are processive, dynamic
agents. Weather, too, is an agent on-site. And the exhibits, as White well
knows, are not really fixed either, even if one encounters them as such
on any given day. They change over time. Many are interactive, and
most encourage individualized interpretations.

The last displays we see before boarding the boat are, in fact, dynamic and didactic ones. "Sadako's cranes" is the site's only mention of
the atomic bombs the U.S. dropped on Hiroshima and Nagasaki,[59] and
it is couched in terms of peace and resilience—in particular, the heroic efforts of a young victim of the bombings, twelve-year-old Sadako
Sasaki, who folded more than 1,300 origami cranes while suffering, and
eventually dying, from leukemia. The significance of the cranes stems
from Japanese legend that folding a thousand will grant one "long life,
good luck or recovery from illness." The cranes are affective objects
meant to carry peace and resilience to today's site. In Sadako's irre-
sistibly heartwarming words, which provide a sort of epigraph for the
display: "I will write peace on your wings and you will fly all over the
world." Perhaps more cynical visitors, like me, are feeling pretty sad-
dened by this, not peaceful or resilient at all. But then, just beside the
Sadako's cranes exhibit, I see video footage of the coral reefs below the
USS *Arizona*, revealing evidence of new life evolving on the sunken

ship. On the screen, tropical fish swim leisurely past brightly colored coral, the vibrant blue water letting rays of sunshine stream through. For those who have snorkeled, especially, the evocative footage conjures an underwater paradise that's as beautiful as the aboveground island.

Elizabeth DeLoughrey attends to the way the ocean "as medium can symbolize the simultaneity or even collapse of linear time, reflecting lost lives of the past."[60] The ocean is, she explains, an "alien environment" for public memory, a uniquely disorienting and unstable place "transformed by salt, currents, pressure, and the rapid occupation by multispecies ecologies."[61] The "multispecies ecologies" shown in the video footage do emphasize the "alien" underwater world below the Memorial. I can't help but worry, though, that they also naturalize the violence of the atomic bombs in their celebration of the resilience of both nonhuman nature and human beings. The displays prepare us to read the USS *Arizona* Memorial as a resilient nature-culture hybrid, as well as a place where we will feel at peace. Like the phoenix Sadako (whose story, the display says, rose "out of the ashes"), our nations, too, can presumably overcome the horrors of war. Rather than "collapsing" that linear, progressive history, though, I think these displays reinforce it. I also suspect the videos set us up for disappointment, since we don't have direct access to that underwater environment ourselves.

As I wait with the other tourists to board the shuttle boat, I find two more screens displaying underwater footage. As I watch—and become aware of the many others watching around me—I wonder how experiencing the Memorial publicly, with these others, will impact the affective atmosphere. I recall Joan Didion's description of witnessing a burial in a different cemetery: Oʻahu's "Punchbowl," the National Memorial Cemetery of the Pacific, where approximately 20,000 soldiers are interred. Didion's prose is marked by environmental reference points: the "tropical sun," the banyan trees, the rain trees, the yellow primavera, the mauve jacaranda, and the "warm trade winds," which she mentions three times in as many pages. The Vietnam War and its casualties become very real to her here. She writes, "Vietnam seemed considerably less chimerical than it had seemed on the Mainland for some months."[62] The grief at the cemetery is palpable in the details she chooses to give us. What

Didion doesn't spell out is how the warm winds and other natural forces shape those emotions. Do they temper the grief, or accentuate it? Do they contrast with the burial site, or harmonize with it? Is nature's agency ironic or dissonant in some sense? Or does the more-than-human world confirm human emotions? And what about the built environment? I'm keen to resolve these questions for myself, and I hope the USS *Arizona* Memorial will be the place to find answers.

———•◆•———

The USS *Arizona* Memorial is the most popular destination on Oʻahu, hosting an average of 4,000 visitors a day and more than 1.7 million each year.[63] No wonder they require tickets. All morning I've been anticipating the time I'd finally get to set foot on it. Before I can do that, I'll need to take a short boat ride. The boat is run by the U.S. Navy, so smartly uniformed armed services members are in charge of us now. Their uniforms feel much more official, stiff, and off-putting, compared to the friendly NPS green and gray. I'm a bit nervous, suddenly, as when I'm driving across a national border or passing through customs at an airport and have that vague fear that surely they'll find something to arrest me for, even if I am not aware of breaking any law. The shuttle offers us a few minutes to make the emotional transition from the hectic mainland complex to this comparatively more peaceful site, to navigate what White describes as a "spatial opposition between the secular activities of the visitor center, onshore, and the 'sacred' site of the memorial."[64] On the way over, U.S. Navy escorts tell us we should treat the Memorial with reverence and respect. No food or drink allowed. We are to avoid texting, and to prepare ourselves for a solemn encounter at this "sacred" site. I hear Jamie Lee Curtis's voice in my ear, reminding me the USS *Arizona* is a "living symbol for all who gave their lives here," but it is also a mass grave, a "tomb" for the more than 900 soldiers buried within it.

Architect Alfred Preis designed the Memorial to provide "a serene and non-coercive atmosphere for contemplation."[65] It floats above the sunken battleship, never touching it; Preis said this is so the ship remains "clean, pure . . . holy." The white stone enhances this effect. The common interpretation of the design is that the sagging middle represents the low point of American morale after the attack; the upswings on both sides reflect the nation's resilience and victory afterward. Preis accepted this interpretation, though the design was also utilitarian, in part, having to do with practical concerns over weight distribution.[66]

The affective atmosphere is appropriately subdued, but not exactly somber. If the Memorial has the atmosphere of a cemetery, it's a cemetery where several dozen strangers are visiting at once. Like at most tourist sites, people at the USS *Arizona* Memorial mostly mill about taking photos, but they do it quietly and respectfully. Fewer tourists wear headphones on the Memorial, though many (including me) still take photos with their phones. There seems to be more attentiveness here. People take time to gaze into the "sacred" submerged tomb. As opposed to in the museum galleries, where it sometimes feels like visitors stop in front of displays just long enough to *appear* to be reading them, people here seem to be reading the displays carefully. There is much less text overall, which gives us time to linger at each sign. The whole process seems less forced here than in the galleries on shore.

We are technological tourists, a phrase I coined in my earlier book[67]—cyborgian visitors for whom it isn't unusual to navigate the world wearing headphones, our bodies moving in space but our mental energies someplace else. After all, many of us plug in to our earbuds on everyday commutes already. The headphones accentuate the solitary dimension of public memory; even while we create meaning together, in a sense, we are still fundamentally alone in our thoughts and feelings. Even Curtis's narration begins and ends by saying there is no single way to feel about this site. For me, public tourism like this is awkward. There's something strange about standing atop a floating Memorial with a bunch of strangers, knowing you'll be shuttled back to the complex shortly. On a busy day, time and space conspire to make even the most patient visitor feel either hurried, or crowded, or both. Visitor surveys indicate that nearly all visitors felt at least "somewhat crowded" at some point during their visit, and the "Memorial itself" topped the list of places at which people felt crowded by others.[68]

It is, indeed, a small space. Negotiating the memorial environment involves some awkward moves, including calculating how much room to leave others' bodies so as not to encroach on their commemoration,

FIGURE 4.2. Tourists on board the USS *Arizona* Memorial

patiently waiting your turn to read display signs, and gauging the appropriateness of when, or whether, to take photos. Sometimes this maneuvering includes what White calls "symbolic pollution," the presence of "'contaminants'" like "loud voices on the Memorial" that can disrupt the sacredness. There is no guarantee that "the sacred" will happen. It must be generated anew during each visit, which means, usually, with other people.[69]

On one hand, the NPS instructions, the distance from the mainland, the architecture, and the idyllic natural environment collaborate to facilitate the emergence of a "sacred" experience. On the other hand, though, there is something not quite right about the assumption that a "serene environment encourages contemplation of the incredible violence, destruction and sacrifice made at this very spot."[70] How can serenity make it easier to contemplate violence and destruction? I'd argue the opposite happens: standing on that serene spot, especially while on vacation, and in paradise, actually makes it difficult to imagine such violence and destruction. Perhaps that's why there are so many photos of the burning ship everywhere else: to reinforce the fact that these horrific things did, in fact, occur here. Even on the Memorial, then, there are felt tensions: between life and death, between natural beauty and military technology, between aloha and patriotism. There's something incongruous about a Memorial that is both a "living symbol" and a "tomb."

That incongruity registers elsewhere in the visual landscape. For instance, the rusty gun turret poking above the water's surface may be a form of "symbolic pollution" for some. Its jarring military-industrial aesthetic contrasts with the oceanic environment, the distant mountains, and the calm of the breezy afternoon. Seeing the gun turret pushes me out of my contemplative mood and sets off a conflicted affective reaction in me, a sort of visceral alarm bell. Just like on shore, there's a degree of affective dissonance—a felt sense of disjunction, an environmental irony, that isn't explicitly narrated or maybe conscious for most visitors. I think of a photo of an NPS diver in the park newspaper that reveals these ironies: While the image is of vibrantly colored coral growing on a submerged gun, the caption is a reminder that these guns "could rain 1,500-pound shells as far away as 20 miles." Here, the military technology is out of synch with the mood. Not only that, the guns feel like relics themselves, rusted-over tokens of a distant past that add to the commemorative atmosphere but render both the violence and its victims past tense.

Unlike on shore, there are no nostalgic images of the past here. The horizon line we see from here is fully developed. We are on a working naval base, so industrial and military facilities encircle the Memorial. From here, the Waianae Range looks like a fake backdrop. The mountains may even, for some of us, contribute to a "darker" mood. When Didion honors Jones's memory with a pilgrimage to Schofield Barracks—a site, she adds, that's not on any postcard and is "off the tour"[71]—she describes an atmospheric shift as she approaches it. As she goes inland, she finds "a clouding of the atmosphere, a darkening of the color range. The translucent pastels of the famous coast give way to the opaque greens of interior Oʻahu. Crushed white coral gives way to red dirt, sugar dirt, deep red laterite soil that crumbles soft in the hand and films over grass and boots and hubcaps. Clouds mass over the Waianae Range."[72] She renders this hidden landscape visible with words as poignant as Jones's. This mountain range, this "darker country," can seem "obscurely oppressive" even to the visiting Didion.[73] It's an affective side of O'ahu that isn't readily available at the contemporary Pearl Harbor complex, especially on an idyllic day. But I imagine on a stormy afternoon, without the sparkling sunshine to lift my spirits, this Memorial would feel darker, sadder, more poignant.

I step over to the "wishing well" next, which a directive display tells me is a "sacred site." A photo of three NPS dive team members, one of whom holds an urn and gazes skyward, is captioned with a diver's words about what it feels like to lay a soldier's remains to rest in the water below: "you can kind of feel it release . . . I tell the family, when I feel that pull, it's the ship accepting one of its own back." I've felt the "pull" of an ocean landscape many times before, so I try to conjure my emotional history with this watery environment, which Rebecca Solnit describes (in her distinctly associative way) as "like a metaphor, but one that is always moving, cannot be fixed, like a heart that is like a tongue that is like a mystery that is like a story that is like a border that is like something altogether different and like everything at once."[74] The fluidity of the sea inspires an affective buoyancy, so unlike the desert's stark lines and harsh light. The ocean's cultural ties to the womb, to amniotic fluid, to the "oceanic feeling" Freud associated with the loss of boundary between ego and object, and—in my own emotional memories, to family vacations and to my youth—create a soothing feeling. Looking into these "sacred" waters, I am at a loss to retrieve any of this emotion. To me, the watery tomb looks pretty much like the "large hole" the sign says it is, not "sacred" at all. Unlike what I'd been shown on the video screens, what I actually see when I peer down is murky and dark. There's a small spot of orange that may be coral, but it's hard to tell with the sun glinting off the surface nearby. Nary a fish swims past. An apt metaphor for public memory, perhaps, the "wishing well" presents me, on this day, not with a clear or heroic vision of resilience but with an uncertain glimpse into an opaque abyss.

Preis, to his credit, advocated for an underwater viewing chamber with access to the sky above and portholes to allow the viewing of the ship's remains, including the organisms living there as well as the buried soldiers. He wanted us to "confront the physicality of the sarcophagus" and to feel the "immanent presence of death."[75] James P. Delgado describes the way death changes an environment, rendering it more sacred: "blood-shedding to protect an ideal or defend a nation is a sanctified ritual that creates 'hallowed ground.'"[76] A tomb has more "drawing power" than an "empty" memorial; moreover, Delgado speculates, people "seem to possess an inherent need to confront their own mortality, and visiting a war grave provides a means for doing so."[77] Ideally, we would be able to see the coral for ourselves, from underwater, to look closely at the "multispecies occupations"[78] forming there, and to reflect on the strange confluence of death and new life happening in this underwater environment.

But the Memorial's management doesn't want us to get too close to death; Preis's initial design proposal was "met with a lack of enthusiasm from the Navy."[79] The Memorial as it stands now allows visitors to get close, but not too close—the structure is "inspired by, but not confronting, the reality" of the ship's destruction.[80] This kind of physical distance likely contributes to what, for many of us, is also an emotional distance, an inability to connect with the death and tragedy at a profound affective register. Perhaps if I'd been able to witness one of the interments—which Martinez describes with emotion that's palpable even by phone, eleven time zones away—then I might feel the way Didion did at the Punchbowl Cemetery about the realities of war. Instead, my most affective moment comes from stories about the particular boys who died, stories featured in both the narrative tour and an NPS site bulletin, "USS *Arizona* Brothers." Shockingly, twenty-three sets of brothers, as well as a father and son who signed up to serve together, ultimately died together during the attack. While this invocation of kinship may register as a kind of cheap shot to some visitors—the emotionally manipulative jump from family to nation, from heroism to patriotic sacrifice—to me, a mother of two sons, it is breathtaking, a visceral reminder of my boys' mortality. I don't mind confronting my own death from time to time, but I generally avoid thinking about theirs.

So far, this has been my most profound affective reaction—that is, until everyone boards the next shuttle back to shore and suddenly I'm the only tourist left on the Memorial. My researcher status has earned me a few minutes of solitude in between boat shipments. Before delicately retreating into a side office, Ranger Kary Goetz had given me a lei to throw into the water, the same purple orchid flowers that President Obama and Prime Minister Abe would toss into the "tomb" the following year. That valuable commodity that can make time in a wilderness area so special—solitude—is also nice to have at a tourist site. I go immediately into the shrine room, which has an allure, and a purity, like a church altar transplanted in a garden. The "Tree of Life" design is meant to promote a "universal spirit of renewal." Framing the wall of names like bookends, two renditions of the Tree of Life echo the larger sculpture on the mainland, which also mentions "renewal" but features the common NPS engagement strategy of reaching out to visitors in the second person: "What does this symbol mean to you?" Fresh flowers, with their "translucent pastels" and intoxicating smells, bring aloha into the breezy shrine room. A wall of names adds to the solemn feel. I run my fingers across the letters on the wall in the shrine room. The edges of each word are sharp against my skin. They are not names so much as texture. Narratives fade away for a few minutes, and I am more impacted by the architecture, the breeze, and the water itself, than by any particular stories or instructions about how to feel.[81]

When I move to the Memorial's edge to drop my lei in the water, I've finally reached a point of affective engagement. I watch the flowers, which look so tiny in the harbor, float away toward the USS *Missouri*. Now that I feel something I'm inclined to start intellectualizing it. I'm fascinated by the so-called "black tears," the small drops of oil that leak from the submerged ship at the rate of four drops per minute and are now appearing before my eyes, coloring the surface with impressionistic shapes. The tears are a nature-culture hybrid, I think, troubling the boundary between contamination and purity. Evidence of the world's permeability, they ooze from the tomb, a simultaneously material and discursive instance of a contact zone between life and death. The black tears are a kind of metaphor for the whole site, and a lot hinges on how one reads them. Does the oil remind us of death, or of renewal (or both)? Does it gesture toward the environmental costs of war—costs that are often sidelined when we focus on stories of individual soldiers and their families? Or does it champion nature's resilience, no matter how badly humans treat it? Whose "tears" are they, metaphorically speaking?

Photographer Jerome A. Kaufman, whom I was fortunate to meet and talk with back on shore, describes the tears in agential terms material ecocritics might admire: "like spirits silently ascending from the past . . . swirled by the breeze and tide, they move in a rhythmic dance choreographed by the natural conditions of the day."[82] In one survivor's words, the tears are "like the grief or grudge of the 1,177 people killed on the ship."[83] The USS *Arizona*, like the other victims of the attack, is always referred to as "she,"[84] a personification that suggests "she" may be the one shedding the tears (and she is, in a literal sense; the oil seeps from her hull). The gendered personification of the boat conjures the bodies contained within. The ship could be read as a mourning mother—perhaps, a symbol of the nation itself—who has taken "her own" sons back to her womb. They could also be nonhuman nature's tears, the ocean's metaphorical grief, reminding witnesses of war's costs—environmental as well as human. Even though the NPS assures us no real damage to the ecosystem is being done, this is a discomfiting sight. For me, it conjures memories and images from massive oil spills: photos of dead pelicans and oil-saturated turtles, oil-stained shorelines, and oil slicks spreading across the gulf. The park newspaper assures us that the coral reef and "marine growth coating has become a protectant" for the ship itself. Concerns about what will happen to the 500,000 gallons of oil still inside the ship's lower-level tanks are assuaged, for the time being, since this protective coating—nature's resilience—might enable the ship to last for hundreds of years. The Pearl Harbor complex is a Superfund site, but you won't read about that on any of the displays.[85]

Between the crowds, headphones, selfie sticks, and potential to feel hurried, everyday tourism is often full of distractions and poorly equipped to promote strong emotions. During my fifteen minutes of solitude on the Memorial, I do feel an emotional response, even if I'm not sure it's the "authentic" one. Kaufman believes the site moves us toward peace and renewal, toward the spirit of aloha that Hawai'i is known for. I want to think he is right. Most of the time, the conditions are beautiful and soothing. But this feeling of aloha might facilitate a peace that eludes responsibility as it ushers us too fast to reconciliation. If we are attuned to the "natural conditions of the day"—to the coral reefs and fish, to the breezy trade winds, to the smells of blooming trees and plants, to the vibrantly colored tropical flowers, to the pleasant shrieks of birds—it's tempting to avoid the "engagement" stage of the tourist experience, to minimize the horrible violence of war, and to skip right to feeling peaceful.

The overarching narrative on-site is now supposed to be a story of a nation's transformation: We once used "Remember Pearl Harbor!" as a war slogan, rallying troops in an affective transition from "shock . . . to indignation, then rage, and finally a steely determination to wage total war," but now we've embraced a new global pacifism, where peace and reconciliation guide "the American spirit."[86] While I think the NPS is sincere in its push for peace, the more cynical part of me sees this as just another tool in the settler colonial toolbox: the recruitment of aloha ("love, honor, and respect") as a weapon of colonialism. This is, after all, the WWII Valor in the Pacific National Monument; patriotic pride is the "authentic" affect. For some tourists, the natural beauty adds to the assurance that our country is mighty, that our soldiers did not die in vain, that our nature and our nation are courageous and resilient. Like Teresa Bergman says of the films at Mount Rushmore National Memorial, this site creates a public united around "an uncritical acceptance of past U.S. aggressions, and civic loyalty as little more than an appreciation of physical might."[87]

It's no surprise, then, that world leaders continue to invoke memorials like this one to motivate the public toward nationalistic policies. President George W. Bush drew on the memory of Pearl Harbor to garner public support for invading Iraq, describing how "the nation's grief turned to resolution" the day following the attacks. Some newspaper headlines on September 12, 2001 read "Day of Infamy." I can't help but wonder, though: Does patriotism based on shared grief always have to mutate into nationalistic militarism? What if patriotism could instead by a catalyst for "tolerance and reconciliation" rather than xenophobic nationalism? I'd like to believe it's possible, even though the current political climate suggests otherwise. Like the clashing images of burning battleships and Edenic Waikiki beaches at the NM, my country

often feels schizophrenic in its politics. We need to overcome the de-
lusion of American innocence before any real reconciliation can take
place, and the current World War II Valor in the Pacific NM seems to
encourage our innocence more than question it.

———◆◆◆———

Back on shore, the didactically named Contemplation Circle eases our
reentry to the mainland by providing a designated space to decom-
press, process, and protectively distance oneself from the Memorial
and its grief. From the circle I gaze back toward the USS *Arizona*
Memorial and in other directions too, toward the mountains and at the
busy overpasses shuttling people to Ford Island.[88] The circle features
inspirational quotes engraved in stone. One tells how a lunar rainbow,
"the old Hawaiian omen for victory, arched over the dark city" the first
night after the attack. On another, a survivor of the USS *Oklahoma*
expresses survivor guilt: "Why them and not me?" A more haunting
quote from President Franklin D. Roosevelt implicates viewers: "We
are now in this war. We are all in it—all the way. Every single man,
woman and child is a partner in the most tremendous undertaking of
our American history." Especially in an era of what seems like inevitable, perpetual war, this reminder of complicity is food for thought,
although I suspect few visitors take this emotional baggage with them.

The compartmentalizing of our affective journey encourages the
implied tourist to have a cathartic experience. If you felt grief on
the USS *Arizona* Memorial, you can now take time to contemplate
your way out of it. You can allow your horror about war's tragedy to
be alleviated by the assurance of righteous nationalism, built in to
most other places on shore—including the Remembrance Circle that
stands next to the Contemplation Circle. The Remembrance Circle
signals that we're not here only to contemplate; but we're also here
to remember. Presumably, remembering means honoring. This spot
is the more high profile of the two shoreline circles, featured on the
"Things to Do" page of the website, and it fosters affective resolution
as it "pays tribute to the men, women, and children, both military
and civilian, who were killed as a result of the attack," with special
attention to Medal of Honor recipients. The overall "tone" or "global

organizing affect" is one of serenity, in part because of the ocean environment's affective agency.

Prime Minister Abe seemed to feel the spirit of aloha and the agency of the waters as he stood here: "The inlet gazing at us is tranquil as far as the eye can see," he claimed, pausing on the stand-alone phrase "Pearl Harbor," before adding: "It is precisely this beautiful inlet, shimmering like pearls, that is a symbol of tolerance and reconciliation."[89] It exchanges a "gaze" with us that is not strictly speaking, optic, but more broadly felt, an affective agency that is multisensory. Abe also noted the soundscape in his remarks: "If we listen closely we can make out the sound of restless waves, breaking and then retreating again. The calm inlet of brilliant blue is radiant with the gentle sparkle of the warm sun."[90] The harbor is affective—tranquil, beautiful, seemingly amenable to an agenda of peace.

For Kanaka Maoli, it's not so simple. Because Native Hawaiians' emotions about this ahupua'a are influenced by militarization and tied to loss, they are apt to include nostalgia and grief, as well as love and respect. Sarah Keli'ilolena Nākoa, a revered Kanaka Maoli writer, captures the beauty, the aloha, and nature's agency:

Beautiful Ka'ala, sublime in the calm
Famous mountain of 'Ewa
That fetches the wind of the land
The tradewind calls, "Here I am, beloved"

Osorio cites her book *Leio Momi o Ewa*, a set of stories, or *mo'olelo*,[91] though he admits that "Auntie Sarah" (as she is affectionately known) tells stories that can be "puzzling" even to students of the Hawaiian language. There is clearly an affective component to her prose that hints at a beauty only Kanaka Maoli can really understand, but even these readers "cannot see these places as Nākoa saw them in her youth."[92] The "terrain," Osorio explains, is so altered as to be "unfamiliar" to the younger generations of Hawaiians. I can only imagine how unsettling it feels for Kanaka Maoli to visit Pu'uloa today.

Probably due to some combination of NPS management—which steers us toward catharsis—and the natural environment's transmission of aloha, it's not likely that non-Native tourists walk away from Pearl

FIGURE 4.3. Techno-patriotism at Pearl Harbor

Harbor feeling unsettled, or in Ngai's word, "irritated." Perhaps I do not quite "fit" the implied tourist, though, because that's how I felt. For me, the broader complex raises more questions than it answers about war memorials and patriotism. How can tourists enjoy experimenting with submarine scopes and long-range missiles while, elsewhere in the same monument, grieving for dead soldiers? Can "love of country" coexist alongside the desire for peace at these sites, where military technology overshadows and consoles us for the lives lost in war? Are patriotism and aloha compatible affects? I suspect they can be, and I think again of Williams's "eco-patriotism," a more localized form of environmental love of country that refuses to scale up into a militaristic or fearful nationalism. To fully flesh out this idea will require a better sense of how memorials instantiate an ethics of scale—how the small-scale affects involved in public memory, the particular affective atmospheres formed on-site, turn into large-scale affects, which circulate more broadly.

The process of healing, too, needs to be rethought, with more attention to the ways that human emotions are shaped by our environments.

"Healing," White rightly notes, is "a word that tends to be overused in describing commemorative activities that allow some kind of narrative reworking of wartime conflicts." Not all "narrative reworking" leads to healing. Peace purchased at the expense of elision may provide the illusion of peace, but it is not real healing. Face-to-face encounters with people who are different from oneself is one way to facilitate the "personal and emotional transformations that [are] in fact literally healing."[93] Perhaps, with that in mind, giving more space to Indigenous perspectives on-site would help.[94] Currently, the few attempts to include these perspectives are steeped in nostalgia, which may unsettle viewers by pointing out the tension between an ideal, lost, environment and the real, militarized, one—but at the risk of rendering Native peoples themselves obsolete.

For instance, the display titled "Bountiful and Revered" describes Native Hawaiian uses of the fertile landscape and oyster-filled waters, beginning by telling us Pearl Harbor has always "been valued" as a "place of immense worth." The fact that these waters "were" home to various Hawaiian gods and goddesses renders the culture past tense, along with the "abundant" fish and pipi (pearl oysters) that are no longer so.[95] The story of the *kupuna* (respected elder) and the "warning from Kaʻahupāhau," the shark goddess, reads as a superstitious tale that, together with the photos of fisherpeople on the undeveloped shoreline, come across as a "folkloric remnant of a vanishing culture, a fragile artifact of knowledge to be preserved,"[96] especially when contrasted with the gigantic torpedoes on shore. Kajihiro explains that this *moʻolelo* has been mobilized by the U.S. Navy and the media to legitimize military presence on the island and "represent itself as her successor in the role of benevolent chief and vigilant guardian."[97] Even while the NPS display probably intends to let Native voices tell the story, Kaʻahupāhau risks being appropriated as "a cultural artifact of colonial nostalgia."[98]

One of the biggest challenges for the NPS going forward is how to include these voices and stories without absorbing them in a history that naturalizes military occupation. New generations of Kanaka Maoli, Osorio hopes, might be able to "reclaim" their *aina*, their land, "spiritually and emotionally" if not physically.[99] If the NPS is to have a role in promoting this particular kind of reconciliation—spiritual and emotional reconciliation for Native Hawaiians—then it still has some difficult work to do. Addressing the generational rifts Osorio identifies is one place to start. How best to reach out to the youngest generation, to welcome them back to their homeland, despite its dramatic alterations?[100] How would their presence, their history, complicate things, if they were included more prominently?

Welcoming them in person at the contemporary site, integrating them as a visible and vocal presence in the way survivors of the attack have historically been, might be one way to create a space for Indigenous voices to return and articulate their ancestral claims on this place. Veterans who survived the attacks have been key figures at the site, and they've been able to speak to the military history in ways that often refuse an easy patriotism. As White puts it, many veterans "navigated emotional transitions from antipathy to empathy" and their lives "embody much of the emotional complexity of Pearl Harbor memory."[101] However, the Monument finds itself at a transitional moment today, as more veteran survivors are passing on. White explains we are losing their diverse perspectives on the dominant historical narrative— ironically, at the same time when the NPS is turning to narratives of peace and actively seeking to include more voices.

The loss of survivors means more reliance on veterans' written stories, whether memoir or fiction—such as novels like Jones's—and on images and recordings like those the NPS shows in the galleries and includes on the narrative tour. Without the in-person presence of survivors, other features of the site will wield more emotional impact. The physical environment, including the natural features of the landscape and the "things" in it, are all the more influential in shaping the tourist experience. We need to understand better how things take over the role of the survivors, and so, how "thing power" affects visitors as person-to-person empathy decreases. We must consider how "agentic capacities"[102] are affective as well as, or sometimes instead of, narrative. Torpedoes, missiles, salvaged anchors, and Trees of Life—as well as oceans, trade winds, palm trees, and plumeria flowers—have affective as well as narrative agency. This matters at memorials, certainly, but even at sites that aren't so neatly compartmentalized, and even in environments that aren't paradise.

Notes

1. I'm grateful to Steve Johnson, Geoffrey M. White, Daniel Martinez, Kyle Kajihiro, and Steve Sumida for help with this chapter.

2. Some conservatives derided this diplomatic visit as part of an "apology tour" that reduced U.S. power and influence in the world. For a version of this critique, see John Bolton, "Obama's Shameful Apology Tour Lands in Hiroshima," *The New York Post*, May 26, 2016. http://nypost.com/2016/05/26/obamas-shameful-apology-tour-lands-in-hiroshima/. Accessed 7 February, 2017.

3. Japanese leaders had visited Pearl Harbor prior to Abe's visit, but none had gone to the USS *Arizona* Memorial itself. See "Japan PM Shinzo Abe offers Pearl Harbor condolences," *BBC News*, December 28, 2016. http://www.bbc.co.uk/news/world-asia-38438714. Accessed 1 February, 2017.

4. Citations are from full text of speech as printed in Michael S. Schmidt, "Japanese Leader Offers Condolences in Visit to Pearl Harbor," *The New York Times*, 27 December 27, 2016. https://www.nytimes.com/2016/12/26/world/asia/pearl-harbor-japan-shinzo-abe-visit.html. Accessed 1 February, 2017.

5. http://www.wsj.com/articles/pearl-harbor-survivors-gather-for-75th-anniversary-reunion-1481106611. Accessed 7 December, 2016.

6. http://pearlharbor75thanniversary.com/full-schedule-of-events/. Accessed 7 December, 2016.

7. Sun elaborates: "Anniversary rhetoric forgets how, in an atmosphere of fear and overwhelming, inexplicable defeat, it was impossible to separate the call to remember from vicious, dehumanizing racial stereotypes that compared 'Japs' to apes, rats and vermin. Such racialist imagery contributed to American policies" including internment. Sun's article challenges us to confront our selective memory. Sun, "With 75 years of perspective, we can re-examine the legacy of Pearl Harbor even as we honor those who served." *The Spokesman Review*, 4 December, 2016. http://www.spokesman.com/stories/2016/dec/04/with-75-years-of-perspective-we-can-re-examine-the/. Accessed 7 December, 2016.

8. Chief of Interpretation Daniel Martinez conveyed this history to me by phone on 23 February, 2017.

9. Jon Kamakawiwoʻole Osorio explains that the "hero" designation extends also to the brave men who protested the occupation and ecological destruction of Kahoʻolawe in the late 1970s. Osorio, "Memorializing Puʻuloa and Remembering Pearl Harbor," in *Militarized Currents: Toward a Decolonized Future in Asia and the Pacific*, eds. Setsu Shigematsu and Keith L. Camacho (Minneapolis: University of Minnesota Press, 2010), 9.

10. Mr. Martinez talks about reconciliation and ceremonies in the following public interview as well: http://kcbx.org/post/national-park-service-historian-daniel-martinez-s-30-year-wwii-and-december-7th-odyssey. Accessed 27 February, 2017.

11. https://www.nps.gov/valr/index.htm. Accessed 7 December, 2016.

12. Geoffrey White, *Memorializing Pearl Harbor: Unfinished Histories and The Work of Remembrance* (Durham: Duke University Press, 2016), 125.

13. White, 22 (my emphasis). White's dedicated participation at ceremonies, planning meetings, educational programs, and more—and his interviews with key players involved in site management—make his book a crucial resource. He offers a detailed account of the site's managerial history and nuanced interpretations of key events, strategies, and concerns at the Memorial over time, including the role of veterans and other survivors, the two versions of the documentary film shown to visitors, and a controversial educational program White helped develop.

14. The majority of tourists at Pearl Harbor are visiting as part of a longer vacation on Oahu. NPS survey numbers say 58 percent of visitors are on vacation, another 10 percent are on the island for "other" purposes, including weddings and other social priorities, and only 7 percent are on the island primarily to visit the Memorial. Wayde Morse and Margaret Littlejohn, USS Arizona Memorial Visitor Study, Summer 2000, University of Idaho Cooperative Park Studies Unit, Visitor Services Project (Moscow: University of Idaho, 2001).

15. Kyle Kajihiro. 2014. "'Becoming Pearl Harbor': A 'Lost Geography' of American Empire." Master's thesis, department of geography, University of Hawai'i, 28.

16. For the full text of the law, see: www.capitol.hawaii.gov [L 1986, c 202, §1]. Accessed 22 February, 2017.

17. Kajihiro, 1.

18. Kajihiro, 2. Kajihiro reads the Memorial itself as participating in this project. He suggests the Memorial site reinforces ideals of American innocence and exceptionalism, and rewrites the role of the U.S. in WWII as a defensive and reactionary one, rather than an imperialistic one. For a broader study of the many ways the memory of Pearl Harbor has functioned politically, see Emily S. Rosenberg, A Date Which Will Live: Pearl Harbor in American Memory (Durham: Duke University Press, 2004).

19. For a history of this ahupua'a, see P. Christian Klieger, "Nā Maka O Hālawa: A History of Hālawa Ahupua'a, O'ahu" (Honolulu: Bishop Museum Technical Report 7, 1995).

20. Allan Seiden, From Fishponds to Warships: Pearl Harbor: A Complete Illustrated History (Honolulu: Mutual Publishing, 2001).

21. Osorio, 14, 4.

22. Osorio, 12. He goes on to explain this "grace" as "a recognition of likeness that most of us, engaged in professions that do not require their kind of sacrifice, will never know." He adds that his parents' sense of "solidarity with American soldiers and sailors simply did not cross the boundaries of [his] generations' whole" (13).

23. "Waikā," for instance—a chant "composed to commemorate the warriors of O'ahu who fell from the Pali in the face of Kamehameha's advance almost 150 years before the samurai in their fragile aircraft descended into Pu'uloa"—depicts the "invading warriors express[ing] a great love, respect, and aloha" for their dying opponents. He credits the interpretation of this mele to ethnomusicology student and recording artist Aaron Sala (14).

24. For instance, Jones's soldiers use the slang of their time—gooks, wops, Japs, and other derogatory terms for ethnic groups. At the same time, he was unusually

frank, for his time, about gay sexual encounters. Censored material from Jones's original manuscript, including references to gay sex and abundant four-letter words, has recently been included in a restored version of his novel. See: Julie Bosman, "Author's Heirs Uncensor a Classic War Novel," *The New York Times*, April 4, 2011. http://www.nytimes.com/2011/04/05/books/james-joness-from-here-to-eternity-is-uncensored.html. Accessed 1 March, 2017.

25. Some continue to laud its "shocking" language and its frank "depiction of the casual cruelty and daily repression inflicted by the United States Army." James Ellroy commends the characters, who are "driven by deep hungers," and the book's capacity to "encapsulate huge themes within the brutal framework of daily tedium and the aching restlessness of the spirit." Ellroy calls the text a "wildly exotic picture"— not so much of the "tourist-trap island" itself as of the "tortured men and women" living there. James Ellroy, "Damned 'From Here to Eternity,'" *NPR* "You must read this" series, November 23, 2009. Accessed 5 March, 2017.

26. Jennifer Ladino, *Reclaiming Nostalgia: Longing for Nature in American Literature* (Charlottesville: University of Virginia Press, 2012).

27. James Jones, 1951. *From Here to Eternity* (New York: Penguin, 2011). 225.

28. Thomas Patin, "America in Ruins: Parks, Poetics, and Politics," in *Observation Points: The Visual Poetics of National Parks*, ed. Thomas Patin, (Minneapolis: University of Minnesota Press, 2012), 270.

29. Email interview with Steve Johnson. 4 January, 2015.

30. See White's fourth chapter, "Theming America at War," especially 179–182.

31. White, 199.

32. White, 61.

33. White, 167–8. The word "playground" comes from a local veteran survivor, who commented to White that today's site feels, to him, "like a playground" (284).

34. White, 112.

35. White, 28.

36. Ibid.

37. White, 169.

38. Martinez, phone interview, 23 February, 2017.

39. Stephen H. Sumida, "A Narrative of Kuki'iahu and its Erasures," *Pacific and American Studies* 2 (2002),109.

40. Sumida, 109.

41. Kajihiro, 21.

42. Jones, 224.

43. For comparison, see Joan Didion's description of the hotel as a place at which she and her family are "quarantined" (fighting off a divorce). She describes the Royal not as "exclusive" but rather as "inclusive": its roped-off section of beach says the people inside the rope are "our kind," a spatially enforced elitism and claim to old-money security. Joan Didion, "In the Islands," in *The White Album*, 136.

44. Robert Lacy, "*From Here to Eternity* and the American Experience," *Sewanee Review* (2007): 642.

45. Jones, 861.

46. Kajihiro calls the show "exoticizing," 18. I have not been able to determine how much of Jones's version of Edwards's broadcast is real and how much is invented.

47. Jones, 853.

48. Jones, 853.

49. Jones, 855.

50. Jones, 828.

51. A "flashbulb memory" is a phrase psychologists use to describe the mental "snapshot" we take when we first read, see, or hear about an especially shocking event. Roger Brown and James Kulik, "Flashbulb Memories," *Cognition* 5, no. 1 (1977): 73–99.

52. Jones, 828. Interestingly, one of the first observations the men make—even after seeing a boy shot down right in front of them—is in praise of the Japanese technology. "'Say! That's pretty clever,' somebody said. 'Our planes is still usin web machinegun belts that they got to carry back home!' The two men started showing their finds to the men around them" and collecting "souvenirs" (830–1).

53. Jones, 839.

54. Jones, 845.

55. Jones, 848–50.

56. Jones, 912.

57. Jones, 902.

58. White, 127.

59. Even on the USS *Missouri*, the site of surrender, the bombs aren't mentioned. In White's words, the *Missouri* is less a "Memorial" than a "'gee-whiz' experience conveying the ship's technological capabilities, especially its firepower," 174.

60. The underwater Memorials in her study, sculptures by Jason de Caires Taylor, offer a form of "memorializing—as an anticipatory mourning—the multi-species lives of the future of the Anthropocene." Elizabeth DeLoughrey, "Submarine Futures of the Anthropocene," *Comparative Literature* 69.1 (2017), 36.

61. DeLoughrey, 37.

62. Didion, 141.

63. The park website gives 4,000 as a daily average. https://www.nps.gov/valr/plan-yourvisit/hours.htm. Accessed 10 March, 2017. Visitation statistics for this and other NPS sites are available online at https://irma.nps.gov/Stats/.

64. White, 35.

65. Michael Slackman, *Remembering Pearl Harbor: The Story of the USS* Arizona *Memorial* (Honolulu: Pacific Historic Parks, 2012), 42.

66. Slackman, 45.

67. Updating Edward Abbey's use of "industrial tourism," I suggested "technological tourism" is a more apt phrase to describe today's visitors. *Reclaiming Nostalgia*, xii.

68. Thirty-six percent of survey respondents reported feeling "crowded," and another 27 percent chose "somewhat crowded" to represent their experience. Other choices included "very crowded" (17 percent) and "extremely crowded" (13 percent). Far

fewer felt "hurried," with forty percent reporting feeling "somewhat hurried" but 45 percent saying they felt "not at all hurried." Still, the Memorial was the top location called out for prompting that feeling, with thirty-two mentions—ten times as many as the other handful of places identified in the survey. Morse and Littlejohn, 53–55.

69. As White puts it: "the quality of the sacred is not inherent in the material remains of the ship, the shrine, the museum, or any other part of the physicality of the *Arizona* memorial. It is a feature of the relationship between persons and places—a quality that may or may not emerge as people engage with the site," 168–9.

70. "Pearl Harbor: A Nation Remembers." (Honolulu: *Honolulu Star Advertiser*), 7. This is a souvenir newspaper given out on-site.

71. Didion, 145. At the NM, the Barracks themselves are reduced to flattened out representations on maps and newspapers, even while military technology dominates the shore.

72. Ibid.

73. Didion, 149.

74. Rebecca Solnit, "Water," in *A Companion to American Environmental History*, edited by Douglas Cazaux Sackman (Oxford: Blackwell Publishing Ltd, 2010), 95.

75. Slackman, 42.

76. James P. Delgado, "Significance: Memorials, Myths and Symbols," in *Submerged Cultural Resources Study: USS* Arizona *Memorial and Pearl Harbor National Historic Landmark.* ed. Daniel J. Lenihan (Washington D.C., Department of the Interior), 178.

77. Delgado, 178.

78. DeLoughrey, 38.

79. Delgado, 180.

80. Delgado, 180.

81. I understand there is a narrative display next to the shrine room now, but it was not built when I visited.

82. Kaufman, 3.

83. Cited in Jerome A. Kaufman, *Renewal at the Place of Black Tears* (Issaquah: Visual World Impressions, 2012), 3.

84. I've long wondered about the politics of this gendered language for military ships, but I haven't the space to explore it here.

85. EPA websites provide details on the site, including a lengthy list of contaminants in the 12,600 acres of land and water now occupied by the U.S. military. https://cumulis.epa.gov/supercpad/cursites/csitinfo.cfm?id=0904481.

86. Delgado, 170. Preis apparently believed the U.S. was a "pacifist nation," only roped into war when "aroused by [the] shock" of a "first blow." Delgado, 176.

87. Teresa Bergman, "Can Patriotism Be Carved in Stone?" in *Observation Points: The Visual Poetics of National Parks*, ed. Thomas Patin (Minneapolis: University of Minnesota Press, 2012).

88. The USS *Oklahoma* Memorial is on Ford Island, near the *Missouri*. In the minimalist tradition Maya Lin made famous with the Vietnam Veterans Memorial,

this one features a black granite wall and simple white marble standards meant to symbolize the deceased's eternal "manning the rails," a "display [of] respect and honor." The site bulletin commits an entire side to a rhetorical "wall of names," and it draws on kinship narratives: "These men were not only sailors and Marines, they were 429 brothers, sons, husbands, fathers." The *Oklahoma* is a unique and evocative Memorial, perhaps even more so because it's off the beaten path a bit; I will have to save it for another essay.

89. "Japan PM Shinzo Abe offers Pearl Harbor condolences," *BBC News*, December 28, 2016. Accessed 7 February, 2016. Obama also noted the water at the anniversary commemoration; he referred to the "waters that still weep."

90. His full remarks can be found here: https://www.nytimes.com/2016/12/27/world/asia/shinzo-abe-text-pearl-harbor.html. Accessed 8 September, 2017.

91. Kajihiro notes that this word is "richly suggestive of Foucault's concept of *discourse*," because it alludes to "the power and performativity of language" and the production of knowledge as situated (25).

92. Osorio, 4.

93. White, 96.

94. Indigenous scholars, too, provide useful perspectives on healing and trauma within a colonial, neoliberal context. See, for instance, Dian Million's *Therapeutic Nations: Healing in an Age of Indigenous Human Rights* (Tucson: The University of Arizona Press, 2013).

95. Kajihiro explains that from a Western perspective the loss of the pipi is due to "accelerated sedimentation caused by upland deforestation and erosion"; from the viewpoint of oral historian Mary Kawena Pukui, this resource loss was "due to the broken covenant of reciprocity and care that had previously maintained the environmental balance" (41).

96. Kajihiro, 19.

97. Kajihiro, 39.

98. Kajihiro, 115.

99. Osorio, 14. Kahijiro ends his thesis with a hopeful story about a friend and Native activist, Terrilee Nāpua Kekoʻolani, who finds the strength and a voice with which to tell stories about the land prior to military invasion.

100. Osorio, 13. Osorio suspects that "the United States has created a target on these islands to make certain that the first place attacked will not be part of their homeland"; this justifiable suspicion makes Kanaka Maoli an especially tough audience to engage.

101. White, 240. Emotionality is one of the things that historians and their audiences use to differentiate between a professional, unbiased historical account and a personal memory. Ironically, the very thing that lends authenticity to a survivor—his or her emotional memory of the event—can discount their credibility. As White puts it, their authority is "undercut by the same premises that give it force" (59).

102. Serenella Iovino and Serpil Oppermann, "Material Ecocriticism: Materiality, Agency, and Models of Narrativity," *Ecozon@* 3.1 (2012): 75–91.

CHAPTER FIVE

Mountains, Monuments, and Other Matter

Reckoning with Racism and Simulating Shame at
Manzanar National Historic Site

When seven-year-old Jeanne Wakatsuki Houston arrived at the Manzanar incarceration camp[1] after riding all day on a Greyhound with drawn shades, the first thing she saw was "a yellow swirl across a blurred, reddish setting sun. The bus was being pelted by what sounded like splattering rain. It wasn't rain. This was [her] first look at something [she] would soon know very well, a billowing flurry of dust and sand churned up by the wind through Owens Valley."[2]

Houston describes her first impression of the arid valley that would be her home for the next three-and-a-half years as a "swirl" that is both environmental and emotional. She continues to bring together environment and affect throughout her memoir, *Farewell to Manzanar*, the best-known account of life at this first of ten camps—a site where more than 11,000 Japanese Americans were imprisoned, beginning in March 1942.[3] *Farewell to Manzanar*'s frank, observant young narrator recounts the homesickness, humiliation, and racism, as well as the cultural, economic, and personal losses experienced by those incarcerated. Houston also describes how the incarcerees formed communities and reshaped their environment—a remote 640-acre plot of desert in the shadow of California's Sierra Nevada, crammed with 504 barracks, 72 latrines, 36 mess halls, 36 recreation halls, 36 laundry buildings, and 36 ironing rooms and enclosed by barbed wire—into something more inhabitable, even more beautiful.

In 1992, fifty years after Manzanar opened, the NPS began managing Manzanar as a National Historic Site (NHS). NPS officials worked closely with former incarcerees, including Houston, to design an interpretive center that would accurately represent life in the camp. As chief of interpretation Alisa Lynch explained to me, one of the NPS managers' goals is to make visitors "feel the era," to facilitate a physical and emotional sense of the camp experience that is historically authentic.[4] To this end, the interpretive center, housed in the camp's original auditorium building, collects diverse artifacts: a home plate from the baseball field, a Kendo helmet and gloves, and children's marbles, along with news clippings, ID tags, and other everyday objects from the period. Vintage photos, film footage, and audio recordings re-create the era. The result is more museum than visitor center; education, not recreation, is the priority.

Resonating with Houston's final book chapter title, "Ten Thousand Stories," one particularly tall and bright NPS display panel reads "One Camp, Ten Thousand Lives; One Camp, Ten Thousand Stories." Since, as Houston observes, incarceration relied on homogenizing and dehumanizing people ("You cannot deport 110,000 people unless you have stopped seeing individuals"[5]), making individual stories public is an ethical, political act of recovery, a way of rehumanizing the people involved. It is also savvy strategy since, as psychological research shows, humans respond more emotionally to stories about a single person than they do to statistics or to narratives featuring more than one individual. Knowing that "[o]ur sympathy for suffering and loss declines precipitously when we are presented with increasing numbers of victims," the NPS managers at Manzanar use personal stories to make visitors care about the more than "ten thousand lives" impacted—without risking the "psychic numbing" that can set in when we feel overwhelmed.[6]

Stories are still being unearthed today by archaeologists and historians on-site, while others are gathered in ever-expanding archives such as densho.org. These memoirs, photographic essays, and interviews are intimately connected to the natural and built environment of the place. This chapter foregrounds the environmental features of the relocation experience—the extreme desert weather, the mountain vistas, the rock gardens, the barracks, the guard towers, and the barbed wire—in order to enhance existing accounts of Manzanar with a perspective that accentuates the impacts of the natural and built environments at this complex site. I cite several of the available oral histories, but mostly I use *Farewell to Manzanar* and Houston's recent essay "Crossing Boundaries"[7] to frame my analysis. Not only did her work directly influence my encounter with the site, but it also describes more keenly than most other published accounts I've found the affective agency of physical matter at Manzanar.

A complex "archive of public affect,"[8] Manzanar is ideally suited for analysis of how problematic histories are negotiated publicly and in relation to multiple scales of identity, including personal, cultural, and national. Like the NPS managers, I am invested in the "feel" of this fraught historical site. Specifically, I'm curious to know: How does the physical matter at this historic site generate affect? What kinds of mixed, conflicting, or "noncathartic"[9] emotions are promoted here? How does affect accumulate here—how is it embedded in landscapes, buildings, monuments, and written displays? How do objects—flowers, rocks, origami cranes, broken glass, handwritten letters, and artifacts from the 1940s—that reside, circulate, or are left at this site affect visitors? How do the natural landscapes and built structures at Manzanar facilitate emotions about incarceration and so shape attitudes about nationalism, war, and racism in the contemporary U.S.?

Manzanar is surely, as Erika Doss claims, a "site of shame"[10] that, at least to a degree, troubles American patriotism. At Manzanar, the implied tourist is, among other things, educated (or knowledge-seeking) if perhaps not yet well-informed about the history of incarceration, English speaking, and an outsider to incarceration, *not* a descendant of an incarceree—criteria I happen to fit. In the interpretive center, she will be confronted not just with diverse stories about individual incarcerees but also—on signs like "The Roots of Racism" and in primary documents containing hateful language about Japanese—with the fear and racism that enabled the camps to happen. The implied tourist, then, is also amenable to a critique of racism, not averse to feeling strong emotions about what happened here, and perhaps even open to the shame of implication. This center, with its carefully curated artifacts, provocative visual and written exhibits, and compelling film, *Remembering Manzanar*, deserves a full-length study of its own.

But my focus on landscape and built structures means I will stay outside, where there is plenty to see, to learn, and to feel. The rebuilt

barracks, excavated rock gardens, and cemetery monument exert affective agency in ways that are sometimes ironic, sometimes harmonious,
but always profound. Doss is right that, rather than upholding national
narratives of progress and democracy, Manzanar "admit[s] the compli-
cations, contradictions, and obligations of American national identity"
and "reckon[s] with the nation's ghosts."[11] In what follows, I track how
this "reckoning" happens at affective registers—textual, corporeal, and
especially, environmental—and how "contradictions" are embedded in,
and even emanate from, Manzanar's physical environment. I probe the
connection between shame and patriotism, and I suggest shame is only
one emotion that might "stick" at the site. A closer look at its environments and objects reveals more nuance to this affective archive. The
affective atmosphere at Manzanar is capable of producing a range of
responses, including loss, frustration, or grief, as well as peace, inspiration, vitality, or redemption. While the built environment is designed
to encourage shame through an embodied simulation of what the incarcerees felt at Manzanar, the natural landscapes complicate that feeling. Irony and affective dissonance, rather than a reflexive patriotism,
are the likely result.

When I arrive at Manzanar in June 2014, the first thing that strikes me
is a guard tower, its large searchlight pointed right at the entrance road.
Even without armed gunmen, the imposing tower carries cultural associations of war, machine guns, and Nazi concentration camps. With its
incongruous linear symmetry, its tone is threatening and cold. It feels
unnatural against the textured Owens Valley landscapes: the Alabama
Hills—odd rock formations, reminding me of the seaside drip castles
I made as a child and carrying connotations of Southern pride and
Western film history; the familiar tufts of pastel green against the rust-
brown ground of the sagebrush flats; and the dominant Sierra Nevada
range, where snowfields dot Mt. Williamson, and other "majestic"[12]
pinnacles tower thousands of feet above the valley.

    I am relieved not to be greeted by "a billowing flurry of dust and
sand," like Houston was, although even this early-summer day is threatening to be a hot one. The Owens Valley is arguably a beautiful place,

FIGURE 5.1. Reconstructed guard tower at Manzanar entrance; photo courtesy of the National Park Service

if not an especially comfortable one. Like Houston, many incarcerees recall the agency of the weather in the form of extreme temperatures—the valley reaches temperatures of more than 100 degrees Fahrenheit in summer and drops below freezing in winter—and the persistent wind that swept sand into bunkhouses, mess halls, and bodily crevices.[13] The valley's history is as hostile as its environment. Los Angeles began acquiring water rights to the Owens Valley in 1905 and has since siphoned its water, draining Owens Lake, creating epic dust pollution and displacing the farmers and cattle ranchers who were making a living there. But farmers and ranchers were only the most recently displaced people. The region was originally home to Paiutes, who were forcibly displaced by prospectors and miners, who in turn gave way to the ranchers and farmers whose livelihood evaporated along with the water. This is a classic Western story: Indigenous people pushed out by white settlers, an effort to turn a frontier into a garden, a political battle over water rights, an urban center sucking resources from small towns. Today, the valley's recreational draw obscures the region's history of displacement, much the way the dozens of Western films shot in the

Alabama Hills—and the celebration of these films in the nearby town of Lone Pine—gloss the troubling conflicts of the "Old West."

The Owens Valley feels vast and cinematic enough to accommodate all of these histories. It is a liminal place between the lowest and highest points in the contiguous United States: Death Valley's Badwater Basin (-282 ft.) and Mount Whitney (14,500 ft.).[14] Mount Whitney isn't visible from Manzanar, though I'd spotted it the previous evening when I drove from Las Vegas through Death Valley to Lone Pine, the "small tree-filled town where a lot of mountain buffs turn off for the Mount Whitney Portal."[15] A longtime "mountain buff" myself, I feel the peaks beckoning with the promise of visual and bodily rewards, dramatic views, heightened senses, and access to water. On this trip, though, I am here to interpret the mountains, not to play in them. A scholar-visitor embarking on a grant-funded research project, and with no familial connection to the incarceration experience, I am hyperaware of my outsider status. I feel like an affect alien, bringing an inappropriate love for big mountains to this site of shame. And yet, my personal associations of mountains with freedom, mobility, and the opportunity to reach a summit are not unique. They are also cultural, shared by many other white, economically secure, able-bodied Americans and promoted by dominant versions of Western history. Perhaps I am not an affect alien after all, but an embodiment of the implied tourist, the very demographic hailed by the site. One thing is immediately clear: These associations with mountains are in tension with the barbed wire surrounding the one square-mile housing area. I would soon discover other similar ironies conveyed by the environment itself.

Arriving by vehicle, as most of Manzanar's 85,000 annual visitors do, I drive through two restored sentry posts—like the guard tower, physical reminders that this was a prison—before pulling into the main parking lot. When I get out and close the car door, the sharp sound reverberates for miles. As I crunch across gravel and approach the interpretive center, a light breeze carries the warm smell of sagebrush. A sleek raven caws as it glides overhead. This is a quiet place, with an atmosphere of "loneliness and vulnerability"[16] Wallace Stegner notes is characteristic of small Western towns. It is hard to imagine thousands of people fenced inside. I gather my impressions as I walk slowly toward the interpretive center, unlocking my gaze from the mountains long enough to notice an object in my path: a waist-high conglomerate stone holding the California Registered Historical Landmark plaque. If we haven't yet let ourselves think the phrase "concentration camp," there it is, unapologetically, on the plaque, along with language naming "hysteria, racism and economic exploitation" as causes of incarceration. Bullet holes and hatchet marks on the plaque's surface attest to the local community's own hysteria and racism as well as the perpetual threat of violence embodied by the guard towers. The tone of this marker sets the tone for the site: The rough conglomerate and scarred plaque match the harsh, confrontational narrative. The many visitors who stop to read this text[17] have been fairly warned: This is a solemn place, one where terrible things happened. The plaque sets us up for one of the NPS's primary goals—"getting most visitors to the exhibition to feel compassion and sympathy for the incarcerees."[18]

Guilt, shame, and anger are also appropriate responses. As Martha Nussbaum explains, guilt acknowledges a wrong that can be righted with reparations, whereas shame recognizes a flawed trait in oneself, a "falling short of some desired ideal."[19] Guilt requires an admission of personal responsibility, and I wonder if many visitors to Manzanar NHS really feel that. As I suggested in my analysis of Sand Creek Massacre NHS, some people have a hard time feeling responsible for something they haven't directly done. Even if one does feel guilt, a Manzanar visitor might easily brush it aside upon learning that an official apology, and reparations, have already been made: After a lengthy campaign spearheaded by the Japanese American Citizens League, the Civil Liberties Act was passed in 1998 and signed by Ronald Reagan (over substantial Republican opposition), providing both a formal apology and monetary compensation of $20,000 to surviving victims.[20]

Shame is more complicated but perhaps more likely here. Some incarcerees express shame about their Manzanar experience in Nussbaum's terms, as an internalized flaw. Houston describes feeling shame as a "continuous unnamed ache," a determination to endure racism because "something about [her] deserved it."[21] In the words of former incarceree, activist, and founder of the Manzanar Committee Sue Kunitomi Embrey, many incarcerees "buried depressing camp memories because there was a feeling of shame, that they had done something wrong."[22] Although Nussbaum lists shame as one of "compassion's enemies"—in part because it can be divisive[23]—I would argue that shame is potentially a more useful emotion for engaging American racism than guilt, which implies a quick fix. Shame is also a stronger possibility for visitors to Manzanar who recognize "hysteria, racism and economic exploitation" as ongoing problems—a "falling short" of the "desired ideals" claimed by a liberal democracy—and are willing to see themselves as implicated in them. Ideally, Manzanar has the potential to be a very particular site of shame, then: one that might alleviate the shame of one group (the incarcerees' shame at being racism's objects) and transfer shame—about the enduring reality of racism in the U.S.—to visitors who aren't in that group. But how likely is this affective transfer to occur?

I'm tempted to agree with Doss when she claims redemptive potential for shame: "Shame can be reparative when individuals, communities, and nations recognize that injustices have been committed against others, that those injustices continue to have power, and that current understandings of self and national identity are complicit with those injustices."[24] Still, I'm not convinced that, in practice, Manzanar, or any site of public memory, can facilitate shame in all these ways. The first step of Doss's three-step recognition process, acknowledging injustices against others, is fairly easy; indeed, it's a prerequisite for establishing a memorial site like Manzanar. But the next two steps—recognizing that injustice is ongoing and that the way we think of ourselves and our nation feeds into it in the present—are much more difficult, especially when the NPS, an agency mandated to be both democratic and politically neutral, is responsible for managing the past.

I turn again to Sara Ahmed (whom Doss cites only briefly, in her chapter's concluding remarks about shame's redemptive potential) for help with understanding how shame works collectively, in relation to national identity. Ahmed differentiates between shame and guilt in a similar way as Nussbaum, but Ahmed plays up the bodily dimensions of shame. Derived from the verb "to cover," shame involves the wish to be concealed, to be re-covered after one has been exposed. She explains: "In shame, more than my action is at stake: *the badness of an action is transferred to me*, such that I feel myself to be bad and to have been 'found' or 'found out' as bad by others."[25] Her approach is especially pertinent to sites of memory, at which "we need to think about what shame does to the bodies whose surfaces burn with the apparent immediacy of its affect before we can think about what it means for nations and international civil society to give shame an 'official reality' in acts of speech"[26]—or, I'd add, in other kinds of rhetorical recognitions. With this in mind, I wonder: Does the physical environment at Manzanar transfer shame to the bodies of tourists, or does it constrain that transfer? Does it implicate us in, or alleviate us of, shame by associating shame with the nation itself? If the latter, then any culpability at the individual scale lies in citizenship alone, and that feeling can be quickly dispensed with. A quick "reconciliation" rather than a true "healing" might be the likely outcome.

Shame requires seeing oneself through the eyes of an idealized other—someone "whose view 'matters' to [us]"[27] Who, then, is that "someone" at Manzanar? Does a visitor feel ashamed by the NPS itself, or by the rangers in uniform who represent the agency? Is it other visitors, who might call us out for not performing the authentic affect, whether grief or shame or something else? Ahmed might say we're put in a strange position, as tourists: we are in a "double, if not paradoxical position" of being both the one who's ashamed (exposed, "caught out") and the one who's exposing the shame, who's "catching out" the wrongdoers.[28] She claims that feeling shame for one's country's failure to live up to an ideal—in this case, the failure to uphold ideals of democracy and multiculturalism by giving in to fear and racism—is really a way of expressing patriotism, "the subject's love of nation."[29] At memory sites like this one, then, "our shame *means that we mean well*, and can work to reproduce the nation as an ideal" in the present.[30] This is widely applicable to NPS visitors, many of whom, I'd argue, feel a sense of self-righteousness. After all, we are doing our democratic duty by choosing to spend our leisure time visiting a historic site. At Manzanar NHS, we are educating ourselves about an unsavory aspect of the nation's history. We are always already off the hook, it seems, especially as the incarceration recedes further into the past.

My attention to the material world of Manzanar extends Ahmed's theories of shame (for which her data set are texts and speech acts) with attention to the nondiscursive, to the physical environment that also shapes affective response. There are small ways that the physical environment at Manzanar promotes a shame that is not necessarily slouching toward patriotic pride. Many features of the built environment are designed to inspire "compassion and sympathy" for—or perhaps even empathy with—the incarcerees.[31] The built environment perhaps has the best chance of making visitors actually feel shame. The natural landscape, I find, tends to alleviate our responsibility. At the same time, the enduring mountains might help some visitors connect past and present, prompting us to see continuities between our shameful past and our less-than-just present.

———◆◆◆———

Visitors who, like me, were raised on a cultural diet of Western icons including John Ford Westerns and the Grand Canyon may be conditioned to see the Owens Valley as a kind of narrative agent, sending "messages that seem as true and incontrovertible as the mountains and plains."[32] As Jane Tompkins describes in her classic *West of Everything*, the Western landscape is a place of "power, endurance [and] rugged majesty," and the desert is "a hard place to be," a place where you'll find "no shelter, no water, no rest, no comfort."[33] Incarcerees recount similar stories of hardship; they had some basic comforts—shelter, water—but lacked others, like privacy. Despite the close quarters, many families grew apart. Most poignantly, a few parents mourned the death of a child who had volunteered to fight for the very government that had imprisoned their family.

These individual stories are narratives in a strict sense; they appear throughout the interpretive center and on the outdoor displays. Mountains, however, do not write the "messages" they send, even if our impressions of them are culturally inflected. While taking seriously the material ecocritical move that "broadens and enhances the narrative potentialities of reality in terms of an intrinsic performativity of elements,"[34] I nevertheless contend that much of matter's agency, its "intrinsic performativity," is affective and not, strictly speaking, narrative. I will turn now toward the affective agency of the mountains and other environmental features of Manzanar, to show how affect works sometimes alongside narrative and sometimes in place of it, as an intense corporeal response to environmental features—something felt but not always storied.

Incarcerees lived in an environment that was circumscribed and ironic, a "community built on contradictions."[35] Perhaps the biggest irony of Manzanar, as Karin Higa and Tim B. Wride note, was the "irony that their 'all-American' experience [was] taking place in confinement."[36] The fact that incarcerees worked jobs, founded churches, held dances, went to school, published a newspaper (the ironically named *Manzanar Free Press*), and played sports—all while behind barbed wire—must have given an ironic tinge to daily life. It's not hard to imagine how the incarcerees felt when they danced to the Andrews Sisters' popular song "Don't Fence Me In" on Saturday nights.

Irony tends to be associated with consciously recognized incongruities, a tension between what is said and what is unsaid, a cognitive contradiction of some kind. But Linda Hutcheon has long observed "both intellectual and affective" powers of irony. Irony "'happens' for you (or better, you *make* it 'happen') when two meanings, one said and the other unsaid, come together."[37] There is no reason these meanings can't be conveyed through affect rather than, or prior to, being conveyed through narrative. More recently, Nicole Seymour makes a case for irony as an affective mode "defined by incongruity" and potentially "alarmist."[38] It makes sense to use the term to describe a conflicted, incongruous, affective reaction to a place—an affective dissonance that sounds visceral alarm bells. Irony need not necessarily be a humorous mode, however; nor is it necessarily an "unserious" one.[39] Affective dissonance often registers as felt irony, and it has unpredictable results. It can gel into a specific emotion, like anger, as easily as it can release into laughter. Or it can remain a kind of unsettling tension that simmers for a long time.

Ironies abound at the contemporary site. I stop at the old baseball fields to read a display with the lighthearted title "Play Ball!," which claims this "symbol of an American way of life . . . boosted morale" in camp. As I am imagining the cheering, smiling players on this field (with the help of the historic photo on the display) I glance up and see the reconstructed guard tower lurking just to the east. This quintessential

American sport, with its connotations of democracy and freedom, was played in the shadow of armed guards—guards who pointed their guns inside the camp. Part of this irony is generated by the narrative, the facile suggestion that a sport could "boost morale" in a prison setting. But one also *feels* the irony, in a more bodily sense, since the environment is at odds with the nationalistic text on the display. The "morale"-building field juxtaposed with the fear-inducing tower makes a paradoxical, ironic, affective impression—a corporeal impression that comes from being in this fraught environment.

Complicating things further, 180 degrees opposite the guard tower are the mountains, which either loom or beckon, depending on a visitor's cultural associations and emotional memories. For me, their promise of adventure, exploration, and mobility generates more affective dissonance, as Mount Williamson's alluring affect confronts the guard tower's threatening one. But for some incarcerees—and I imagine, for their descendants who visit today—the landscape's tone is as ominous and daunting as the tower's. The mountain range echoes and compounds the confinement of the built environment, adding a "natural" reinforcement to the government-sponsored perimeter.[40] Houston writes about a night outside the fence for a school-sponsored camping trip, after which she concludes: "Lovely as they were to look at, the Sierras were frightening to think about, an icy barricade."[41] Quite unlike the sense of adventure or risk that today's recreationalists seek in the mountains, Houston is "frightened" at the mere thought of them. She felt more secure inside the barbed wire. For incarcerees, who could be shot for leaving the camp, this was not the open desert of the Western film, in which the leading male "can go in any direction, as far as he can go."[42] Even so, today's implied tourist is likely to sense vastness in the landscape—if not in the mountains, then in the expansive desert valley. A strong impression of incongruity emerges, a tension between confinement and openness that the environment generates whether one reads the "Play Ball!" display or not.

The barracks and mess hall replicas work in a similar way, creating affective tension at environmental and corporeal registers. Visitors can sit in the small dining area and feel how cramped and loud a mess hall would be with hundreds of people inside, three times a day, as thousands of meals are served. I step inside a barracks building, an accurately sized twenty-by-twenty-five-foot room with eight metal cots and a lone bulb dangling from the low ceiling, and immediately feel the stifling loss of privacy. Especially if one sits on the tiny beds, or squeezes a rough corner of the straw-filled "mattresses," or fondles a kitchen utensil above the enormous cast-iron stove, one senses what it was like inside these buildings for the incarcerees. The timing of my visit allows me to read the posted design plans for the not-quite-finished barracks. Placeholders for exhibits to come, words like "powerful," "immersive," and "personalized" recur in the written plans, echoing the intentions for the interpretive center. Although the goal is to evoke a range of personalized stories and responses to them, the plans do name specific affects: "loss" and "frustration." The buildings are affective agents that facilitate these goals, "material *inducement*[s]" capable of "drawing out the appropriate memories *in that location*."[43]

In other words, while NPS displays make "overt rhetorical appeals"— through compelling stories about individual incarcerees, among other things—"the material form is a silent instructor" that makes appeals "at the level of the body, where things may be felt and responded to without necessarily being verbalized or visualized."[44] What's striking to me is the feeling of being confined inside one of the barracks, then stepping outside into the bright, dry air and seeing the mountains. This inside-outside contrast—the affective dissonance between the cramped quarters and the vast natural spaces outside—hits me "at the level of the body." I'm not sure what I feel is the sense of the "loss" and "frustration" the NPS plans aspire to, nor is it "shame" exactly, but I'm certainly unsettled, anxious, and uncomfortable while inside, and relieved to get out. For incarcerees like Houston, the natural environment didn't provide that relief; instead, it accentuated the sense of entrapment enforced by the built environment. For me, there is irony in the contrast between the connotation of freedom in my cultural associations with big mountains and the confinement I feel in the barracks. In both cases, built and natural environments collaborate to generate strong affective dissonance, though the emotional content is different for different visitors.

Being inside the buildings makes one pause and "feel the era" in a more affectively profound way. I do sense what life was like here.

Ahmed warns that too often *"what is shameful is passed over through the enactment of shame."*[45] This "quick fix" affective resolution risks not only absolution but also a disconnecting of the past from the present, as we move too fast to patriotic pride rather than fully acknowledging the shameful acts themselves. The kind of phenomenological experience in the barracks makes it hard to "pass over" the shameful events that happened here. I am implicated, affectively, through playing a role, performing a simulation of a life that was never mine. Simply walking around alone is unlikely to prompt that affect. All affective response is relational, when bodies come into contact with each other. Even a mountain range can implicate us, particularly if we empathize with Houston's perspective on it as an "icy barricade."

Park officials play up spatial ironies in their tours. I happen upon one tour group just as Ranger Rose Masters is asking a handful of teenage students to position themselves atop the remains of a camp latrine. As they balance awkwardly on rusty circles of pipe peeking out from a concrete foundation in the sandy earth, the students feel firsthand the shameful closeness of the toilets. I recall a poster-size photo of a latrine inside the interpretive center's bathroom: a close-up of three toilets practically touching. Quotations from incarcerees describe the bathroom as "humiliating" and "embarrassing." Seeing the poster and reading these words next to a modern-day private stall gives one pause, certainly. But standing over the original latrines in this embodied way, outdoors, is more striking. The teenagers giggle nervously, their self-consciousness likely masking profound affects. I stand apart from the group and out of earshot, but, even with no narrative to guide my emotional response, I nevertheless register affect corporeally. Similar to the irony I felt at the baseball field, the competing scales here—the enormous Sierra Nevada as backdrop for our small bodies, the imaginary walls of the tiny latrines within an otherwise vast valley—create an unsettled atmosphere, implicitly calling into question the democratic pretensions of a country that could barricade thousands of people within a tiny section of such a vast space.

Suddenly, I hear Ranger Master's voice: "Will it happen again? We don't know. We hope not. We have to stand up for what is right." Her ominous words conjure a darker environmental affect, and I sense the

FIGURE 5.2. Tourists at latrines at Manzanar NHS, Sierra Nevada in background

daunting tone that the young Houston felt when she looked at the peaks. I suspect the other tourists sense it too. The affective atmosphere emerging from these assembled bodies is an agitated, anxious one. Ranger Master, at this moment, becomes Ahmed's agent of shame; her uniformed gaze "'matters' to us," and it implicates us, for a moment, transferring to our bodies the shame of the incarcerees. Ranger Master's authoritative voice, backed by her official uniform, works with the physical environment to both shame her young audience and inspire them to "stand up for what is right." By catching visitors with their (imaginary) pants down, she is able to use shame to convey a powerful message of anti-racist activism.

Ranger Master's strategy is effective because, as Teresa Bergman and Cynthia Duquette Smith argue about a different prison, Alcatraz, "the more fully engaged visitors are with the spaces and experiences [of the place], the more likely they are to leave with a lasting impression."[46] Sue Embrey makes a similar claim for Manzanar. Cited on an interpretive center panel called "A Place for History," Embrey notes: "No one could really learn from the books. You have to walk through the blocks, see the gardens, and the remains of the stone walls and rocks." Her use of the word "walk" implies an able-bodied visitor who

can get around on foot, while in reality the unstable sand at much of
the site prevents wheelchair access. Still, Embrey's insight is accurate.
Part of Manzanar's impact comes from exploring the deserted blocks
and discovering signs of life, and of history, in these "remains." Again,
I feel fortunate to fit the demographic of the implied tourist, including being able-bodied.[47] I embark on a scavenger hunt for the "off the
beaten path" rock gardens that Ranger Patricia Biggs has marked in
blue ballpoint pen on my 8x11 paper map. Each discovery is a pleasurable surprise, like the charge one feels when snapping two puzzle
pieces together.

Searching for the gardens is a rewarding process. As I wander
among cottonwood and locust trees and the remaining orchards, objects shimmer in the dry heat. William Least Heat Moon describes how
the West's "apparent emptiness . . . makes matter look alone, exiled,
and unconnected." Put simply: *"Things show up out here."*[48] For Jane
Bennett, things show up when matter becomes vibrant, unconcealed,
provocative in its "impossible singularity."[49] As I walk alone through
the site, I experience what she calls "thing-power," the affective force of
things. Things that show up for me include rusted tin can lids (which
incarcerees used to nail over the knotholes in their floors and walls to
try to keep the dust out); small bits of broken glass; a slew of bent, rusty
nails (especially around the latrines); and a few brightly colored origami cranes blown from the cemetery and lodged in some sagebrush.
I spot the highly toxic, hallucinogenic datura plant flowering around
the camp with its large white petals, a suggestion of succulence in an
otherwise dry land. A jackrabbit sprints through locusts, and a lizard
does what look like little pushups for me ("posturizing," Ranger Mark
Hachtmann explains later). These bits of matter—animate and inanimate, both—enhance my loneliness, my own sense of being "alone, exiled, and unconnected." They make the site feel deserted, melancholy,
and empty.

I am struck again by how hard it is to imagine thousands of people
going about their busy lives, making the best of their imprisonment.
And yet, they were here, and they made amazing improvements to this
environment. Collecting rocks from the Inyo Mountains, east of camp,
replanting trees from the camp nursery, and finding creative ways to

acquire cement (which was in short supply),[50] incarcerees created dozens, if not hundreds, of gardens, including rock, flower, and "victory" gardens in their blocks, in fire breaks, and outside mess halls. Some of the gardens were practical—incarcerees produced two-thirds of their own food by the time the camp closed—and others were works of art, which NPS archaeologists are carefully excavating. Camp managers supported the gardens—deeming them acceptable subject matter for photographers, probably because they cast relocation in a positive light[51]—and incarcerees reaped their benefits. An outdoor display at the impressive Block 34 garden, titled "Waiting in Beauty," describes the mess hall gardens as "soothing troubled spirits and easing the monotony of long mealtime lines." They also "served as a source of block identity and pride." Creating the gardens brought families and neighbors together, fostered community, and, some argue, took advantage of this acceptable, attractive, form of Japanese cultural expression to mitigate racial tensions.[52]

Gardening and landscape design were an "ethnic niche" for Japanese Americans in the L.A. area beginning in the 1920s.[53] As former incarceree Hank Umemoto quips, "Japanese were the Cadillacs of yard maintenance."[54] Approximately 400 of the incarcerees at Manzanar already had landscape design skills, and many others acquired them in camp. The gardens are informed by a distinctive Japanese aesthetic tradition that aims to produce a "scenic and ambient mood through asymmetrical balance."[55] Block 34's display panel explains that its garden, like several others around camp, contains "three distinct levels aligned north to south: A hill of earth represents the mountains from which water flows south to a pond, symbolizing an ocean or lake." This garden is special for its rock animals—crane- and tortoise-shaped rock sculptures, which, the interpretive display narrative tells us, "are said to ensure ageless vitality." This sense of vitality is echoed at Merritt Park, a 1.5-acre refuge created in 1943 near the camp's northwest corner, initially called Pleasure Park but later renamed for Manzanar project director Ralph Merritt. This display calls the park "an oasis of beauty and solitude" and cites Houston: facing away from the barracks and toward the park, she writes, you could "for a while not be a prisoner at all."

While incarceree Arthur Ogami recalls how the gardens "just gave you a good feeling," the displays narrate specific good feelings: peace, vitality, a temporary sense of freedom in the midst of confinement. These affects are tied explicitly to national identity. The display at Block 22's garden site, titled "Islands of Beauty, Seeds of Resistance," claims that "Ancient Japan, the frontier West, and the Owens Valley environment all met in this garden." Some display narratives foreground the frontier component of this triad. Tsuyako Shimizu recalls, for instance: "When we entered it was a barren desert . . . When we left camp, it was a garden that had been built up without tools." On a different display, a quote from the *Manzanar Free Press* invokes both the frontier West and ancient Japan: "Six months ago Manzanar was a barren uninhabited desert. Today, beautiful green lawns, picturesque gardens with miniature mountains, stone lanterns, bridges over ponds . . . attest to the Japanese people's love of nature." One could argue that these narratives play into "Orientalist expectations" that saw Japanese as close to nature and, accordingly, as "inactive, passive, and uncivilized."[56] But the descriptions tap into "good feelings" that are equally valued in the U.S.: freedom, love of nature, the desire for "beauty and solitude" in an otherwise crowded place. The narratives take quintessentially American affects and recast them as emerging from a Japanese cultural tradition. It is hard to say which country can lay greater claim to a "love of nature," and tourists can align themselves with either nation.

Any feelings at the site today emerge at the confluence of personal, cultural, and national identities. The rhetoric of the displays evokes affects that manifest differently depending on how that confluence comes together. For the implied tourist, the dominant story of the gardens is one in which Japanese aesthetics combine with an American pioneer work ethic to create a pastoral garden. While the implied tourist needs to have emotions explained, textually, a tourist familiar with Japanese gardens might feel the vitality and other affects more directly. For a Japanese or Japanese American visitor, especially one familiar with garden aesthetics, I imagine the pioneer rhetoric takes a back seat to the agency of the Japanese features—like the fish ponds, waterfalls, bridges, and animal rock sculptures—in the gardens.

The "Owens Valley environment" is the most powerful force in my own encounter with the gardens. For me, there is tension between the emotions represented in the nationalistic narratives—the textual register—and the affective agency of the rock gardens themselves, the environmental register. While the displays celebrate the lush beauty of the gardens, it is hard for me, standing dry-throated in the heat, to imagine an "oasis" here, or even to think of these as "gardens" at all. The display panel at Merritt Park claims: "While the water that flowed through the pond and the plants that once graced the park are gone, these stones remain as a testament to beauty created behind barbed wire." The rocks are "testaments," indeed, but not to "ageless vitality." With the help of historic photos, displays encourage tourists to "visualize" objects that once existed—a cottonwood stump, a wagon, and fish swimming in the pond, for instance. But I find that visualization difficult. Instead, the atmosphere—especially if we compare the photos of "beautiful green lawns" to the present-day landscape—is one of desertification. If there is an "ambient and scenic mood," it is elegiac. Another spatial irony, then: Even while archeologists work to revive these brilliant gardens, the atmosphere is one of loss and desolation, not life.

———◆◆◆———

While the gardens feel like memorials of sorts,[57] there is one designated memorial I'm eager to reach: the cemetery monument, a white obelisk with black Kanji letters that Ansel Adams's photographs have made Manzanar's most recognizable icon. I arrive early on my second day and am lucky to spend over an hour alone at the cemetery. Here, at the western edge of camp, I had expected to encounter affective dissonance between the human-made monument and the mountain range. However, I find a surprising synchronicity instead. Unlike Manzanar's ironic spaces, the cemetery emits a harmonious, peaceful atmosphere, where the sacred, serene tone of the human-built obelisk is matched and accentuated by the sublimity of the Sierra Nevada, and the quiet, stillness of the desert parallels the repose of the graves.

For more than forty years pilgrims have gathered here for "an interfaith memorial service, guided tours, displays, presentations, and

FIGURE 5.3. Manzanar obelisk and cemetery

music."⁵⁸ The first pilgrimage,⁵⁹ spearheaded in 1969 by Sansei activists who were eager to learn about the camps, entailed a lot of cleanup work at the cemetery. The bitter cold—it was the coldest day of the year— "humbled" the younger generation and reminded those who'd lived in the camps of the valley's harsh climate.⁶⁰ In interviews archived on densho.org, former incarcerees describe their impressions of the camp's remoteness and emptiness (the obelisk was initially one of the few remains), and they recall the pilgrimages as primarily educational, crucial for keeping history alive and not repeating the mistakes of the past. While some, like Robert A. Nakamura, who took photographs at the 1969 pilgrimage, describe the return as "very, very emotional," most downplay—or perhaps struggle to narrate—their specific emotional responses.⁶¹ Few of the interviewees I've seen in the densho.org archive mention the kinds of things Sue Embrey discusses: the "trauma of that first return," the "nightmares," the "tears that fell unchecked," and "the need to know about the pain, the psychological effects" of imprisonment.⁶²

In "Crossing Boundaries," Houston grapples with her own trauma as she describes her intense affective response to revisiting Manzanar with her daughter, more than fifty years after living there. Initially she is "irritated at her[self]" for her constricting throat and stinging tears upon seeing the Alabama Hills. Hadn't her "years of therapeutic work" and cathartic memoir writing, she wonders, "healed the trauma?"[63] Accompanied by a Paiute docent, Richard Stewart, on this return trip, Houston revises her childhood feelings about the Sierra Nevada as an "icy barricade" and recalls how her father and some of the other Issei had found comfort in the "stately aura" of Mount Williamson, which reminded them of Mount Fuji.[64] She now senses "a grandfather's protective power" and "unconditional acceptance" in the peaks.[65]

Without the shared experience of being imprisoned, I can't claim empathy for these perspectives. But I do feel a "protective power" in today's cemetery. The interpretive display at the entrance tells us this is "Sacred Space," and it translates the obelisk's Kanji letters for an English-speaking audience: *I REI TO*, "Soul Consoling Tower."[66] For the implied tourist, and for me, a mountain peak can also be a kind of "soul consoling tower," a place to seek rejuvenation. Outside of the five-foot-tall barbed-wire fence that surrounds the camp's living area, the cemetery's smaller reconstructed locust fence forms a comforting enclosure. Its durable wood looks soft, and the fence's "X" pattern complements the site's other geometrical shapes: the triangular mountains, the trapezoidal slab at the base of the obelisk, the rectangular gravestones, and the circles of rocks that mark the grave sites. The NPS designed the interpretive center, in part, to "compel visitors to contemplate their own feelings of the Manzanar experience, what it's like to be forcibly displaced against your will, removed from all your possessions and placed in a guarded, barb-wire [sic] camp,"[67] but it is here in the cemetery that tourists are most compelled to contemplation. The implied tourist should be "somber" and reverent, ready to reflect on intense feelings.

Inside the cemetery itself, there are no informational panels. Even though the echoes of the stories I just read influence my encounter, narrative details fade into the background, and physical matter becomes a more powerful agent in the affective atmosphere. The obelisk dominates. Obelisks are traditionally symbols of power, whether in ancient Egypt or in our nation's capitol, in the form of the

Washington Monument. Their tone tends to be solemn and digni-
fied. Unlike the marker at Coronado NM along the U.S./Mexico border—another barbed-wire fence punctuated by an obelisk, meant to
seem natural in its delineation of a national boundary—Manzanar's
barbed-wire fence is meant to feel *unnatural* in order to highlight the
racially- and fear-motivated injustice that happened there. Quite unlike the Washington Monument, with its tone of phallic nationalism,
the Manzanar cemetery's relatively small obelisk is humble and cross-
cultural: The Buddhist Young People's organization worked alongside
Catholic stonemason Ryozo Kado to erect this monument. For those
who (like me) do not read or speak Japanese, the Kanji letters are
more art than narrative—like the gardens, a mark of Japanese culture
on the Western landscape. Even without knowing the story of the
obelisk's construction, Japanese and dominant American-Western
affects collide, as the Kanji characters mark a distinctive presence
in a landscape the implied tourist associates with American identity,
perhaps even national pride.[68]

As I walk toward this obelisk, it grows larger and more pronounced,
bright white against the brilliant blue sky. By the time I reach the glossy
rock at its base, it obscures Mount Williamson entirely and relegates
the range to a hazy backdrop. Yi-Fu Tuan identifies the aesthetic tension between vertical and horizontal as a kind of "basic polarity" that
can "excite emotions that are widely shared." Specifically, the vertical
evokes "a sense of striving, a defiance of gravity, while the horizontal
elements call to mind acceptance and rest."[69] The obelisk does seem
to "strive"; its design draws the visitor's gaze upward, from the angular
rock at the base to the three increasingly smaller tiers, then skyward.
The horizon could certainly conjure "acceptance and rest." Still, I sense
not a polarity but a congruity between this horizontal range and this
vertical obelisk. Both possess a "monolithic, awe-inspiring character"
that can "reflect a desire for self-transcendence."[70] Tompkins sees an
"architectural quality" in desert spaces, the way a landscape's "monumental" qualities can "resembl[e] man-made space."[71] The obelisk
matches the range in its monumentality; both affect visitors with a tone
of longevity, permanence, and a kind of sublime self-transcendence.
Since I have been prepped by the narrative display to be "somber," my

mood fits. Built environment and landscape, too, collaborate in this meditative, contemplative atmosphere.

Perhaps this is an atmosphere common to all cemeteries, what Houston describes as "the antiquity, the calm energy that accumulates with years of undisturbed tranquility."[72] For me, it is especially calming to feel my mortality, my smallness, against this immense mountain range. When viewed from the cemetery, the distinctive Western landscape asks us to retrain our perception—as Stegner puts it, to "get used to an inhuman scale" and to "understand geologic time."[73] The lack of human presence and sparse vegetation accentuate the vast scale and facilitate this retraining. Strangely, expanding our sense of time belies the sense of "undisturbed tranquility." Houston hints at this, in fact, when she remarks that the obelisk seems "miraculous, as if some block of stone had fallen from the peaks above and landed upright in the brush, chiseled, solitary, twelve feet high."[74] The obelisk did not fall from the peaks, of course, but if we consider them not in our time scale but in theirs, then we remember that mountains do move. All landscapes are processive and dynamic, to the point that even rocks are agents and should be thought of as "*immigrant* rocks."[75]

Sometimes, humans assist with rocks' migrations. Here, visitors have moved rocks from camp blocks to the base of the obelisk in a process Carole Blair calls "supplementing."[76] This way of adding to the archive of affect allows visitors to participate in the process of making public memory—a process the NPS display "Legacy" describes as "ongoing, unspoken conversations about America's past and its future." The tiered base of the obelisk acts as a sort of shrine for what the display calls "offerings," and I find coins, bits of glass from the blocks, and wreaths of multicolor origami cranes, which—as noted in the previous chapter's discussion of the "Sadako's Cranes" exhibit at Pearl Harbor—symbolize peace, long life, and good fortune.[77] Some of these offerings are subsequently gathered in the interpretive center, where they are encased and narrated within the genre of the museum. Seeing them outdoors, framed against the landscape, is powerful in a different way. Outside, we are not bound to any single story of the objects. Their "thing-power" adds an affective dimension to the "unspoken conversations" happening here. The corporeal register, what actual visitors feel here, must vary drastically. For many of us, though, I suspect the temporary nature of this vibrant matter adds to the contemplative atmosphere: Like all our lives, these objects are transient and fragile.

Only after the obelisk and its offerings relinquish their authoritative hold on my gaze do I finally notice the actual graves. The small piles of rocks placed by visitors blend in with the sand, their circular form suggesting continuity and contributing to the sense of comfort at the site. A solitary red rose accents the former grave of "Baby Jerry Ogata." Reading the name of a victim—and the word "Baby"—is one of the most moving moments of my day. Even before reading this baby's story,[78] the gravesite triggers a profound and anxious sadness in me. My darkest fears stir in the pit of my stomach, fears about my own children's health and safety; dreadful, unformed affects that I rarely allow myself to narrate or even become conscious of. Cultural and national identity boundaries are, for the moment, unimportant; we will all lose loved ones in our lifetimes. After the gut-punch moment has passed, the atmosphere slowly becomes serene again: Environmental, textual, and corporeal affective registers come back into alignment. The rings of rocks fit naturally in this desert landscape, and the mountains offer the supportive sense of "acceptance and rest" in death, even as their vastness accentuates the tininess of a baby's too-short life. Physical matter can both comfort and unsettle us, providing geologic perspective, inciting distress or compassion, and confronting us with the transience of all lives.

For the moment, things appear stable—so still in fact that a scrap of paper fluttering at the obelisk's base catches my eye. The only English-language narrative within the cemetery that day, it is a handwritten note held in place by some loose change. It reads: "As Americans it is our responsibility to our fellow citizens who were used unjustly here to fight every day to stop our country from repeating this shameful chapter. We must learn from our past, especially the painful parts." These words express one potential lesson learned at Manzanar, a sentiment that recurs in the visitor comment books inside the interpretive center.[79] It seems to replicate the nationalism Ahmed argues is so often the end game of shame: "the re-cover[y of] the national subject" and of "'civil society.'"[80] Interestingly, though, it refuses "the endless deferral of responsibility for injustice in the present"[81] by insisting "it is our responsibility" and locating injustice in our "every day" context. The visitor also seems to complete the final step Doss says is essential for shame to be redemptive: "the affirmation of others—those to whom shameful things were done—being perceived as legitimate members of society."[82] I'd like to believe that, face-to-face with a baby's grave, this particular visitor felt something other than the shame-pride binary, something more complex and unsettling, but something inspiring and redemptive.

Whether this visitor's note conveys genuine feelings of compassion, shame, or repentance, or whether it performs a perfunctory patriotism, these narrated emotions fail to fully account for, even as they respond to, the messiness of the affective atmosphere. Rocks are as powerful as words, here: I hear Tompkins again, calling deserts "the place where language fails and rocks assert themselves." Language is only a small part of a greater affective assemblage, including the mountains, the obelisk, the gravestones, the sagebrush, the wind, the raven's caws, the dry heat, and our own bodies.

———————

As archaeologists continue to excavate the gardens, as the NPS continues to educate visitors about what happened there, as former incarcerees—or increasingly, their descendants—continue to make pilgrimages to the valley, and as new stories continue to be told and archived, Manzanar's legacy is, like all public memory, "subject to continual reassessment and revision."[83] When I drove out of Lone Pine at the end of my trip, I knew I might never settle on an answer to the NPS's probing question: "What does Manzanar mean to YOU?" As the all-caps pronoun insists, affective experiences are always, to some degree, subjective. In Tuan's formulation, "the affective bond between people and place," which he famously calls "topophilia," is "[d]iffuse as concept, vivid and concrete as personal experience."[84] While my account is constrained by my positionality and my corporeality, as a white, cis-gendered, middle-aged, economically stable, tenured academic mother of two who is (for the time being) able-bodied, I hope it exemplifies an approach to affect that grounds it in "entanglements of agential

beings."[85] Rock animals, origami cranes, grave markers, cemetery offerings, mountain ranges, and baseball fields framed by guard towers
are all "agential beings," of sorts, and I contend that the affects they
carry—"ageless vitality," peace, sorrow, solemnity, and irony—complicate the reading of Manzanar NHS as a "site of shame."

For me, there was no cathartic emotional experience to be had
here.[86] The unsettling impressions linger. I suspect this is a good
thing—that noncathartic affects might be more useful for political
awareness than an open-and-shut encounter with sadness or a temporary feeling of guilt that dissipates off-site. Intellectually, too, there
is no "magical closure," no decisive arguable claim, for affect theorists.[87] For Stewart, Bennett, and others, standard ideology critique
is insufficient and even detrimental to writing about affect: always
focused on the human, the common scholarly approach of "demysti-
fication tends to screen from view the vitality of matter."[88] As ecocritics continue to think about matter's agency, we should turn to affect
theory to consider physical matter as "a corporeal palimpsest" that is
not only "storied"[89] but also deeply affective. Getting at that affective
register might require more acceptance of intellectual ambiguity and
more experimental methodologies.

For environmental humanities scholars who refuse to separate
ecological and social issues, it is important to ask how physical environments shape feelings about injustice. Manzanar's "dark energy," the
valley's "saturat[ion] with sorrows of the past,"[90] confronts the dominant American culture of optimism. We tend to assume that "good feelings are open and bad feelings are closed," an assumption that "allows
historical forms of injustice to disappear."[91] But instead of mandating
that we "be affirmative," sites like Manzanar ask us to cultivate *bad* feelings, at least while on-site, and to reflect precisely on historical injustice. If we are encouraged to feel shame or even outrage at Manzanar,
then what are the prospects for turning these so-called negative emotions into compassionate political action in the present?

Answering this requires a better understanding of the process by
which affects—those gut punch moments at a baby's grave, for instance—acquire the "narrative complexity of emotions" and how, in-
versely, the emotions we read about and contemplate at sites of public

memory "denature into affects" once we depart, leaving us with an ambient sense of the place that we take home.[92] The next chapter takes up eco-affective entanglements in another California landscape: the Presidio of San Francisco, in Golden Gate National Recreation Area. I'll use this final case study to think more about how negative affects can turn positive, how even sites of recreation can generate profound emotional responses, and how paying attention to affective agency in all environments can help clarify the intricacies of contemporary politics at larger scales. I'll suggest it's incumbent on all of us, whether on public lands or not, to excavate and attend to the layered histories that are too often invisible.

Notes

1. While the camps are usually called "internment camps," the word "internment" is legally and ethically problematic. In the legal sense, internment technically applies to the imprisonment of noncitizens in the Department of Justice internment centers. More than two-thirds of the Japanese at Manzanar were citizens. Densho. org, a website that preserves testimonies of incarcerees and compiles historical information, suggests internment is a euphemism and prefers incarceration. Some suggest "concentration camp" is most accurate, a point to which I return. With respect for these ongoing debates, I use "incarceration camps" and "incarcerees" to affirm the reality of imprisonment. Thanks to Manzanar ranger-historian Dr. Patricia Biggs for her insights about terminology.

2. Jeanne Wakatsuki Houston, *Farewell to Manzanar* (New York: Ember, 2012), 18–19.

3. The Manzanar site brochure clarifies that "11,070 Japanese Americans were processed through Manzanar," and that the population peaked at 10,046 in September of 1942. National Park Service, *Manzanar*, 2003.

4. Alisa Lynch (chief of interpretation), in discussion with the author, June 1, 2014.

5. Houston, *Farewell*, 159. 110,000 refers to the total number of people incarcerated in all ten camps.

6. One especially inventive "exhibit" invites visitors to take one of the identification tags that incarcerees were given—which named and numbered the individuals and instructed them to report to a particular destination, "ready to travel"—and match it with an interpretive center display, at which that individual's story is revealed. For analysis of psychic numbing and other psychological barriers to compassion, see "The Arithmetic of Compassion," Scott Slovic and Paul Slovic. *The New York Times*. December 6, 2015. http://www.nytimes.com/2015/12/06/opinion/the-arithmetic-of-compassion.html. In their book *Numbers and Nerves: Information, Emotion, and Meaning in a World of Data* (Corvallis: Oregon State University Press, 2015), Slovic and Slovic explore these challenges in more detail.

7. Jeanne Wakatsuki Houston, "Crossing Boundaries," in *The Colors of Nature: Culture, Identity, and the Natural World*, eds. Alison H. Deming and Lauret E. Savoy (Minneapolis: Milkweed Editions, 2011).

8. Erika Doss, *Memorial Mania: Public Feeling in America* (Chicago: The University of Chicago Press, 2010), 13.

9. Sianne Ngai, *Ugly Feelings* (Cambridge: Harvard University Press, 2007), 6.

10. Doss, 302.

11. Doss, 303.

12. I cite Houston here ("Crossing", 35), but this is a common way to describe large mountains.

13. Comfort was not a criterion for the War Relocation Authority (WRA) in choosing locations for the camps, though remoteness and proximity to water were. The WRA thought Manzanar could draw on Shepherd Creek, to the north, for its water. When that water quickly proved inadequate to satisfy the camp's needs, L.A. contractors funded the construction of an 800,000-gallon reservoir. The internee labor crew that helped build the reservoir carved political graffiti into the wet concrete, including "pro-Japanese and anti-American sentiments" that are captured in the concrete to this day. NPS, *Manzanar Reservoir*, 2009.

14. Death Valley NP is also notable for being the only U.S. national park where land has been returned to its Indigenous inhabitants, the Timbisha Shoshone Tribe. This occurred with the help of the Homeland Act of 2000. For discussion of this, see Grebowicz.

15. Houston, *Farewell*, 188.

16. Wallace Stegner, "Living Dry," in *Where The Bluebird Sings To The Lemonade Springs* (New York: Random House, 1992), 74.

17. Initially located by the restored sentry posts to the south, the historical landmark plaque was relocated to this prominent spot in February 2014 in order to be more visible for all visitors.

18. NPS, "Focus Group Notes," October 3, 2011. Thanks to Alisa Lynch for providing these.

19. Martha Nussbaum, *Political Emotions: Why Love Matters for Justice* (Cambridge: The Belknap Press of Harvard University Press, 2013).

20. Survivors continue to note both shame and guilt. John Tateishi says, in a 2013 interview, that he left camp "with a sense of shame and guilt" for "having been considered betrayers of our country." http://www.npr.org/sections/codeswitch/2013/08/09/210138278/japanese-internment-redress. Accessed 15 December, 2016. Reparations of this sort still have not been made to descendants of the victims of the Sand Creek Massacre.

21. Houston, *Farewell*, 188.

22. Bahr, *Unquiet Nisei*, 115.

23. Nussbaum, *Political Emotions*, 359–364.

24. Doss, 311.

25. Ahmed, *Cultural Politics*, 105.

26. Ibid., 103.

27. Ibid., 104.

28. Ibid., 108.

29. Ibid., 108.

30. Ibid., 109.

31. Suzanne Keen helpfully identifies the difference between sympathy (a feeling *for* someone) and empathy (a feeling *with* another). I'd argue the embodied simulation tourists participate in here is more empathy than sympathy, though I don't pursue that argument in detail here. Keen, *Empathy and the Novel* (New York: Oxford University Press, 2007).

32. Jane Tompkins, *West of Everything: The Inner Life of Westerns* (New York: Oxford University Press, 2010), 71.

33. Ibid., 71–2.

34. Iovino and Oppermann, "Material Ecocriticism," 459.

35. Bahr, *Unquiet Nisei*, 61–69.

36. Karen Higa and Tim B. Wride, "Manzanar Inside and Out: Photo Documentation of the Japanese Wartime Incarceration," in *Reading California: Art, Image, Identity, 1900–2000*, eds. Stephanie Barron, Sheri Bernstein, and Ilene Susan Fort (Los Angeles: Los Angeles County Museum of Art, and Berkeley: University of California Press, 2000), 330.

37. Linda Hutcheon, "Irony, Nostalgia, and the Postmodern," in *Methods For The Study of Literature as Cultural Memory*, eds. Raymond Vervliet and Annemarie Estor (Atlanta: Rodopi, 2000), 199. Hutcheon claims "there is little irony in most memorials" (206), and she is right if you think of their design and intended impact. But accounting for how matter itself can contribute a "critical edge" to the atmosphere in question, bumping up against the written text directed at the implied tourists who visit, suggests otherwise.

38. Nicole Seymour, "Irony and Contemporary Ecocinema: Theorizing a New Affective Paradigm," in *Moving Environments: Affect, Emotion, Ecology, and Film*, ed. Alexa Weik von Mossner (Waterloo: Wilfrid Laurier Press, 2014), 63.

39. Ibid., 73.

40. Hank Umemoto's book is a notable exception here; even as an incarceree he was drawn to the mountains, and he eventually summited Mount Whitney in his 70s. *Manzanar to Mount Whitney: The Life and Times of a Lost Hiker* (Berkeley: Heyday, 2013).

41. Houston, *Farewell*, 107–8.

42. Tompkins, *West of Everything*, 75.

43. Casey, "Public Memory," 32, original emphasis.

44. Robert M. Bednar, "Being Here, Looking There: Mediating Vistas in the National Parks of the Contemporary American West," in *Observation Points: The Visual Poetics of National Parks*, ed. Thomas Patin (Minneapolis: University of Minnesota Press, 2012), 2.

45. Ahmed, *Cultural Politics*, 120.

46. Teresa Bergman and Cynthia Duquette Smith, "You Were on Indian Land:

Alcatraz Island as Recalcitrant Memory Space," in *Places of Public Memory: The Rhetoric of Museums and Memorials*, eds. Carole Blair, Greg Dickinson, and Brian L. Ott (Tuscaloosa: The University of Alabama Press, 2010), 182.

47. NPS literature, too, occasionally implies an able-bodied tourist. The interpretive center is accessible and much of the site can be seen from your car. But mandates to "Stop occasionally and walk through the site" and reminders to "Wear comfortable shoes" and "Watch your step" suggest a tourist who can walk easily. NPS, *Manzanar: After Hours Guide*, 2011.

48. Cited in Stegner, "Living Dry," 75, original emphasis.

49. Bennett, *Vibrant Matter*, 4.

50. Embrey recalls how Harry Ueno, a kitchen worker, and his mess hall crew built a garden and pond outside by resubmitting the same receipt for three bags of cement. Incarcerees nicknamed it the "Three-Sacks Garden." Bahr, *Unquiet Nisei*, 64.

51. Laura W. Ng, "Altered Lives, Altered Environments: Creating Home at Manzanar Relocation Center, 1942–1945" (M.A. Thesis, University of Massachusetts, Boston, 2014), 81–82.

52. Ng suggests the gardens were a strategic effort by incarcerees to "appear compliant" and ease tensions in camp (87). Debates about to what degree the gardens were acts of "defiance" are ongoing. See, for instance, Kenneth I. Helphand, *Defiant Gardens: Making Gardens in Wartime* (San Antonio: Trinity University Press, 2006).

53. NPS, *Cultural Landscape Report: Manzanar National Historic Site*, 2006, 115. This is my primary source for information about the gardens. Uncited quotations in this section of the essay are from NPS displays around the site.

54. Umemoto, *Manzanar to Mount Whitney*, 121. Gardening and landscaping were the "primary livelihood for Nisei men" after the war as well (Bahr, *Unquiet Nisei*, 97).

55. NPS, *Cultural Landscape Report*, 117.

56. Brett Esaki, "Multidimensional Silence, Spirituality, and the Japanese American Art of Gardening," *Journal of Asian American Studies* 16, no.3 (2013): 235–265. Cited in Ng, "Altered Lives."

57. Madelon Arai Yamamoto calls her father's recently excavated fish pond a "tremendous memorial for his respect for the Japanese garden and the heritage that he brought from Japan to Manzanar." NPS, *Aria Fish Pond*, 2013.

58. NPS, *Manzanar War Relocation Center Cemetery*, 2001.

59. Two Issei ministers, Sentoku Mayeda and Shoichi Wakahiro, had been going annually for more than two decades "to pray for those who had died at Manzanar," prior to this first group pilgrimage, (Bahr, *Unquiet Nisei*), 119.

60. Bahr, *Unquiet Nisei*, 118.

61. For instance, Matsue Watanabe does not use a single emotion word to describe her return to Manzanar, even after two direct questions about her "feeling and emotions." She acknowledges it was "probably more emotional" for her daughter, then talks in unemotional terms about showing her daughter and some other visitors around the site. Densho Digital Archive, interview with Debra Grindeland from 7 October, 2006, accessed 16 April 2015, archive.densho.org.

62. Bahr, *Unquiet Nisei*, 119. One exception is Miho Shiroishi, who describes her return in 2004 (for the NPS dedication) as "very emotional" and tells how she "just started crying"—and continued to cry—throughout the interpretive center, but she does not specify her reactions to the outdoor environment. Video footage shows her moving from chuckling to tears as she describes seeing personal photos and her family's names on the wall inside. Analyzing the video interviews could be the subject of yet another potential project: a study of how emotions are displayed, and how affect is transmitted, through archival footage. Densho Digital Archive, interview with Kristen Luetkemeier from 21 August, 2012, archive.densho.org, accessed 16 April 2015.

63. Houston, "Crossing," 35.

64. Ibid., 37.

65. Ibid., 39. Watanabe remarks, similarly, that the Sierra Nevada were "the most beautiful sight" upon her return to Manzanar, though she "[didn't] ever remember seeing it as a beautiful sight when [she] lived in camp."

66. The NPS brochure lists other translations, my favorite being "this is the place of consolation for the spirit of all mankind." NPS, *Manzanar War Relocation Center Cemetery*, 2001.

67. "Manzanar Front End Evaluation Focus Group Results," prepared for the NPS by Harris H. Shettel Evaluation, February 2001.

68. I think here of Ansel Adams's *Born Free and Equal*, a text that elicits pride in the pioneer spirit of the incarcerees, framed and reinforced by the mountains, to promote shame for the fear and nationalism that allowed their imprisonment. I explore Adams's text in *Reclaiming Nostalgia: Longing for Nature in American Literature* (Charlottesville: University of Virginia Press, 2012), 86–93.

69. Yi–Fu Tuan, *Topophilia: A Study of Environmental Perception, Attitudes, and Values* (Englewood Cliffs: Prentice-Hall, Inc., 1974), 28.

70. Tompkins, *West of Everything*, 76.

71. Ibid., 76.

72. Houston, "Crossing," 36.

73. Stegner, "Living Dry," 54.

74. Houston, *Farewell*, 189.

75. Doreen Massey, "Landscape as a Provocation: Reflections on Moving Mountains," *Journal of Material Culture* 11, no. 1-2 (2006): 35, original emphasis.

76. Carole Blair, "Contemporary U.S. Memorial Sites as Exemplars of Rhetoric's Materiality," in *Rhetorical Bodies* eds. Jack Selzer and Sharon Crowley (Madison: The University of Wisconsin Press, 1999), 40.

77. In Japanese legend, cranes are said to live for 1,000 years. Japanese Americans fold *Senbazuru*, 1,000 cranes—one for each year of life—and string them together to give as gifts, with wishes for longevity and luck. Tamiko Nimura, "For A Sister Getting Married: *Senbazuru*—1,000 Cranes," *Discover Nikkei*, 28 June, 2013, http://www.discovernikkei.org/en/journal/2013/6/28/senbazuru/ accessed 23 January, 2015.

78. Baby Jerry's story is told in the interpretive center and on the site bulletin: he

died of a congenital heart defect at the age of two months. NPS, *Manzanar War Relocation Center Cemetery*, 2001. His remains were removed from the cemetery after WW II, along with those of eight others.

79. I glance through the current book and find comments on everything from Obamacare to Hitler, present politics and past. Coding and assessing the comment books is yet another potential project at Manzanar.

80. Ahmed, 22.

81. Ibid.

82. Doss, 312.

83. Casey, 29.

84. Tuan, 4.

85. Deborah Bird Rose, et al., "Thinking Through the Environment, Unsettling the Humanities," *Environmental Humanities* 1 (2012), 3.

86. I imagine a quite different result for, say, pilgrims who visit the cemetery.

87. Stewart, *Ordinary Affects*, 5.

88. Bennett, *Vibrant Matter*, xv.

89. Iovino and Oppermann, "Material Ecocriticism," 4, 51.

90. Houston, "Crossing," 38.

91. Ahmed, "Happy Objects," 50.

92. Ngai, 27.

CHAPTER SIX

"We have died. Remember us."

Fear, Wonder, and Overlooking the Buffalo Soldiers at Golden Gate National Recreation Area

Even with the growing number of places for tourists to "remember, to learn, to contemplate the challenges and gifts of social change,"[1] not all historical traumas are adequately commemorated. As Toni Morrison said shortly after the publication of her masterpiece, *Beloved*:

> There is no place you or I can go, to think about or not think about, to summon the presences of, or recollect the absences of slaves. . . . There is no suitable memorial, or plaque, or wreath, or wall, or park, or skyscraper lobby. There's no 300-foot tower, there's no small bench by the road. There is not even a tree scored, an initial that I can visit or you can visit in Charleston or Savannah or New York or Providence or better still on the banks of the Mississippi. And because such a place doesn't exist . . . [*Beloved*] had to.[2]

The Toni Morrison Society's "Bench By The Road Project" confronts the relative invisibility of slavery's history in the U.S. South and East by creating visible markers of that past: memorial benches in key places where the slave trade flourished. More recently, the Equal Justice Initiative opened the National Memorial for Peace and Justice outside of Montgomery, Alabama, to provide a "sacred space for truthtelling and reflection about racial terror in America and its legacy."[3] While the National Park System contains nothing like this striking new memorial (about which I'll say more at the end of this chapter), the NPS has designated a handful of sites at which visitors could conceivably contemplate slavery and its legacy: at the Martin Luther King Jr. National Historic Site (or at the foot of the memorial dedicated to him, on the National Mall in Washington, D.C.), or along the Selma to Montgomery National Historic Trail, or at the Boston African American National Historic Site. Still, there is not yet a "suitable memorial" to slavery itself within the National Park System.

In the West, commemorations of African American history are especially scarce. The Nicodemus National Historic Site in Kansas, the "oldest and only remaining Black settlement west of the Mississippi River," offers a place to reflect on African Americans who headed to the "promised land" of Kansas following emancipation.[4] The Homestead National Monument in southeast Nebraska recognizes the Exodusters and others who settled west of the Mississippi following the Homestead Act of 1862. The Charles Young Buffalo Soldiers National Monument in Ohio, while not located in the West, commemorates the "buffalo soldiers," the nickname American Indians gave to the Army's four all-black regiments, the 9th and 10th Cavalry and the 24th and 25th Infantry. And the three years that the buffalo soldiers' Company L spent securing the U.S.-Canada border and "taming the frontier" is one of Klondike Gold Rush National Historical Park's interpretive themes.[5] The NPS has begun to compile online resources documenting the history of African American military service in the West. Some of those documents note the ironies of that service. For instance, a link on the Presidio's website called "On the Western Frontier" explains how black soldiers were "frequently ordered to return hostile tribes to their appointed reservations." Especially for those who had lived through the Fugitive Slave Law, it is no wonder that following these orders "created feelings of moral dilemma and a sense of irony for many of the Black troops."[6] It is perhaps no wonder, too, that the NPS struggles to commemorate such a troubling national past.

Morrison's comments remind us that memorials take many forms—from formal plaques and prominent towers to humble trees etched with initials—and that *literature* can be counted among the most powerful memorials to a traumatic past, especially when there's no other "suitable" place to contemplate that trauma. In the tradition of *Beloved*, Shelton Johnson's novel *Gloryland* could be considered a memorial to slavery and its aftermath. In this unique work of historical fiction, Johnson chronicles the life of Elijah Yancy, a young man of African American, Seminole, and Cherokee descent, as he rebels against racism in Spartanburg, South Carolina (where he's born, symbolically, on Emancipation Day, 1863), heads West, joins the Army, serves in the 9th Cavalry, and is eventually stationed in Yosemite National Park. Through Elijah's compelling first-person point of view, readers hear a little-known story of the American past: the story of the buffalo soldiers and their role not just in "winning the West" but also in establishing the national parks. Many Americans aren't aware that black soldiers were among the first NPS rangers or that Captain Charles Young became the first African American superintendent when he was stationed in Sequoia National Park in 1903. Johnson is a ranger in Yosemite National Park, a charismatic living historian featured in Ken Burns's documentary *The National Parks: America's Best Idea*. While it's perhaps more likely that one would encounter Johnson there, or via one of his podcasts,[7] his obscure but one-of-a-kind novel provides an insightful depth to the history of black and mixed-race people in the West. *Gloryland* also brings together NPS history and frontier history, reminding readers that the creation of the parks, and our enjoyment of them today, are products of settler colonialism.

Attention to this history, including a surge of scholarly interest in the "black West," has increased in recent years.[8] As Michael K. Johnson explains, narratives about African American experiences in the West tend to fit into one of two ideological frames: those that "repeat the dominant myths of western history and tell stories of an exceptional West where the limitations of race can be transcended and the African American individual can find prosperity and equality" *or* those that "tell the opposite story—of hopes for a new life crushed by the existence of unexceptional western prejudice."[9] Of course, as Johnson quickly acknowledges, this is a false binary, one that glosses over the complexities of a region with space enough to accommodate opportunity and prejudice, both. *Gloryland*, I'll argue, is a novel that reveals that complexity, even as it courts the first of these narratives. That is, while the book depicts moments of racial tension in the Yosemite Valley, the national park itself is upheld as a place of transcendence influenced by an entrenched, mythical notion of parks as places of spiritual freedom. By spatializing emotions such as fear, anger, joy, and awe, Johnson's novel shows how some NPS sites are, as Carolyn Finney puts it, "overlaid with histories seen and unseen; *geographies of fear* that can make a 'natural' place in the United States suspect to an African American."[10] However, while Johnson recognizes public lands as places "where African Americans experience insecurity, exclusion, and fear born out of historical precedent, collective memory, and contemporary concerns"[11] he also reclaims them as places where John Muir-caliber awe is possible for people of any skin color. People of color belong here, *Gloryland* affirms, and they have for a long time.

I'll read *Gloryland* in dialogue with Finney's *Black Faces, White Spaces: Reimagining the Relationship of African Americans to the Great Outdoors*, which filled a gap in scholarship by collecting stories of black environmental experience that have been largely neglected.[12] I'll also read it alongside Margret Grebowicz's slim but potent *The National Park to Come* and its critique of the exclusionary "wilderness affect" that has traditionally shaped the designation and protection of parks in the National Park System. Grebowicz cautions, rightly, that our typical understanding of "wilderness-as-spectacle" makes it easy to ignore the history and politics of public lands. I'll suggest that Johnson's novel, and his work for the NPS, should be seen as correctives to the wilderness affect Grebowicz laments: They reintegrate history and politics while uncovering how people of color have maintained positive emotional connections to nonhuman nature.[13]

At the turn of the twentieth century, Muir and other champions of nature preservation—including, beginning in 2016, the NPS itself—were boasting that parks were for all people. Meanwhile, as Finney reminds us, "enslaved people had just gotten freed, were given land, had that land taken away, and then were living under the threat of Jim Crow segregation for all those years afterward. That's a real cognitive dissonance: There were words on paper saying these protected spaces were meant for everyone, but we know they weren't really meant for everyone, because everything else that was going on in the country at the time indicated that."[14] These ironies, I suggest, also have a felt dimension, *affective* dissonance. It's no wonder that fear, hatred, and anger characterize so many of Elijah's experiences.

By situating racist encounters in the early Yosemite National Park, *Gloryland* renders racism, and the negative affects that fuel it, unnatural. Fear and anger, in particular, are exposed as double-edged: Both are reasonable responses to racism *and* the very emotions that often fuel it. Because fear is typically immobilizing, anger is perhaps more useful for political action.[15] Yet Finney warns that, "while justified," anger "becomes part of people's identity, and they fear if they lose that, they have nothing, no power. Anger becomes the only vehicle in which to explore their feelings and thoughts around these issues, but it is often damaging to others and to themselves."[16] Both fear and anger can be harmful to the one feeling them, and particularly exhausting for a person of color plagued by ignorance, microaggressions, or worse. *Gloryland* confronts these complexities, charting a movement through negative affective territories (fear, anger, hatred) into positive ones: awe, wonder, and joy. Elijah's affective evolution models possibilities for individual and perhaps collective healing in natural environments. The novel certainly walks the line Finney lays out: acknowledging the very real fear that exists as "a by-product of white supremacy and oppression" while also opening a space for the "black imagination to create and construct a rich reality that is not grounded primarily in fear, but in human ingenuity and the rhythms and flows of life."[17]

Compared to the preceding chapters, the organization of this final chapter is inverted: It gives the priority to literature. Because Golden Gate NRA and the Presidio only obliquely include the experiences of black people in the West, my argument in this chapter depends more heavily on written texts. Golden Gate NRA is also a bit of an outlier in my project for being (with the exception of Alcatraz, perhaps)[18] more recreationally focused than the other sites in this study. With these factors in mind, I make two moves. First, I position Johnson's novel as a memorial to a history that hasn't yet found a secure home at a specific NPS site in the West: the role of buffalo soldiers in frontier expansion and the formation and management of the national parks.[19] Second, I suggest that even at a site of recreation, disruptions to tourists' experiences can trigger unexpected affective responses, which can lead to reflection that's every bit as powerful as what happens at a memorial explicitly designed for education or contemplation.

Like Morrison's protagonists in *Beloved*, Elijah leaves the South looking for freedom. Elijah's quest is similar to Sethe's and to Paul D.'s, insofar as he must discover how to claim, and love, himself. Like Paul D., the young Elijah—armed only with an innocent sense of justice that makes him instantly likable—wants to become "a man who owns himself completely."[20] Whereas Paul D. keeps his feelings packed safely away in a tightly sealed tobacco tin heart for most of the novel, and readers are given only glimpses of his years on the road, Elijah expresses strong emotions from the day of his birth. Those feelings intensify as he leaves home—heading not north but west—and travels through diverse American environments.

Fear and anger structure much of Elijah's journey. As he makes his way out of the South, he describes how his fear is "like something living, the shadow of everything you're seeing and feeling." Elijah feels "like a deer, like whatever gets hunted" and his body responds in kind: his heart is "always beating hard," and he breathes rapidly, sweats profusely, and gets fatigued easily. The upside to this constant state of fear is that it "can clear your mind so you see that squirrel in the elm overhead or hear a quail bolting out of the bushes," which makes it "easier to get food."[21] This hyper-attunement to his surroundings—and the fear that prompts it—set the stage for his later appreciation of the beauty of the newly minted Yosemite National Park when he arrives there in 1903.

Also like *Beloved*, *Gloryland* operates in the tension between remembering and forgetting, and Elijah tells us his book contains the things he can't forget. One of those things is his participation in the Indian Wars, which Johnson outlines in the chapter "buffalo soldier." On the one hand, his Seminole and Cherokee ancestry makes him hyperaware that he has something in common with the Indians he's instructed to fight. He doesn't feel the "hate" many of the other "colored soldiers" feel.[22] On the other hand, Elijah takes pride in the 9th Cavalry and enjoys the respect the uniform gives him. He thinks he might prove his patriotism and his humanity by his efforts, that even if he dies fighting for "the same country that enslaved Mama and Daddy, [and] that made war against Grandma Sara's people," his death might still "prove that all of us deserve to be treated like Americans."[23] While he shows tremendous capacity for empathy, whether it's feeling the loneliness and pain of Indians on the plains who've had their lands and their freedom stolen from them, or imagining that white people might be "just as afraid of the colored people around them" as his fellow soldiers are of the Indians,[24] Elijah also confesses to a kind of relief that, for once, the target of racialized hate is someone else.

In the story of U.S. imperialism that Elijah's character reenacts for readers, that "someone else" is Indigenous, Mexican, Cuban, and Filipino. The buffalo soldiers were enlisted in all of these wars of empire. But Johnson pulls off an interesting move—again, like Morrison does with Sethe in *Beloved*—by which he asks readers to withhold our judgment of Elijah and his fellow soldiers' choices and redirect it toward the country that constrained those choices, the nation that limited people's freedom to shape an identity and a life for themselves. One way Johnson does this is by recasting affects as beyond the individual. Elijah is not ashamed of choosing to enlist in the armed forces. As he explains it, his shame is "not at myself but at such a world where it was so easy to make the wrong choice and then choose to go on living."[25] Shame becomes not about a flaw in oneself but rather about flaws in one's country. Externalizing shame in this way, as a response to how things are, at a systemic level, in "such a world," can pose a challenge to the current social order. It's also a unique way to conceive of an affect that, as I discussed in chapter five, is typically internalized.

Gloryland reconceives of other familiar affects by highlighting their environmental dimensions. For Elijah, "anger is a country inside" with a distinct topography: "a flat, empty land."[26] Johnson's novel imagines emotions not just as emplaced, then, but as actual *places*, geographical entities one can inhabit or pass through. In a chapter on the Tampa Riots of 1898, Elijah explains that anger is "a place to live in" and that he "moved all the way there" the summer white soldiers used a two-year-old black child for target practice.[27] When Elijah arrives in Yosemite, he discovers that he's reached the country of "Truth," a "country of high mountains" more conducive to "Happy" than to anger or fear.[28] Sounding a bit like Edward Abbey, Johnson writes: "Everyone's got a favorite place, a place that's who you are, and you can move through it, breathe the air, walk the ground, and be home in a way that you're not anyplace else. I found a place like that in Yosemite, or it found me." The chapter "Horse Heaven" describes his "giddy" feelings in a particularly magical high mountain meadow, a place where God not only walked but also "lingered." In the tradition of John Muir, Johnson often uses religious language to talk about nonhuman nature, and he acknowledges that tradition with a nod to Muir's knowledge of "the name of every bird and every flower" and his ability to "talk about them as if they were people he knew."[29]

Johnson seems to have read Leopold, too. Elijah imagines the world "from the Big Trees' point of view," in which "we're just shadows moving round and not adding up to much of anything." "How long do you have to be there," he wonders, "to be noticed by those mountains?" To them, he muses, the presence of the 9th Cavalry might be "like that cloud of butter-flies [he] saw one spring down in the canyon of the Merced . . . so beautiful, fluttering round like the sun broken up into tiny pieces, pieces that were alive and aware they weren't going to be here for a long time and they might as well spend it all dancing in the air." Elijah notes a kind of indifference in the natural world, a sense that the trees and the mountains "would never know [they were] being taken care of and probably would be just fine if every human being walked away and never came back."[30]

But on rare occasions Elijah suspects that nonhuman nature does take an interest in human activity. On the night he and his fellow black soldiers sing "I Couldn't Hear Nobody Pray," he reflects: "Even the ponderosas and cedars seemed to be leaning over to hear the music, and the mountains around brought it all back, shaped different from how it went out into the world." In a fine example of an agency that isn't strictly narrative but rather affective—part of an atmosphere created by an assemblage of human and nonhuman bodies in, and with, their environment—Johnson describes how the music was visible, something you could see "in the eyes across from you with fire coming up in between," and how that night the mountains finally "recognized us, welcomed us for the first time."[31] This musical collaboration between the soldiers and the mountains resonates with ecocritical conceptions of matter's agential capacities—capacities I've been arguing are every bit as affective as they are narrative.

Not every day affords such spiritual highs. Most of Elijah's duties patrolling the backcountry—checking for poachers or trespassers, greeting the public, and when necessary, enforcing regulations about fires and food gathering—are more banal. Some of the duties aren't much different from what I did during my summers in the Tetons a century later, on the rare occasions I found myself being paid to hike. Of course, since I am a privileged twenty-first-century white woman with no law enforcement commission, Elijah's patrols differ from mine in fundamental ways: His military authority and his skin color sometimes prompt outrage from the people he encounters. Aside from the irate visitor who resented the presence of horses on the trails—a local white man who barged into the visitor center and up to my desk hollering: "Do you like the smell of horse shit?!"—I was never subjected to the negative affects Elijah occasionally faces at work.

Elijah is confronted with that "mix of hate and fear" his whole life, and not just in the South.[32] The West is no stranger to racism. There's the young redheaded boy Elijah meets at the Presidio parade, who can't fathom that Elijah is "a nigger . . . and a soldier."[33] There's the bartender, Mr. William Dunn, who is "close to exploding" when the 9th Cavalrymen come into the bar for a drink and issues a pistol shot to the gut of one soldier who is angry enough to call him out for his racism.[34] And there's the white hunter who neglects to put out his campfire and, when confronted by Elijah and his fellow patrollers, is so angry he looks "like he was going to die from what was boiling inside him."[35] Johnson uses "explosive" imagery—fuses, fires, heat, and bulging veins—to illustrate the anger in these scenes (even the young boy has red hair). In each instance Elijah responds with polite patience and a willingness to do work that isn't part of his job description: the work of exposing the offenders' racism.

Because of his uniform, Elijah occasionally finds himself the object of fear. While out on patrol one day, he spots what he thinks at first are two deer but soon realizes are Indians, an older woman and a young girl. He is "used to coming across Indians in Yosemite Valley, members of a tribe called Ahwahneechee," but these two are wary of him; they watch Elijah and his coworkers "the way you eye a rattlesnake that's about to strike."[36] He soon senses that "along with the fear was anger, too." He listens to the woman as she recounts how her people were killed, displaced, and infected with illness. These Ahwahneechee have every right to be afraid and angry given their history in the valley—a history Mark David Spence details in *Dispossessing the Wilderness*.[37] By placing Indians in the Yosemite Valley, Johnson's book reinforces a lesson Spence's project lays out: that "Americans are able to cherish their national parks today largely because native peoples either abandoned them involuntarily or were forcefully restricted to reservations."[38] Strangely, Spence neglects to mention that the buffalo soldiers were among the U.S. Cavalry enlisted to "forcefully" patrol the early Yosemite NP. *Gloryland* foregrounds that historical fact, giving faces, bodies, stories, and feelings to the people who lived this history.

Elijah's life story exposes how, as Terry Tempest Williams puts it, "America's national parks were a vision seen through the horrors of war."[39] The lands in Yosemite Valley were the first to receive federal protection (although Yosemite wasn't the first national park), and that protection was concurrent with the Civil War. That federal legislation was enabled by events fourteen years prior when, in 1851, a California state militia known as the Mariposa Battalion burned Yosemite Indians' villages, destroyed their food supplies, and forced them from their homes, setting the stage for the colonization of the valley and the expulsion of its Indigenous peoples. This "chapter buried in America's history"[40] has been unearthed and is legible (among other places) on a Yosemite National Park web page, "Destruction and Disruption." There, the NPS asks us to "Imagine strangers invading your neighborhood, burning your house to the ground, and ransacking your local grocery store, and taking over your town. Could you make a living in a foreign culture that invaded your world? Could you hold your family together? Could you survive?"[41] Johnson's novel asks readers for a similar kind of compassionate response while helping us imagine the Ahwahneechee people and their struggles more vividly.

In the encounter with the Yosemite Indians and other racially charged scenes, *Gloryland* dwells on the affective dimensions of racism. Racism, a toxic brew of hatred, anger, and fear, perhaps spiked with a dash of disgust, is felt in bodies as a constellation of negatively charged affects, affects that compound and intensify each other. Racially motivated violence and the affects that enable it are features of an affective atmosphere, something a person of color learns to "smell" or otherwise sense in the air, even if no words are spoken. Elijah explains: "Animals that get hunted know . . . that violence is a thought before it's a deed, a kind of stink mixed in with sweat that you got to learn to smell. It's what it feels like the second before stacked logs burst into flame. You got to know the fire's coming if you don't want to get burned."[42] Johnson echoes what higher profile writers like Frantz Fanon, Audre Lorde, Claudia Rankine, and Ta-Nehisi Coates have also shown: that people of color are exposed to countless large- and small-scale moments of racism (what Rankine and others call "microaggressions"[43]), and that they learn to sense a potentially violent atmosphere from a young age.

While it doesn't shy away from depicting intense, racialized affects within and between humans, *Gloryland* insists the more-than-human-world has little tolerance for emotions like hate, anger, and fear. The Yosemite Valley and its nonhuman residents are indifferent to race: "Trees don't lie bout how they feel bout air. Trees don't care that you're colored. A bear or a river or a canyon or a bird don't care that you're colored. It don't even matter to a rattlesnake that you're colored."[44] Although fear and awe are etymologically linked (think "fear of God")[45] in the tradition of the sublime, Elijah's historical record suggests that negative emotions such as fear are unnatural when they're products of racism. The mix of hate and fear that inspires racism "sounded funny here under the great trees, like it was lost."[46] Racist emotions are inappropriate, out of place in the Yosemite Valley.

Of course, *Gloryland*'s broader message is that racist emotions should have no place *anywhere*, and its protagonist deftly defuses racist confrontations in various environments. Just after being questioned by the young redheaded boy (whom Elijah has calling him "soldier" by the end of their brief conversation), Elijah watches Captain Charles Young escort President Theodore Roosevelt through the Presidio in 1903. Elijah detects "pride" in the way the cavalry holds themselves on their horses, but "it wasn't just pride. I still can't put a name to it," he admits. He leaves us with the simple image of a straight-backed Captain Young "all alone out in that road, in that parade, in that city, in all the brightness, a West Point graduate and a colored officer," but somehow transcendent in his ability to be "in command of [himself]." He struggles to find words for his feelings, but the atmosphere is an intense one full of pride and patriotism.[47] Later, in one of the book's more mystical

chapters, Elijah sees a vision of his future self and describes how the
"air [is] heavy with joy."[48] *Gloryland* is ultimately an optimistic story of
resilience and strength, enabled by Yosemite's grandeur and wildness.

Elijah's candid thoughts and visceral experiences in the Yosemite
Valley invite everyone—not just people of color but all humans—to
rediscover beauty and "Truth" in the more-than-human world. As
Johnson puts it in an interview, "it's not a cultural thing in terms of
being Euro-American or being Hispanic or being African-American.
It's a human thing to respond to beauty."[49] Elijah's posting in the
Yosemite is "not just a physical posting, it was also a spiritual posting,"
and it taught him that "being in the presence of mountains can trans-
figure oneself, can change the way that one looks at the world and how
one looks at oneself in the world."[50] A fictional account like *Gloryland*
is a stirring way to learn about the buffalo soldiers' presence in the
West, to make it relevant to anyone who needs a refresher course on
the longstanding cultural connections African Americans have to the
natural world. Johnson grew up in inner-city Detroit, and his main
audience, the one he thinks about when he puts on his NPS uniform
each day, is young urban blacks who don't see themselves as connected to nonhuman nature. For them, he hopes, the buffalo soldier
story might be a "bridge" that reminds African Americans they "have a
place here."[51] This story of healing and resilience is not just Elijah's; it is
meant to have a broader, collective reach.

I haven't had the good fortune to see Johnson do his living history
reenactment, but from what Burns' *National Parks* documentary shows
and what I've heard in Johnson's podcasts, he must be stunning in his
role as Sergeant Elizy Boman. With an intense, sincere voice and dressed
sharply in a historically accurate uniform, Johnson embodies authenticity. As I argued in my discussion of Golden Spike NHS, reenacts
can romanticize authenticity in a way that risks eliding the violent aspects of the past. Despite that risk, Johnson's visibility at Yosemite NP
naturalizes and affirms a black presence in the U.S. West, including in
the spectacular mountain landscapes so closely identified with the region and with recreational tourism. His novel and his life are valuable
reminders of the important roles black people have played, and continue
to play, in the West. Johnson's visibility is still the exception, and one has

to look closely to detect the legacies of the black West. But traces of the history are there, as I found out when I went to the Presidio in 2013.

——◆◆——

The Presidio was the first site I visited for this book. At the time, I had no idea it would pull together so many of its strands. I had a dim sense of it as a place where "world and local events, from military campaigns to World Fairs and earthquakes, left their mark."[52] A quick online search told me its history in brief. Designated a National Historic Landmark in 1962, the Presidio was later absorbed into Golden Gate National Recreation Area in 1994. A "Post to Park" ceremony was held in October of that year, but the Presidio itself still has a military feel, as if it hasn't quite made the leap to "park" status. This is appropriate, since the Presidio is deeply implicated in a history of war and empire. The Native Ohlone people lived on this land for thousands of years prior to Spanish colonization; then Spain and, following its independence, Mexico, used it as a northern military outpost; finally, the U.S. acquired the site during the Mexican-American War and transformed it dramatically "from mostly windswept dunes and scrub to a verdant, preeminent military post."[53] Like the story of the Owens Valley, this plot struck me as all too familiar, another tale of displacement and military conquest in the American West.

I hadn't yet read the story of Elijah Yancy. I knew next to nothing about the buffalo soldiers who were stationed here or about Captain Young's stint as superintendent of Sequoia NP. I didn't know how many people of African ancestry were among the "Californios" who colonized this part of California.[54] Nor was I thinking about the fact that the Presidio was used as a staging ground for imperial efforts in the Philippines, or that Franklin Delano Roosevelt signed Executive Order 9066 here in 1942, in yet another exercise of federal power bolstered by fear and racism, which restricted the freedoms of yet another minority group.[55] I knew that President Nixon approved the addition of Golden Gate National Recreation Area to the NPS in 1972, partly to preserve the "recreational open space necessary to urban environment and planning" and that this marked a new development in NPS management: it placed the agency "squarely in the business of urban mass recreation for essentially local populations—not previously a federal responsibility." Golden

Gate NRA now encompasses more than 80,000 acres, including "re-stored native habitat, a coastal redwood forest, historical coastal defenses, [and] Alcatraz," in addition to the Muir Woods National Monument, the Marin Headlands, a Nike Missile Site, and the Presidio.[56] The Presidio's history means it, too, contains an eclectic mix of natural and cultural sites: the San Francisco National Cemetery, various military buildings, installation art by Andy Goldsworthy, and even a golf course.

I'd traveled to the Presidio to see an obscure memorial I'd discovered during a rabbit-hole Internet search: the West Coast Memorial to the Missing. This WWII memorial, dedicated to those who died or were buried at sea during that conflict, was built in the late 1950s by the American Battle Monuments Commission. It features a curved wall of California granite bearing the inscribed names of 412 soldiers who lost their lives and/or were buried at sea during WWII. A statue of Columbia, which the Presidio's website calls "the female personification of America," gazes out over the Pacific.[57] The Memorial to the Missing is not a central feature of the NPS website, and there's only a brief mention of it in *The Presidio Experience* newspaper. It's partly this subtlety that appealed to me. I expected it to be off the beaten path. I expected to see a peaceful scene that looked something like this:

FIGURE 6.1. WWII Memorial to the Missing; photo by Jay Graham, Presidio Trust

I arrive breathless and pleasantly flushed after biking up the large hill from the Golden Gate Bridge, and I am excited (as tourists tend to be) to see what I'd come to see. But I do not feel a powerful emotional impact here. For one thing, the memorial is much smaller than I'd imagined, which leaves me feeling (as tourists at Mount Rushmore often do) a bit deflated. Because they're making it ADA accessible—which is great—there is active construction going on at the site, and the scene is abuzz with a handful of friendly construction workers, a mini excavator, and a chaotic visual landscape filled with temporary fences and neon flagging. There is also, to my surprise, a fairly busy road just below this purportedly "serene" spot.[58] The road isn't in any of the pictures I've seen of the site. Architect James Mayo describes the memorial as "situated on a rather quiet promontory site,"[59] but it is anything but quiet today.

Much like the USS *Arizona* Memorial's wall of the missing, the visual rhetoric of this memorial is meant to signal peace, justice, sacrifice, and honor. Its "general disposition" (to return to Ngai's conception of tone) conveys national strength, bravery, coherence, and confidence in a way that, with its orientation toward the Pacific, implicitly celebrates imperialistic Westward migrations and reinscribes U.S. dominance. We may feel small and perhaps sheltered when we look up at Columbia, and when we turn around we are aligned with her Westward gaze—a phenomenological experience that encourages a kind of unity with the site itself and implicitly, with the nation. The statue stands in metonymically for the U.S., inviting visitors to interpret the memorial as telling the nation's story. The nation is feminized both in the inscription and via the statue, who watches over the lost sailors (identified in the wall's text as "sons" who now "sleep" in the sea) like a world-weary mother.

The written text on the granite wall spells out two emotions we are meant to feel: pride and gratitude for the service of the fallen soldiers. I do not feel these things, however. Instead, I find myself intellectualizing. This memorial site stakes its claim on a contested Western landscape, and in doing so, risks relegating ongoing conflicts to the past. The landscape is complicit with this elision, too, I think: The Monterey pine and cypress grove offers itself as a refuge, and the view of the placid-looking ocean—from this vantage point, a passive sea-scape rather than an agential force—smooths over the bodies buried there. These natural features work with the built structures to ease the mourning process and render violence historical. Especially with the grass all torn up, the built environment takes the center of the affective stage, dominating the site and the overall tone of strength, confidence, and endurance. The trauma and loss of war are "missing" here, along with the soldiers' bodies that "sleep" in the sea. The built structure assures us that American dominance continues, sturdy as a wall, devoted as a mother. The fact is conveniently overlooked that this protective ideal of safety, kinship, and love—the kind of love implied in conventional understandings of patriotism—is an unfulfilled promise for so many who inhabit the nation.[60]

The next day, I take a tip from a Presidio Trust employee and set out for an overlook above the San Francisco National Cemetery. Funded by private donors and dedicated on Veterans Day in 2009, the overlook is situated on the cemetery's upper edge. The cemetery itself, I'd read online, contains the graves of some 30,000 soldiers and family members from most major battles in U.S. history. The overlook is, the website had promised, "tucked in the woods." Sure enough, the forest here is denser than at the Memorial to the Missing. My thoughts meander as I stroll up the Bay Area Ridge Trail toward the overlook, content as can be amidst the intoxicating eucalyptus and Monterey pines.

Recent research suggests recreational hiking can instantiate what psychologists call "soft fascination," a "reflective mode" marked by a "mixture of fascination and pleasure."[61] Light hiking feels satisfying, calming, and rejuvenating because the natural stimuli that encourage soft fascination—things like "the play of light on foliage, the patterns created by long shadows, [and] the different moods of a nature oasis with changes in weather and season"[62]—engage our default mode network, allow our minds to wander, and have "emotionally positive and low-arousing" impacts on our bodies.[63] It may be tempting to want to ignore or skim over park displays if you've achieved this pleasant state, since narratives would disrupt soft fascination by challenging us to read and think historically. Even so, recreational hiking can make us attuned to forms of knowledge that aren't, at least initially, intellectually taxing. If anxiety predisposes us to feel fear—as I argued in chapter one—then perhaps soft fascination provides an affective foundation for moments of awe or wonder, as well as for other unsettling, dissonant responses.

The physical environment offers plenty of prompts for wonder. Whether it's the startling 100-foot-tall "Spire" installed by Andy Goldsworthy or a flustered California quail crossing your path, a surprise encounter in a natural setting can inspire wonder—an affective response that's unscripted, unexpected, and for a moment at least, unprocessed. Jane Bennett describes moments like this in terms of "enchantment," which entails "a temporary suspension of chronological time and bodily movement."[64] Other researchers study "awe," and recent work in psychology has produced some intriguing results. In particular, a research lab in Berkeley led by Jonathan Haidt and Dacher Keltner has published a series of studies suggesting that awe is evolutionarily useful: It makes us happier and healthier, encourages collaboration, and might even foster altruistic behavior.[65] Awe has even been linked to an increased awareness of the agency of the more-than-human world.[66]

Especially compelling to me is the likelihood that "[m]omentary experiences of awe stimulate wonder and curiosity."[67] But this description positions wonder as a mere side effect of awe, something awe "stimulates." What if wonder is something else, something not *awe*-ful exactly, and so not tethered to the problematic associations with fear, domination, and masculinity that have plagued the sublime?[68] It seems to me that wonder has the advantage of being a less magical-sounding word than enchantment and a more accurate one for the scaled-down version of awe that's probably more common for today's technological tourists. Wonder's noun-verb flexibility is also appealing. I'll define wonder, for now, as a break in the ordinary, a way of stepping out of time and inhabiting, for a long moment or two, an affectively charged exchange, a feeling of fascination, or amazement, a kind of *felt* curiosity (the noun, "wonder") with the potential to become *intellectual* curiosity (the verb, "to wonder")—to figure out what things are called, how they work, and why things are the way they are.[69]

As I crest the hill on the final approach to the overlook, I have a moment of wonder when I come upon a waist-high rock wall with words carved on it in all caps: "THEY SAY: WE WERE YOUNG. WE HAVE DIED. REMEMBER US."

FIGURE 6.2. Archibald MacLeish poetry on rock wall at the San Francisco National Cemetery overlook; photo courtesy of Presidio Trust

I'd been expecting an overlook, not a wall, and its sudden presence stops me in my tracks for a second. As I resume walking, now with halting, tentative steps along the path, I encounter three more walls, with more words on them. The last of the three identifies the words as a poem by Archibald MacLeish, "The Young Dead Soldiers Do Not Speak." Etched on the memorial structure, they embody his modernist mantra from "Ars Poetica": "a poem should not mean, but *be*." Written on rock, on a piece of matter, this poem *is*. It becomes an affective object, an object with agency or what Bennett calls "thing-power." It arrests me, momentarily backgrounding the other features of the affective atmosphere: the smell of eucalyptus, the inviting benches, the neatly spaced grave markers, and the bay below.

Reading these lines of verse on the rock is by far the most powerful affective conversion point of my day. Wonder, sparked by the encounter with the rock walls, has converted my peaceful mood to something very different. When I get to the wall that says "Whether our lives and our deaths were for peace and a new hope or for nothing we cannot say; it is *you* who must say this," I feel pensive and melancholy. I am stunned by the direct address, the confrontational challenge to justify wars that take the lives of the young, the collective voice of the "we" who have been the victims. My inability to find justification registers corporeally, as an unsettling affective response, an anxious feeling in the pit of my stomach that disturbs an otherwise peaceful day of walk-ing the trails. That arresting feature, that visceral impact, of memorials often comes when the textual and environmental dimensions of affect are in tension, and that tension takes hold of one's body. In this case, my happy-go-lucky hiker mood has been exposed, called out, and con-verted into an uneasy dissonance.

Sure, as an English professor, I'm predisposed to appreciate the gut punch of good poetry. But the second-person addresses and the frank mandate of the verse speak not only to me but also to the implied tourist directly, not in the generic (and occasionally, condescending) way that most NPS displays do but as human beings. The tone here is solemn, not in the symbolic sense of honoring bravery—too often an uncritical, nationalistic ritual—but rather in the more personal, direct sense of re-minding us of mortality. Beyond the words, the physical environment, like all overlooks, directs our experience toward particular visual and affective ends. As Robert Bednar explains, overlooks "present the land-scape as if it were already a picture, and present themselves as a place to take pictures."[70] However, gazing out across the hillside at the graves, over at the Golden Gate Bridge, and down at the bay and the ferries to Alcatraz Island doesn't encourage me to snap a photo. The neatly spaced grave markers overshadow the rest—they are a visual body count and a reminder that mortality is a condition we all share, complicate the kind of landscape aesthetic typically encouraged at park overlooks. It's hard to feel a sense of mastery over a landscape that is occupied by deceased human beings. This particular overlook situates you in an "embodied relation"[71] to a landscape full of other humans—and they have died. This brutal fact reinforces the site's broader message about war and death: Death is final, and the living must take responsibility for it, make mean-ing out of it, and account for this sacrifice.

FIGURE 6.3. View from the overlook; photo courtesy of Presidio Trust

The website lauds this is as a "contemplative" view, and I agree. I sit on one of the benches and look out at the bay and think. I can hear distant traffic but it's not loud, and there is no visible road. While mulling over the poetry, I start to notice things again: the pleasant aroma of the eucalyptus, the rustle of the breeze disturbing the fallen leaves, the sound of a group of schoolchildren coming toward me. The moment of wonder compelled my initial interest, and what followed was a gradual immersion, a slow moving down the path, directed by the poem's words and the gentle spacing of the walls. Because the overlook is spread out, not compact and unified like the West Coast Memorial, you encounter it experientially, as a kind of process—and it encourages a more open-ended affective encounter. I'm not sure I can pinpoint a singular emotional response.

A unique combination of narrative and affective agency has created a powerful affective dissonance. I feel the grief of mortality and the shame of the ruthlessness with which the U.S. conducts its nation-building projects, and, at the same time, the incongruous sense of peacefulness a silent cemetery emits and the compassion many humans have for each other in the face of our inevitable deaths. I'm not sure if these are the things I'm supposed to feel. Military cemeteries are places where visitors should respect the sacrifice, the "ultimate price," these citizens made for us. Sacrifice, as I discussed in chapter five, can feel like a necessary part of being a good citizen—even, or maybe especially, when we are grieving others who've died for our country. If it weren't for the confrontational poetry, I'd suspect that the overlook is meant to prompt something closer to the pride and patriotism embodied in the statue of Columbia.

As it turns out, the Presidio's landscape *was* originally designed to inspire confidence in the nation. I'd walked by a sign along the trail that told me the Presidio is the product of "the largest landscaping effort ever attempted and completed by the U.S. Army." Later I'd learn that the goal of that landscape management was to "accentuate the idea of the power of Government." According to Major William A. Jones, who was in charge of the forestation project:

> The main idea is to crown the ridges, border the boundary fences, and cover the areas of sand and marsh waste with a forest that will generally seem continuous, and thus appear immensely larger than it really is. By leaving the valleys uncovered . . . the contrast of height will be strengthened . . . In order to make the contrast from the city seem as great as possible, and indirectly accentuate the idea of the power of Government, I have surrounded all the entrances with dense masses of wood.[72]

Trying to make the Presidio seem "larger and more continuous than it really was" (and to mitigate winds that swept through the post), the Army transformed the native sand dunes and coastal scrub into strategic groves of Monterey cypress, Monterey pines, and (all the way from Australia) the fragrant eucalyptus trees that so enchant me. The Presidio Trust's *Cultural Landscape Report* explains that, in the nineteenth century, a forest landscape was "considered an 'ideal landscape.' It was considered more appealing, comfortable, and familiar to people used to the tree-covered eastern landscapes."[73] The report confirms what I'd read on the sign, that the park's natural landscapes were designed in accordance with "military values": "hierarchy, consistency, order, utility, discipline, and functionality."[74] There is a sense in which the trees are like sentinels, a powerful infantry poised to keep watch over the water and protect the country from invaders.

Certainly one could glean "the power of the Government" at the Presidio today, especially if holistically mapped, or seen from an aerial view. But sitting amidst these trees as an embodied visitor, the groves don't register that way. Despite being planted in rows (and in some areas, rows that were too close together for the trees' health), these forests don't seem orderly or disciplined now. Eucalyptus bark peels and falls to the ground, as do its long leaves. Large cones from the Monterey pines lie around haphazardly. We might think of these as small-scale examples of nonhuman nature's agency—natural tactics that undermine the strategic uses humans put them to. Like the tourists who come here, the more-than-human world exerts itself in unpredictable, sometimes messy, ways. Tracing the affective atmosphere at a particular site, at a particular moment, can reveal the intersections between natural and cultural history and the shifty, intense conversions of affects, even at a site of recreation.

——◆◆——

Whether they take distinct emotional forms or not, moments of affect often prompt contemplation. A startling encounter with a snake can lead to insights about other anxieties. A steam engine's high-pitched whistle can inspire patriotic pride or painful nostalgia, which may engender counterfactual reflection. A baseball field overshadowed by a guard tower, or a tiny toothbrush lying beside a baby's grave, can trigger sadness tinged with anger about racist injustices. Sometimes our affective responses are mixed feelings we can't put a name to or mold into narrative form. My emotional response at the cemetery overlook was complex and hard to articulate. I'm not sure there's an emotion word, for instance, for the feeling of sensing one's mortality by measuring one's own tiny life against a particular landscape or under a particular sky. Or for the feeling of being overwhelmed by the too-many lives lost to war and the too-many other unnecessary forms of suffering.

But affective dissonance is unsettling; it wants to resolve. Like wonder, affective dissonance may be especially conducive to curiosity, in that it makes us search for answers. The wonder that precipitated my complex feelings at the overlook made me want to read the signs care-fully, to know whose graves I was looking at and why they lost their lives. If I couldn't say whether they died for something or "for nothing" at least I could find out who they were. Although the display at the overlook didn't mention them, I'd later discover on the website that 450 of the white headstones in those carefully arranged rows mark the bodies of buffalo soldiers. These soldiers, I'd learn, were called upon to carry out a range of military duties.

In addition to escorting President Roosevelt in the Presidio, pa-trolling in the Yosemite Valley, and superintending in Sequoia National Park, the buffalo soldiers participated in the destruction of Indigenous peoples, fought in the Spanish-American War, had a hand in secur-ing the U.S.-Canada border in southeastern Alaskan boom towns, and were stationed periodically at Fort Huachuca, near the present-day Coronado National Memorial. The history of the buffalo soldiers in the West debunks the "deracinated Anglo frontier myth"[75] and reveals a military that "tolerated" black presence but "preferred to use 'colored' soldiers in remote outposts."[76] It also illustrates the migrations and re-verberations of racialized violence—how it moves from region to re-gion, how it pits people of color groups against each other, and how it underscores international imperial projects. Seeing the graves at the San Francisco National Cemetery makes these connections real for me, even if the black presence there is far from the most visible feature of the site. Other ghostly echoes of violent histories can be heard if you're listening. For instance, a typo on the cemetery website—a link to "fa-mous internments" where it should say "interments"[77]—accidentally reminds us that the incarceration of Japanese Americans was autho-rized at the Presidio. While it has yet to fully acknowledge its role as a settler colonial institution, the NPS is getting savvier about how to uncover and interpret these diverse and intertwined histories.

NPS sites have the capacity to move visitors of any demographic from negative affects to positive ones, as they did for Shelton Johnson. Terry Tempest Williams imagines a similar shift from fear to resilience when visitors come to these "places of poetry": "Rather than fear the wilderness ahead, even climate change, we are present inside it. Fear is replaced with engagement. Relationships are forged, resiliency as a species is enhanced." Within the extreme ecological and political conditions we find ourselves, Williams believes "our greatest transformation as a species will be spiritual. The word 'we' must include all species."[78] She elaborates:

> When we enter places of grandeur and sites of suffering, and inhabit landscapes of historical import and ecological splendor, we stand on the periphery of awe. How did this happen? Who were the witnesses? And what are we seeing now? The American landscape has a voice, many voices. It becomes us. Our national parks are a burning bush of identities.[79]

Williams is right, of course, about the need to listen to the many voices of the American landscape, about the need to ask better questions about the histories embedded there, and about the need to contemplate a more democratic future. But her solution is less clear about *how* we get from there to here, from fear to engagement, from divisive to harmonious multispecies relationships. What, exactly, will bring about the kind of "[h]umility in the face of humanity"[80] she proposes? What affective responses are most likely to make us ask "How did this happen"?

I have been suggesting that a better understanding of emotions like fear, shame, and anxiety, as well as lesser-known affects like regret, wonder, and Williams's own eco-patriotism, might help. Discourse about "emotional intelligence" is gaining momentum, although the *Harvard Business Review* model seems to prioritize self-discipline in the service of a pro-capitalist agenda.[81] A more deliberate awareness of how we feel, and a more coherent vocabulary to talk about our feelings, could be beneficial not just for turning a profit but also for promoting justice. It seems appropriate to expect NPS managers to become more fluent in the language of affect in the service of the agency's own not-for-profit agenda. This fluency must be accompanied by a more sophisticated sense of how affective responses are not universal but rather are deeply informed by personal experiences and emotional memories, as well as by factors related to our identities—including race, gender, class, and sexuality.

Indeed, environmental and social justice might be productively reconnected around the category of affect, but only if we attend more closely to the racialized, gendered, sexualized, and classed aspects of affect *in regard to environments*. Being "outdoorsy" can signal belonging to the nation, for some tourists; for others, like the "black hiker" in a recent "Funny or Die" video, your skin color marks you as out of place in a public park.[82] As Evelyn White and others have long noted, wilderness is haunted by historical trauma for African Americans in particular. Finney puts it this way: "the memory of slavery and segregation has manifested in many ways, including in the form of an *emotional residue* that has the capacity to be a roadblock in the pursuit of healthy human/environment relationships." There is, she says, "an emotional and psychological 'trickle-down effect'" that passes from generation to generation and crystallizes in places.[83]

Yet fear, as Finney insists and Johnson's novel reiterates, is not the only way people of color connect to natural environments. Camille Dungy, Audrey Peterman, LaTasha N. Nevada Diggs, Percival Everett, and bell hooks, are among the many African American writers expanding the options for affective engagement with the more-than-human world. I've been suggesting that most people don't live perpetually in the grips of fear or other basic emotions, which is one reason we need a broader, more precise vocabulary for our feelings. Yet some people do endure negative emotions on a near-constant basis—depression, anxiety, and other unpleasant moods and background feelings—and some people of color do live with the terrifying feeling of being a target, of being "hunted," that Johnson attributes to his protagonist. Given these complexities, everyday, "ordinary" affects are every bit as essential to track as those rare moments in which we find ourselves "on the periphery of awe."

As we enter a new epoch many geologists agree should be called the Anthropocene, it is more urgent than ever to assess feelings about loss, change, and trauma. As Williams writes about a different kind of change—her mother's impending death—in *Refuge*, "It's strange to feel change coming. It's easy to ignore. An underlying restlessness seems to accompany it like birds flocking before a storm. We go about our business with the usual alacrity, while in the pit of our stomach there is a sense of something tenuous."[84] In the face of the restlessness, the visceral tenuousness of life in the Anthropocene—a tenuousness that often manifests as anxiety, melancholia, or grief—the choice between hope and despair seems more pronounced than ever.[85] Some say we have no alternative but to soldier on and hope for the best, while some cast doubt on the efficacy of hope itself.[86]

Others wonder: Is it really a matter of leaving a legacy for the future—a future in which we (humans) may not exist—or is our task in the present to resign ourselves to dying with dignity? For Iraq War veteran and writer Roy Scranton, the latter may be our only option. "Learning how to die" means refusing the tendency of the psyche to "rebel against the idea of its own end." We must, Scranton argues, live life in close contemplation of our probable death.[87] This is a difficult task.[88] Strangely enough, public memorials can help us face our emotions about death in a way that facilitates concern for the present. In fact, the moving part of the MacLeish poem, for me, was its visceral reminder that these soldiers have died—we can see their graves below— and also that we, too, are dying. "Learning how to die as an individual means letting go of our predispositions and fear," says Scranton," and learning how to die as a civilization will require much more than that.[89]

The National Memorial for Peace and Justice opened on April 26, 2018, near Montgomery, Alabama, and it is one of the more honest, confrontational public memory sites in recent history. Developed by the Equal Justice Initiative (EJI), the site demands a "reckoning with one of the nation's least recognized atrocities: the lynching of thousands of black people in a decades-long campaign of racist terror."[90] A total of 800 large steel columns hang from a roof along a "grim cloister" of a walkway; each column represents a county in which lynchings are known to have occurred, and each is engraved with victims' names. These belated graves (a *NYT* article describes them as "like the headstones that lynching victims were rarely given") start at eye level but end by dangling above you as you walk a slowly descending floor, and you're put "in the position of the callous spectators in old photographs of public lynchings."[91] The memorial (which I haven't had the chance to visit yet) combines names, stories, details of lynchings, and writing by Toni Morrison and others, with a powerful architectural design intended to make visitors feel unsettled. The physical environment aids in that project:

> A grassy hillock rises in the middle of the memorial. From here you can see the Montgomery skyline through the thicket of hanging columns, the river where the enslaved were sold and the State Capitol building that once housed the Confederacy, whose monuments the current Alabama governor has vowed to protect. It is a striking view. But Mr. Stevenson [founder of EJI] pointed out that when standing here, you are on view as well, faced on all sides by the names of the thousands who were run down, instantly judged and viciously put to death.
>
> "You might feel judged yourself," he said. "What are you going to do?"

The physical environment exposes the benevolent "city on the hill" narrative of American identity as a sham and turns the optic tables on visitors, who are exposed and "judged" by the ghosts of those who were "viciously" killed. The memorial physically puts visitors on the spot, makes us complicit in the nation's violent history, and forces us to contemplate our implication in the politics of the present.

The memorial has far-reaching aims, both ideological and physical. Physically, the long-term plan is that counties will come and "claim" their column, then install it in a public space.[92] Ideologically, we are urged to connect past violence with its contemporary legacy, especially the instant "judgments" made by police officers whose racially inflected fear leads them to "put to death" black men. The fact that the memorial is dedicated to "victims of white supremacy" suggests we should extend the reach of our concern to other people of color, in addition to African Americans. Interestingly, this memorial's design was inspired not by other U.S. sites but rather by European models—Berlin's Holocaust Memorial and Johannesburg's Apartheid Museum—suggesting it might require a healthy dose of international perspective to tell more honest stories about our nation's past and our present.

Stevenson's challenge reminds me of the NPS's question at Manzanar NHS: "What does Manzanar mean to you?" What if NPS memory sites could be designed, like the EJI memorial, to confront us more directly, and to clearly connect past and present injustices? What would it take for NPS memory sites to avoid being "colonized by the compulsory optimism that has a stranglehold on all our attempts at life-building today"?[93] The agency's hands are, to some degree, tied due to its democratic mission and enforced political neutrality. But they can partner with organizations who are at liberty to speak more freely about politics, such as the International Coalition of Sites of Conscience.[94] The physical environment, too, can be enlisted in what we might call a "tourism without optimism." Manzanar's barracks compel us to simulate a humiliating lack of privacy within an uncomfortable living space. The Presidio's cemetery overlook confronts us with our mortality. These sorts of human-environment interactions avoid reproducing ideals of sacrifice and honor or the ideologies about progress and nationality that too often help support war in the present and future. They leave us feeling ambivalent, affectively dissonant, and so, I've been suggesting here, more likely to ask hard questions and seek hard answers.

Memorials have the potential to remind us of environmental losses in conjunction with traumatic human histories. Heavily managed landscapes like the ones in this study remind us that all landscapes are dynamic processes that humans shape, or manufacture, then exploit for various aesthetic, affective, and ideological purposes. Even built structures are dynamic, with their own material histories of design, construction, and transportation and often—as happened when the statue of Columbia's toe was damaged and needed to be rebuilt—decay and/ or restoration. Affect theory helps us to see all environments as processive, in flux, and ongoing, and so is a useful tool for destabilizing and demystifying memorial spaces, giving the lie to the apparent permanence and completion signified there. Memorials also raise questions of scale—both spatial and temporal—in provocative ways, inspiring visitors to think across geologic and anthropocentric time scales, sometimes both at once. The kind of geological thinking many memorials encourage reduces human agency to a negligible level, which could inspire all sorts of generative emotions in an epoch in which humans are both "exceptional," insofar as we self-identify as a force of nature, *and* subject to geologic forces in scary new ways.

Whether an iconic site, like Mount Rushmore National Memorial, or a lesser-known one, like Coronado National Memorial, sites of public memory are accretive, geologically, culturally, and emotionally. Memorials matter, clearly, but so do the environments—neighborhoods, city streets, offices, classrooms, parks, roads—we use and live in every day. Ideally, then, the attention to affective agency I've been thinking through in this book will be useful in becoming more attuned to how affect circulates in, is embedded in, and impacts us in, our daily worlds. The micromoments in which affect "happens" are often the breaks in our routines that matter most. Because affect disrupts the ordinary, it's a crucial catalyst for extraordinary thought and action— precisely what the Anthropocene requires.

Notes

1. NPS website featured link, "National Park Getaway: César E. Chávez National Monument." https://www.nps.gov/articles/getaway-cech.htm. Accessed 4 July, 2017.

2. Toni Morrison, interview in *The World*, 1989. Cited in *The Toni Morrison Society*, "Bench By The Road Project." http://www.tonimorrisonsociety.org/bench.html. Accessed 2 July, 2017.

3. https://museumandmemorial.eji.org/. Accessed 4 May, 2018.

4. https://www.nps.gov/nico/index.htm. Accessed 6 July, 2017.

5. "Buffalo Soldiers of Company L," at https://www.nps.gov/klgo/index.htm. Accessed 6 July, 2017.

6. NPS site, "On The Western Frontier." https://www.nps.gov/prsf/learn/historyculture/on-the-western-frontier.htm. Accessed 4 July, 2017.

7. NPS site, "A Buffalo Soldier Speaks." https://www.nps.gov/yose/learn/historyculture/buffspodcast16-30.htm. Accessed 4 July, 2017.

8. Useful resources include: Philip Durham and Everett Jones's *The Negro Cowboys* (New York: Dodd, Mead & Company, 1965); William Loren Katz, *The Black West* (New York: Doubleday, 1971); Sara Massey, ed., *Black Cowboys of Texas* (College Station, TX: Texas A&M University Press, 2000); Michael K. Johnson, *Black Masculinity and the Frontier Myth in American Literature* (Norman, OK: University of Oklahoma Press, 2002); Dan Moos, *Outside America: Race, Ethnicity, and the Role of the American West in National Belonging* (Hanover, NH: Dartmouth College Press, 2005); *Black Cowboys in the American West: On the Range, On the Stage, Behind the Badge*, ed. Bruce Glasrud and Michael Searles (Norman: University of Oklahoma Press, 2016); and Emily Lutenski, *West of Harlem: African American Writers and the Borderlands* (Lawrence: University Press of Kansas, 2016).

9. Michael K. Johnson, *Hoo-Doo Cowboys and Bronze Buckaroos: Conceptions of the African American West* (Jackson, MS, University Press of Mississippi, 2014), 12.

10. Carolyn Finney, *Black Faces, White Spaces: Reimagining the Relationship of African Americans to the Great Outdoors* (Chapel Hill: University of North Carolina Press, 2014), 117, my emphasis.

11. Finney, 28.

12. Finney has worked closely with the NPS and other federal agencies to provide valuable perspective on the agencies' goals of diversifying their staff and sites. She explains the exhausting nature of this work, in which people of color are constantly tasked with providing that perspective; however, she finds the patience and energy to continue. Audrey Peterman is another black woman who has done incredibly important work for the NPS.

13. Strangely, Grebowicz pays no attention to Johnson's role there or to his novel, despite her treatment of the Burns's documentary.

14. Finney, 117.

15. I nod to Audre Lorde here, whose "The Uses of Anger" is a black feminist classic.

16. Finney, 65.

17. Finney, 123.

18. Even Alcatraz can be experienced recreationally, as little more than a "must-see attraction," at which challenging historical events, including the Native American Occupation of November 1969 - June 1971, are elided. See Teresa Bergman and Cynthia Duquette Smith, "You Were on Indian Land: Alcatraz Island as Recalcitrant Memory Space" (in *The Places of Public Memory: The Rhetoric of Museums and Memorials*), 160–188.

19. In addition to the sites I mention in the first pages of this chapter, Yosemite National Park—primarily relying on Johnson himself—is another high-profile location for telling this history. However, visitors to Yosemite NP are even more likely to go there for recreational purposes, and Golden Gate NRA serves the purposes of this project better.

20. Shelton Johnson, *Gloryland* (San Francisco: Sierra Club Books, 2009). The quote is from the book jacket description, but there are references to being "a man" throughout the novel as well.

21. Johnson, *Gloryland*, 82.

22. Johnson, *Gloryland*, 105.

23. Johnson, *Gloryland*, 109–10.

24. Johnson, *Gloryland*, 94.

25. Johnson, *Gloryland*, 112.

26. Johnson, *Gloryland*, 191–2.

27. Johnson, *Gloryland*, 117. For one historical account of the shooting at a black child and the ensuing Tampa riot, see Willard B. Gatewood Jr., "Negro Troops in Florida, 1898," *Florida Historical Quarterly* XLIX (1970), 7–9.

28. Johnson, *Gloryland*, 192, 209.

29. Johnson, *Gloryland*, 225–6.

30. Johnson, *Gloryland*, 232.
31. Johnson, *Gloryland*, 236–7.
32. Johnson, *Gloryland*, 174.
33. Johnson, *Gloryland*, 142.
34. Johnson, *Gloryland*, 167–8.
35. Johnson, *Gloryland*, 173.
36. Johnson, *Gloryland*, 201.
37. See Spence's chapter "The Heart of the Sierras, 1864–1916" for an overview of that history in relation to the designation of Yosemite National Park, 101–113.
38. Spence, 101.
39. Williams, *The Hour*, 7.
40. Williams, *The Hour*, 8.
41. "Destruction and Disruption," Yosemite National Park website. https://www.nps.gov/yose/learn/historyculture/destruction-and-disruption.htm. Accessed 31 May, 2018.
42. Johnson, *Gloryland*, 167.
43. Rankine talks about this term in "Using Poetry to Uncover the Moments that Lead to Racism," *PBS Newshour*, December 4, 2014. http://www.pbs.org/newshour/bb/using-poetry-uncover-moments-lead-racism/. Accessed 18 August, 2017.
44. Johnson, *Gloryland*, 193.
45. The online Oxford English Dictionary contains one definition of fear as "A mingled feeling of dread and reverence towards God (formerly also, towards any rightful authority)." This definition seems to have fallen out of favor since the nineteenth century.
46. Johnson, *Gloryland*, 174.
47. Johnson, *Gloryland*, 145.
48. Johnson, *Gloryland*, 246.
49. Kurt Repanshek, "*Gloryland* Brings Yosemite National Park Ranger Shelton Johnson Full Circle," *National Parks Traveler*, September 30, 2009. https://www.nationalparktraveler.org/2009/09/gloryland-brings-yosemite-national-park-ranger-shelton-johnson-full-circle4649. Accessed 10 July, 2017.
50. Repanshek, "*Gloryland.*"
51. "Shelton Johnson," *The National Parks*, pbs.org. http://www.pbs.org/national-parks/people/nps/johnson/. Accessed 11 July, 2017.
52. http://www.presidio.gov/visit. Accessed 13 October, 2013.
53. https://www.nps.gov/prsf/learn/historyculture/index.htm. Accessed 6 July, 2017. For a more thorough study of the Presidio's colonial history, see Barbara Voss, *The Archeology of Ethnogenesis: Race and Sexuality in Colonial San Francisco* (Berkeley: University of California Press, 2008).
54. The Golden Gate NRA apparently led an educational hike about the "African Californios" at least once, in February of 2017. https://www.nps.gov/goga/plan-yourvisit/event-details.htm?event=FE7CE2BC-1DD8-B71B-0BEF581B1E21815A. Accessed 15 May, 2018. I couldn't find another place on the website focused on "the untold stories of African-Latino in California's colonial period," but presumably their "legacy" is on the NPS's radar. I suspect Golden Gate NRA's archives contain

much more information, although only .1 percent of the more than five million documents are available to online researchers. https://www.nps.gov/goga/learn/historyculture/research.htm. Accessed 15 May, 2018.

55. A year-long 75th anniversary exhibit (which unfortunately didn't coincide with my visit) commemorates this "dark moment in history." https://www.nps.gov/goga/anniversary-executive-order-9066.htm. Accessed 17 July, 2017.

56. *The National Parks*, 79.

57. http://www.presidio.gov/places/world-war-ii-memorial-to-the-missing. Accessed 15 October, 2013.

58. James Mayo, *War Memorials as Political Landscape: The American Experience and Beyond* (New York: Praeger, 1988), 110.

59. Ibid.

60. For an insightful analysis of how narratives of protective love support hate group ideology, see Ahmed, "In the Name of Love," *Cultural Politics*, 122–143.

61. Rachel Kaplan and Stephen Kaplan, *The Experience of Nature: A Psychological Perspective* (New York: Cambridge University Press, 1989), 192. For another definition of soft fascination, see Peter Aspinall, Panagiotis Mavros, Richard Coyne, and Jenny Roe, "The urban brain: analyzing outdoor physical activity with mobile EEG," *British Journal of Sports Medicine*, vol. 49 (2015): 272–276. Accessed 22 May, 2017.

62. Kaplan and Kaplan, 193.

63. Ruth Ann Atchley, David L. Strayer, and Paul Atchley, "Creativity in the Wild: Improving Creative Reasoning through Immersion in Natural Settings," *PLoS ONE* 7:12 (2012): 1. Although research on the default mode network is still in its infancy, it is linked to creativity, memory, and "restful introspection" (Atchley, Strayer, and Atchley, 2). A related term is "flow," a concept introduced by psychologist Mihaly Csikszentmihalyi to describe the dynamic absorption in a physical task in which we float between boredom and anxiety in a kind of harmony with our environment and temporarily silence our internal monologue. I count recreational hiking as soft fascination rather than flow, since hiking is generally done at a lower intensity than most flow activities and does not shut down linguistic thought. An overview of Csikszentmihalyi's ideas can be found here: http://www.pursuit-of-happiness.org/history-of-happiness/mihaly-csikszentmihalyi/.

64. Bennett, *The Enchantment of Modern Life: Attachments, Crossings, and Ethics* (Princeton: Princeton University Press, 2001), 5.

65. For an overview, see Dacher Keltner and Jonathon Haidt, "Approaching awe, a moral, spiritual, and aesthetic emotion," *Cognition & Emotion*, 17 (2003), 297–314. For a study on awe's altruistic capacity, see Claire Prade and Vassilis Saroglou, "Awe's effects on generosity and helping," *The Journal of Positive Psychology* 11.5 (2016).

66. See Piercarlo Valdesolo and Jesse Graham, "Awe, Uncertainty, and Agency Detection," *Psychological Science*, November 18, 2013.

67. Their research findings are summarized at the Berkeley lab's site in accessible language, which is where I found this quote. Dacher Keltner, "Why Do We Feel Awe?"

May 10, 2016. http://greatergood.berkeley.edu/article/item/why_do_we_feel_awe. Accessed 1 September, 2017.

68. I plan to explore wonder, awe, and soft fascination in greater depth in a separate publication. Certainly more research needs to be done on wonder as an affect distinct from awe, especially now that mobile EEG machines are available to track brain activity as we move through environments.

69. For a recent exploration of wonder in relation to the sublime, see Louise Economides, *The Ecology of Wonder in Romantic and Postmodern Literature* (New York: Palgrave MacMillan, 2016). Houser's *Ecosickness* reads several Richard Powers novels for their treatment of wonder, exposing how the affect can provoke curiosity and concern, or vulnerability and paranoia, if taken to the extreme (77–116).

70. Robert Bednar, "Being Here, Looking There: Mediating Vistas in the National Parks of the Contemporary American West" (in *Observation Points*), 20.

71. Ibid.

72. Royston Hanamoto Alley & Abey, Landscape Architects, *Main Post Cultural Landscape Report: Presidio of San Francisco* (San Francisco CA: The Presidio Trust, 2012), 30.

73. Ibid., 202.

74. Ibid., 11.

75. Lutenski, 29.

76. Savoy, 142. Savoy discovers that "all four African American regiments had called the fort home by the early 1930s" (144). Her archival research fleshes out a more complicated history than the one told at the Fort Huachuca post museum, which "praises the Buffalo Soldiers for their gallantry and self-sacrifice, their rise above prejudice and 'quiet dignity lacking outright protest'" (154). She uncovers evidence of racism, discrimination, and protests.

77. San Francisco National Cemetery, https://www.nps.gov/prsf/learn/historyculture/san-francisco-national-cemetery.htm. Accessed 11 July, 2017.

78. Williams, *The Hour*, 360–1.

79. Williams, 363.

80. Williams, 362.

81. During a recent visit to an airport bookstore, I found a conspicuously placed compilation of ten "must-read" articles from *Harvard Business Review*, titled *On Emotional Intelligence*. Daniel Goleman's widely cited work on the subject has helped bring it into the mainstream. The brief table in *On Emotional Intelligence* called "Idea in Brief" doesn't name a single emotion—aside from empathy, which (as I've suggested) is a gateway to a shared emotional experience, not an emotion itself. They list "self-awareness," "self-regulation," "motivation," and "social skill" as the "abilities" we need to hone (3).

82. "Black Hiker, with Blair Underwood," November 23, 2009. http://www.funnyordie.com/videos/24b56caf3e/black-hiker-with-blair-underwood. Accessed 19 May, 2018.

83. Finney, 50, my emphasis.

84. Williams, *Refuge*, 24.

85. Many of the authors compiled in my recent co-edited collection explore affects that are emerging, or being redefined, in the Anthropocene. Kyle Bladow and Jennifer Ladino, *Affective Ecocriticism: Emotion, Embodiment, Environment* (Lincoln: University of Nebraska Press, 2018). Timothy Morton deserves mention for his treatment of melancholia in his well-known *Ecology without Nature* (Cambridge: Harvard University Press, 2007).

86. For a recent take on hope, see Derrick Jensen, "Beyond Hope." *Orion Magazine*. https://orionmagazine.org/article/beyond-hope/. Accessed 6 February, 2017. For an alternate (more "hopeful") view of hope, see Rebecca Solnit's *Hope in the Dark*.

87. Roy Scranton, "Learning How to Die in The Anthropocene," *The New York Times*, November 10, 2013. https://opinionator.blogs.nytimes.com/2013/11/10/learning-how-to-die-in-the-anthropocene/. Accessed 17 July, 2017.

88. For one study that links reluctance to think about our morality with resistance to climate change, see George Marshall's *Don't Even Think About It: Why Our Brains Are Wired to Ignore Climate Change* (New York: Bloomsbury, 2014).

89. The "more" is the subject of Scranton's book, *Learning to Die in the Anthropocene: Reflections on the End of a Civilization* (San Francisco: City Lights, 2015), 24.

90. Campbell Robertson, "A Lynching Memorial Is Opening. The Country Has Never Seen Anything Like It." *The New York Times* April 25, 2018. https://www.nytimes.com/2018/04/25/us/lynching-memorial-alabama.html. Accessed 8 May, 2018.

91. Robertson, "A Lynching Memorial."

92. https://eji.org/national-lynching-memorial. Accessed 5 June, 2018.

93. Grebowicz, 66.

94. For information about this organization, see https://www.sitesofconscience.org/en/home/. Accessed 5 June, 2018.

"Going Rogue" with the Alt-NPS

Managing Love and Hate
for an Alternative Anthropocene

The NPS is well positioned to help craft an alternative future in this scary new epoch. Together, today's NPS sites attract roughly 300 million visitors every year. Those 417 sites (and counting) still protect some of the nation's most distinctive natural resources, but the number and diversity of cultural and historical resources the NPS preserves have increased in recent decades. Since 1973, the agency has not only more than doubled the size of the area it manages, but it has also added dozens of historical sites, complementing its protection of military and presidential sites with "themes that formerly received less attention": sites devoted to literature and the arts; social and humanitarian sites, including several focused on women; sites commemorating traumatic events, such as terrorist attacks and the incarceration of Japanese Americans; and sites dedicated to civil rights history, including struggles for justice by farmworkers, LGBTQ communities, and African Americans.[1]

As the NPS looks ahead to its next 100 years, becoming more relevant to an increasingly diverse demographic is a top priority.[2] The recently formed Office of Relevancy, Diversity, and Inclusion strategizes about how to make its titular terms priorities. A recent agency document called *A Call to Action: Preparing for a Second Century of Stewardship Engagement* (2012) explains that a "second-century" NPS will be "relevant and valued" in part because it will "invite new publics into the parks, from recent immigrants to those serving in our Armed Forces to young people."[3] The agency is making sincere efforts to engage people of color as partners in planning how to meet these goals.

A 2014 conference called "Co-Creating Narratives in Public Spaces" (available online in archived videos) brought together scholar-experts in African American studies, sociology, anthropology, and history, alongside NPS interpreters, educators, and museum curators. The event's main goal was to ensure that "the narratives at [NPS] sites are informed by up-to-date scholarship that is inclusive and incorporates issues of race, ethnicity, gender, and power." Some panels explicitly named "healing in the community" as a priority.[4] It's good to see humanities and social science scholars being invited to participate in the "healing" work of recasting the nation's most powerful stories.

The NPS itself is doing some recasting, too: It has spawned a "rogue" branch in response to the climate-denying Trump administration's attempts to silence the agency.[5] The "Alt-NPS," a social media organization claiming origins in Badlands National Park, now has more than two million followers on its Facebook page. Its posts are provocative and overtly political. A representative cartoon features Trump, with his too-long red tie and much-pilloried orange toupee, adrift on a broken bit of iceberg, sucking his thumb.[6] One of its first posts (shared more than 27,000 times at the time of this writing) adapts anti-Nazi poetry with hip slang and popular social media acronyms: "First they came for the scientists. And the National Park Service said, 'Lol. No.' And went rogue, and we were all, like, 'I was not expecting the park rangers to lead the resistance. None of the dystopian novels I read prepared me for this. But, cool.'"[7]

The mission of the Alt-NPS (according to its Facebook page) sounds a lot like that of the mainstream NPS: "to help protect and preserve the environment for future generations to come." But there's a sleight of hand in this paraphrase of the agency's founding legislation, the Organic Act, which calls for the *enjoyment* of these public lands as well as their conservation.[8] Telling only half the story is a radical move by the Alt-NPS, since it takes a stand on which part of the notoriously ambivalent mandate is more important: conservation. The "story" section of the Alt-NPS Facebook page spells out its politics even more explicitly. This section claims the movement was "created by a coalition of National Park Service employees, state park employees, National Forest Service employees, EPA employees, USDA employees, and environmental scientists" in order to "resist" an administration that has "shown little mercy for the environment." With its embrace of the term "resist," the Alt-NPS aligns itself with the Women's March and other global resistance movements around the world, as well as with Black Lives Matter advocates and the water protectors at Standing Rock. Like these movements, the Alt-NPS insists that "Resistance is not futile" and that "In unity, we find power."[9]

The Trump administration is not the first to try to ignore park scientists.[10] Nevertheless, the NPS has persisted for more than a century, despite inconsistent funding and support. Today, in a nation that seems anything but united, the NPS seems poised to reframe its sites and their stories, many of which are steeped in whiteness and a history of expulsion, violence, and more banal discriminatory practices so that they are welcoming to all visitors. Its training manual makes connections between ecology and social justice, maintaining that "biodiversity boosts ecosystem productivity and helps improve nature's ability to adapt to changing environmental conditions. Likewise, nationally significant events in our nation's past tell the stories of diverse cultures and perspectives that make our nation what it is today."[11] Many NPS employees are getting training that emphasizes these connections and positions diversity at the root of national identity.

The NPS identifies two of its "critical needs of the future" as "a civil, informed social discourse and building a national community" and "an understanding of our vulnerable natural world and what we must do to maintain it." As important is discovering "a model of sustainability where commerce and heritage are not mutually exclusive."[12] Somewhere at the nexus of these goals—informed social discourse, a national community, and a model of sustainability that synthesizes economic and historical priorities—lies an environmentalism that appeals to diverse demographics because it is committed to social justice. That the NPS is linking biodiversity to social diversity, as well as to productivity and sustainability, is an indication of the agency's and the nation's progress.

So far, NPS visitor-use data is not showing an increase in visitation among minority groups.[13] But Shelton Johnson's high-profile position in Yosemite is a marker of change. So is the presence of Betty

Reid Soskin, the oldest NPS ranger, who leads interpretive programs at Rosie the Riveter/WWII Homefront National Historical Park in Richmond, California, near San Francisco—a site established in 2000 to highlight the role of African Americans and women in war industries. So is the work of Audrey Peterman, whose environmental consulting firm and passionate writing are helping to position NPS sites as historically significant to *all* people, and parks and park science as resistant to "alternative facts."[14] The NPS must find ways to center this typically marginalized knowledge, especially at sites of public memory.

More Indigenous presence is crucial. Non-Natives must learn to listen to and learn from the experiences of this country's Indigenous peoples—to value the traditional ecological knowledge that scholars like Kyle Powys Whyte remind us are essential for planning our collective future. This kind of work requires more than just good intentions. As Finney cautions, "building relationships across difference means you have to do the internal work, both within the organization and within oneself," to assess one's limitations, before one is able to "meet someone else with honesty and clarity."[15] In this spirit, NPS managers must find nonappropriative ways to invite and foreground the knowledge of people of color if the agency is to effectively connect past to present, avoid erasing contemporary violence, and enable a broader range of affective responses, beyond obligatory patriotism.

The NPS is mandated to be democratic and sensitive when discussing politics; however, as the Alt-NPS shows, this doesn't mean it has to be silent. The agency is populated by diplomats, many of whom are inclined—by mandate or by temperament—to bridge the ideological chasms that polarize the country. Because they are trained in performing neutrality, many NPS employees are ideal mediators. And mediators are in high demand as the twenty-first century heats up, in terms of both temperature and political tensions. Indeed, in this age of "alts," some argue we need more diplomats than protesters, more mediators then militants, more activists in Smokey Bear hats (or Smokey Bear "Resist" T-shirts, which this ex-ranger happens to wear proudly) than in Antifa black.[16]

Public memory is often at the heart of contemporary political rifts. A case in point was the "Unite the Right" rally in Charlottesville, Virginia on August 11 and 12, 2017. Led by white nationalist groups including the KKK and neo-Nazis, who dressed like militia, armed themselves accordingly, and gathered after dark wielding tiki torches, the rally ended in tragedy when a member of those groups deliberately drove a car into a crowed of counter-protesters, killing one young woman and injuring many others; two state troopers died in a helicopter accident while monitoring the event.[17] The group had gathered to protest the taking down of a statue of Confederate War general Robert E. Lee and the renaming of the park that houses it "Emancipation Park." Those on the so-called "alt right" see such moves as sanitizing history, but many others insist it's an appropriate, indeed long overdue, response to a symbol of white supremacy and ongoing domestic terrorism.[18] Meanwhile, our current president claimed there was "violence on both sides," defended the "very fine people" he insists were among the crowd of white nationalists, and wondered publicly whether statues of George Washington and Thomas Jefferson would be the next to topple.[19]

The Lee statue and the surrounding controversy remind us that statues can still generate as much "mania" as other kinds of memorials, and that sites of public memory are still among the most significant stages for the performance and negotiation of national identity. To take an example in the American West, the forty-one-day occupation of Oregon's Malheur National Wildlife Refuge by a white militia group in early 2016 was partly about who belongs in public lands, whose heritage counts.[20] In October of that year, many of the men involved—all white, well-armed, and self-fashioned as defenders of Western lands from government overreach—were acquitted. Simultaneously, unarmed water protectors in South Dakota were treated as rioters, shot with tear gas and water cannons, and arrested for engaging in unarmed political action on behalf of clean water and the protection of indigenous lands. As Black Lives Matter founder Alicia Garza noted on Facebook, "So let me get this correct. If you're white, you can occupy federal property . . . and get found not guilty. No teargas, no tanks, no rubber bullets . . . If you're Indigenous and fighting to protect our earth, and the water we depend on to survive, you get tear gassed, media blackouts, tanks and all that." Even mainstream media sources noted the irony; the Garza quote was picked up by *USA Today*.[21]

There remains considerable disagreement over what counts as national "heritage" and how we should commemorate it. As a teacher in north Idaho, a region with a history of white supremacist organizations and a diehard allegiance to the Second Amendment, I am not alone in feeling anxious. I can only imagine how it feels to be a black woman, or a Jewish one, or any person of color, in any region of a country where marchers can carry swastika flags alongside the national one, gather at night by torchlight, and wield assault weapons in defense of a "heritage" with institutionalized slavery, torture, and the murder of people of color at its core. The foundation of the Charlottesville statue still bears traces of the words "Black Lives Matter," which show through dimly, in a haunting palimpsest that could be a metaphor for our fraught nation and the people of color that bravely continue to insist on their centrality, even in the face of lived experience marked by erasure, microaggressions, and other forms of violence.[22]

Sara Ahmed provides a useful lens for making sense of how the Charlottesville marchers positioned themselves as protectors of national heritage, their whiteness as under threat, and their affective politics as politics of love, not hate, and how the Bundys and other Oregon militia members saw themselves as defenders of the Constitution—not haters, but lovers. In her chapter "The Organisation of Hate,"[23] Ahmed explores how hate groups claim love: "it is love for the nation that makes the white Aryans feel hate towards others who, in 'taking away' the nation, are taking away their history, as well as their future."[24] Hate is "distributed," she explains, across a range of figures—in her study, the "mixed race couple, the child-molester, the rapist, aliens and foreigners"—who, in a tricky "metonymic slide," come to "embody the threat of loss: lost jobs, lost money, lost land."[25] Who gets to claim love, and which people (and what sorts of actions) are marked as hateful, demands more scrutiny.

As I discussed in regard to fear in chapter one, hate "does not reside in a given subject or object"; rather, like all affects, it "is produced as an effect of its circulation."[26] If "the more signs circulate, the more affective they become," then the affective economies of love and hate demand evaluation with an eye toward social media, where signs circulate fast and affects quickly grow to hurricane-force intensity. As immigration crises intensify, especially at national borders, questions about who belongs in which nations, and who can claim hate as a response to love of country, are also intensifying. Questions are crucial to address about who gets to claim the past, how that past is commemorated, and how certain affectively charged objects, like a Confederate flag or a statue of Robert E. Lee, gesture toward a particular history as they circulate hate, anger, pride, and other affects.

Shortly after Charlottesville, former president Barack Obama's tweet of a line from Nelson Mandela's 1994 autobiography, *Long Walk to Freedom*, became the most liked tweet ever: "No one is born hating another person because of the color of his skin or his background or his religion. People must learn to hate, and if they can learn to hate, they can be taught to love, for love comes more naturally to the human heart than its opposite."[27] It's heartening to see so much "like" for such a love-filled message. Love, as Martha Nussbaum argues, is an affect we should deliberately try to amplify, and we need political leaders who embrace love in the name of justice. The Alt-NPS—and perhaps the mainstream NPS—might be one such leader, if it continues to connect environmental and social justice with an eye toward a sustainable and truly democratic future. My hope is that other leaders will emerge to help heal this fractured nation.[28]

The politics of love and hate bear upon issues of environmental justice as well as issues of race and nation. If love is to promote justice, it must extend across lines of difference to forge a truly "affectionate solidarity"—the kind that, in Jodi Dean's words, "lets our disagreements provide the basis for connection."[29] Nussbaum, Williams, and many other scholars suggest that at the core of social and environmental justice lies a more expansive view of love and a minimizing and eventual elimination of hate. In a recent essay, Stephanie LeMenager argues that love in the Anthropocene must operate at both small and large scales. "Love, in the time of climate change," she writes, "inheres in attachment to other life—but necessarily small attachments to limited life forms and places, attachments that can be enacted through local conservation or appreciation." At the same time, she insists that Anthropocenic love "demands memory and speculation," including "attachment to multiple generations, distant futures as well as distant pasts."[30] NPS sites seem ideal for promoting both small-scale attachments, perhaps in the form of wonder, as well as the opportunity for contemplation that might promote concern and care capable of reaching across generations and time scales.

Americans love to *claim* love, especially in public. But loving across boundaries of race, class, species, and other lines of difference—to say nothing of the tricky task of loving future generations—is easier said than done. More research needs to be done to tease out the affects that inform racism, and perhaps the ways in which racism is itself a kind of affect. Studying affects in constellations rather than as isolated emotional responses, as I've been doing here, is one way to unravel the complicated tangles in which hate, disgust, and shame, or fear, anger, and guilt, stick to objects and bodies, accrete in landscapes, circulate in cultural texts, and have material impacts in the world. Understanding how affects work—not just the negative ones but also love, compassion, and wonder—is an essential step on what sometimes seems like a very long, slow walk toward freedom and justice.

The physical environments—statues, parks, museums, and memorials, but also schools, offices, neighborhoods, and other everyday environments—in which we negotiate our relationships with others are agents in shaping our affective lives and our politics. As I've been suggesting, finding out how different people feel when they visit different kinds of landscapes and engage in public memory creation is important, not only for NPS management but for building a national community of inclusion. We must confront the conflicts embedded in the foundations of even relatively popular agencies like the NPS, including the logic of "violence and dispossession" that enabled the parks to form and, Grebowicz argues, still shapes our experiences of them today.[31] The NPS must deal with this charge if it's to attract broader demographics and become the democratic agency it has always wanted to be.

As more visitor centers engage today's technological tourists with hands-on, interactive exhibits, there are new kinds of opportunities to prompt more honest, and more powerful affective connections to places. Trying on chain mail armor, or sitting inside a barracks at Manzanar—these are good starts, and these sorts of simulative experiences might be enhanced with new technologies. Ideally, technology might be used creatively to combat the tendency toward romanticization and historicization that makes violence feel perpetually past tense. The agency might diversify its approach to traditional displays and overlooks, which tend to register as "historical" in tone. Citations from literature—Simon Ortiz's moving poetry about the Sand Creek Massacre, for instance—could be used to enhance historical narratives. But there are bolder options, too. What if, for example, NPS divers showed video footage that allowed visitors to see (as its designer originally suggested) inside the "watery tomb" of the USS *Arizona* Memorial, forcing us to consider our mortality? What if, instead of emphasizing only the spectacular, aesthetically pleasing aspects of nonhuman nature, the NPS created displays and overlooks that featured the less savory ones, as Jeffrey Lockwood recommends: "not only lookout points for folks to contemplate the abyss but [also] gross-out points with a decomposing deer seething with maggots, a pile of coyote scat, or a hawked-up owl pellet?"³² What if the agency developed more honest signage, as Daniel Duane imagines for Yosemite National Park: We could "relabel Yosemite Valley itself Ahwahnee and sprinkle the park with new historical plaques saying things like 'On this spot, in 1851, American militiamen shot Tenaya's son in the back, let him bleed out in the grass, then dragged Tenaya up to have a look and enjoyed watching him weep."³³ This would implicate viewers in a much more powerful way than, say, taking a virtual photo of yourself in a hardhat "working" on the Golden Gate Bridge or manning the controls of a torpedo launcher at Pearl Harbor. Perhaps more confrontational signage would lead to the noncathartic affects I've been championing.

If disgust and violence are too extreme, perhaps the NPS could start by administering social justice lessons with a dose of humor. NPS literature has been slow to include images of people of color recreating, or working, at their sites, and this relative lack of representation in the NPS and in popular media more broadly "perpetuates their invisibility in conversations about environmental management."³⁴ What if NPS rangers developed interpretive programs about, and ideally *with*, people of color in public lands? I can imagine a self-reflective (and self-deprecating) ranger-led program featuring Funny or Die's "Black Hiker" video, in which white liberal tourists (one wears an Obama T-shirt) treat the black hiker like a rare wildlife sighting—even the park rangers ask to take his picture to prove he was there.[35] Maybe the Canada-based *Lesbian National Parks and Services* artists could be persuaded to do a tour of U.S. national parks and "insert a lesbian presence into the landscape" down here.[36] The NPS should work with groups such as Outdoor Afro and Latino Outdoors to find engaging ways to make visitors more aware of our own biases about who "belongs" in public lands.[37] Perhaps such awareness training could even be part of the permit process—an educational entrance fee to accompany the financial one.

Confrontation isn't what we've come to expect at an NPS site, and it would be uncomfortable, especially for the most privileged of us. But honest confrontation is essential if we are to move forward as a united country and work with other countries to survive the Anthropocene. Love of country will need to adapt to an epoch marked by distressing forms of "psychoterratic distress": Glenn Albrecht's umbrella term that bundles ailments such as "ecoanxiety, nature deficit order, ecoparalysis, solastalgia, eco-nostalgia and global dread."[38] It will entail learning how to live in a maelstrom of shifting affects, how to cope with negative feelings, how to be resilient as individuals and communities, and how to harness affects in ways that might promote a more just world in the present, however uncertain its future. Public land management in the Anthropocene might require a "tourism after optimism," including emancipation from "the fantasies that created capital-N Nature long ago,"[39] and a "rogue" management style to match the extremities of the epoch.

At the heart of all this is a willingness to see and feel from another person's perspective. Imagining what it feels like for a black person to walk by a statue of Robert E. Lee every day, or for a Lakota to look at the faces on Mount Rushmore, isn't a matter of political correctness. It's a matter of compassion. It's a matter of recognizing that place names can be "the linguistic equivalents of Confederate statues,"[40] painful reminders of past trauma that should outweigh any claims to "heritage." The recent renaming of the tallest mountain in South Dakota, Harney Peak, which I climbed with my son Evan when we visited Mount Rushmore at the start of this project, suggests an affective maturation, a growing capacity for compassion in this nation. It was a pleasure to see the joy on Evan's face when I told him the mountain is now called Black Elk Peak.[41]

Notes

1. For details, see the NPS website's "National Park Service Overview" document, a downloadable brochure available at https://www.nps.gov/aboutus/upload/NPS-Overview-02-09-17.pdf. Testifying to its commitment to diversity, one of the two uniformed rangers the brochure features on its cover is a young black woman. For a fuller accounting of the agency's shifting priorities, see the chapter "Rounding Out the System, 1973–2004" in *The National Parks,* 84–103.

2. Lucy Rock's "Call of the Wild: Can America's National Parks Survive?" *The Guardian.* 15 January, 2017, rightly identifies three major challenges for NPS managers today: severe underfunding, climate change, and shifting visitor demographics. https://www.theguardian.com/environment/2017/jan/15/call-of-the-wild-can-americas-national-parks-survive. Accessed 18 January, 2017.

3. Cited in *Golden Spike National Historic Site Long-Range Interpretive Plan: 2014–2023.* (Harper's Ferry: Department of the Interior, June 2013), 13.

4. https://www.nps.gov/history/narratives/Narratives_in_Public_Spaces.html. Accessed 16 August, 2017.

5. See, for instance, "National Parks [sic] Service 'goes rogue' in response to Trump Twitter ban," *The Guardian,* January 25, 2017. https://www.theguardian.com/technology/news-blog/2017/jan/25/national-parks-service-goes-rogue-in-response-to-trump-twitter-ban. Accessed 17 August, 2017.

6. The caption, "Trump isolated on G20 and climate change," refers to President Trump's stance on the Paris Climate Agreement. He was the only leader at the July 2017 G20 meeting to refuse to sign. For one of the many news reports on this, see: Angela Dewan and Stephanie Halasz, "G20 closes with rebuke to Trump's climate change stance," *CNN,* July 9, 2017. http://edition.cnn.com/2017/07/08/europe/g20-merkel-trump-communique/index.html. Accessed 17 July, 2017.

7. The beginning of the post refers to the poem "First they came . . ." by German Lutheran pastor Martin Niemöller, which he wrote in response to the lack of resistance to the Nazis. The poem has been adapted in multiple speeches and at the New England Holocaust Memorial in Boston, Massachusetts. For a capsule history, see Harold Marcuse's university website: http://www.history.ucsb.edu/faculty/marcuse/niem.htm. Accessed 17 July, 2017.

8. The legislation is cited in many places, including the recent survey data compilation: Patricia A. Taylor, Burke D. Grandjean, and James H. Gramann, "National Park Service Comprehensive Survey of the American Public, 2008–9: Racial and Ethnic Diversity of National Park System Visitors and Non-Visitors." (Fort Collins: U.S. Department of the Interior, 2011): 3. https://www.nature.nps.gov/socialscience/docs/CompSurvey2008_2009RaceEthnicity.pdf. Accessed 16 August, 2017.

9. Facebook page, accessed 17 July, 2017. There are many news articles on the "resistance." See, for example, Dana R. Fisher, Dawn Marie Dow, and Rashawn Ray, "The demographics of the #resistance," *Salon,* June 3, 2017. http://www.salon.com/2017/06/03/the-demographics-of-the-resistance_partner/. Accessed 17 July, 2017.

10. For a history of the agency's struggle to base policy on the knowledge of biologists and other scientists, see Sellars.

11. https://www.nps.gov/training/essentials/html/relev_div_inc_topic.html. Accessed 16 August, 2017.

12. Ibid.

13. See Taylor, Grandjean, and Gramann. They note that another survey is required before a trend can be established (10).

14. For information about Peterman's consulting and publishing firm, Earthwise Productions, Inc., and her writing projects, see https://www.humansandnature.org/audrey-peterman and http://www.legacyontheland.com/. She also writes for the *Huffington Post* and has used that platform to critique the Trump administration. For instance, see "The Land Doesn't Lie: National Parks Vaporize 'Alternative Facts,'" http://www.huffingtonpost.com/entry/the-land-doesnt-lie-national-parks-vaporize-alternative_us_58c96669e4b02c06957328f5. Accessed 18 August, 2017.

15. Finney, 132.

16. It's beyond the scope of my research to provide a map for social justice movements. For one perspective on the argument that we need "more mayors" and fewer marchers, see Mark Lilla, *The Once and Future Liberal: After Identity Politics* (New York: Harper Collins, 2016). For an equally controversial but perhaps more interesting critical take on contemporary protest movements, see Nick Srnicek and Alex Williams, *Inventing the Future: Postcapitalism and a World Without Work* (Verso: 2016).

17. For one account of the rally, see Joe Heim, "Recounting a day of rage, hate, violence and death," *The Washington Post*, August 14, 2017. https://www.washingtonpost.com/graphics/2017/local/charlottesville-timeline/?utm_term=.c4c31b70ad79. Accessed 20 May, 2018.

18. A few days after Charlottesville, Baltimore officials removed several Confederate statutes overnight, and other cities are following suit. Russell Goldman, "Baltimore Removes Confederate Statues in Overnight Operation," *The New York Times*, August 16, 2017. https://mobile.nytimes.com/2017/08/16/us/baltimore-confederate-statues.html?mwrsm=Facebook&referer=http%3A%2F%2Fm.facebook.com. Accessed 16 August, 2017.

19. White nationalist leaders seem emboldened by the events in Charlottesville and encouraged by the president's response. See, for instance, Byron Wolf, "Trump's defense of the 'very fine people' at Charlottesville white nationalist march has David Duke gushing," *CNN*, August 15, 2017. http://www.cnn.com/2017/08/15/politics/donald-trump-david-duke-charlottesville/index.html. Accessed 16 August, 2017.

20. For one account with a timeline and links, see Les Jaitz, "Militia takes over Malheur National Wildlife Refuge headquarters," *The Oregonian*, January 2, 2016. http://www.oregonlive.com/pacific-northwest-news/index.ssf/2016/01/drama_in_burns_ends_with_quiet.html. Accessed 20 May, 2018.

21. https://www.usatoday.com/story/news/2016/10/28/dakota-access-pipeline-protests-continue-questions-fairness-emerge/92913148/. Accessed 2 June, 2018.

22. For one news article on the statue and a compelling image of the palimpsest I refer to, see Jacey Fortin, "The Statue at the Center of Charlottesville's Storm," *The New York Times*, August 13, 2017. https://www.nytimes.com/2017/08/13/us/ charlottesville-rally-protest-statue.html. Accessed 15 August, 2017.

23. Ahmed's chapter, originally published in 2004, applies seamlessly to our current politics, and she reprinted parts of it on her blog on November 9, 2016. Ahmed, "Fascism as Love," *feministkilljoys*, November 9, 2016. https://feministkilljoys. com/2016/11/09/fascism-as-love/. Accessed August 19, 2017.

24. Ahmed, *Cultural Politics*, 43.

25. Ahmed, 44.

26. Ahmed, 44–45.

27. Hunter Schwarz, "Obama's Charlottesville tweet is most liked in Twitter history," *CNN*, August 16, 2017. http://www.cnn.com/2017/08/15/politics/obamas- charlottesville-tweet/index.html. Accessed 16 August, 2017.

28. The mayor of New Orleans, Mitch Landrieu, is one local leader to watch. He gave a speech about statue removal in May of 2017 that went viral after Charlottesville. Greg Fisher, the mayor of Louisville, Kentucky, explicitly pledged to make his city a "compassionate" one. See "Watch New Orleans Mayor Mitch Landrieu defend removal of monuments to heroes of a 'four-year historical aberration,'" *MarketWatch*, August 16, 2017. http://www.marketwatch.com/story/ watch-new-orleans-mayor-mitch-landrieu-defend-removal-of-monuments-to- heroes-of-a-four-year-historical-aberration-2017-08-15/, and Teresa Mathew, "Can a City Be Compassionate?" *City Lab*, August 15, 2017. https://www.citylab. com/equity/2017/08/can-a-city-be-compassionate/536841/?utm_source=nl__ link1_081517. Accessed 18 August, 2017.

29. Jodi Dean, *Solidarity of Strangers: Feminism after Identity Politics* (Berkeley: University of California Press, 1996). Cited in Ahmed, *Cultural Politics*, 141.

30. Stephanie LeMenager, "Climate Change and the Struggle for Genre," in *Anthropocene Reading: Literary History in Geologic Times*, eds Tobias Meneley and Jesse Oak Taylor (University Park: The Pennsylvania State University Press), 236.

31. Grebowicz, 37.

32. Jeffrey A. Lockwood, "A Six-Legged Guru: Fear and Loathing in Nature," in *Trash Animals: How We Live with Nature's Filthy, Feral, Invasive, and Unwanted Species*, ed. Kelsi Nagy and Philip David Johnson, 2013), 282.

33. Daniel Duane, "Goodbye Yosemite, Hello What?" *The New York Times*, September 2, 2017. https://www.nytimes.com/2017/09/02/opinion/sunday/goodbye-yosemite- hello-what.html?emc=eta1. Accessed 3 September, 2017. Duane's op-ed examines issues of renaming in regard to Yosemite's Ahwahnee Hotel—now called the Majestic Yosemite Hotel—and other sites in the Yosemite Valley.

34. Finney, 69.

35. "Black Hiker, with Blair Underwood," November 23, 2009. http://www.funny- ordie.com/videos/24b56caf3e/black-hiker-with-blair-underwood. Accessed 19

May, 2018. A related video is *PBS*'s "Black Folks Don't Camp" (which features a clip from Oprah), though this one seems to reinforce rather than interrogate the idea that black people don't "do" nature. https://www.pbs.org/video/black-folk-dont-camp/. Accessed 19 May, 2018. Black Public Media's "Black Folk Don't . . ." series includes a longer and more probing episode on camping. "Black Folk Don't: Go Camping" (documentary episode), directed by Angela Tucker. *Black Folk Don't* (New York City: National Black Programming Consortium, 2012). Thanks to Nicole Seymour for making me aware of these texts.

36. Shawna Dempsey and Lorri Millan are performance artists, who've also published a *Handbook of the Junior Lesbian Ranger*. The quote here comes from their website, which also describes their ongoing projects: http://www.shawnadempseyandlorrimillan.net/#/alps/. Accessed 20 May, 2018.

37. Outdoor Afro describes itself as a "cutting edge network that celebrates and inspires African American connections and leadership in nature." http://outdoorafro.com/about/. Latino Outdoors' mission statement is similar: [they] "bring cultura into the outdoor narrative and connect Latino communities and leadership with nature and outdoor experiences." http://latinooutdoors.org/about-us/. Indigenous activist groups are also staking claims to public lands; for instance, Indigenous Geotags urges all outdoor enthusiasts to acknowledge "public land as stolen Native land" and reminds us that "this is an environmental justice issue." https://www.indigenousgeotags.com/. Accessed 30 October, 2018.

38. Glenn Albrecht, "Tipping Points in the Mind: The Drama of Solastalgia and Soliphilia." *Tedx Sydney*, June 2, 2010. https://www.youtube.com/watch?v=-GUG-W8rOpLY. Accessed 15 October, 2017.

39. Grebowicz, 66.

40. The phrase is Daniel Duane's, "Goodbye Yosemite."

41. For one article about the renaming, including some comments, see "Feds rename Harney Peak, South Dakota's highest peak, to Black Elk Peak," *Rapid City Journal*, August 12, 2016. http://rapidcityjournal.com/news/local/feds-rename-harney-peak-south-dakota-s-highest-peak-to/article_2234e9de-c1fc-5a44-91b2-e39f3bfb76e4.html. Accessed 2 September, 2017.

Acknowledgments

A seed for this project was planted in the summer of 1996, when I first donned a National Park Service (NPS) uniform, but the research began in earnest in autumn of 2013, when I took the first of eight trips to NPS sites as far-flung as Hawai'i and South Dakota. I'm grateful to the organizations that funded my travel: the National Endowment for the Humanities, the Charles Redd Center for Western Studies, the Idaho Humanities Council, and the University of Idaho, especially the College of Letters, Arts, and Social Sciences and the Department of English.

The University of Nevada Press has been wonderful to work with; Justin Race was enthusiastic and motivating from the start, and Alrica Goldstein was expert at shepherding the manuscript through production. My two readers—Nicole Seymour and an anonymous second reader—gave brilliant feedback that has improved the project immeasurably. I owe a debt of gratitude to Sylvan Goldberg and Erin James, who read portions of the book, as well as to Scott Slovic and Stacy Alaimo, who wrote the letters of support that helped me get grants. Alexandra Teague, Jodie Nicotra, Tara MacDonald, Ryanne Pilgeram, and Jon Hegglund also offered insightful perspectives, as did the students in my graduate and undergraduate seminars on affect theory. My NPS supervisors, especially Joan Anzelmo, Jackie Skaggs, and Sara Petsch, and fellow seasonal rangers Ron Steffens, Shelagh Forester, Dave Bywater, and Wendy Koelfgen, inspired me to think about emotional engagement at NPS sites.

Friends who visited sites with me (and tolerated my constant photo taking and incessant intellectualization), helped shape my impressions, especially Amy Vidali, Kerry and Albert Renner, and the Renner kids. And a shout-out to Alexandra Teague and Michele Waltz: even if, as we suspected, peace is boring, our trip to San Juan Island National Historical Park will always make me think about wonder, especially in the forms of eagles eating crabs and otters trotting by with fresh fish.

I'm grateful to my older son, Evan—whose awe of the steam engine in Keystone and the faces on Mount Rushmore inspired me then, and whose creative mind continues to amaze me—and to my younger son, Elliott, for releasing me from his clutches long enough to take these trips and for the many emotions he bravely wears on his sleeve, especially love. And again, to Doug, for supporting my scholarship and teaching since our grad school days, even when they've taken me away from home, and for being my intrepid travel partner (and travel agent). I am grateful, always, to my dad, who has passed along to me his love of travel, intellectual curiosity, and appreciation for well-crafted prose.

An earlier version of chapter five was published as "Mountains, Monuments, and Other Matter: Environmental Affects at Manzanar," in *Environmental Humanities* (2015).

Bibliography

Abbey, Edward. *Desert Solitaire: A Season in the Wilderness.* New York: Ballantine Books, 1968.

Acorn, Annelise E. *Compulsory Compassion: A Critique of Restorative Justice.* Vancouver: University of British Columbia Press, 2004.

Adams, Ansel. *Born Free and Equal: The Story of Loyal Japanese-Americans at Manzanar Relocation Center, Inyo County, California.* New York: U.S. Camera, 1944, Accessed 18 June 2010. http://memory.loc.gov/ammem/collections/anse-ladams/aamborn.html

Ahmed, Sara. *The Cultural Politics of Emotion.* New York: Routledge, 2004.

———. "Happy Objects." In *The Affect Theory Reader,* edited by Melissa Gregg and Gregory J. Seigworth, 29–51. Durham: Duke University Press, 2010.

———. *The Promise of Happiness.* Durham: Duke University Press, 2010.

Alaimo, Stacy. *Bodily Natures: Science, Environment, and the Material Self.* Bloomington: Indiana University Press, 2010.

Alexie, Sherman. "Vilify." In *Face.* New York: Hanging Loose Press, 2009. 29–38.

Anderson, Ben. "Affective Atmospheres," *Emotion, Space and Society* 2 (2009): 77–81.

Andrews-Hanna, Jessica R. "The brain's default network and its adaptive role in internal mentation." *The Neuroscientist* 18.3 (2012): 251–270.

Aspinall, Peter, Panagiotis Mavros, Richard Coyne, and Jenny Roe. "The urban brain: analyzing outdoor physical activity with mobile EEG." *British Journal of Sports Medicine,* vol. 49 (2015): 272–276.

Atchley, Ruth Ann, David L. Strayer, and Paul Atchley. "Creativity in the Wild: Improving Creative Reasoning through Immersion in Natural Settings." *PLoS ONE* 7:12 (2012): 1–3.

Bednar, Robert M. "Being Here, Looking There: Mediating Vistas in the National Parks of the Contemporary American West." In *Observation Points: The Visual Poetics of National Parks,* edited by Thomas Patin, 1–28. Minneapolis: University of Minnesota Press, 2012.

———. "Killing Memory: Roadside Memorial Removals and the Necropolitics of Affect." *Cultural Politics* 9.3 (2013): 337–356.

Bennett, Jane. *The Enchantment of Modern Life: Attachments, Crossings, and Ethics.* Princeton: Princeton University Press, 2001.

———. *Vibrant Matter: A Political Ecology of Things.* Durham: Duke University Press, 2010.

Bergman, Teresa, "Can Patriotism Be Carved in Stone?" In *Observation Points:*

The Visual Poetics of National Parks, edited by Thomas Patin. Minneapolis: University of Minnesota Press, 2012.

Berlant, Lauren. "Cruel Optimism." *differences: A Journal of Feminist Cultural Studies*, 17, no. 3 (2006): 20–36.

Blair, Carole. "Contemporary U.S. Memorial Sites as Exemplars of Rhetoric's Materiality." In *Rhetorical Bodies*, edited by Jack Selzer and Sharon Crowley, 16–57. Madison: The University of Wisconsin Press, 1999.

Blair, Carole and Neil Michel, "The Rushmore Effect: Ethos and National Collective Identity." *The Ethos of Rhetoric*, edited by Michael J. Hyde. Columbia: University of South Carolina Press, 2004.

Blair, Carole, Greg Dickinson, and Brian L. Ott, eds. *Places of Public Memory: The Rhetoric of Museums and Memorials*. Tuscaloosa: The University of Alabama Press, 2010.

Bloom, Paul. *Against Empathy: The Case for Rational Compassion*. New York: Ecco, 2016.

———. "Empathy and Its Discontents." In *Trends in Cognitive Sciences* (January 2017): 21.1. 24–31.

Bowden, Charles. "Snaketime." In *The Charles Bowden Reader*, edited by Erin Almeranti and Mary Martha Miles. Austin: University of Texas Press, 2010.

Bowman, Michael S. "Tracing Mary Queen of Scots." In *Places of Public Memory: The Rhetoric of Museums and Memorials*, edited by Carole Blair, Greg Dickinson, and Brian L. Ott, 191–215. Tuscaloosa: The University of Alabama Press, 2010.

Boym, Svetlana. *The Future of Nostalgia*. New York: Basic Books, 2001.

Brennan, Teresa. *The Transmission of Affect*. Ithaca: Cornell University Press, 2004.

Butler, Judith. *Gender Trouble: Feminism and The Subversion of Identity*. New York: Routledge, 1990.

Casey, Edward. "Public Memory in Place and Time." In *Framing Public Memory*, edited by Kendall R. Phillips. Tuscaloosa: University of Alabama Press, 2007.

Clance, Pauline Rose and Suzanne Imes. (1978). "The Impostor Phenomenon in High Achieving Women: Dynamics and Therapeutic Interventions." *Psychotherapy: Theory Research and Practice*, 15: 241247.

Cohen, Jeffrey Jerome. *Stone: An Ecology of the Inhuman*. Minneapolis: University of Minnesota Press, 2015.

Cornelius, Wayne A. "Death at the Border: Efficacy and Unintended Consequences of US Immigration Control Policy." *Population and Development Review*. 27.4 (2001): 661–685.

Cresswell, Tim. *Place: A Short Introduction*. 2004. New York: Wiley Blackwell, 2015.

Cvetkovich, Ann. *An Archive of Feelings: Trauma, Sexuality, and Lesbian Public Cultures*. Durham: Duke University Press, 1998.

———. "Affect." In *Keywords for American Cultural Studies*, edited by Bruce Burgett and Glenn Hendler, 13–16. 2007. New York: New York University Press, 2014.

Damasio, Antonio. *The Feeling of What Happens: Body and Emotion in the Making of Consciousness*. Orlando: Harcourt, Inc., 1999.

Delgado, James P. "Significance: Memorials, Myths and Symbols." In *Submerged Cultural Resources Study: USS* Arizona *Memorial and Pearl Harbor National Historic Landmark*, edited by Daniel J. Lenihan. Washington D.C., Department of the Interior.

DeLillo, Don. *White Noise*. New York: Penguin, 1984.

DeLoughrey, Elizabeth. "Ordinary Futures: Interspecies Worldings in the Anthropocene." In *Global Ecologies and the Environmental Humanities*, edited by Elizabeth DeLoughrey, Jill Didur, and Anthony Carrigan. New York: Routledge, 2015.

———. "Submarine Futures of the Anthropocene." *Comparative Literature* 69.1 (2017): 32–44.

Dickinson, Greg, Brian Ott, and Eric Aoki. "Spaces of Remembering and Forgetting: The Reverent Eye/I at the Plains Indian Museum." *Communication and Critical/Cultural Studies* 3 (2006): 27–47.

Didion, Joan. "In the Islands." In *The White Album*. New York: Farrar, Straus, and Giroux, 2009.

Doss, Erika. *Memorial Mania: Public Feeling in America*. Chicago: The University of Chicago Press, 2010.

Duran, Bonnie and Eduardo. *Native American Post-Colonial Psychology*. Albany: SUNY Press, 1995.

Economides, Louise. *The Ecology of Wonder in Romantic and Postmodern Literature*. New York: Palgrave MacMillan, 2016.

Eisenberger, Naomi I., Gable, S.L., and Lieberman, M.D. (2007). "fMRI responses relate to differences in real-world social experience." *Emotion*, 7, 745–754.

Evans, Jessica, Michael A. Schuett, and Steven J. Hollenhorst. "Golden Spike National Historic Site Visitor Study." University of Idaho Park Studies Unit. U.S. Department of Interior, 2006.

Felski, Rita. *The Limits of Critique*. Chicago: The University of Chicago Press, 2015.

Finney, Carolyn. *Black Faces, White Spaces: Reimagining the Relationship of African Americans to the Great Outdoors*. Chapel Hill: University of North Carolina Press, 2014.

Fojas, Camilla. *Border Bandits: Hollywood on The Southern Frontier*. Austin: University of Texas Press, 2010.

Frankenberger, Robert and James Garrison. "From Rustic Romanticism to Modernism, and Beyond: Architectural Resources in the National Parks." *Forum Journal: The Journal of the National Trust for Historic Preservation*, 2002. http://forum.savingplaces.org/viewdocument/from-rustic-romanticism-tomodernism. Accessed 26 March, 2017.

Gareth, John. "Image/Text/Geography: Yellowstone and the Spatial Rhetoric of Landscape." In *Observation Points: The Visual Poetics of National Parks*, edited by Thomas Patin, 140–164. Minneapolis: University of Minnesota Press, 2012.

Gibbs, Jules. "In the Beautiful, Violent Swirl of America: Simon Ortiz's *From Sand Creek*, Thirty Years Later." *American Poetry Review* (July/August 2012).

Gilpin, Lyndsey. *High Country News*. http://www.hcn.org/articles/how-we-investigated-the-national-park-services-long-history-of-sexual-harassment-and-discrimination. Accessed 12 December, 2016.

Golden Spike National Historic Site Long-Range Interpretive Plan: 2014–2023. Harper's Ferry: Department of the Interior, June 2013.

Grebowicz, Margret. *The National Park to Come*. Palo Alto: Stanford University Press, 2015.

Gregg, Melissa and Gregory J. Seigworth, eds. *The Affect Theory Reader*. Durham: Duke University Press, 2010.

Grossberg, Lawrence, Cary Nelson, and Paula Treichler, eds. *Cultural Studies*. New York: Routledge, 1991.

Hamilton, Amy. *Peregrinations: Walking in American Literature*. Reno: University of Nevada Press, 2018.

Heise, Ursula. *Sense of Place and Sense of Planet: The Environmental Imagination of the Global*. Cambridge: Oxford University Press, 2008.

Helstern, Linda Lizut. "Shifting the Ground: Theories of Survivance in *From Sand Creek* and *Hiroshima Bugi: Atomu 57*." In *Survivance: Narratives of Native Presence*, edited by Gerald Vizenor, 163–189. Lincoln: University of Nebraska Press, 2008.

Hemmings, Clare. "Invoking Affect: Cultural Theory and the Ontological Turn." *Cultural Studies* 19.5 (2005): 548–567.

Higa, Karen and Tim B. Wride. "Manzanar Inside and Out: Photo Documentation of the Japanese Wartime Incarceration." In *Reading California: Art, Image, Identity, 1900–2000*, edited by Stephanie Barron, Sheri Bernstein, and Ilene Susan Fort, 315–338. Los Angeles: Los Angeles County Museum of Art, and Berkeley: University of California Press, 2000.

Hogan, Patrick. "On Being Moved: Emotion and Cognition in Literature and Film." In *Introduction to Cognitive Cultural Studies*, edited by Lisa Zunshine. Baltimore: The Johns Hopkins University Press, 2010.

———. *Understanding Nationalism: On Narrative, Cognitive Science, and Identity*. Columbus: Ohio State University Press, 2009.

Hooks, bell. "Touching the Earth." 360–362. In *At Home on This Earth: Two Centuries of U.S. Women's Nature Writing*, edited by Lorraine Anderson and Thomas S. Edwards. New York: UPNE, 2002.

Houser, Heather. *Ecosickness in Contemporary U.S. Fiction: Environment and Affect*. New York: Columbia University Press, 2014.

Houston, Jeanne Wakatsuki. "Crossing Boundaries." In *The Colors of Nature*, edited by Lauret E. Savoy and Alison H. Deming, 33–41. Minneapolis: Milkweed Editions, 2011.

———. *Farewell to Manzanar*. New York: Ember, 2012.

Hutcheon, Linda. "Irony, Nostalgia, and the Postmodern." In *Methods For The Study of Literature as Cultural Memory*, edited by Raymond Vervliet and Annemarie Estor, 189–207. Atlanta: Rodopi, 2000.

Huyssen, Andreas. "Monumental Seduction." In *Acts of Memory: Cultural Recall in the Present*, edited by Mieke Bal, Jonathan Crewe, and Leo Spitzer, 191–207. Hanover: Dartmouth College, 1999.

Imhoff, Roland, Michal Bilewicz and Hans-Peter Erb. "Collective regret versus collective guilt: Different emotional reactions to historical atrocities." *European Journal of Social Psychology* 42 (2012): 729–742.

Interdisciplinary Center for Narratology. "Living Handbook of Narratology." http://wikis. sub.uni-hamburg.de/lhn/index.php/Implied_Reader. Accessed 8 January, 2015.

Iovino, Serenella and Serpil Oppermann. "Material Ecocriticism: Materiality, Agency, and Models of Narrativity," *Ecozon@* 3.1 (2012): 75–91.

———. "Theorizing Material Ecocriticism: A Diptych." *Interdisciplinary Studies in Literature and Environment* 19.3, Summer (2012): 448–57.

James, Erin. *The Storyworld Accord: Econarratology and Postcolonial Narratives.* Lincoln: University of Nebraska Press, 2015.

Johnson, Michael K. *Hoo-Doo Cowboys and Bronze Buckaroos: Conceptions of the African American West.* Jackson: University Press of Mississippi, 2014.

Johnson, Shelton. *Gloryland.* San Francisco: Sierra Club Books, 2009.

Jones, James. 1951. *From Here to Eternity.* New York: Penguin, 2011.

Kajihiro, Kyle. "'Becoming Pearl Harbor': A 'Lost Geography' of American Empire." Master's thesis, Department of Geography, University of Hawaiʻi, 2014.

Kammen, Michael. *Mystic Chords of Memory: The Transformation of Tradition in American Culture.* New York: Alfred A. Knopf, 1991.

Kaufman, Jerome A. *Renewal at the Place of Black Tears.* Issaquah: Visual World Impressions, 2012.

Keen, Suzanne. *Empathy and the Novel.* Oxford: Oxford University Press, 1992.

Kelman, Ari. *Misplaced Massacre: Struggling over the Memory of Sand Creek.* Boston: Harvard University Press, 2013.

Keltner, Dacher and Jonathan Haidt. "Approaching awe, a moral, spiritual, and aesthetic emotion." *Cognition & Emotion*, 17 (2003): 297–314.

Kemeny, Margaret E., Carol Foltz, Margaret Cullen, Patricia Jennings, Omri Gillath, B. Alan Wallace, James F. Cavangh, Janine Giese-Davis, Erika L. Rosenberg, Phillip R. Shaver, and Paul Ekman. "Contemplative/Emotion Training Reduces Negative Emotional Behavior and Promotes Prosocial Responses." *Emotion* 12.2 (2012): 338–350.

Kingston, Maxine Hong. *China Men.* New York: Alfred A. Knopf, Inc., 1977.

Klieger, P. Christian. "Nā Maka O Hālawa: A History of Hālawa Ahupuaʻa, Oʻahu." Honolulu: Bishop Museum Technical Report 7, 1995.

Kübler-Ross, Elisabeth. *On Death and Dying.* New York: Routledge, 1969.

Lacy, Robert. "*From Here to Eternity* and the American Experience." *Sewanee Review* (2007).

Ladino, Jennifer K. *Reclaiming Nostalgia: Longing for Nature in American Literature.* Charlottesville: University of Virginia Press, 2012.

Landman, Janet. *Regret: The Persistence of the Possible*. Oxford: Oxford University Press, 1993.

Leary, Mark R. "Affect, Cognition, and the Social Emotions." In *Feeling and Thinking: The Role of Affect in Social Cognition*, edited by Joseph P. Forgas, 331–356. Cambridge: Cambridge University Press, 2000.

Ledbetter, Resa. "Memorials Matter: The Impressions History Leaves Behind." Interview with Jennifer Ladino. Utah Public Radio interview, June 27, 2016. http://upr.org/post/memorials-matter-impressions-history-leaves-behind. Accessed May 17, 2017.

Lee, Julia H. "The Railroad as Message in Maxine Hong Kingston's *China Men* and Frank Chin's 'Riding the Rails with Chickencoop Slim." *Journal of Asian American Studies* 13.3 (2015).

Leopold, Aldo. 1949. *A Sand County Almanac, with Other Essays on Conservation from Round River*. New York: Ballantine Books, 1970.

Leys, Ruth. "The Turn to Affect: A Critique." *Critical Inquiry* 37.3 (2001): 434–472.

Littlejohn, Margaret and Yen Le. "Mount Rushmore National Memorial Visitor Study." University of Idaho Park Studies Unit. U.S. Department of Interior, 2013.

Lorde, Audre. "The Uses of Anger." *Women's Studies Quarterly* 9.3 (1981): 7–10.

Lutenski, Emily. *West of Harlem: African American Writers and the Borderlands*. Lawrence: University Press of Kansas, 2016.

Marshall, George. *Don't Even Think About It: Why Our Brains Are Wired to Ignore Climate Change*. New York: Bloomsbury, 2014.

Massey, Doreen. "Landscape as a Provocation: Reflections on Moving Mountains." *Journal of Material Culture* 11, 1-2 (2006): 33–48.

Massumi, Brian. "Fear (The Spectrum Said)," *positions* 13.1 (2005).

———. *Parables for the Virtual: Movement, Affect, Sensation*. Durham: Duke University Press, 2002.

Mayo, James M. *War Memorials as Political Landscape: The American Experience and Beyond*. New York: Praeger, 1988.

Milton, Kay. *Loving Nature: Towards an Ecology of Emotion*. New York: Routledge, 2002.

Morrison, Toni. *Beloved*. 1987. New York: Random House, 2004.

Morse, Wayde and Margaret Littlejohn. *USS* Arizona *Memorial Visitor Study*, Summer 2000, University of Idaho Cooperative Park Studies Unit, Visitor Services Project. Moscow: University of Idaho, 2001.

Nash, Linda. "The Agency of Nature or the Nature of Agency?" *Environmental History* 10 (2005), 67–69.

The National Parks: Shaping the System. Washington, D.C.: U.S. Department of the Interior, 2005.

Ng, Laura W. "Altered Lives, Altered Environments: Creating Home at Manzanar Relocation Center, 1942–1945." M.A. Thesis, University of Massachusetts, Boston, 2014.

Ngai, Sianne. *Ugly Feelings*. Cambridge: Harvard University Press, 2005.

Nimura, Tamiko. "For A Sister Getting Married: *Senbazuru*—1,000 Cranes." *Discover*

Nikkei (28 June, 2013), http://www.discovernikkei.org/en/journal/2013/6/28/sen-bazuru/. Accessed 23 January, 2015.

Nora, Pierre. "Between Memory and History: *Les Lieux de Mémoire.*" *Representations* 26 (Spring 1989): 7–24.

Nussbaum, Martha. *Political Emotions: Why Love Matters for Justice.* Boston: Harvard University Press, 2015.

Nye, David. *American Technological Sublime.* Boston: The MIT Press, 1994.

Ortiz, Simon J. *from Sand Creek: rising in this heart which is our America.* Oak Park: Thunder's Mouth Press, 1981.

Ortiz, Simon. "Towards a National Indian Literature: Cultural Authenticity in Nationalism." *MELUS* 8.2 (1981).

Ortiz, Simon, Kathleen Manley, and Paul W. Rea. "An Interview with Simon Ortiz." *Journal of the Southwest* 31.3 (1989).

Osorio, Jon Kamakawiwoʻole. "Memorializing Puʻuloa and Remembering Pearl Harbor." In *Militarized Currents: Toward a Decolonized Future in Asia and the Pacific*, edited by Setsu Shigematsu and Keith L. Camacho. Minneapolis: University of Minnesota Press, 2010.

Patin, Thomas. "America in Ruins: Parks, Poetics, and Politics." In *Observation Points: The Visual Poetics of National Parks*, edited by Thomas Patin, 267–290. Minneapolis: University of Minnesota Press, 2012.

Percy, Walker. "The Loss of the Creature." *The Message in the Bottle: How Queer Man Is, How Queer Language Is, and What One Has to Do with the Other.* New York: Farrar, Straus, and Giroux, 1975.

Perillo, Lucia. *I've Heard the Vultures Singing: Field Notes on Poetry, Illness, and Nature.* San Antonio: Trinity University Press, 2007.

Peterman, Audrey. *Our True Nature: Finding a Zest for Life in the National Park System.* Fideli Publishing, Inc., 2012.

Phelan, James, "Rhetoric/Ethics," *The Cambridge Companion to Narrative* 14 (2007).

Prade, Claire and Vassilis Saroglou. "Awe's effects on generosity and helping." *The Journal of Positive Psychology* 11.5 (2016).

Rankine, Claudia. *Don't Let Me Be Lonely.* Minneapolis: Graywolf Press, 2004.

Rose, Deborah Bird, Thom van Dooren, Matthew Churlew, Stuart Cooke, Matthew Kearnes, and Emily O'Gorman. "Thinking Through the Environment, Unsettling the Humanities." *Environmental Humanities* 1 (2012): 1–5.

Royston Hanamoto Alley & Abey, Landscape Architects. *Main Post Cultural Landscape Report: Presidio of San Francisco.* San Francisco CA: The Presidio Trust, 2012.

Sánchez, Joseph P., Jerry L. Gurule, and Bruce A. Erickson. *Between Two Countries: A History of Coronado National Memorial: 1939–1990.* Albuquerque: Rio Grande Books, 2007.

Savoy, Lauret Edith. *Trace: Memory, History, Race, and the American Landscape.* Berkeley: Counterpoint Press, 2015.

Scranton, Roy. *Learning to Die in the Anthropocene: Reflections on the End of a Civilization*. San Francisco: City Lights, 2015.

Seamon, David. *A Geography of the Lifeworld*. London: Croom Helm, 1979.

Sedgwick, Eve Kosofsky, and Adam Frank, eds. *Shame and Its Sisters: A Silvan Tomkins Reader*. Durham: Duke University Press, 1995.

Seiden, Allan. *From Fishponds to Warships: Pearl Harbor: A Complete Illustrated History*. Honolulu: Mutual Publishing, 2001.

Sellars, Richard West. *Preserving Nature in the National Parks: A History*. New Haven: Yale University Press, 1997.

Seymour, Nicole. "Irony and Contemporary Ecocinema: Theorizing a New Affective Paradigm." In *Moving Environments: Affect, Emotion, Ecology, and Film*, edited by Alexa Weik von Mossner, 61–78. Waterloo: Wilfrid Laurier Press, 2014.

Shackel, Paul A. *Myth, Memory, and the Making of the American Landscape*. Gainesville: University Press of Florida, 2001.

Silko, Leslie Marmon. "Landscape, History, and the Pueblo Imagination." In *At Home on the Earth: Becoming Native to Our Place: A Multicultural Anthology*, edited by David Landis Barnhill. Berkeley: University of California Press, 1999.

Slackman, Michael. *Remembering Pearl Harbor: The Story of the USS* Arizona *Memorial*. Honolulu: Pacific Historic Parks, 2012.

Slovic, Scott and Paul Slovic. *Numbers and Nerves: Information, Emotion, and Meaning in a World of Data*. Corvallis: Oregon State University Press, 2015.

Solnit, Rebecca. *Storming the Gates of Paradise: Landscapes for Politics*. Berkeley: U C Press, 2007.

———. "Water." In *A Companion to American Environmental History*, edited by Douglas Cazaux Sackman. Oxford: Blackwell Publishing, Ltd., 2010.

Spence, Mark David. *Dispossessing the Wilderness: Indian Removal and the Making of the National Parks*. New York: Oxford University Press, 1999.

Spinoza, Baruch. "The Ethics." In *A Spinoza Reader: The Ethics and Other Works*, edited and translated by Edwin Curley. 85–265 (Princeton: Princeton University Press).

Spurlock, Cindy. "America's Best Idea: Environmental Public Memory and the Rhetoric of Conservation Civics." In *Observation Points: The Visual Poetics of National Parks*, edited by Thomas Patin, 247–266. Minneapolis: University of Minnesota Press, 2012.

Stegner, Wallace. "Living Dry." In *Where The Bluebird Sings To The Lemonade Springs*. New York: Random House, 1992.

Stewart, Kathleen. *Ordinary Affects*. Durham: Duke University Press, 2007.

———. "Worlding Refrains." In *The Affect Theory Reader*, edited by Melissa Gregg and Gregory J. Seigworth, 339–353. Durham: Duke University Press, 2010.

Stewart, Susan. *On Longing: Narratives of the Miniature, the Gigantic, the Souvenir, the Collection*. Durham: Duke University Press, 1993.

Sumida, Stephen H. "A Narrative of Kuki'iahu and its Erasures." *Pacific and American Studies* 2 (2002): 101–110.

Sutter, Paul. "The World with Us: The State of American Environmental History." *Journal of American History* (2013), 94–119.

Taliaferro, John. *Great White Fathers: The Story of the Obsessive Quest to Create Mount Rushmore.* New York: Perseus, 2002.

Taylor, David. *Monuments.* Radius Books, Nevada Museum of Art, 2015.

Taylor, Patricia A., Burke D. Grandjean, and James H. Gramann. "National Park Service Comprehensive Survey of the American Public, 2008–9: Racial and Ethnic Diversity of National Park System Visitors and Non-Visitors." Fort Collins: U.S. Department of the Interior, 2011.

Thornber, Karen Laura. *Ecoambiguity: Environmental Crises and East Asian Literatures.* Ann Arbor: University of Michigan Press, 2012.

Tompkins, Jane. *West of Everything: The Inner Life of Westerns.* New York: Oxford University Press, 1992.

Tuan, Yi-Fu. *Topophilia: A Study of Environmental Perception, Attitudes, and Values.* Englewood Cliffs: Prentice-Hall, Inc., 1974.

Urrea, Luis Alberto. *The Devil's Highway: A True Story.* New York: Little, Brown and Company, 2004.

Valdesolo, Piercarlo and Jesse Graham. "Awe, Uncertainty, and Agency Detection." *Psychological Science* (November 18, 2013).

Vizenor, Gerald. *Fugitive Poses: Native American Scenes of Absence and Presence.* Lincoln: University of Nebraska Press, 2000.

Voss, Barbara. *The Archeology of Ethnogenesis: Race and Sexuality in Colonial San Francisco.* Berkeley: University of California Press, 2008.

Wallace, Gwynn, J. *Commonly Asked Questions About Utah's Great Salt Lake and Ancient Lake Bonneville.* Utah Geological Survey, 1996.

Weik von Mossner, Alexa. *Affective Ecologies: Empathy, Emotion, and Environmental Narrative.* Columbus: The Ohio State University Press, 2017.

———. *Moving Environments: Affect, Emotion, Ecology, and Film.* Waterloo: Wilfrid Laurier University Press, 2014.

Wheeler, Wendy. *Expecting the Earth: Life/Culture/Biosemiotics.* Dagenham: Lawrence & Wishart, 2016.

White, Evelyn. "Black Women and the Wilderness." In *Literature and the Environment: A Reader on Nature and Culture,* edited by Lorraine Anderson, Scott Slovic, and John P. O'Grady. New York: Addison Wesley Longman, 1999.

White, Geoffrey. *Memorializing Pearl Harbor: Unfinished Histories and The Work of Remembrance.* Durham: Duke University Press, 2016.

White, Richard. *Railroaded: The Transcontinentals and the Making of Modern America.* New York: W.W. Norton & Company, 2012.

Whyte, Kyle Powys. "Resurgence within the Rust: Indigenous Science (Fiction) for the Anthropocene." https://echo360.org/media/76adf527-126c-459d-b86e-9672970ea7aa/public. Accessed 2 September, 2017.

Wildcat, Daniel. *American Indians and the Civil War.* Eastern National, 2013.

Wilke, Sabine. "How German is the American West?: The Legacy of Caspar David

Friedrich's Visual Poetics in American Landscape Painting." In *Observation Points: The Visual Poetics of National Parks*, edited by Thomas Patin, 100–118. Minneapolis: University of Minnesota Press, 2012.

Williams, Terry Tempest. *Refuge: An Unnatural History of Family and Place*. New York: Vintage, 2015.

———. *The Hour of Land: A Personal Topography of America's National Parks*. New York: Sarah Crichton Books, 2016.

Winter, Jay. "Historical Remembrance in the Twenty-First Century." *Annals of the American Academy of Political and Social Science*, vol. 617 (2008): 6–13.

———. "Sites of Memory and the Shadow of War." In *Media and Cultural Memory Studies: An International and Interdisciplinary Handbook*, edited by Astrid Erll and Ansgar Nünning, 61–74. Berlin: DEU. Walter de Gruyter. 2008.

———. *Sites of Memory; Sites of Mourning: The Great War in European Cultural History*. Cambridge: Cambridge University Press, 1995.

Wyckoff, William. *How to Read the American West: A Field Guide*. Seattle: University of Washington Press, 2014.

Zepeda, Ofelia. *Ocean Power: Poems From The Desert*. Tucson: University of Arizona Press, 1995.

Index

Abbey, Edward, xi, xvii, 54, 233

affect: as attunement, 13, 21; 59, 243; definitions of, 12, 35n46; *vs.* emotion, 12, 40n128, 56, 133, 220–21; as impression, 12, 35n50, 56, 94, 206; as intensity, 12, 22, 56; and narrative, 15–16; noncathartic affects, 22, 107, 111, 148, 197, 220, 248; relationship to form, 16, 65; transmission of, 17, 21, 39n101, 39n102, 160; *See also* emotion

affect alien, 90, 110, 125, 167, 200; definition of, 24

affect imposter syndrome, 24–25, 40n123, 91

affective agency: and built environment, 63, 197–8; definition of, 16; and landscape, 87, 96, 109, 144, 148; and multisensory factors, 185; *vs.* narrative agency, 144, 204, 213, 246; political significance, 221; and thing-power, 21

affective atmosphere, 17, 45, 62, 248; and affective dissonance, 198; and anxiety, 28, 60, 209; and fear, 172, 189n7, 236; and the more-than-human world, 215, 244; and patriotism, 128, 130, 148, 171; and scale, 186; and serenity, 65; and solemnity, 87, 90; and tourism, 23, 24, 96, 174, 176, 219

affective dissonance, 22, 29, 166, 168, 205; *vs.* cognitive dissonance; *vs.* discord, 22–23; as embodied tourist feeling; 99, 178, 207, 246; and environment, 206, 213; and irony, 205,

230; and patriotism, 30, 148, 198; resolution of, 163, 248

affective itinerary, 19, 59, 92, 162, 167

affective registers, 11, 51, 65, 220; tension in, xvii, 99–100, 163, 198, 206, 213; alignment of, 87, 148, 218

affect theory: critiques of, 13–14, 79n69; and environmental humanities, 16, 25, 45; as methodology, xviii, 11, 33n16, 108, 254; overview of, 12–14; and physical matter, 132, 220

Ahmed, Sara: affect alien, 24; conversion points, 19, 84; on fear and anxiety, 57, 59, 60, 76n22; on hate, 266; on love of nation, 8–9, 156n71; moodiness, 7, 21; on shame and patriotism, 30, 202–203, 208, 218–19; sticky objects, 21, 58, 77n30, 159; women's bodies, 61

Albrecht, Glenn, 270

Alcatraz Island, 209, 231, 240, 245, 256n18

Alexie, Sherman, 18, 24, 33n20; "Vilify," 3–5

aloha: 159, 166, 168, 181–2, 190n23; as affect transmission, 160; and natural environment, 185; and patriotism, 163, 172, 178, 186; as weapon of colonialism, 183

Alt-NPS, xviii, 31, 263, 264, 267; mission, 262

American West, xii, xvi xxin15, 84, 93; black West, 31, 228–9, 231, 238; Civil War in, 114, 116n27; diversity in, 18, 28, 67; Western frontier

About the Author

JENNIFER LADINO is an associate professor of English at the University of Idaho, where she specializes in American literature and the environmental humanities. Her first book *Reclaiming Nostalgia: Longing for Nature in American Literature* (University of Virginia Press, 2012) was a finalist for the ASLE book award in 2013. She has also co-edited a volume of essays called *Affective Ecocriticism: Emotion, Embodiment, Environment* (University of Nebraska Press, 2018). She has published on a range of authors and topics, including Wallace Stegner's frontier rhetoric, Marianne Moore's collage poem about Mount Rainier, the films *Grizzly Man* and *March of the Penguins*, and Maya Lin's memorial website, "What is Missing?" Happiest when she's adventuring or traveling (or both), Ladino worked as a National Park Service ranger for thirteen summers, all of them in Grand Teton National Park—the place that initiated her love of the West when she accepted an entrance station job on a romantic whim and found herself transplanted from Virginia to Wyoming at age 20. She has also been a Fulbright Lecturer at the University of Bergen, in Norway, and a visiting fellow at Bath Spa University, in England.